CAMBRIDGE

Brighter Thinking

A Level Further Mathematics for OCR A

Pure Core 2 Student Book (Year 2)

Vesna Kadelburg, Ben Woolley, Stephen Ward, Paul Fannon

CAMBRIDGE
UNIVERSITY PRESS

University Printing House, Cambridge CB2 8BS, United Kingdom

One Liberty Plaza, 20th Floor, New York, NY 10006, USA

477 Williamstown Road, Port Melbourne, VIC 3207, Australia

314–321, 3rd Floor, Plot 3, Splendor Forum, Jasola District Centre, New Delhi – 110025, India

103 Penang Road, #05-06/07, Visioncrest Commercial, Singapore 238467

Cambridge University Press is part of the University of Cambridge.

It furthers the University's mission by disseminating knowledge in the pursuit of education, learning and research at the highest international levels of excellence.

www.cambridge.org
Information on this title: www.cambridge.org/9781316644393 (Paperback)
www.cambridge.org/9781316644249 (Paperback with Cambridge Elevate edition)

First published 2018

20 19 18 17 16 15 14 13 12 11 10 9 8 7 6 5 4

Printed in Great Britain by CPI Group (UK) Ltd, Croydon CR0 4YY

A catalogue record for this publication is available from the British Library

ISBN 978-1-316-64439-3 Paperback
ISBN 978-1-316-64424-9 Paperback with Cambridge Elevate edition

Additional resources for this publication at www.cambridge.org/education

· ·

· ·

This resource is endorsed by OCR for use with specification AS Level Further Mathematics A (H235)
and specification A Level Further Mathematics A (H245). In order to gain OCR endorsement,
this resource has undergone an independent quality check. Any references to assessment
and/or assessment preparation are the publisher's interpretation of the specification
requirements and are not endorsed by OCR. OCR recommends that a range of teaching
and learning resources are used in preparing learners for assessment. OCR has not paid for
the production of this resource, nor does OCR receive any royalties from its sale. For more
information about the endorsement process, please visit the OCR website, **www.ocr.org.uk.**

Contents

Introduction

You have probably been told that mathematics is very useful, yet it can often seem like a lot of techniques that just have to be learnt to answer examination questions. You are now getting to the point where you will start to see where some of these techniques can be applied in solving real problems. However, as well as seeing how maths can be useful, we hope that anyone working through this book will realise that it can also be incredibly frustrating, surprising and ultimately beautiful.

The book is woven around three key themes from the new curriculum:

Proof

Maths is valued because it trains you to think logically and communicate precisely. At a high level, maths is far less concerned about answers and more about the clear communication of ideas. It is not about being neat – although that might help! It is about creating a coherent argument that other people can easily follow but find difficult to refute. Have you ever tried looking at your own work? If you cannot follow it yourself it is unlikely anybody else will be able to understand it. In maths we communicate using a variety of means – feel free to use combinations of diagrams, words and algebra to aid your argument. And once you have attempted a proof, try presenting it to your peers. Look critically (but positively) at some other people's attempts. It is only through having your own attempts evaluated and trying to find flaws in other proofs that you will develop sophisticated mathematical thinking. This is why we have included common errors in our 'work it out' boxes – just in case your friends don't make any mistakes!

Problem solving

Maths is valued because it trains you to look at situations in unusual, creative ways, to persevere and to evaluate solutions along the way. We have been heavily influenced by a great mathematician and maths educator, George Polya, who believed that students were not just born with problem solving skills – these skills were developed by seeing problems being solved and reflecting on the solutions before trying similar problems. You may not

realise it but good mathematicians spend most of their time being stuck. You need to spend some time on problems you can't do, trying out different possibilities. If after a while you have not cracked it then look at the solution and try a similar problem. Don't be disheartened if you cannot get it immediately – in fact, the longer you spend puzzling over a problem the more you will learn from the solution. You may, for example, never need to integrate a rational function in future, but we firmly believe that the problem solving skills you will develop by trying it can be applied to many other situations.

Modelling

Maths is valued because it helps us solve real-world problems. However, maths describes ideal situations and the real world is messy! Modelling is about deciding on the important features needed to describe the essence of a situation and turning that into a mathematical form, then using it to make predictions, compare to reality and possibly improve the model. In many situations the technical maths is actually the easy part – especially with modern technology. Deciding which features of reality to include or ignore and anticipating the consequences of these decisions is the hard part. Yet some fairly drastic assumptions – such as pretending a car is a single point or that people's votes are independent – can result in models that are surprisingly accurate.

More than anything else, this book is about making links. Links between the different chapters, the topics covered and the themes just discussed, links to other subjects and links to the real world. We hope that you will grow to see maths as one great complex but beautiful web of interlinking ideas.

Maths is about so much more than examinations, but we hope that if you take on board these ideas (and do plenty of practice!) you will find maths examinations a much more approachable and possibly even enjoyable experience. However, always remember that the results of what you write down in a few hours by yourself in silence under exam conditions is not the only measure you should consider when judging your mathematical ability – it is only one variable in a much more complicated mathematical model!

How to use this book

Throughout this book you will notice particular features that are designed to aid your learning. This section provides a brief overview of these features.

In this chapter you will learn how to:

- use de Moivre's theorem to derive trigonometric identities
- find sums of some trigonometric series.

Before you start…

Chapter 2, Section 1	You should be able to use de Moivre's theorem to raise a complex number to a power.	1 Find $\left(2\left(\cos\frac{\pi}{7}+i\sin\frac{\pi}{7}\right)\right)^{5}$ in modulus-argument form.
Chapter 2, Section 2	You should be able to use the exponential form of a complex number.	2 a Write $4e^{\frac{i\pi}{3}}$ in exact Cartesian form. b Write down the complex conjugate of $2+e^{3i}$.

Learning objectives
A short summary of the content that you will learn in each chapter.

Before you start
Points you should know from your previous learning and questions to check that you're ready to start the chapter.

WORKED EXAMPLE

The left-hand side shows you how to set out your working. The right-hand side explains the more difficult steps and helps you understand why a particular method was chosen.

Key point

A summary of the most important methods, facts and formulae.

PROOF

Step-by-step walkthroughs of standard proofs and methods of proof.

Explore

Ideas for activities and investigations to extend your understanding of the topic.

WORK IT OUT

Can you identify the correct solution and find the mistakes in the two incorrect solutions?

Tip

Useful guidance, including on ways of calculating or checking and use of technology.

Each chapter ends with a **Checklist of learning and understanding** and a **Mixed practice** exercise, which includes **past paper questions** marked with the icon 📝.

In between chapters, you will find extra sections that bring together topics in a more synoptic way.

Focus on …

Unique sections relating to the preceding chapters that develop your skills in proof, problem solving and modelling.

CROSS-TOPIC REVIEW EXERCISE

Questions covering topics from across the preceding chapters, testing your ability to apply what you have learnt.

You will find **practice questions** towards the end of the book, as well as a **glossary** of key terms (picked out in colour within the chapters), and **answers** to all questions. Full **worked solutions** can be found on the Cambridge Elevate digital platform, along with a **digital version** of this Student Book.

Maths is all about making links, which is why throughout this book you will find signposts emphasising connections between different topics, applications and suggestions for further research.

⏮ **Rewind**

Reminders of where to find useful information from earlier in your study.

📷 **Focus on ...**

Links to problem solving, modelling or proof exercises that relate to the topic currently being studied.

⏭ **Fast forward**

Links to topics that you may cover in greater detail later in your study.

ⓘ **Did you know?**

Interesting or historical information and links with other subjects to improve your awareness about how mathematics contributes to society.

Colour-coding of exercises

The questions in the exercises are designed to provide careful progression, ranging from basic fluency to practice questions. They are uniquely colour-coded, as shown here.

② For each equation from question 1, write the roots in exact Cartesian form.

⑤ Let $z = 2e^{\frac{i\pi}{12}}$ and $w = 4e^{\frac{i\pi}{3}}$. Show that $z^2 + w = 2(1+i)(1+\sqrt{3})$.

⑦ Solve the equation $z^3 - \sqrt{2}(4-4i) = 0$, giving your answers in Cartesian form.

⑧ Multiply out and simplify $(a + b\omega)(a - b\omega^2)$, where $\omega = e^{\frac{i\pi}{3}}$.

⑭ In the derivation of $\cosh^{-1} x$ you found that two possible expressions were $\ln(x + \sqrt{x^2 - 1})$ and $\ln(x - \sqrt{x^2 - 1})$. Show that their sum is zero and hence explain why the expression chosen in Proof 3 is non-negative.

㉒ Point A represents the complex number $3 + i$ on an Argand diagram. Point A is rotated through $\frac{\pi}{3}$ radians anticlockwise about the origin to point B. Point B is then translated by $\begin{pmatrix} -2 \\ 1 \end{pmatrix}$ to obtain point C.

Black – drill questions. Some of these come in several parts, each with subparts i and ii. You only need attempt subpart i at first; subpart ii is essentially the same question, which you can use for further practice if you got part i wrong, for homework, or when you revisit the exercise during revision.

Green – practice questions at a basic level.

Blue – practice questions at an intermediate level.

Red – practice questions at an advanced level.

Yellow – designed to encourage reflection and discussion.

Purple – challenging questions that apply the concept of the current chapter across other areas of maths.

1 Series and induction

In this chapter you will learn how to:

- use the principle of mathematical induction to prove results about sequences, series and differentiation
- use given results for the sums of integers, squares and cubes to find expressions for sums of other series
- use a technique called the method of differences to find an expression for the sum of n terms of a series
- use the expression for the sum of the first n terms to determine whether an infinite series converges and find its limit.

Before you start…

Pure Core Student Book 1, Chapter 6	You should be able to use mathematical induction to prove results about matrices, divisibility and inequalities.	1 Prove that $\begin{pmatrix} 1 & 3 \\ 0 & 1 \end{pmatrix}^n = \begin{pmatrix} 1 & 3n \\ 0 & 1 \end{pmatrix}$.
GCSE	You should be able to use the nth term formula to generate terms of a sequence.	2 A sequence is defined by $u_n = n^2 + 3n - 1$. Find the first three terms.
GCSE	You should be able to simplify expressions by factorising.	3 Simplify $n(n+1)(2n+3) + n(n+1)(n-3)$.
A Level Mathematics Student Book 2, Chapter 4	You should be able to use sigma notation to write a series.	4 Find $\sum_{k=1}^{5} 2^k$.
A Level Mathematics Student Book 2, Chapter 10	You should know how to differentiate using the product rule and chain rule.	5 Given that $y = (2x+1)e^{3x}$, find $\dfrac{dy}{dx}$.
A Level Mathematics Student Book 2, Chapter 5	You should know how to write an expression in partial fractions.	6 Write $\dfrac{1}{r(r+1)}$ in partial fractions.

Introduction

In Pure Core Student Book 1, Chapter 6, you learnt about the method of proof by induction, which you can use to prove that observed patterns continue forever. The sorts of patterns you looked at included powers of matrices (for example, prove that $\begin{pmatrix} 1 & 0 \\ 1 & 1 \end{pmatrix}^n = \begin{pmatrix} 1 & 0 \\ n & 1 \end{pmatrix}$

for all $n \in \mathbb{N}$), divisibility (for example, prove that $7^n - 3^n$ is divisible by 4 for all $n \in \mathbb{N}$) and inequalities (for example, prove that $2^n > 2n$ for $n \geqslant 3$).

In this chapter you will revisit these ideas, including examples where you need to conjecture (guess) the pattern first, and then see how to extend them to other contexts, such as sums of series and differentiation.

Finding expressions for sums of series is one of the most difficult problems in mathematics as there is no general method that always works. For example, you know how to find the sum of the first n terms of a geometric series: $5^1 + 5^2 + \ldots + 5^n = \dfrac{5(5^n - 1)}{4}$. But what about a series such as $1^5 + 2^5 + \ldots + n^5$?

The method of mathematical induction is useful for proving that a conjectured formula for the sum of a series is correct, but it offers no help in finding what the formula might be. Sometimes you can guess the formula by looking at some examples, but most of the time the general expression is far from obvious. In this chapter you will meet the method of differences, which allows you to find the formula in some cases. You will also learn how to derive formulae for sums of more complicated series by combining results you have already derived.

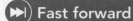 **Fast forward**

In Chapter 2 you will use induction to prove de Moivre's theorem, a result about powers of complex numbers.

Fast forward

In Chapter 8 you will learn about another type of series called the Maclaurin series.

Section 1: Review of proof by induction

You can use induction to prove statements about a sequence or a pattern, where the statement holds for every natural number n. The proof involves two steps:

1 Prove that the statement is true for some starting value of n (usually, but not always, $n = 1$).
2 Assuming that the statement is true for some k, prove that it is also true for $k + 1$.

Then the principle of mathematical induction states the statement is true for all values of n.

Sometimes you need to conjecture the pattern for yourself before using induction to prove it.

Rewind

You will need to use the product rule for differentiation. This was covered in A Level Mathematics Student Book 2, Chapter 10.

WORKED EXAMPLE 1.1

Let $y = x e^x$.

a Find $\dfrac{dy}{dx}, \dfrac{d^2 y}{dx^2}$ and $\dfrac{d^3 y}{dx^3}$.

b Conjecture an expression for $\dfrac{d^n y}{dx^n}$ and prove it by induction.

Continues on next page …

a $\dfrac{dy}{dx} = e^x + xe^x = (1+x)e^x$

Use the product rule to differentiate.

$\dfrac{d^2 y}{dx^2} = e^x + (1+x)e^x = (2+x)e^x$

The factorised form makes it easier to spot the pattern.

$\dfrac{d^3 y}{dx^3} = e^x + (2+x)e^x = (3+x)e^x$

b Conjecture:

$\dfrac{d^n y}{dx^n} = (n+x)e^x$

Proof:

When $n = 1$:

Start by showing that the statement is true when $n = 1$.

$\dfrac{dy}{dx} = (1+x)e^x$

So the statement is true for $n = 1$.

Assume it is true for $n = k$:

$\dfrac{d^k y}{dx^k} = (x+k)e^x$

Write down the statement with $n = k$.

When $n = k + 1$,

Think about what you are trying to prove. Remember that you cannot use this result!

You are working towards: $\dfrac{d^{k+1} y}{dx^{k+1}} = (x+k+1)e^x$

$\dfrac{d^{k+1} y}{dx^{k+1}} = \dfrac{d}{dx}\left(\dfrac{d^k y}{dx^k}\right)$

Relate $\dfrac{d^{k+1} y}{dx^{k+1}}$ to $\dfrac{d^k y}{dx^k}$.

$= \dfrac{d}{dx}\left((x+k)e^x\right)$

Use the result you have assumed for $n = k$.

$= e^x + (x+k)e^x$

Differentiate using the product rule.

$= e^k(1+x+k)$

$= e^k(x+(k+1))$

This the the required result for $n = k + 1$.

Hence the result is also true for $n = k + 1$.

The result is true for $n = 1$, and if true for $n = k$ it is also true for $n = k + 1$.

Remember to write the conclusion.

Therefore, the result is true for all $n \in \mathbb{Z}^+$ by the principle of mathematical induction.

Sequences are often given by a term-to-term rule, but you might want to know a formula for the nth term. You might be able to guess the formula by looking at the numbers and then you can use induction to prove that it works for all n.

For example, the term-to-term rule $u_{n+1} = 3u_n + 2, u_1 = 2$ describes a sequence whose first four terms are 2, 8, 26, 80. You might notice that these are all one less than a power of 3, so the formula for the nth term could be $u_n = 3^n - 1$. You can prove by induction that this formula indeed works for all n.

WORKED EXAMPLE 1.2

A sequence is given by $u_1 = 2$ and $u_{n+1} = 3u_n + 2$ for $n \geqslant 1$. Prove that the nth term of the sequence is $u_n = 3^n - 1$.

When $n = 1$:

$u_1 = 2 = 3^1 - 1$ Show that the result is true for $n = 1$.
So the formula works when $n = 1$.

Assume that the formula works when $n = k$:

$u_k = 3^k - 1$ Assume that the formula works for some k.

When $n = k + 1$,   Think about what you are trying to prove.

$u_{k+1} = 3u_k + 2$ You are working towards: $u_{k+1} = 3^{k+1} - 1$

$\quad = 3(3^k - 1) + 2$

$\quad = 3^{k+1} - 1$ Use the result you assumed for $n = k$.

So, the formula also works when $n = k + 1$.

The formula works when $n = 1$, and if it works for some $n = k$ then it also works for $n = k + 1$.   Remember to write the conclusion.

Hence, by the principle of mathematical induction, the formula works for all $n \in \mathbb{N}$.

Sometimes each term in the sequence depends on more than one previous term. For example, the term-to-term rule

$$u_{n+2} = 5u_{n+1} - 6u_n \text{ with } u_1 = 5 \text{ and } u_2 = 13$$

produces this sequence:

$$u_1 = 5$$
$$u_2 = 13$$
$$u_3 = 5 \times 13 - 6 \times 5 = 35$$
$$u_4 = 5 \times 35 - 6 \times 13 = 97$$

and so on. You can still use proof by induction, but you need to show that the formula works for two starting values of n.

WORKED EXAMPLE 1.3

A sequence is given by the recurrence relation $u_1 = 5$ and $u_2 = 13$, $u_{n+2} = 5u_{n+1} - 6u_n$ for $n \geqslant 2$. Prove that the formula for the nth term of the sequence is $u_n = 2^n + 3^n$.

When $n = 1$: $\quad$ RHS $= 2^1 + 3^1$ $\qquad = 5$ $\qquad = u_1$ So, the formula works for $n = 1$. When $n = 2$: $\quad$ RHS $= 2^2 + 3^2$ $\qquad = 13$ $\qquad = u_2$ So, the formula works for $n = 2$.	Check that the formula works for $n = 1$ and $n = 2$.
Assume the formula works for $n = k$ and $n = k + 1$:	Assume that the formula works for $n = k$ **and** $n = k + 1$, and prove that it works for $n = k + 2$.
$u_k = 2^k + 3^k$ $u_{k+1} = 2^{k+1} + 3^{k+1}$	Think about the formula with $n = k$ and $n = k + 1$.
When $n = k + 2$,	Think about what you are trying to prove. You are working towards: $u_{k+2} = 2^{k+2} + 3^{k+2}$
$u_{k+2} = 5u_{k+1} - 6u_k$	Express u_{k+2} in terms of u_k and u_{k+1}.
$\quad = 5\left(2^{k+1} + 3^{k+1}\right) - 6\left(2^k + 3^k\right)$	Use the results for $n = k$ and $n = k + 1$.
$\quad = 5 \times 2^{k+1} + 5 \times 3^{k+1} - 6 \times 2^k - 6 \times 3^k$	
$\quad = (5 \times 2 \times 2^k - 6 \times 2^k) + (5 \times 3 \times 3^k - 6 \times 3^k)$ $\quad = 4 \times 2^k + 9 \times 3^k$ $\quad = 2^2 \times 2^k + 3^2 \times 3^k$ $\quad = 2^{k+2} + 3^{k+2}$	Look at what you are working towards; group the powers of 2 and the powers of 3.
So, the formula also works for $n = k + 2$.	
The formula works for $n = 1$ and $n = 2$, and if it works for $n = k$ and $n = k + 1$ then it also works for $n = k + 2$. Therefore, the formula works for all $n \in \mathbb{Z}^+$ by the principle of mathematical induction.	Write a conclusion.

EXERCISE 1A

1 Given that $u_{n+1} = 5u_n - 8, u_1 = 3$, prove by induction that $u_n = 5^{n-1} + 2$.

2 A sequence has first term 1 and subsequent terms defined by $u_{n+1} = 3u_n + 1$. Prove by induction that

$u_n = \dfrac{3^n - 1}{2}$.

3 Given that $u_{n+1} = 5u_n + 4, u_1 = 4$,

  a find the first four terms of the sequence

  b conjecture a formula for the nth term and prove it by induction.

4 Let $A = \begin{pmatrix} 1 & 0 \\ 1 & 1 \end{pmatrix}$.

  a Find A^2, A^3 and A^4.

  b Conjecture an expression for A^n and prove it by induction.

5 Let $f(n) = 5^n - 1$.

  a Find $f(n)$ for $n = 1, 2, 3, 4$.

  b Which natural number do all $f(n)$ seem to be multiples of?

  c Use mathematical induction to prove your conjecture from part **b**.

> **📷 Focus on ...**
>
> Powers of matrices have many interesting applications. To explore one of them see Focus on ... Modelling 1.

6 A sequence is given by the term-to-term rule $u_{n+2} = 5u_{n+1} - 6u_n$ with $u_1 = 1$ and $u_2 = 5$.

Prove that the general term of the sequence is $u_n = 3^n - 2^n$.

7 Given that $u_1 = 3, u_2 = 36, u_{n+2} = 6u_{n+1} - 9u_n$, prove by induction that $u_n = (3n-2)3^n$.

8 Let $A = \begin{pmatrix} 1 & 1 \\ 1 & 1 \end{pmatrix}$.

  a Find A^2, A^3 and A^4.   **b** Conjecture an expression for A^n and prove it by induction.

9 **a** Suggest which natural number is a factor of all the numbers of the form $9^n - 4^n$.

  b Prove your claim by induction.

10 Given that $y = \dfrac{1}{1-x}$, use induction to prove that $\dfrac{d^n y}{dx^n} = \dfrac{n!}{(1-x)^{n+1}}$.

11 Given that $f(x) = \dfrac{1}{1-3x}$, prove by induction that $f^{(n)}(x) = \dfrac{3^n n!}{(1-3x)^{n+1}}$.

12 Use mathematical induction to show that $\dfrac{d^n}{dx^n}(xe^{2x}) = (2^n x + n2^{n-1})e^{2x}$.

13 Prove by induction that $\dfrac{d^n}{dx^n}(x^2 e^x) = (x^2 + 2nx + n(n-1))e^x$ for $n \geqslant 2$.

14 Given that $y = x\sin x$, use mathematical induction to prove that $\dfrac{d^{2n}y}{dx^{2n}} = (-1)^n(x\sin x - 2n\cos x)$.

15 The Fibonacci sequence is defined by $u_1 = u_2 = 1, u_n = u_{n-1} + u_{n-2}$ for $n \geqslant 3$. Show that the nth term of the

Fibonacci sequence is given by $u_n = \dfrac{1}{\sqrt{5}}\left(\left(\dfrac{1+\sqrt{5}}{2}\right)^n + \left(\dfrac{1-\sqrt{5}}{2}\right)^n\right)$.

Explore

Leonardo Fibonacci (c. 1170 - c. 1250) was an extremely influential mathematician in the Middle Ages, largely responsible for spreading the number system you use today. He also gave his name to the famous Fibonacci sequence. The formula in question 15 shows the link between the Fibonacci sequence and the golden ratio, a quantity $\frac{1+\sqrt{5}}{2}$ which appears in many surprising places in mathematics.

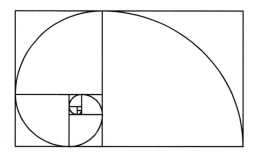

Section 2: Induction and series

A **series** is a sum of the terms of a sequence. If you add the terms up to a certain point you get a **finite series**, such as $\frac{1}{2}+\frac{1}{3}+\frac{1}{4}+\frac{1}{5}$. You can also try to form an **infinite series**, for example $\frac{1}{2}+\frac{1}{4}+\frac{1}{8}+\frac{1}{16}+\ldots$. Some infinite series, such as the geometric series given here, have a finite sum. In this section you will only look at finite series; you will meet some infinite series in Section 4.

⏪ Rewind

You met sequences, series and sigma notation in A Level Mathematics Student Book 2, Chapter 4.

You can use **sigma notation** as a shorter way of writing a series. For example,

$$\frac{1}{2}+\frac{1}{3}+\frac{1}{4}+\frac{1}{5}=\sum_{k=2}^{5}\frac{1}{k}$$

$$\frac{1}{2}+\frac{1}{4}+\frac{1}{8}+\frac{1}{16}+\ldots=\sum_{k=1}^{\infty}\frac{1}{2^k}$$

In the A Level Mathematics course you learnt how to find the general formula for the sum of the first n terms of an arithmetic and a geometric series:

$$\sum_{k=1}^{n}\left(a+(k-1)d\right)=\frac{n}{2}\left(2a+(n-1)d\right)$$

$$\sum_{k=1}^{n}ar^{k-1}=\frac{a\left(r^n-1\right)}{r-1}$$

You also learnt about finite and infinite binomial series, for example:

$$1+4x+6x^2+4x^3+x^4 = \sum_{k=0}^{4} {}^4C_k x^k = (1+x)^4$$

$$1-2x+3x^2-4x^3+\dots = \sum_{k=0}^{\infty} \frac{(-2)(-3)\dots(-2-(k-1))}{k!} x^k = (1+x)^{-2}$$

In Chapter 8 of this book you will learn about Maclaurin series, which you can use to write a function as an infinite series, for example:

$$\sum_{k=0}^{\infty} \frac{(-1)^k}{(2k+1)!} x^{2k+1} = \sin x$$

These are some examples of finite and infinite series where it is possible to find an exact expression for the sum. In general, finding an expression for the sum of the first n terms of a series can be surprisingly difficult, if not impossible. For example, it is not possible to express a formula for the sum $\displaystyle\sum_{k=1}^{n} \frac{1}{k^2} = \frac{1}{1^2} + \frac{1}{2^2} + \dots + \frac{1}{n^2}$ in terms of standard functions.

In cases where you manage to guess the formula for the sum of a series, you can then try to prove it by induction. The inductive step relies on making the connection between the sum of the first k terms and the sum of the first $k+1$ terms; this is done simply by adding the next term of the series.

Rewind

Binomial series were covered in A Level Mathematics Student Book 1, Chapter 9, and A Level Mathematics Student Book 2, Chapter 6.

Explore

Although it is not possible to find a general expression for $\displaystyle\sum_{k=1}^{n} \frac{1}{k^2}$, it is possible to find its exact sum to infinity, $\displaystyle\sum_{k=1}^{\infty} \frac{1}{k^2}$. Find out what it is: the result may surprise you!

Key point 1.1

If $S_k = u_1 + u_2 + \dots + u_k$ then

$$S_{k+1} = S_k + u_{k+1}$$

WORKED EXAMPLE 1.4

Prove by induction that

$$\sum_{r=1}^{n} r(r+2) = \frac{n(n+1)(2n+7)}{6} \text{ for all } n \in \mathbb{Z}^+.$$

For $n = 1$:

Show that the statement is true for the starting value (in this case, $n = 1$).

LHS $= 1 \times 3 = 3$

RHS $= \dfrac{1(1+1)(2\times1+7)}{6} = \dfrac{1\times2\times9}{6} = 3$

So, the result is true for $n = 1$.

Continues on next page ...

Assume that the result is true for $n = k$:

$$\sum_{r=1}^{k} r(r+2) = \frac{k(k+1)(2k+7)}{6}$$

State the assumption for $n = k$.

Let $n = k + 1$:

$$\sum_{r=1}^{k+1} r(r+2) = \sum_{r=1}^{k} r(r+2) + (k+1)(k+3)$$

Consider S_{k+1} and relate it to S_k by using $S_{k+1} = S_k + u_{k+1}$.

$$= \frac{k(k+1)(2k+7)}{6} + (k+1)(k+3)$$

Substitute in the result for $n = k$ (assumed to be true).

$$= (k+1)\left(\frac{2k^2 + 7k}{6} + \frac{6k+18}{6} \right)$$

$$= \frac{(k+1)(2k^2 + 13k + 18)}{6}$$

Combine this into one fraction and simplify. It is always a good idea to take out any common factors.

$$= \frac{(k+1)(k+2)(2k+9)}{6}$$

$$= \frac{(k+1)((k+1)+1)(2(k+1)+7)}{6}$$

Show that this is in the required form by separating out $k+1$ in each place it occurs.

So, the result is also true for $n = k + 1$.

The result is true for $n = 1$, and if it is true for $n = k$ it is also true for $n = k + 1$. Therefore, the result is true for all $n \in \mathbb{Z}^+$, by induction.

Make sure you write a conclusion.

EXERCISE 1B

1. Prove by induction that, for all $n \in \mathbb{Z}^+$:

$$\sum_{r=1}^{n} 2 \times 3^{r-1} = 3^n - 1$$

2. Prove by induction that, for all integers $n > 1$:

$$\sum_{r=1}^{n} r^2 = \frac{n(n+1)(2n+1)}{6}$$

3. Using mathematical induction prove that, for all positive integers:

$$\sum_{r=1}^{n} r^3 = \frac{n^2(n+1)^2}{4}$$

4. Prove by induction that, for all integers $n > 1$:

$$\sum_{r=1}^{n} \frac{1}{r(r+1)} = \frac{n}{n+1}$$

5. Use mathematical induction to show that, for all integers $n > 1$:

$$\sum_{r=1}^{n} r2^r = 2\left[(n-1)2^n + 1 \right]$$

6 Prove by induction that, for all $n \in \mathbb{Z}^+$:

$$\frac{1}{1 \times 3} + \frac{1}{3 \times 5} + \frac{1}{5 \times 7} + \ldots + \frac{1}{(2n-1)(2n+1)} = \frac{n}{2n+1}$$

7 Using mathematical induction prove that, for all integers $n > 1$:

$$\sum_{r=1}^{n} r(r!) = (n+1)! - 1$$

8 Prove by induction that, for all positive integers:

$$1^2 - 2^2 + 3^2 - 4^2 + \ldots + (-1)^{n+1} n^2 = (-1)^{n+1} \frac{n(n+1)}{2}$$

9 Prove using mathematical induction that, for all $n \in \mathbb{Z}^+$:

$$(n+1) + (n+2) + (n+3) + \ldots + (2n) = \frac{1}{2}n(3n+1)$$

10 Prove by induction that, for all integers $n > 1$:

$$\sum_{k=1}^{n} k \, 2^k = (n-1)2^{n+1} + 2$$

Section 3: Using standard series

You will now look at finding expressions for the sums of series such as $\sum_{k=1}^{n} \left(2n^3 - 5n\right)$ by combining some standard results.

You can use the following formulae without proof (unless the question explicitly asks you to prove them).

Key point 1.2

Formulae for the sums of integers, squares and cubes:

- $\displaystyle\sum_{r=1}^{n} r = \frac{1}{2}n(n+1)$

- $\displaystyle\sum_{r=1}^{n} r^2 = \frac{1}{6}n(n+1)(2n+1)$

- $\displaystyle\sum_{r=1}^{n} r^3 = \frac{1}{4}n^2(n+1)^2$

The second and third formulae will be given in your formula book.

◄◄ Rewind

You proved the second and third formulae in Exercise 1B, Questions 2 and 3.

The first formula in Key Point 1.2 is just a special case of an arithmetic series.

Explore

The formula for the sum of the first n integers, $\frac{1}{2}n(n+1)$, is the formula for the nth term in the sequence of triangular numbers: 1, 3, 6, 10, 15, 21....

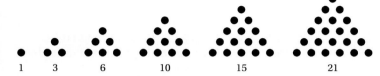

| 1 | 3 | 6 | 10 | 15 | 21 |

Explore pictorial representations of the other two formulae from Key point 1.2.

Before you use these results, notice how you can split up sums and take out constants. For example:

$$\sum_{r=1}^{n}(3r+2) = (3\times1+2)+(3\times2+2)+(3\times3+2)+(3\times4+2)+\cdots+(3n+2)$$

$$= 3(1+2+3+4+\cdots+n)+\underbrace{2+2+2+2+\cdots+2}_{n \text{ times}}$$

$$= 3\sum_{r=1}^{n}r+\sum_{r=1}^{n}2$$

where $\sum_{r=1}^{n}2 = 2n$.

Key point 1.3

You can manipulate series in several ways.

- $\sum(u_r+v_r)=\sum u_r+\sum v_r$
- $\sum cu_r=c\sum u_r$
- $\sum_{r=1}^{n}c=nc$

where c is a constant.

Tip

Remember that a constant, c, summed n times is nc and not just c. For example, $\sum_{r=1}^{n}2 = 2n$ and not 2.

WORKED EXAMPLE 1.5

a Use the formula for $\sum_{r=1}^{n} r$ to show that $\sum_{r=1}^{n}(4r+3)=n(2n+5)$.

b Hence find $\sum_{r=8}^{20}(4r+3)$.

a $\sum_{r=1}^{n}(4r+3)=\sum_{r=1}^{n}4r+\sum_{r=1}^{n}3$

> You need to rearrange the expression into a form to which you can apply the standard formulae. Start by splitting up the sum.

$=4\sum_{r=1}^{n}r+\sum_{r=1}^{n}3$

> Then take 4 out of the first sum as a factor.

$=4\times\frac{1}{2}n(n+1)+3n$

> $\sum_{r=1}^{n}r=\frac{1}{2}n(n+1)$ and $\sum_{r=1}^{n}3=3n$

$=n[2(n+1)+3]$

$=n(2n+5)$

> Notice that it's always a good idea to factorise first. In this case only n factorises, but in more complicated examples this will avoid having to expand and then factorise a higher order polynomial later.

b $\sum_{r=8}^{20}(4r+3)=\sum_{r=1}^{20}(4r+3)-\sum_{r=1}^{7}(4r+3)$

> You can only use the formula in part **a** if the sum starts from $r=1$. Therefore, work out the sum of the first 20 terms and subtract the sum of the first 7 terms.

$=20(2\times20+5)-7(2\times7+5)$

$=900-133$

$=767$

> Now use the formula $n(2n+5)$ with $n=20$ and $n=7$.

WORKED EXAMPLE 1.6

a Use the formulae for $\sum_{r=1}^{n}r$, $\sum_{r=1}^{n}r^2$ and $\sum_{r=1}^{n}r^3$ to show that $\sum_{r=1}^{n}r(2r-5)(r+1)=\frac{1}{2}n(n+1)(n+2)(n-3)$.

b Hence find an expression for $\sum_{r=1}^{2n}r(2r-5)(r+1)$, simplifying your answer fully.

a $\sum_{r=1}^{n}r(2r-5)(r+1)=\sum_{r=1}^{n}r(2r^2-3r-5)$

> Expand the brackets.

$=\sum_{r=1}^{n}(2r^3-3r^2-5r)$

$=\sum_{r=1}^{n}2r^3-\sum_{r=1}^{n}3r^2-\sum_{r=1}^{n}5r$

> Split up the series into separate sums.

Continues on next page ...

$$= 2\sum_{r=1}^{n} r^3 - 3\sum_{r=1}^{n} r^2 - 5\sum_{r=1}^{n} r$$

> Take out constants.

$$= 2\left[\frac{1}{4}n^2(n+1)^2\right] - 3\left[\frac{1}{6}n(n+1)(2n+1)\right] - 5\left[\frac{1}{2}n(n+1)\right]$$

> Substitute in the standard formulae.

$$= \frac{1}{2}n^2(n+1)^2 - \frac{1}{2}n(n+1)(2n+1) - 5\left[\frac{1}{2}n(n+1)\right]$$

> Simplify the first two terms.

$$= \frac{1}{2}n(n+1)[n(n+1) - (2n+1) - 5]$$

> Now factorise as many terms as possible. Note that this is much easier than expanding everything first.

$$= \frac{1}{2}n(n+1)[n^2 + n - 2n - 1 - 5]$$

$$= \frac{1}{2}n(n+1)[n^2 - n - 6]$$

$$= \frac{1}{2}n(n+1)(n+2)(n-3)$$

b $$\sum_{r=1}^{2n} r(2r-5)(r+1) = \frac{1}{2}2n(2n+1)(2n+2)(2n-3)$$

> Substitute $2n$ for n in the formula found in part **a**.

$$= n(2n+1)(2n+2)(2n-3)$$
$$= 2n(2n+1)(n+1)(2n-3)$$

> Simplify and factorise, taking out a 2 from the second bracket.

WORK IT OUT 1.1

Given that $\displaystyle\sum_{r=1}^{n}(r^2 - 2r) = \frac{n}{6}(n+1)(2n-5)$, find an expression for $\displaystyle\sum_{r=n+1}^{2n}(r^2 - 2r)$.

Which is the correct solution? Identify the errors made in the incorrect solutions.

Solution 1	$\displaystyle\sum_{r=n+1}^{2n}(r^2 - 2r) = \frac{2n}{6}(2n+1)(2(2n)-5)$ $\displaystyle = \frac{n}{3}(2n+1)(4n-5)$
Solution 2	$\displaystyle\sum_{r=n+1}^{2n}(r^2 - 2r) = \sum_{r=1}^{2n}(r^2 - 2r) - \sum_{r=1}^{n}(r^2 - 2r)$ $\displaystyle = \frac{2n}{6}(2n+1)(2(2n)-5) - \frac{n}{6}(n+1)(2n-5)$ $\displaystyle = \frac{n}{6}[2(2n+1)(2(2n)-5) - (n+1)(2n-5)]$ $\displaystyle = \frac{n}{6}[2(8n^2 - 6n - 5) - (2n^2 - 3n - 5)]$ $\displaystyle = \frac{n}{6}(14n^2 - 9n - 5)$ $\displaystyle = \frac{n}{6}(14n + 5)(n - 1)$

Continues on next page ...

Solution 3

$$\sum_{r=n+1}^{2n}(r^2-2r)=\sum_{r=1}^{2n}(r^2-2r)-\sum_{r=1}^{n+1}(r^2-2r)$$

$$=\frac{2n}{6}(2n+1)(2(2n)-5)-\frac{n}{6}((n+1)+1)(2(n+1)-5)$$

$$=\frac{n}{6}[2(2n+1)(2(2n)-5)-(n+2)(2n-3)]$$

$$=\frac{n}{6}[2(8n^2-6n-5)-(2n^2+n-6)]$$

$$=\frac{n}{6}(14n^2-13n-4)$$

EXERCISE 1C

In this exercise, you can assume the formulae for $\sum_{r=1}^{n}r$, $\sum_{r=1}^{n}r^2$ and $\sum_{r=1}^{n}r^3$.

1 Evaluate each expression.

    a i $\displaystyle\sum_{r=1}^{30}r^2$ **ii** $\displaystyle\sum_{r=1}^{20}r^3$ **b i** $\displaystyle\sum_{r=32}^{50}r^3$ **ii** $\displaystyle\sum_{r=25}^{100}r$

2 Find a formula for each series, giving your answer in its simplest form.

    a i $\displaystyle\sum_{r=1}^{4n}r$ **ii** $\displaystyle\sum_{r=1}^{3n}r^2$ **b i** $\displaystyle\sum_{r=1}^{n-1}r^2$ **ii** $\displaystyle\sum_{r=1}^{n+1}r^3$

3 Show that $\displaystyle\sum_{r=1}^{n}r(3r-5)=n(n+1)(n-2)$.

4 Show that $\displaystyle\sum_{r=1}^{n}3r(r-1)=n(n^2-1)$.

5   **a** Find an expression for $\displaystyle\sum_{r=1}^{n}(6r+7)$.

    b Hence find the least value of n such that $\displaystyle\sum_{r=1}^{n}(6r+7)>2400$.

6   **a** Show that $\displaystyle\sum_{r=1}^{n}(r+1)(r+5)=\frac{n}{6}(n+7)(2n+7)$.

    b Hence evaluate $\displaystyle\sum_{r=16}^{40}(r+1)(r+5)$.

7 Show that $\displaystyle\sum_{r=1}^{n}r^2(r-1)=\frac{n}{12}(n^2-1)(kn+2)$, where k is an integer to be found.

8   **a** Show that $\displaystyle\sum_{r=1}^{n}r(r^2-3)=\frac{n}{4}(n+1)(n-2)(n+3)$.

    b Hence find a formula for $\displaystyle\sum_{r=1}^{2n}r(r^2-3)$, fully simplifying your answer.

9 **a** Show that $\displaystyle\sum_{r=1}^{n} r(r+1) = \frac{n}{3}(n+1)(n+2)$.

   b Hence find, in the form $\ln 3^k$, the exact value of $2\ln 3 + 3\ln 3^2 + 4\ln 3^3 + \cdots + 20\ln 3^{19}$.

10 Show that the sum of the squares of the first n odd numbers is given by $S = \dfrac{n}{3}(an^2 - 1)$, where a is an integer to be found.

Section 4: The method of differences

Whenever you are investigating a series, start by writing out a few terms to see if any patterns develop.

For example, for the series $\displaystyle\sum_{r=1}^{n} u_r = \sum_{r=1}^{n}[r(r+1) - r(r-1)]$:

$$u_1 = 1(2) - 1(0)$$
$$u_2 = 2(3) - 2(1)$$
$$u_3 = 3(4) - 3(2)$$
$$u_4 = 4(5) - 4(3)$$
$$\vdots$$

You can see that each term shares a common element with the next; in the first term, this element is positive and in the next it is negative. Therefore, when you complete the sum, these common elements will cancel out.

This cancellation continues right through to the nth term.

$$1(2) - 1(0)$$
$$+2(3) - 2(1)$$
$$+3(4) - 3(2)$$
$$+4(5) - 4(3)$$
$$\vdots$$
$$+(n-1)n - (n-1)(n-2)$$
$$+n(n+1) - n(n-1)$$

$$\therefore \sum_{r=1}^{n} r(r+1) - r(r-1) = n(n+1) - 1(0) = n(n+1)$$

In fact, because

$$r(r+1) - r(r-1) = r^2 + r - r^2 + r = 2r$$

you have just shown that

$$\sum_{r=1}^{n} 2r = n(n+1) \Rightarrow \sum_{r=1}^{n} r = \frac{n}{2}(n+1)$$

which is the result for the sum of the first n integers that you used in Section 3.

This process for finding a formula for the sum of the first n terms of a sequence is called the **method of differences**.

Key point 1.4

Method of differences

If the general term of a series, u_r, can be written in the form $u_r = \mathrm{f}(r+1) - \mathrm{f}(r)$, then:

$$\sum_{r=1}^{n} u_r = \mathrm{f}(n+1) - \mathrm{f}(1)$$

 Tip

The series won't always take exactly this form, so write out several terms to see how the cancellation occurs.

WORKED EXAMPLE 1.7

a Show that $(2r+1)^3 - (2r-1)^3 \equiv 24r^2 + 2$.

b Hence show that $\displaystyle\sum_{r=1}^{n} r^2 = \frac{1}{6}n(n+1)(2n+1)$.

a $(2r+1)^3 - (2r-1)^3$

$= (2r)^3 + 3(2r)^2 1 + 3(2r)1^2 + 1^3$

  $- [(2r)^3 + 3(2r)^2(-1) + 3(2r)(-1)^2 + (-1)^3]$

$= 8r^3 + 12r^2 + 6r + 1 - [8r^3 - 12r^2 + 6r - 1]$

$= 24r^2 + 2$

> Use the binomial expansion to expand the cubed brackets.

> Simplify to give the result required.

b $\displaystyle\sum_{r=1}^{n}(24r^2 + 2) = \sum_{r=1}^{n}[(2r+1)^3 - (2r-1)^2]$

> Sum both sides of the result from **a**.

$\text{RHS} = (3)^3 - (1)^3$

  $+ (5)^3 - (3)^3$

  $+ (7)^3 - (5)^3$

  $\vdots$

  $+ (2n-1)^3 - (2n-3)^2$

  $+ (2n+1)^3 - (2n-1)^2$

> The RHS is a difference, so you expect cancellation.

> Write out the first few terms ($r = 1, 2, 3, \ldots$) and the last couple of terms ($r = n-1, n$).

$= (2n+1)^3 - 1^3$

> Everything cancels except the terms shown.

$\text{LHS} = 24\displaystyle\sum_{r=1}^{n} r^2 + 2n$

> For the LHS, remember that $\displaystyle\sum_{r=1}^{n} 2 = 2n$.

$\therefore 24\displaystyle\sum_{r=1}^{n} r^2 + 2n = (2n+1)^3 - 1^3$

> Make the expressions for the LHS and RHS equal.

Continues on next page ...

$$24\sum_{r=1}^{n}r^2 + 2n = (2n)^3 + 3(2n)^2 1 + 3(2n)1^2 + 1^3 - 1^3$$

$$24\sum_{r=1}^{n}r^2 + 2n = 8n^3 + 12n^2 + 6n$$

$$24\sum_{r=1}^{n}r^2 = 8n^3 + 12n^2 + 4n$$

$$6\sum_{r=1}^{n}r^2 = 2n^3 + 3n^2 + n$$

$$6\sum_{r=1}^{n}r^2 = n(2n^2 + 3n + 1)$$

$$6\sum_{r=1}^{n}r^2 = n(n+1)(2n+1)$$

$$\sum_{r=1}^{n}r^2 = \frac{1}{6}n(n+1)(2n+1)$$

> You now need to make $\sum_{r=1}^{n}r^2$ the subject.
>
> Start by expanding the RHS and then simplify.

> Factorise the RHS.

> Finally, divide by 6.

Sometimes the cancellation occurs two terms apart.

WORKED EXAMPLE 1.8

a Write $\dfrac{2}{(k+1)(k+3)}$ in partial fractions.

b Find an expression for $\displaystyle\sum_{k=1}^{n}\dfrac{2}{(k+1)(k+3)}$.

a $\dfrac{2}{(k+1)(k+3)} = \dfrac{A}{k+1} + \dfrac{B}{k+3}$

> Each factor in the denominator corresponds to one partial fraction.

$\Rightarrow 2 = A(k+3) + B(k+1)$

> Multiply through by the common denominator.

$k = -1: \ 2 = A(2) + B(0) \Rightarrow A = 1$
$k = -3: \ 2 = A(0) + B(-2) \Rightarrow B = -1$

> Use suitable values of k to make each bracket equal to zero.

$\therefore \dfrac{2}{(k+1)(k+3)} = \dfrac{1}{k+1} - \dfrac{1}{k+3}$

Continues on next page ...

Rewind

You learnt about partial fractions in A Level Mathematics Student Book 2, Chapter 5.

b $\displaystyle\sum_{k=1}^{n}\frac{2}{(k+1)(k+3)}=\sum_{k=1}^{n}\frac{1}{k+1}-\frac{1}{k+3}$ $\qquad$ Sum both sides of the result in **a**.

$$=\frac{1}{2}-\frac{1}{4}$$
$$+\frac{1}{3}-\frac{1}{5}$$
$$+\frac{1}{4}-\frac{1}{6}$$
$$+\frac{1}{5}-\frac{1}{7}$$
$$\vdots$$

Writing out several terms ($k = 1, 2, 3, \ldots$) shows that the cancellations in the series occur two terms apart.

$$+\frac{1}{n-1}-\frac{1}{n+1}$$
$$+\frac{1}{n}-\frac{1}{n+2}$$
$$+\frac{1}{n+1}-\frac{1}{n+3}$$

Continue the pattern of cancellation for the last few terms ($k = n-2, n-1, n$).

$$=\frac{1}{2}+\frac{1}{3}-\frac{1}{n+2}-\frac{1}{n+3}$$

This leaves part of the first two terms and part of the last two. You could put this all over a common denominator and combine into one fraction but, as the question doesn't specifically require this, there is no need to do anything else.

As you keep adding more and more terms of a series, the sum could keep increasing without a limit, or it could approach a finite value. In the latter case you say that the series **converges** (is convergent) and you could try to find its sum to infinity. To do this, you can find an expression for the sum of the first n terms and consider what this expression tends to when n gets very large.

WORKED EXAMPLE 1.9

Use the result from Worked example 1.8 to evaluate $\displaystyle\sum_{k=1}^{\infty}\frac{2}{(k+1)(k+3)}$.

From Worked example 1.8:

$$\sum_{k=1}^{n}\frac{2}{(k+1)(k+3)}=\frac{1}{2}+\frac{1}{3}-\frac{1}{n+2}-\frac{1}{n+3}$$

Let $n \to \infty$ in this result. Then:

$$\frac{1}{n+2}\to 0$$
$$\frac{1}{n+3}\to 0$$

As the denominator tends to ∞, these fractions tend to zero.

$$\therefore \sum_{k=1}^{\infty}\frac{2}{(k+1)(k+3)}=\frac{1}{2}+\frac{1}{3}=\frac{5}{6}$$

EXERCISE 1D

1 **a** Show that $(r+1)^2 - r^2 \equiv 2r+1$.

    b Hence show that $\displaystyle\sum_{r=1}^{n}(2r+1) = n(n+2)$.

2 **a** Show that $r^2(r+1)^2 - (r-1)^2 r^2 \equiv 4r^3$.

    b Hence show that $\displaystyle\sum_{r=1}^{n} r^3 = \frac{1}{4}n^2(n+1)^2$.

3 **a** Show that $\dfrac{1}{k+1} - \dfrac{1}{k+2} \equiv \dfrac{1}{(k+1)(k+2)}$.

    b **i** Hence show that $\displaystyle\sum_{k=1}^{n} \frac{2}{(k+1)(k+2)} = \frac{n}{n+2}$.

       ii Find $\displaystyle\sum_{k=11}^{24} \frac{2}{(k+1)(k+2)}$.

4 **a** Express $\dfrac{2}{(2r-1)(2r+1)}$ in partial fractions.

    b Use the method of differences to show that $\displaystyle\sum_{r=1}^{n} \frac{2}{(2r-1)(2r+1)} = \frac{2n}{2n+1}$.

    c Find $\displaystyle\sum_{r=1}^{\infty} \frac{2}{(2r-1)(2r+1)}$.

5 **a** Show that $(r+1)! - (r-1)! \equiv (r^2+r-1)(r-1)!$

    b Use the method of differences to show that $\displaystyle\sum_{r=1}^{n}(r^2+r-1)(r-1)! = (n+2)n! - 2$.

6 **a** Show that $\dfrac{1}{k} - \dfrac{1}{(k+2)} \equiv \dfrac{2}{k(k+2)}$.

    b Hence, find $\displaystyle\sum_{k=1}^{\infty} \frac{2}{k(k+2)}$.

7 **a** Show that $\dfrac{1}{2k+1} - \dfrac{1}{2k+3} \equiv \dfrac{2}{(2k+1)(2k+3)}$.

    b Find an expression for $\displaystyle\sum_{k=1}^{n} \frac{2}{(2k+1)(2k+3)}$.

    c Hence show that $\dfrac{1}{3\times 5} + \dfrac{1}{5\times 7} + \dfrac{1}{7\times 9} + \ldots = \dfrac{1}{6}$.

8 Use the method of differences to find $\displaystyle\sum_{r=1}^{n} \frac{1}{(r+1)(r+2)(r+3)}$.

9 **a** Show that $\dfrac{1}{2k} - \dfrac{1}{k+1} + \dfrac{1}{2(k+2)} \equiv \dfrac{1}{k(k+1)(k+2)}$.

    b Use the method of differences to show that

$$\sum_{k=1}^{2n} \frac{1}{k(k+1)(k+2)} = \frac{n(an+b)}{c(n+1)(2n+1)}$$

    where a, b and c are constants to be found.

    c Find $\dfrac{1}{11\times 12\times 13} + \dfrac{1}{12\times 13\times 14} + \ldots + \dfrac{1}{20\times 21\times 22}$

10 **a** Use the method of differences to find $\displaystyle\sum_{k=1}^{n} \ln\left(1+\frac{1}{k}\right)$.

b Hence, prove that the series $\displaystyle\sum_{k=1}^{\infty} \ln\left(1+\frac{1}{k}\right)$ diverges.

 Checklist of learning and understanding

- You can use proof by induction to prove results concerning matrices, divisibility, inequalities, sequences, series, powers and differentiation.
- When working with series, use $S_{k+1} = S_k + u_{k+1}$.
- The formulae for the sums of integers, squares and cubes are:

  - $\displaystyle\sum_{r=1}^{n} r = \frac{1}{2}n(n+1)$

  - $\displaystyle\sum_{r=1}^{n} r^2 = \frac{1}{6}n(n+1)(2n+1)$

  - $\displaystyle\sum_{r=1}^{n} r^3 = \frac{1}{4}n^2(n+1)^2$

- You can manipulate series in these ways:

  - $\displaystyle\sum(u_r + v_r) = \sum u_r + \sum v_r$

  - $\displaystyle\sum cu_r = c\sum u_r$

  - $\displaystyle\sum_{r=1}^{n} c = nc$

  where c is a constant.

- **Method of differences**

  If the general term of a series, u_r, can be written in the form $u_r = \mathrm{f}(r+1) - \mathrm{f}(r)$, then:

  $$\sum_{r=1}^{n} u_r = \mathrm{f}(n+1) - \mathrm{f}(1)$$

  - You might need to split an expression into partial fractions before using the method of differences.
  - You can check whether an infinite series converges, and find its sum to infinity, by finding an expression for the first n terms of the series and considering what happens to it as n gets very large.

Mixed practice 1

1 Let $f(n) = 3^{2n} + 7$.

    a Evaluate $f(n)$ for $n = 1, 2, 3$ and 4. Hence suggest a natural number which is a factor of each $f(n)$.

    b Prove by induction that your conjecture from part **a** is correct for all $n \in \mathbb{N}$.

2 Prove by induction that, for $n \geqslant 1$

$$\sum_{r=1}^{n} r(r+1) = \frac{n}{3}(n+1)(n+2).$$

© OCR AS Level Mathematics, Unit 4725 Further Pure Mathematics 1, June 2010

3 Let $f(x) = e^{3x}$.

    a Find $f'(x), f''(x)$ and $f'''(x)$. Suggest an expression for $f^{(n)}(x)$.

    b Use mathematical induction to prove your conjecture from part **a**.

4 Find an expression for $\displaystyle\sum_{r=n+1}^{2n} (2r+1)$.

5 Use the formulae for $\displaystyle\sum_{r=1}^{n} r$ and $\displaystyle\sum_{r=1}^{n} r^2$ to show that $\displaystyle\sum_{r=1}^{n}(r+2)(r-1) = \frac{n}{3}(n+4)(n-1)$.

6 Use the formulae for $\displaystyle\sum_{r=1}^{n} r^2$ and $\displaystyle\sum_{r=1}^{n} r^3$ to find the value of $\displaystyle\sum_{r=5}^{40} r^2(2r-3)$.

7   **a** Show that $\dfrac{1}{k+4} - \dfrac{1}{k+5} \equiv \dfrac{1}{k^2 + 9k + 20}$.

    b Hence show that $\displaystyle\sum_{k=1}^{n} \dfrac{1}{k^2 + 9k + 20} = \dfrac{an}{b(n+5)}$, where a and b are integers to be found.

8 Find $\displaystyle\sum_{r=1}^{2n}\left(3r^2 - \frac{1}{2}\right)$, expressing your answer in a fully factorised form.

© OCR AS Level Mathematics, Unit 4725 Further Pure Mathematics 1, June 2011

9 Use induction to prove that, for all integers $n \geqslant 1$,

$$\frac{1}{2!} + \frac{2}{3!} + \frac{3}{4!} + \frac{4}{5!} + \dots + \frac{n}{(n+1)!} = \frac{(n+1)! - 1}{(n+1)!}$$

10 Prove by induction that, for all $n \in \mathbb{N}$,

$$\sum_{r=1}^{n} \frac{r}{2^r} = 2 - \left(\frac{1}{2}\right)^n (n+2)$$

11   **a** Show that $\cos\left(x + \dfrac{\pi}{2}\right) = -\sin x$.

    b Prove that $\dfrac{d^n}{dx^n}(\cos x) = \cos\left(x + \dfrac{n\pi}{2}\right)$.

12   **a** Show that $\displaystyle\sum_{r=2}^{n} r(r-1)(r+1) = \frac{n}{4}(n^2 - 1)(n+2)$.

    b Hence find the sum of $(11 \times 12 \times 13) + (12 \times 13 \times 14) + (13 \times 14 \times 15) + \dots + (38 \times 39 \times 40)$.

13 a Show that $\dfrac{1}{r^2} - \dfrac{1}{(r+1)^2} \equiv \dfrac{2r+1}{r^2(r+1)^2}$.

b Hence show that $\displaystyle\sum_{r=1}^{n} \dfrac{2r+1}{r^2(r+1)^2} = \dfrac{n(n+2)}{(n+1)^2}$.

14 a Show that $\dfrac{1}{r!} - \dfrac{1}{(r+1)!} \equiv \dfrac{r}{(r+1)!}$.

b Find $\dfrac{1}{2!} + \dfrac{2}{3!} + \dfrac{3}{4!} + \ldots + \dfrac{n}{(n+1)!}$.

c Hence find $\displaystyle\sum_{r=1}^{\infty} \dfrac{r}{(r+1)!}$.

15 The sequence $u_1, u_2, u_3, \ldots$ is defined by $u_n = 5^n + 2^{n-1}$.

i Find u_1, u_2 and u_3.

ii Hence suggest a positive integer, other than 1, which divides exactly into every term of the sequence.

iii By considering $u_{n+1} + u_n$, prove by induction that your suggestion in part **ii** is correct.

© OCR AS Level Mathematics, Unit 4725/01 Further Pure Mathematics 1, June 2014

16 i Show that $\dfrac{1}{3r-1} - \dfrac{1}{3r+2} \equiv \dfrac{3}{(3r-1)(3r+2)}$.

ii Hence show that $\displaystyle\sum_{r=1}^{2n} \dfrac{1}{(3r-1)(3r+2)} = \dfrac{n}{2(3n+1)}$.

© OCR AS Level Mathematics, Unit 4725/01 Further Pure Mathematics 1, June 2013

17 Use mathematical induction to prove that $\dfrac{1}{\sqrt{1}} + \dfrac{1}{\sqrt{2}} + \ldots + \dfrac{1}{\sqrt{n}} > \sqrt{n}$ for all $n > 1$.

18 Prove by induction that $\dfrac{1}{\sqrt{1}} + \dfrac{1}{\sqrt{2}} + \ldots + \dfrac{1}{\sqrt{n}} > 2(\sqrt{n+1} - 1)$ for all $n \geqslant 1$.

19 Find the smallest positive integer N for which $3^N < N!$. Prove that $3^n < n!$ for all $n \geqslant N$.

20 Show that $(1+x)^n \geqslant 1 + nx$ for $n \in \mathbb{N}$ and $x \in \mathbb{R}$.

21 Prove by induction that, for any positive integer n:

$$2 \times 6 \times 10 \times \ldots \times (4n-2) = \dfrac{(2n)!}{n!}.$$

22 i Show that $\dfrac{r}{r+1} - \dfrac{r-1}{r} \equiv \dfrac{1}{r(r+1)}$.

ii Hence find an expression, in terms of n, for $\dfrac{1}{2} + \dfrac{1}{6} + \dfrac{1}{12} + \ldots + \dfrac{1}{n(n+1)}$.

iii Hence find $\displaystyle\sum_{r=n+1}^{\infty} \dfrac{1}{r(r+1)}$.

© OCR AS Level Mathematics, Unit 4725 Further Pure Mathematics 1, January 2012

23   **a**   Express $\dfrac{3}{(r-1)(r+2)}$ in partial fractions.

     b   Hence show that $\displaystyle\sum_{r=2}^{3n+1} \dfrac{1}{(r-1)(r+2)} = \dfrac{n(an^2+bn+c)}{6(3n+1)(3n+2)(3n+3)}$ where a, b and c are constants to be found.

24   Use the method of differences to show that $\displaystyle\sum_{k=1}^{n} \dfrac{3k+4}{k(k+1)(k+2)} = \dfrac{n(an+b)}{c(n+1)(n+2)}$,

where a, b and c are coprime integers to be found.

Powers and roots of complex numbers

In this chapter you will learn how to:

- raise complex numbers to integer powers (de Moivre's theorem)
- work with complex exponents
- find roots of complex numbers
- use roots of unity
- find quadratic factors of polynomials
- use a relationship between complex number multiplication and geometric transformations.

Before you start…

Pure Core Student Book 1, Chapter 4	You should know how to find the modulus and argument of a complex number.	1 Find the modulus and argument of $-3 + 4i$.
Pure Core Student Book 1, Chapter 4	You should be able to represent complex numbers on an Argand diagram.	2 Write down the complex numbers corresponding to the points A and B.
Pure Core Student Book 1, Chapter 2, Section 2, Chapter 4	You should know how to work with complex numbers in Cartesian form.	3 Given that $z = 3 - 2i$ and $w = 2 + i$, evaluate: a $z - w$ b $\dfrac{z}{w}$.
Pure Core Student Book 1, Chapter 4	You should be able to multiply and divide complex numbers in modulus–argument form.	4 Given that $z = 10\left(\cos\dfrac{3\pi}{4} + i\sin\dfrac{3\pi}{4}\right)$ and $w = 2\left(\cos\dfrac{2\pi}{3} + i\sin\dfrac{2\pi}{3}\right)$, find: a zw b $\dfrac{z}{w}$. Give the arguments in the range $(-\pi, \pi)$.

Continues on next page …

Pure Core Student Book 1, Chapter 4	You should be able to work with complex conjugates.	5	Write down the complex conjugate of: a $5i - 3$ b $3\left(\cos\dfrac{\pi}{4} + i\sin\dfrac{\pi}{4}\right)$.
Pure Core Student Book 1, Chapter 4	You should know how to relate operations with complex numbers to transformations on an Argand diagram.	6	Let $a = 2 + i$ and z be any complex number. Describe a geometrical transformation that maps: a z to z^* b z to $z + a$.

Extending arithmetic with complex numbers

You already know how to perform basic operations with complex numbers, both in Cartesian and in modulus–argument form. Modulus–argument form is particularly well suited to multiplication and division. In this chapter you will see how you can utilise this to find powers and roots of complex numbers. This chapter also includes a definition of complex powers which can make calculations even simpler.

You will also meet roots of unity, which are the solutions of the equation $z^n = 1$. They have some useful algebraic and geometric properties. Some of the applications include finding exact values of trigonometric functions.

Because you can represent complex numbers as points on an Argand diagram, operations with complex numbers have a geometric interpretation. You can use this to solve some problems that at first sight have nothing to do with complex numbers. This is just one example of the use of complex numbers to solve real-life problems.

> ⏮ **Rewind**
>
> You met complex numbers in Pure Core Student Book 1, Chapter 4.

> ⏭ **Fast forward**
>
> You will learn more about links between complex numbers and trigonometry in Chapter 3.

Section 1: De Moivre's theorem

In Pure Core Student Book 1, Chapter 4, you learnt that you can write complex numbers in Cartesian form, $x + iy$, or in modulus–argument form, $r(\cos\theta + i\sin\theta)$, or $r\,\mathrm{cis}\,\theta$. You also learnt the rules for multiplying complex numbers in modulus–argument form:

$$|zw| = |z||w| \text{ and } \arg(zw) = \arg z + \arg w$$

You can apply this result to find powers of complex numbers. If a complex number has modulus r and argument θ, then multiplying $z \times z$ gives that z^2 has modulus r^2 and argument 2θ. Repeating this process, you can see that

$$|z^n| = |z|^n \text{ and } \arg(z^n) = n\arg z$$

In other words, when you raise a complex number to a power, you raise the modulus to the same power and multiply the argument by the power.

Key point 2.1

De Moivre's theorem

For a complex number, z, with modulus r and argument θ:

$$z^n = \left(r\left(\cos\theta + i\sin\theta\right)\right)^n = r^n\left(\cos n\theta + i\sin n\theta\right)$$

for every integer power n.

 Tip

De Moivre's theorem can also be written as $(r\operatorname{cis}\theta)^n = r^n\operatorname{cis}(n\theta)$ or $\left[r, \theta\right]^n = \left[r^n, n\theta\right]$.

For positive integer powers, you can prove this result by induction.

Rewind

For Proof 1 you will also need the compound angle formulae from A Level Mathematics Student Book 2, Chapter 8.

Focus on …

See Focus on … Proof 1 for a discussion of how to extend de Moivre's theorem to all rational n.

PROOF 1

When $n = 1$:
$$\left(r\left(\cos\theta + i\sin\theta\right)\right)^1 = r\left(\cos\theta + i\sin\theta\right)$$
so the result is true for $n = 1$.

Check that the result is true for $n = 1$.

Assuming that the result is true for some k:
$$\left(r\left(\cos\theta + i\sin\theta\right)\right)^k = r^k\left(\cos k\theta + i\sin k\theta\right)$$

Assume that the result is true for some k and write down what that means. (Remember, you will need to use this later.)

Then for $n = k + 1$:
$$\left(r\left(\cos\theta + i\sin\theta\right)\right)^{k+1} = r^k\left(\cos k\theta + i\sin k\theta\right) \times r\left(\cos\theta + i\sin\theta\right)$$

Make a link between $n = k$ and $n = k + 1$. In this case use $z^{k+1} = z^k z$.

$$= r^{k+1}\left(\cos k\theta \cos\theta + i\cos k\theta \sin\theta + i\sin k\theta \cos\theta - \sin k\theta \sin\theta\right)$$

Expand the brackets, remembering that $i^2 = -1$.

$$= r^{k+1}\left(\left(\cos k\theta \cos\theta - \sin k\theta \sin\theta\right) + i\left(\cos k\theta \sin\theta + \sin k\theta \cos\theta\right)\right)$$

Group real and imaginary parts.

$$= r^{k+1}\left(\cos(k+1)\theta + i\sin(k+1)\theta\right)$$

Recognise the compound angle formulae:

$\cos(A + B) = \cos A \cos B - \sin A \sin B$ and
$\sin(A + B) = \sin A \cos B + \cos A \sin B$.

This is the result you are trying to prove, but with n replaced by $k + 1$.

Hence the result is true for $n = k + 1$.

The result is true for $n = 1$, and if it is true for some k then it is also true for $k + 1$. Therefore, it is true for all $n \geqslant 1$ by induction.

Remember to write the full conclusion.

You can use **de Moivre's theorem** to evaluate powers of complex numbers.

WORKED EXAMPLE 2.1

Evaluate, without a calculator, $\dfrac{(1+i)^{22}}{4i}$.

$|1+i| = \sqrt{1^2 + 1^2} = \sqrt{2}$ .... First find the modulus and argument of each number.

$\arg(1+i) = \arctan\left(\dfrac{1}{1}\right) = \dfrac{\pi}{4}$

$\therefore 1+i = \sqrt{2}\left(\cos\dfrac{\pi}{4} + i\sin\dfrac{\pi}{4}\right)$

$|4i| = 4, \arg(4i) = \dfrac{\pi}{2}$

$\therefore 4i = 4\left(\cos\dfrac{\pi}{2} + i\sin\dfrac{\pi}{2}\right)$

By *de Moivre's theorem*:

$\left(\sqrt{2}\left(\cos\dfrac{\pi}{4} + i\sin\dfrac{\pi}{4}\right)\right)^{22} = \left(\sqrt{2}\right)^{22}\left(\cos\dfrac{22\pi}{4} + i\sin\dfrac{22\pi}{4}\right)$

$= 2^{11}\left(\cos\dfrac{11\pi}{2} + i\sin\dfrac{11\pi}{2}\right)$

$= 2048\left(\cos\dfrac{\pi}{2} + i\sin\dfrac{\pi}{2}\right)$ .... The argument needs to be between $-\pi$ and π: $\dfrac{11\pi}{2} - 5\pi = \dfrac{\pi}{2}$.

Dividing the moduli and subtracting the arguments:

$\dfrac{(1+i)^{22}}{4i} = \dfrac{2048\left(\cos\dfrac{\pi}{2} + i\sin\dfrac{\pi}{2}\right)}{4\left(\cos\dfrac{\pi}{2} + i\sin\dfrac{\pi}{2}\right)}$

$= \dfrac{2048}{4}(\cos 0 + i\sin 0)$

$= 512$

💡 **Tip**

If the power of (1 + i) had been smaller, you might have been able to use the binomial expansion with the fact that $i^2 = -1$, $i^3 = -i$ and $i^4 = 1$. For example:

$$(1 + i)^6 = 1 + 6i + 15i^2 + 20i^3 + 15i^4 + 6i^5 + i^6$$
$$= 1 + 6i - 15 - 20i + 15 + 6i - 1$$
$$= -8i$$

The usefulness of complex numbers is that the calculation does not get any longer or more difficult with larger powers.

You can also prove that de Moivre's theorem works for negative integer powers.

WORKED EXAMPLE 2.2

Let $z = r(\cos\theta + i\sin\theta)$.

a Find the modulus and argument of $\dfrac{1}{z}$.

b Hence prove de Moivre's theorem for negative integer powers.

a Multiplying top and bottom by the complex conjugate:

$$\frac{1}{z} = \frac{1}{r(\cos\theta + i\sin\theta)} \times \frac{(\cos\theta - i\sin\theta)}{(\cos\theta - i\sin\theta)}$$

$$= \frac{\cos\theta - i\sin\theta}{r(\cos^2\theta + \sin^2\theta)}$$

$$= \frac{1}{r}(\cos\theta - i\sin\theta) \quad\cdots\cdots\cdots\quad \text{Use } \cos^2\theta + \sin^2\theta \equiv 1.$$

$$= \frac{1}{r}(\cos(-\theta) + i\sin(-\theta)) \quad\cdots\cdots$$

> To find the modulus and argument, you need to write the number in this form.
>
> Remember that $\cos(-\theta) \equiv \cos\theta$ and $\sin(-\theta) \equiv -\sin\theta$.

Hence $\left|\dfrac{1}{z}\right| = \dfrac{1}{r}$ and $\arg\left(\dfrac{1}{z}\right) = -\theta.$ $\cdots\cdots$

> This means that you can write
> $\dfrac{1}{z} = \dfrac{1}{r}(\cos(-\theta) + i\sin(-\theta)).$

b Using de Moivre's theorem for positive powers:

$$\left(\frac{1}{z}\right)^n = \left(\frac{1}{r}(\cos(-\theta) + i\sin(-\theta))\right)^n \quad\cdots\cdots$$

$$= \left(\frac{1}{r}\right)^n (\cos(-n\theta) + i\sin(-n\theta))$$

> Since you have already proved de Moivre's theorem for positive powers, you can use
> $z^{-n} = (z^{-1})^n = \left(\dfrac{1}{z}\right)^n$ with the modulus and argument of $\dfrac{1}{z}$ found in part **a**.

Hence $z^{-n} = r^{-n}(\cos(-n\theta) + i\sin(-n\theta))$, as required.

WORKED EXAMPLE 2.3

Find the modulus and argument of $\dfrac{1}{\left(1-i\sqrt{3}\right)^{7}}$.

Modulus and argument of $z = 1 - i\sqrt{3}$:

The best way to find the modulus and argument is to sketch a diagram.

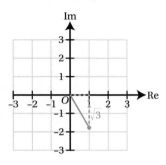

$$\sqrt{1^2 + \sqrt{3}^2} = 2$$

$$\tan^{-1}\left(-\frac{\sqrt{3}}{1}\right) = -\frac{\pi}{3}$$

$$\text{So } z = 2\,\text{cis}\left(-\frac{\pi}{3}\right)$$

Applying de Moivre's theorem for negative powers:

$$z^{-7} = 2^{-7}\,\text{cis}\left(-7 \times -\frac{\pi}{3}\right)$$

$$= \frac{1}{128}\,\text{cis}\,\frac{7\pi}{3}$$

This is in the form $r\,\text{cis}\,\theta$ so you can just read off the modulus and the argument.

The modulus is $\dfrac{1}{128}$ and the argument is

$$\frac{7\pi}{3} - 2\pi = \frac{\pi}{3}.$$

The argument needs to be between 0 and 2π, so you need to take away 2π.

EXERCISE 2A

1 Evaluate each expression, giving your answer in the form $r(\cos\theta + i\sin\theta)$.

a **i** $\left(2\cos\dfrac{\pi}{5} + 2i\sin\dfrac{\pi}{5}\right)^{6}$ **ii** $\left(3\left(\cos\left(-\dfrac{\pi}{3}\right) + i\sin\left(-\dfrac{\pi}{3}\right)\right)\right)^{4}$

b **i** $\left(\text{cis}\dfrac{\pi}{6}\right)^{2}\left(\text{cis}\dfrac{\pi}{4}\right)^{3}$ **ii** $\left(\text{cis}\dfrac{\pi}{8}\right)^{4}\left(\text{cis}\dfrac{\pi}{3}\right)^{2}$

c **i** $\dfrac{\left(\cos\dfrac{2\pi}{3}+\mathrm{i}\sin\dfrac{2\pi}{3}\right)^{6}}{\left(\cos\dfrac{\pi}{6}+\mathrm{i}\sin\dfrac{\pi}{6}\right)^{3}}$ **ii** $\dfrac{\left(\cos\dfrac{\pi}{4}+\mathrm{i}\sin\dfrac{\pi}{4}\right)^{2}}{\left(\cos\dfrac{\pi}{3}+\mathrm{i}\sin\dfrac{\pi}{3}\right)^{6}}$

2   Given that $z = \cos\dfrac{\pi}{6} + \mathrm{i}\sin\dfrac{\pi}{6}$:

    a   write z^2, z^3 and z^4 in the form $r(\cos\theta + \mathrm{i}\sin\theta)$

    b   represent z, z^2, z^3 and z^4 on the same Argand diagram.

3   **a**   Given that $z = \left[1, \dfrac{2\pi}{3}\right]$:

       i   write z^2, z^3 and z^4 in modulus–argument form

       ii   represent z, z^2, z^3 and z^4 on the same Argand diagram.

    b   For which natural numbers n is $z^n = z$?

In questions 4 and 5 you must show detailed reasoning.

4   **a**   Find the modulus and argument of $1 + \mathrm{i}\sqrt{3}$.

    b   Hence find $\left(1 + \mathrm{i}\sqrt{3}\right)^{5}$ in modulus–argument form.

    c   Hence find $\left(1 + \mathrm{i}\sqrt{3}\right)^{5}$ in Cartesian form.

5   **a**   Write $-\sqrt{2} + \mathrm{i}\sqrt{2}$ in the form $r\,\mathrm{cis}\,\theta$.

    b   Hence find $\left(-\sqrt{2} + \mathrm{i}\sqrt{2}\right)^{6}$ in simplified Cartesian form.

6   Find the smallest positive integer value of n for which $\left(\cos\dfrac{5\pi}{12} + \mathrm{i}\sin\dfrac{5\pi}{12}\right)^{n}$ is real.

7   Find the smallest positive integer value of k such that $\left(\mathrm{cis}\,\dfrac{3\pi}{28}\right)^{k}$ is purely imaginary.

Section 2: Complex exponents

The rules for multiplying complex numbers in modulus–argument form look just like the rules of indices:

Compare

$$r_1\,\mathrm{cis}\,\theta_1 \times r_2\,\mathrm{cis}\,\theta_2 = r_1 r_2\,\mathrm{cis}(\theta_1 + \theta_2)$$

with

$$k_1\,\mathrm{e}^{x_1} \times k_2\,\mathrm{e}^{x_2} = k_1 k_2\,\mathrm{e}^{x_1 + x_2}.$$

You can extend the definition of powers to imaginary numbers so that all the rules of indices still apply.

Key point 2.2

Euler's formula:

$$e^{i\theta} \equiv \cos\theta + i\sin\theta$$

It is important to realise that Euler's formula is a definition, and so it makes no sense to ask why it is true or how to prove it. You can, however, note that it seems to be a sensible definition, since it ensures that imaginary powers follow the same rules as real powers.

You can write a complex number with modulus r and argument θ in **exponential form** as $re^{i\theta}$. You now have four different ways of writing complex numbers with a given modulus and argument.

 Key point 2.3

$$re^{i\theta} = r(\cos\theta + i\sin\theta) = r\operatorname{cis}\theta = [r, \theta]$$

When working with complex numbers in exponential form you can use all the normal rules of indices.

 Fast forward

With this definition of imaginary powers, all the usual properties of the exponential function still hold. For example, it turns out that the Maclaurin series, which you will meet in Chapter 8, can be extended to include imaginary powers.

 Did you know?

Substituting $\theta = \pi$ into Euler's formula and rearranging gives $e^{i\pi} + 1 = 0$. This equation, called Euler's identity, connects five important numbers from different areas of mathematics. It is often cited as 'the most beautiful' equation in mathematics.

WORKED EXAMPLE 2.4

Given that $z = 2e^{\frac{i\pi}{12}}$ and $w = \dfrac{1}{2}e^{\frac{i\pi}{4}}$, find $z^5 w^3$ in the form $x + iy$.

$z^5 w^3 = \left(2e^{\frac{i\pi}{12}}\right)^5 \left(\dfrac{1}{2}e^{\frac{i\pi}{4}}\right)^3$

> You can do all the calculations in exponential form and then convert to Cartesian form at the end.

$= 2^5 e^{\frac{5i\pi}{12}} \times \dfrac{1}{2^3} e^{\frac{3i\pi}{4}}$

$= 4e^{\frac{7i\pi}{6}}$

> Use rules of indices for the powers:
> $\dfrac{5}{12} + \dfrac{3}{4} = \dfrac{7}{6}$

$= 4\left(\cos\left(\dfrac{7\pi}{6}\right) + i\sin\left(\dfrac{7\pi}{6}\right)\right)$

> Now write in terms of trigonometric functions and evaluate.

$= 4\left(-\dfrac{\sqrt{3}}{2} - \dfrac{1}{2}i\right)$

$= -2\sqrt{3} - 2i$

You can combine Euler's formula with rules of indices to raise any real number to any complex power.

WORKED EXAMPLE 2.5

Find, correct to three significant figures, the value of:

a e^{2+3i} **b** 3^{2+3i}.

a $e^{2+3i} = e^2 e^{3i}$

> Use rules of indices to separate the real and imaginary parts of the power.

$= e^2(\cos 3 + i \sin 3)$

> Use Euler's formula for the imaginary power.

$= -7.32 + 1.04i$

> Expand the brackets and give the answer to 3 s.f. Remember that the arguments of the trigonometric functions are in radians.

b $3^{2+3i} = (e^{\ln 3})^{2+3i}$

> You only know how to raise e to a complex power, so express 3 as a power of e.

$= e^{2\ln 3} e^{(3\ln 3)i}$

> Use rules of indices and then Euler's formula. Note that $e^{2\ln 3} = e^{\ln 9} = 9$ and $3\ln 3 = \ln 27$.

$= 9(\cos(\ln 27) + i \sin(\ln 27))$

$= -8.89 - 1.38i$

The complex conjugate of a number is easy to find when written in exponential form. This is best seen on an Argand diagram, where taking the complex conjugate is represented by a reflection in the real axis. In this case it is best to take the argument between $-\pi$ and π.

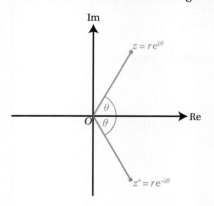

▶▶| **Fast forward**

You will use the exponential form of complex numbers when solving second order differential equations in Chapter 10.

🔑 **Key point 2.4**

The complex conjugate of $z = re^{i\theta}$ is $z^* = re^{-i\theta}$.

💡 **Tip**

Note that if $r = 1$, you also have
$z^* = \dfrac{1}{z} = e^{-i\theta}$.

In Pure Core Student Book 1, Chapter 5, you used complex conjugates when solving polynomial equations.

WORKED EXAMPLE 2.6

A cubic equation has real coefficients and two of its roots are 1 and $2e^{\frac{i\pi}{3}}$. Find the equation in the form $x^3 + ax^2 + bx + c = 0$.

The roots are:

$1, 2e^{\frac{i\pi}{3}}$ and $2e^{-\frac{i\pi}{3}}$.

> Complex roots occur in conjugate pairs, so you can write down the third root.

$-a = 1 + 2e^{\frac{i\pi}{3}} + 2e^{-\frac{i\pi}{3}}$

> Use the formulae for sums and products of roots to find the coefficients of the equation:
>
> $-a = x_1 + x_2 + x_3$

$= 1 + 4\cos\dfrac{\pi}{3}$

> Remember that $z + z^* = 2\text{Re}(z)$, and that
>
> $\text{Re}\left(e^{\frac{i\pi}{3}}\right) = \cos\dfrac{\pi}{3} = \dfrac{1}{2}$

$= 3$

$\therefore a = -3$

$b = \left(1 \times 2e^{\frac{i\pi}{3}}\right) + \left(1 \times 2e^{-\frac{i\pi}{3}}\right) + \left(2e^{\frac{i\pi}{3}} \times 2e^{-\frac{i\pi}{3}}\right)$

> $b = x_1 x_2 + x_2 x_3 + x_3 x_1$

$= 4\cos\left(\dfrac{\pi}{3}\right) + 4$

$= 6$

$-c = 1 \times 2e^{\frac{i\pi}{3}} \times 2e^{-\frac{i\pi}{3}} = 4$

> $-c = x_1 x_2 x_3$

$\therefore c = -4$

Hence the equation is $x^3 - 3x^2 + 6x - 4 = 0$.

EXERCISE 2B

You can use your calculator to perform operations with complex numbers in Cartesian, modulus–argument and exponential forms, as well as to convert from one form to another. Do the questions in this exercise without a calculator first, then use a calculator to check your answers.

1 Write each complex number in Cartesian form without using trigonometric functions.

   a **i** $3e^{i\frac{\pi}{6}}$ **ii** $4e^{\frac{i\pi}{4}}$

   b **i** $4e^{i\pi}$ **ii** $5e^{2\pi i}$

   c **i** $e^{\frac{2\pi i}{3}}$ **ii** $2e^{\frac{3\pi}{2}i}$

2 Write each complex number in the form $re^{i\theta}$.

   a **i** $5 + 5i$ **ii** $2\sqrt{3} - 2i$

   b **i** $-\dfrac{1}{2} + \dfrac{1}{2}i$ **ii** $2 + 3i$

   c **i** $-4i$ **ii** -5

3 Write the answer to each calculation in the form $re^{i\theta}$.

a **i** $4e^{i\frac{\pi}{6}} \times 5e^{i\frac{\pi}{4}}$ **ii** $\dfrac{5e^{i\frac{3\pi}{4}}}{10e^{i\frac{\pi}{4}}}$

b **i** $\dfrac{\left(2e^{i\frac{\pi}{4}}\right)^3}{\left(5e^{i\frac{\pi}{3}}\right)^2}$ **ii** $\dfrac{2e^{i\frac{\pi}{3}}}{\left(e^{i\frac{\pi}{6}}\right)^5}$

4 Represent each complex number on an Argand diagram.

a **i** $e^{i\frac{\pi}{3}}$ **ii** $e^{i\frac{3\pi}{4}}$

b **i** $5e^{i\frac{\pi}{2}}$ **ii** $2e^{-i\frac{\pi}{3}}$

5 Let $z = 2e^{\frac{i\pi}{12}}$ and $w = 4e^{\frac{i\pi}{3}}$. Show that $z^2 + w = 2(1+i)(1+\sqrt{3})$.

6 **In this question you must show detailed reasoning.**

Let $z = 2e^{\frac{i\pi}{3}}$ and $w = 3e^{-\frac{i\pi}{6}}$. Write each complex number in the form $x + iy$.

a $\dfrac{z}{w}$ **b** $z^5 w^3$

7 Write e^{4+3i} in the form $x + iy$, where x and y are real, giving your answer correct to three significant figures.

8 Write $e^{2-\frac{i\pi}{3}}$ in exact Cartesian form.

9 The equation $x^3 + ax^2 + bx + c = 0$ has real coefficients, and two of its roots are 2 and $e^{\frac{i\pi}{3}}$. Find the values of a, b and c.

10 A quartic equation has real coefficients and two of its roots are $e^{\frac{i\pi}{6}}$ and $2e^{\frac{i\pi}{3}}$. Find the equation in the form $x^4 + ax^3 + bx^2 + cx + d = 0$.

11 Find 5^i in the form $x + yi$.

12 Find 3^{2-i} in the form $x + yi$.

Section 3: Roots of complex numbers

Now that you can use de Moivre's theorem to find powers of complex numbers, it makes sense to ask whether you can also find roots.

In Pure Core Student Book 1, you learnt how to find the two square roots of a complex number by writing $z = x + iy$ and comparing real and imaginary parts. You also know that a polynomial equation of degree n has n complex roots. Just as a complex number has two square roots, it will have three cube roots, four fourth roots, and so on.

You can't always use the algebraic method to find all those roots. De Moivre's theorem gives an alternative method.

 Rewind

See Pure Core Student Book 1, Chapter 4, for an example of finding square roots of a complex number.

WORKED EXAMPLE 2.7

Solve the equation $z^3 = 4\sqrt{3} + 4\mathrm{i}$.

Let $z = r(\cos\theta + \mathrm{i}\sin\theta)$.

> Use the modulus–argument form since raising to a power is easier in this form than in Cartesian form.

Then the equation is equivalent to
$$r^3(\cos 3\theta + \mathrm{i}\sin 3\theta) = 4\sqrt{3} + 4\mathrm{i}$$

> Use de Moivre's theorem and then compare the modulus and the argument of both sides.

> Find the modulus and argument of the RHS.

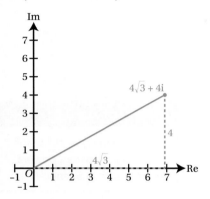

$$\left|4\sqrt{3} + 4\mathrm{i}\right| = \sqrt{\left(4\sqrt{3}\right)^2 + 4^2} = 8$$

$$\arg\left(4\sqrt{3} + 4\mathrm{i}\right) = \arctan\left(\frac{4}{4\sqrt{3}}\right) = \frac{\pi}{6}$$

Therefore,

$$r^3(\cos 3\theta + \mathrm{i}\sin 3\theta) = 8\left(\cos\frac{\pi}{6} + \mathrm{i}\sin\frac{\pi}{6}\right)$$

Comparing the moduli:

$$r^3 = 8 \Rightarrow r = 2$$

> Remember that, by definition, r is a positive real number.

Comparing the arguments:

$$3\theta = \frac{\pi}{6}, \frac{13\pi}{6} \text{ or } \frac{25\pi}{6}$$

$$\theta = \frac{\pi}{18}, \frac{13\pi}{18}, \frac{25\pi}{18}$$

> If $0 < \theta < 2\pi$ then $0 < 3\theta < 6\pi$.

> Since adding 2π to the argument returns to the same complex number, there are 3 possible values for 3θ between 0 and 6π.

The roots are:

$$z_1 = 2\left(\cos\frac{\pi}{18} + \mathrm{i}\sin\frac{\pi}{18}\right)$$

> Write down all three roots in modulus–argument form.

$$z_2 = 2\left(\cos\frac{13\pi}{18} + \mathrm{i}\sin\frac{13\pi}{18}\right)$$

$$z_3 = 2\left(\cos\frac{25\pi}{18} + \mathrm{i}\sin\frac{25\pi}{18}\right)$$

If you plot the three roots from Worked example 2.7 on an Argand diagram, you will notice an interesting pattern. They all have the same modulus so they lie on a circle of radius 2. The arguments differ by $\frac{2\pi}{3}$ so they are equally spaced around the circle. Therefore, the three points form an equilateral triangle.

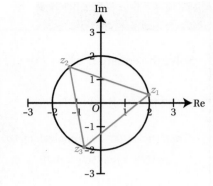

 Key point 2.5

To solve $z^n = w$:

- write w in modulus–argument form
- use de Moivre's theorem to write $z^n = r^n(\cos n\theta + i\sin n\theta)$
- compare moduli, remembering that they are always real
- compare arguments, remembering that adding 2π to the argument does not change the number
- write n different roots in modulus–argument form.

All n roots of the equation $z^n = w$ will have the same modulus, and their arguments will differ by $\frac{2\pi}{n}$. This means that the Argand diagram will always show the pattern you noticed in Worked example 2.7.

 Fast forward

You will learn more about the connection between powers and rotations in Section 6.

 Key point 2.6

The roots of $z^n = w$ form a regular polygon with vertices on a circle centred at the origin.

WORKED EXAMPLE 2.8

Draw an Argand diagram showing the roots of the equation $z^6 = 729$.

One root is

$z_1 = \sqrt[6]{729} = 3$

There are six roots, forming a regular hexagon.
You only need to find one of them and then complete the diagram.

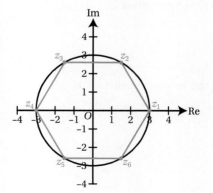

You can also find the equation whose roots form a given regular polygon.

WORKED EXAMPLE 2.9

The diagram shows a regular pentagon inscribed in a circle on an Argand diagram. One of the vertices lies on the positive imaginary axis.

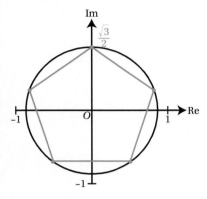

The five vertices of the pentagon correspond to the solutions of an equation of the form $z^n = w$, where w is a complex number. Find the values of n and w.

There are five roots, so $n = 5$.	Any equation of the form $z^n = w$ has n complex roots.
From the diagram: $z = \dfrac{\sqrt{3}}{2}$ i is a root.	Use the fact that one root is given in the question.
Hence	Remember that $i^5 = i$.
$w = \left(\dfrac{\sqrt{3}}{2}i\right)^5 = \dfrac{9\sqrt{3}}{32}i$	

EXERCISE 2C

In this exercise you must show detailed reasoning.

1   Find all three cube roots of each number, giving your answers in the form $r\,e^{i\theta}$.

   a i 27   **ii** 100

   b i 8i   **ii** i

   c i 1+i   **ii** $2 - \sqrt{3}i$

2 Find the fourth roots of each number. Give your answers in the form $r\operatorname{cis}\theta$ and show them on an Argand diagram.

a i -16　　　　　　　　　　　　**ii** 81i

b i $8\sqrt{2}+8\sqrt{2}$i　　　　　　　**ii** $-\dfrac{1}{2}+\dfrac{\sqrt{3}}{2}$i

3 Solve the equation $z^3=-8$ for $z\in\mathbb{C}$. Give your answers in the form $x+y$i.

4 a Find the modulus and the argument of $8\sqrt{3}-8$i.

　b Solve the equation $z^4=8\sqrt{3}-8$i, giving your answers in the form $r\left(\cos\left(\dfrac{p}{q}\pi\right)+\mathrm{i}\sin\left(\dfrac{p}{q}\pi\right)\right)$, where p and q are integers.

5 Solve the equation $z^3-\sqrt{2}\left(4-4\mathrm{i}\right)=0$, giving your answers in Cartesian form.

6 Find all complex roots of the equation $z^4+81\mathrm{i}=0$, giving your answers in the form $r\left(\cos\left(\dfrac{p}{q}\pi\right)+\mathrm{i}\sin\left(\dfrac{p}{q}\pi\right)\right)$, where p and q are integers.

7 a Write $4+4\sqrt{3}\mathrm{i}$ in the form $r\mathrm{e}^{\mathrm{i}\theta}$.

　b Hence solve the equation $z^4=4+4\sqrt{3}\mathrm{i}$, giving your answers in the form $r\mathrm{e}^{\mathrm{i}\theta}$.

　c Show your solution on an Argand diagram.

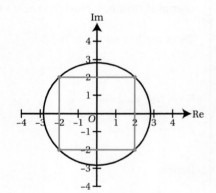

8 The diagram shows a square with one vertex at $(2, 2)$. The complex numbers corresponding to the vertices of the square are solutions of an equation of the form $z^n=w$, where $n\in\mathbb{N}$ and $w\in\mathbb{R}$.

Find the values of n and w.

9 a Solve the equation $z^4=-16$, giving your answers in Cartesian form.

　b Hence express z^4+16 as a product of two real quadratic factors.

10 a Find all the roots of the equation $z^3=-8$i.

　b Hence solve the equation $w^3+8\mathrm{i}(w-1)^3=0$. Give your answers in exact Cartesian form.

11 Consider the equation $z^3+\left(4\sqrt{2}-4\sqrt{2}\mathrm{i}\right)=0$.

　a Solve the equation, giving your answers in the form $r(\cos\theta+\mathrm{i}\sin\theta)$.

The roots are represented on an Argand diagram by points A, B and C, labelled anticlockwise with A in the first quadrant. D is the midpoint of AB and the corresponding complex number is d.

　b Find the modulus and argument of d.

　c Write d^3 in exact Cartesian form.

12 a Find, in exponential form, the three roots of the equation $z^3=-1$.

　b Expand $(x+2)^3$.

　c Hence or otherwise solve the equation $z^3+6z^2+12z+9=0$, giving any complex root in exact Cartesian form.

Section 4: Roots of unity

In Section 3 you learnt a method for finding all complex roots of a number. A special case of this is solving the equation $z^n = 1$. Its roots are called **roots of unity**.

WORKED EXAMPLE 2.10

Find the fifth roots of unity, giving your answers in exponential form.

Let the roots be $z = r\,e^{i\theta}$.

Write z in exponential form and use de Moivre's theorem.

Then:

$$\left(re^{i\theta}\right)^5 = 1$$

$$\Rightarrow r^5 e^{5i\theta} = 1e^{0i}$$

1 has modulus 1 and argument 0.

Comparing the moduli:

$r = 1$

Comparing the arguments:

Remember that there should be five roots.

$5\theta = 0, 2\pi, 4\pi, 6\pi, 8\pi$

$$\theta = 0, \frac{2\pi}{5}, \frac{4\pi}{5}, \frac{6\pi}{5}, \frac{8\pi}{5}$$

The fifth roots of unity are:

$$1, e^{\frac{2\pi i}{5}}, e^{\frac{4\pi i}{5}}, e^{\frac{6\pi i}{5}}, e^{\frac{8\pi i}{5}}$$

As in Section 3, the five roots form a regular pentagon on the Argand diagram:

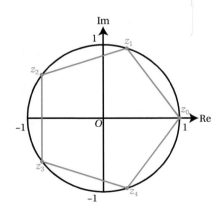

The same procedure works for any power n: there will be n distinct roots, each with modulus 1, and with arguments differing by $\dfrac{2\pi}{n}$. Remembering that one of the roots always equals 1, you can write down the full set of roots.

 Key point 2.7

The nth roots of unity are:

$$1, e^{\frac{2\pi i}{n}}, e^{\frac{4\pi i}{n}}, \ldots, e^{\frac{2(n-1)\pi i}{n}}$$

They form a regular n-gon on an Argand diagram.

Notice that all the arguments are multiples of $\dfrac{2\pi}{n}$. But multiplying an argument by a number k corresponds to raising the complex number to the power of k. Hence all the nth roots of unity are powers of $e^{\frac{2\pi i}{n}}$. It is usual to denote the n roots $\omega_0, \omega_1, \ldots, \omega_{n-1}$.

Key point 2.8

You can write the nth root of unity as:

$$\omega_k = \left(e^{\frac{2\pi i}{n}} \right)^k = \omega_1^k, \text{ where } k = 0, 1, \ldots, n-1.$$

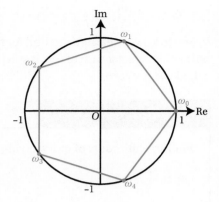

You can use the fact that the roots form a regular polygon to deduce various relationships between them. For example, for $n = 5$, you can use the symmetry of the pentagon to see that $\omega_4 = \omega_1^*$ and $\omega_3 = \omega_2^*$.

One of the most useful results concerns the sum of all n roots. You know from Pure Core Student Book 1, Chapter 4, that adding complex numbers corresponds to adding vectors on an Argand diagram. Since the points corresponding to the n roots of unity are equally spaced around the circle, the sum of the corresponding vectors should be zero.

You can also prove this result algebraically.

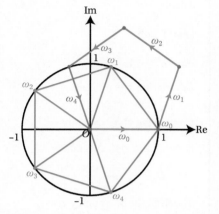

WORKED EXAMPLE 2.11

Let n be a natural number, and let $\omega = e^{\frac{2\pi i}{n}}$. Let $1, \omega_1, \omega_2, \ldots, \omega_{n-1}$ be the nth roots of unity.

a Express ω_k in terms of ω.

b Hence show that $1 + \omega_1 + \ldots + \omega_{n-1} = 0$.

a $\omega_k = \omega^k$ | This is the result from Key point 2.8.

b $1 + \omega_1 + \ldots + \omega_{n-1} = 1 + \omega + \omega^2 + \ldots + \omega^{n-1}$

$$= \frac{1 - \omega^n}{1 - \omega}$$

This is a geometric series with first term 1 and common ratio ω.

Note that $\omega \neq 1$ so you can use the formula for the sum of the geometric series.

$$= 0 \ (\text{since } \omega^n = 1)$$

ω is an nth root of unity, which means that $\omega^n = 1$.

 Key point 2.9

If $1, \omega_1, \omega_2, \ldots, \omega_{n-1}$ are the nth roots of unity, then

$$1 + \omega_1 + \ldots + \omega_{n-1} = 0.$$

Tip

You could also prove the result in Key point 2.9 by using the result about the sum of the roots of a polynomial: these are the roots of the equation $z^n - 1 = 0$, so their sum equals minus the coefficient of z^{n-1} which is 0.

You can use the result in Key point 2.9 with a specific value of n to find some special values of trigonometric functions.

⏩ Fast forward

You will learn more about the links between complex numbers and trigonometry in Chapter 3.

⏪ Rewind

You learnt about sums and products of roots of polynomials in Pure Core Student Book 1, Chapter 5.

WORKED EXAMPLE 2.12

Let $\omega = e^{\frac{2\pi i}{5}}$.

a Show that $\text{Re}(\omega) + \text{Re}(\omega^2) = -\dfrac{1}{2}$.

b Hence find the exact value of $\cos\dfrac{2\pi}{5}$.

a

The five points form a regular pentagon.

From the diagram:

$\omega^4 = \omega^*$ and $\omega^3 = \left(\omega^2\right)^*$

Hence $\text{Re}\left(\omega^4\right) = \text{Re}(\omega)$ and $\text{Re}\left(\omega^4\right) = \text{Re}(\omega)$

You are interested in the real parts.

Using the result $1 + \omega + \omega^2 + \omega^3 + \omega^4 = 0$

This is the result from Key point 2.9.

and taking the real part:

$1 + \text{Re}(\omega) + \text{Re}\left(\omega^2\right) + \text{Re}\left(\omega^3\right) + \text{Re}\left(\omega^4\right) = 0$

$\Rightarrow 1 + 2\text{Re}(\omega) + 2\text{Re}\left(\omega^2\right) = 0$

Pair up the terms with equal real parts.

$\Rightarrow \text{Re}(\omega) + \text{Re}\left(\omega^2\right) = -\dfrac{1}{2}$

Continues on next page ...

b $Re(\omega)=\cos\dfrac{2\pi}{5}, Re(\omega^2)=\cos\dfrac{4\pi}{5}$

> Use the fact that $\omega = e^{\frac{2\pi i}{5}} = \cos\dfrac{2\pi}{5}+i\sin\dfrac{2\pi}{5}$
> and $\omega^2 = \cos\dfrac{4\pi}{5}+i\sin\dfrac{4\pi}{5}$.

But $\cos\dfrac{4\pi}{5}=2\cos^2\dfrac{2\pi}{5}-1$, so:

> Use the double angle formula to relate the two values.

$$\cos\dfrac{2\pi}{5}+\cos\dfrac{4\pi}{5}=-\dfrac{1}{2}$$

$$\Rightarrow \cos\dfrac{2\pi}{5}+2\cos^2\dfrac{2\pi}{5}-1=-\dfrac{1}{2}$$

$$\Rightarrow 4\cos^2\dfrac{2\pi}{5}+2\cos\dfrac{2\pi}{5}-1=0$$

> This is a quadratic equation in $\cos\dfrac{2\pi}{5}$.

$$\Rightarrow \cos\dfrac{2\pi}{5}=\dfrac{-2+\sqrt{4+16}}{8}$$

> Take the positive root since $\cos\dfrac{2\pi}{5}>0$.

$$=\dfrac{-1+\sqrt{5}}{4}$$

EXERCISE 2D

1 Write down, in the form $r(\cos\theta+i\sin\theta)$, all the roots of each equation.

    a   **i** $z^3=1$ **ii** $z^2=1$

    b   **i** $z^6=1$ **ii** $z^4=1$

2 For each equation from question 1, write the roots in exact Cartesian form.

3   **a** Write down, in the form $e^{i\theta}$, the roots of the equation $z^5=1$.

    b Represent the roots on an Argand diagram.

4 The diagram shows all the roots of an equation $z^n=1$.

    a Write down the value of n.

    b Write down the value of $\omega_1+\omega_2+\omega_3+\omega_4$.

    c Which of these statements are correct?

        A $\omega_3=\omega_1^3$ **B** $\omega_4=\omega_2^2$

        C $\omega_3^5=1$ **D** $\omega_1^3=-\omega_1^2$

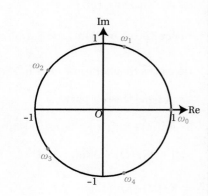

5 Let $\omega=e^{\frac{2\pi i}{7}}$.

    a Express the seventh roots of unity in terms of ω.

    b Is there an integer k such that $\omega^k=-\omega$? Justify your answer.

   c Write down the smallest positive integer p such that $\omega^{17} = \omega^p$.

   d Write down an integer m such that $\omega^m = \left(\omega^2\right)^*$.

6 Let $1, \omega_1, \omega_2, \omega_3, \omega_4, \omega_5$ be the distinct sixth roots of unity.

   a Show that $\omega_n = \omega_1^n$ for $n = 2, 3, 4, 5$.

   b Hence show that $1 + \omega + \omega^2 + \omega^3 + \omega^4 + \omega^5 = 0$.

7 **In this question you must show detailed reasoning.**

   a Find, in exact Cartesian form, all the complex roots of the equation $z^3 = 1$.

   b Hence find the exact roots of the equation $(z-1)^3 = (z+2)^3$.

8 Multiply out and simplify $\left(a + b\omega\right)\left(a - b\omega^2\right)$, where $\omega = e^{\frac{i\pi}{3}}$.

9 **In this question you must show detailed reasoning.**

Let $\omega = e^{\frac{2\pi i}{5}}$.

   a Write, in terms of ω, the complex roots of the equation $z^5 = 1$.

Consider the equation $(z-1)^5 = (z+1)^5$.

   b Find, in terms of ω, all roots of the equation.

   c Show that the roots can be written as $i\cot\left(\dfrac{k\pi}{5}\right)$ for $k = 1, 2, 3, 4$.

   d Show that $(z-1)^5 = (z+1)^5$ is equivalent to $5z^4 + 10z^2 + 1 = 0$.

   e Hence show that $\cot^2\dfrac{\pi}{5} + \cot^2\dfrac{2\pi}{5} = 2$.

10 Let $1, \omega, \omega^2, \omega^3, \omega^4, \omega^5$ be the roots of the equation $z^6 = 1$, where ω is the solution with the smallest positive argument.

   a Show these roots on an Argand diagram.

   b Write in the form $re^{i\theta}$:

     i $\dfrac{1 + \omega}{2}$ **ii** $\dfrac{\omega^3 + \omega^4}{2}$.

11 **a** Show that $\cos 3\theta = 4\cos^3\theta - 3\cos\theta$.

Let $\omega = \cos\dfrac{2\pi}{7} + i\sin\dfrac{2\pi}{7}$.

   b **i** Show that $1 + \omega + \omega^2 + \omega^3 + \omega^4 + \omega^5 + \omega^6 = 0$.

     ii Hence deduce the value of $\cos\dfrac{2\pi}{7} + \cos\dfrac{4\pi}{7} + \cos\dfrac{6\pi}{7}$.

   c Show that $\cos\dfrac{2\pi}{7}$ is a root of the equation $8t^3 + 4t^2 - 4t - 1 = 0$.

Section 5: Further factorising

In Pure Core Student Book 1, Chapter 5, you learnt that complex roots of a real polynomial come in conjugate pairs, and how you can use this fact to factorise a polynomial. You used the important result that, for any complex number w,

$$(z-w)(z-w^*)=z^2-2z\operatorname{Re}(w)+|w|^2$$

You can now combine this with your knowledge of roots of complex numbers to factorise expressions of the form z^n+c.

WORKED EXAMPLE 2.13

a Find all the complex roots of $z^4=-81$, giving your answers in Cartesian form.

b Hence write z^4+81 as a product of two real quadratic factors.

a Let $z=re^{i\theta}$.

> Write z in exponential form to find the roots, then turn answers into Cartesian form.

Then $r^4e^{i4\theta}=-81=81e^{i\pi}$

> The argument of -81 is π.

Comparing the moduli:

$r^4=81$, so $r=3$

Comparing the arguments:

$4\theta=\pi, 3\pi, 5\pi, 7\pi$

> You are looking for four roots, so add 2π three times.

$\theta=\dfrac{\pi}{4}, \dfrac{3\pi}{4}, \dfrac{5\pi}{4}, \dfrac{7\pi}{4}$

The roots are:

> Find the Cartesian form
>
> $x+iy=(r\cos\theta)+i(r\sin\theta)$

$z_1=\dfrac{3\sqrt{2}}{2}+\dfrac{3\sqrt{2}}{2}i$

$z_2=-\dfrac{3\sqrt{2}}{2}+\dfrac{3\sqrt{2}}{2}i$

$z_3=-\dfrac{3\sqrt{2}}{2}-\dfrac{3\sqrt{2}}{2}i$

$z_4=\dfrac{3\sqrt{2}}{2}-\dfrac{3\sqrt{2}}{2}i$

b $z^4+81=(z-z_1)(z-z_2)(z-z_3)(z-z_4)$

> The factors of z^4+81 correspond to the roots of the equation $z^4+81=0$, which you found in part **a**.

$(z-z_1)(z-z_4)=z^2-2\operatorname{Re}(z_1)z+|z_1|^2$

$=z^2-3\sqrt{2}z+9$

$(z-z_2)(z-z_3)=z^2-2\operatorname{Re}(z_2)z+|z_2|^2$

$=z^2+3\sqrt{2}z+9$

> To get real quadratic factors you need to pair up the factors corresponding to the conjugate roots.
>
> You can use the shortcut
>
> $(z-w)(z-w^*)=z^2-2z\operatorname{Re}(w)+|w|^2$ and $|z_k|=3$.

$\therefore z^4+81=\left(z^2-3\sqrt{2}z+9\right)\left(z^2+3\sqrt{2}z+9\right)$

EXERCISE 2E

In this exercise you must show detailed reasoning.

1 **a** Find, in exponential form, all the complex roots of the equation $z^4 = -16$.

    b Write your answers from part **a** in exact Cartesian form.

    c Hence express $z^4 + 16$ as a product of two real quadratic factors.

2 By solving the equation $z^8 = 16$, express $z^8 - 16$ as a product of four real quadratic factors.

3 Show that $z^5 - 1 = (z-1)\left(z^2 - (2\cos\theta)z + 1\right)\left(z^2 - (2\cos\phi)z + 1\right)$, where $\theta, \phi \in (0, \pi)$.

4 Let $\omega = e^{\frac{2i\pi}{5}}$.

    a Write the roots of the equation $z^5 - 1 = 0$ in terms of ω.

    b Hence evaluate $(2-\omega)\left(2-\omega^2\right)\left(2-\omega^3\right)\left(2-\omega^4\right)$.

5 **a** Show that $t^2 + t + 1 = \left(t - e^{\frac{2i\pi}{3}}\right)\left(t - e^{-\frac{2i\pi}{3}}\right)$.

    b Solve the equation $z^4 = e^{\frac{2i\pi}{3}}$.

    c Hence write $z^8 + z^4 + 1$ as a product of four real quadratic factors.

6 Let $\omega = e^{\frac{2i\pi}{7}}$.

    a Write down the non-real roots of the equation $z^7 = 1$ in terms of ω.

    b Show that $\cos\dfrac{2\pi}{7} + \cos\dfrac{4\pi}{7} + \cos\dfrac{6\pi}{7} = -\dfrac{1}{2}$.

    c Hence show that $\cos\dfrac{2\pi}{7}$ is a root of the equation $8t^3 + 4t^2 - 4t - 1 = 0$.

Section 6: Geometry of complex numbers

Multiplication of complex numbers has an interesting geometrical interpretation. On an Argand diagram, let A be the point corresponding to the complex number $z_1 = r_1 \text{cis}\,\theta_1$, and let B be the point corresponding to the complex number $z_1 \times r_2 \text{cis}\,\theta_2 = r_1 r_2 \text{cis}(\theta_1 + \theta_2)$.

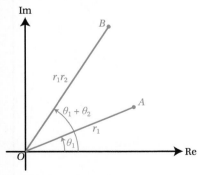

Then $OA = r_1$, $OB = r_1 r_2$, and $\angle AOB = (\theta_1 + \theta_2) - \theta_1 = \theta_2$. Hence the transformation that takes point A to point B is a rotation through angle θ_2 followed by an enlargement with scale factor r_2.

Key point 2.10

Multiplication by $r \operatorname{cis} \theta$ corresponds to a rotation about the origin though angle θ and an enlargement with scale factor r.

 Rewind

You already know, from Pure Core Student Book 1, Chapter 4, that adding a complex number $a + ib$ corresponds to a translation with vector $\begin{pmatrix} a \\ b \end{pmatrix}$, and that taking the complex conjugate corresponds to a reflection in the real axis.

WORKED EXAMPLE 2.14

Points A and B on an Argand diagram represent complex numbers $a = \sqrt{3} + i$ and $b = 2\sqrt{2} + 2i\sqrt{2}$, respectively.

a Find the modulus and argument of a and b.

b Hence describe a combination of two transformations which maps A to B.

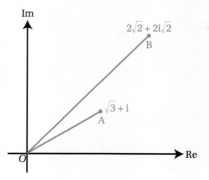

A diagram helps to find the modulus and the argument.

a $|a| = \sqrt{3+1} = 2$, $\arg(a) = \arctan\left(\dfrac{1}{\sqrt{3}}\right) = \dfrac{\pi}{6}$

$|b| = \sqrt{8+8} = 4$, $\arg(b) = \arctan\left(\dfrac{2\sqrt{2}}{2\sqrt{2}}\right) = \dfrac{\pi}{4}$

b Enlargement with scale factor 2

$|b| = 2|a|$

and rotation through $\dfrac{\pi}{4} - \dfrac{\pi}{6} = \dfrac{\pi}{12}$ about the origin.

The angle of rotation is the difference between the arguments.

The result from Key point 2.10 is remarkably powerful in some situations that have nothing to do with complex numbers.

WORKED EXAMPLE 2.15

An equilateral triangle has one vertex at the origin and another at $(1, 2)$. Find one possible set of coordinates of the third vertex.

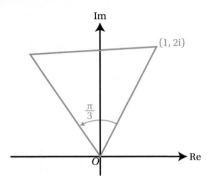

On an Argand diagram the point $(1, 2)$ corresponds to the complex number $1 + 2i$.

You can obtain the third vertex by rotation through $60°$ anticlockwise about the origin and no enlargement. This corresponds to multiplication by the complex number with modulus 1 and argument $\frac{\pi}{3}$.

The complex number corresponding to the third vertex is

$$(1+2i)\left(\cos\frac{\pi}{3}+i\sin\frac{\pi}{3}\right) = (1+2i)\left(\frac{1}{2}+\frac{\sqrt{3}}{2}i\right)$$

$$= \left(\frac{1}{2}-\sqrt{3}\right)+\left(\frac{\sqrt{3}}{2}+1\right)i$$

So the coordinates are

$$\left(\frac{1}{2}-\sqrt{3}, \frac{\sqrt{3}}{2}+1\right)$$

Tip

There is another equilateral triangle with vertices $(0, 0)$ and $(1, 2)$. You can obtain it by rotating clockwise through $60°$, corresponding to multiplication by $\cos\left(-\frac{\pi}{3}\right)+i\sin\left(-\frac{\pi}{3}\right)$.

Focus on ...

You can use several different approaches to solve the problem from Worked example 2.15. You could use coordinate geometry and trigonometry, or you could use a matrix to carry out the rotation. In Focus on ... Problem solving 1 you will explore different approaches to similar problems.

Rewind

You studied rotation matrices in Pure Core Student Book 1, Chapter 3.

Division by $\text{cis}\,\theta_2$ is the same as multiplication by $\text{cis}(-\theta_2)$:

$$(r_1\text{cis}\,\theta_1) \div (\text{cis}\,\theta_2) = r_1\text{cis}(\theta_1 - \theta_2) = (r_1\text{cis}\,\theta_1) \times (\text{cis}(-\theta_2))$$

Geometrically, this represents a rotation through angle $-\theta_2$.

 Key point 2.11

Division by $r\,\text{cis}\,\theta$ corresponds to a rotation about the origin though angle $-\theta$ and an enlargement with scale factor $\dfrac{1}{r}$.

Tip

If the angle θ is positive then multiplication corresponds to an anticlockwise rotation and division corresponds to a clockwise rotation.

Since raising to a positive integer power is repeated multiplication, in an Argand diagram it corresponds to repeated rotation and enlargement.

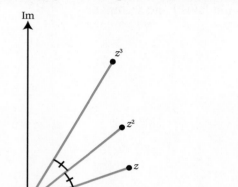

Although you can solve Worked example 2.16 just by doing the algebra, thinking about rotations might help you visualise what's going on.

WORKED EXAMPLE 2.16

Find the smallest positive integer value of n for which $\left(3\text{cis}\left(\dfrac{3\pi}{16}\right)\right)^n$ is pure imaginary.

$\left(\text{cis}\left(\dfrac{3\pi}{16}\right)\right)^n$ has argument $\dfrac{3n\pi}{16}$.

If $\dfrac{3n\pi}{16} = \dfrac{\pi}{2}$, $n = \dfrac{8}{3}$ which is not an integer.

If $\dfrac{3n\pi}{16} = \dfrac{3\pi}{2}$, $n = 8$.

Raising $3\text{cis}\left(\dfrac{3\pi}{16}\right)$ to a power corresponds to repeated rotation through $\dfrac{3\pi}{16}$ (combined with an enlargement with scale factor 3).

The question is therefore: how many rotations through $\dfrac{3\pi}{16}$ are needed to reach either $\dfrac{\pi}{2}$ or $\dfrac{3\pi}{2}$?

EXERCISE 2F

1 Points A and B represent complex numbers $a = 4 + i$ and $b = 5 + 3i$ on an Argand diagram.

   a Find the modulus and argument of a and b.

   b Point A is mapped to point B by a combination of an enlargement and a rotation. Find the scale factor of the enlargement and the angle of rotation.

2 Points P and Q represent complex numbers $p = 3 + 5i$ and $q = -\sqrt{30} + 2i$, respectively.

   a Show that $|p| = |q|$.   **b** Describe a single transformation that maps P to Q.

3 The complex number corresponding to the point A in the diagram is $z_1 = 3 + 2i$. The distance $OB = OA$. Find, in surd form, the complex number corresponding to the point B.

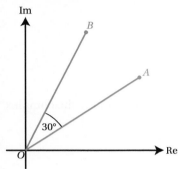

4 The diagram shows a square $OABC$, where A has coordinates $(5, 2)$.

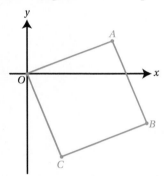

Find the exact coordinates of B and C.

5 Point A in the diagram corresponds to the complex number a. The complex number z equals $\operatorname{cis}\left(\dfrac{\pi}{6}\right)$.

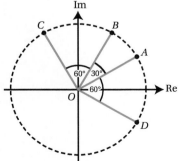

Write the complex numbers b, c and d corresponding to the points B, C and D in terms of a and z.

6 The diagram shows a right angled triangle OAB with angle $AOB = 30°$. The coordinates of A are $(6, 3)$.

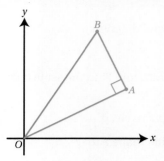

a Find the exact length OB.

b Using complex numbers, or otherwise, find the coordinates of B.

7 Let $z = 0.6 + 0.8i$.

a Represent z, z^2 and z^3 on an Argand diagram.

b Describe fully the transformation mapping z to z^3.

8 The diagram shows line l through the origin with gradient $\sqrt{3}$ and the point A representing the complex number $\sqrt{2} + \sqrt{2}i$.

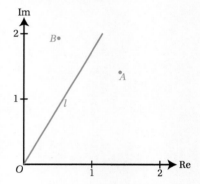

a The line l is the locus of $z \in \mathbb{C}$ which satisfy $\arg z = \theta$. Find the exact value of θ.

Point B is the reflection of point A in the line l.

b Find the size of the angle AOB.

c Use complex numbers to find the exact coordinates of B.

9 The diagram shows an equilateral triangle with its centre at the origin and one vertex $A(4, -1)$.

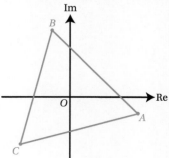

   a Write down the complex number corresponding to the vertex A.

   b Hence find the coordinates of the other two vertices.

10 The diagram shows a regular pentagon with one vertex at $z = 2$.

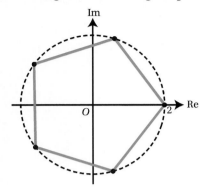

Write down, in the form $r\operatorname{cis}\theta$, the complex numbers corresponding to the other four vertices.

11 **a** The point representing a complex number z on an Argand diagram is reflected in the real axis and then rotated 90° anticlockwise about the origin. Write down, in terms of z, the complex number representing the resulting image.

   b If the rotation is applied before the reflection, show that the resulting image represents the complex number $-iz^*$.

12 **a** The point representing the complex number p on an Argand diagram is rotated through angle θ about the point representing the complex number a. The resulting point represents complex number q. Explain why $q - a = (p - a)e^{i\theta}$.

   b Find the exact coordinates of the image when the point $P(1, 3)$ is rotated 60° anticlockwise about the point $A(2, -1)$.

13 **a** On an Argand diagram, points A, B and C represent complex numbers a, b and c, respectively. C is the image of B after a rotation through angle θ, anticlockwise, about A.

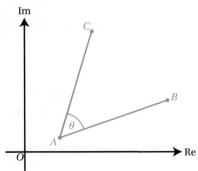

Express the complex number $c - a$ in terms of $b - a$.

   b The point $(4, 1)$ is rotated 45° anticlockwise about the origin. The image is then rotated 30° anticlockwise about the point $(-1, 2)$. Find the coordinates of the final image.

14 The diagram shows two equilateral triangles on an Argand diagram.

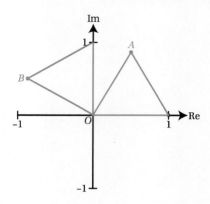

Find the complex number corresponding to the midpoint of *AB*.
Give your answer in exact Cartesian form.

Checklist of learning and understanding

- De Moivre's theorem: $\left(r\left(\cos\theta + \mathrm{i}\sin\theta\right)\right)^{n} = r^{n}\left(\cos n\theta + \mathrm{i}\sin n\theta\right)$ for $n \in \mathbb{Z}$.
- Exponential form of a complex number: $re^{\mathrm{i}\theta} = \left[r, \theta\right] = r\operatorname{cis}\theta = r\left(\cos\theta + \mathrm{i}\sin\theta\right)$.
- To solve $z^{n} = w$:
  - write w in modulus–argument form and write $z^{n} = r^{n}\left(\cos n\theta + \mathrm{i}\sin n\theta\right)$
  - compare moduli, remembering that they are always real
  - compare arguments, remembering that adding 2π to the argument does not change the number
  - the n roots form a regular polygon on an Argand diagram.
- The nth roots of unity (solutions of $z^{n} = 1$):
  - You can write them as ω^{k}, where $\omega = e^{\frac{2\pi \mathrm{i}}{n}}$ and $k = 0, 1, 2, ..., n-1$.
  - $1 + \omega_{1} + ... + \omega_{n-1} = 0$.
- You can use roots of the equation $z^{n} = a$ to factorise the expression $z^{n} - a$. Real quadratic factors are found by combining each root with its complex conjugate:

$$\left(z - re^{\mathrm{i}\theta}\right)\left(z - re^{-\mathrm{i}\theta}\right) = z^{2} - 2r\cos\theta\, z + r^{2}$$

- Multiplication by $re^{\mathrm{i}\theta}$ corresponds to an enlargement with scale factor r and a rotation through θ anticlockwise about the origin. Division by $r\operatorname{cis}\theta$ corresponds to rotation around the origin through angle $-\theta$ and an enlargement with scale factor $\dfrac{1}{r}$.

Mixed practice 2

1. If $z^* = r\mathrm{e}^{\mathrm{i}\theta}$, write $\dfrac{1}{z}$ in exponential form.

2. **a** Find the modulus and argument of $-1+\mathrm{i}\sqrt{3}$.

   b Hence find $\left(-1+\mathrm{i}\sqrt{3}\right)^5$ in exact Cartesian form.

3. **a** Write down, in the form $r\mathrm{e}^{\mathrm{i}\theta}$, all the roots of the equation $z^5 = 1$.

   b Show the roots on an Argand diagram.

4. Find $\left(\cos\dfrac{\pi}{3}+\mathrm{i}\sin\dfrac{\pi}{3}\right)^4\left(\cos\dfrac{\pi}{4}+\mathrm{i}\sin\dfrac{\pi}{4}\right)^5$ in the form $r\mathrm{e}^{\mathrm{i}\theta}$, where $-\pi < \theta \leqslant \pi$.

5. **a** Find the modulus and argument of $8-8\mathrm{i}$.

   b Hence solve the equation $z^4 = 8-8\mathrm{i}$, giving your answers in the form $r\mathrm{e}^{\mathrm{i}\theta}$.

6. **a** Find the modulus and argument of $1+\mathrm{i}$.

   b A regular hexagon is inscribed in a circle on an Argand diagram, centred at the origin, and one of its vertices is $1+\mathrm{i}$. Find an equation whose roots are represented by the six vertices of the hexagon.

7. **i** Express $\dfrac{\sqrt{3}+\mathrm{i}}{\sqrt{3}-\mathrm{i}}$ in the form $r\mathrm{e}^{\mathrm{i}\theta}$, where $r>0$ and $0\leqslant\theta<2\pi$.

   ii Hence find the smallest positive value of n for which $\left(\dfrac{\sqrt{3}+\mathrm{i}}{\sqrt{3}-\mathrm{i}}\right)^n$ is real and positive.

© **OCR A Level Mathematics, Unit 4727 Further Pure Mathematics 3, January 2009**

8. If $\arg\left((a+\mathrm{i})^3\right)=\pi$, where a is real and positive, find the exact value of a.

9. Find the exact value of $\dfrac{1}{\left(\sqrt{3}+\mathrm{i}\right)^6}$, clearly showing your working.

10. **a** Express $\dfrac{\sqrt{3}}{2}-\dfrac{1}{2}\mathrm{i}$ in the form $r(\cos\theta+\mathrm{i}\sin\theta)$.

    b Hence show that $\left(\dfrac{\sqrt{3}}{2}-\dfrac{1}{2}\mathrm{i}\right)^9 = c\mathrm{i}$ where c is a real number to be found.

    c Find one pair of possible values of positive integers m and n such that
    $$\left(\dfrac{\sqrt{3}}{2}-\dfrac{1}{2}\mathrm{i}\right)^m = \left(\dfrac{\sqrt{2}}{2}+\dfrac{\sqrt{2}}{2}\mathrm{i}\right)^n.$$

11. Use trigonometric identities to show that

    a $\dfrac{1}{\operatorname{cis}\theta}=\operatorname{cis}(-\theta)=\operatorname{cis}(2\pi-\theta)$　　**b** $\dfrac{\operatorname{cis}\theta_1}{\operatorname{cis}\theta_2}=\operatorname{cis}(\theta_1-\theta_2)$

12. If ω is a complex third root of unity and x and y are real numbers, prove that:

    a $1+\omega+\omega^2 = 0$

    b $(\omega x+\omega^2 y)(\omega^2 x+\omega y)=x^2-xy+y^2$.

13. If $0<\theta<\dfrac{\pi}{2}$ and $z=\left(\sin\theta+\mathrm{i}(1-\cos\theta)\right)^2$, find in its simplest form $\arg z$.

14. If $z=\cos\theta+\mathrm{i}\sin\theta$, prove that $\dfrac{z^2-1}{z^2+1}=\mathrm{i}\tan\theta$.

15. **a** Express i in the form $r\mathrm{e}^{\mathrm{i}\theta}$.

    b Hence state the exact value of i^i.

16 The complex numbers 0, 3 and $3e^{\frac{1}{3}\pi i}$ are represented in an Argand diagram by the points O, A and B respectively.

   i Sketch the triangle OAB and show that it is equilateral.

   ii Hence express $3 - 3e^{\frac{1}{3}\pi i}$ in polar form.

   iii Hence find $\left(3 - 3e^{\frac{1}{3}\pi i}\right)^5$, giving your answer in the form $a + b\sqrt{3}i$ where a and b are rational numbers.

© **OCR A Level Mathematics, Unit 4727/01 Further Pure Mathematics 3, June 2013**

17 Let $\omega = e^{\frac{2i\pi}{5}}$.

   a Write ω^2, ω^3 and ω^4 in the form $e^{i\theta}$.

   b Explain why $\omega^1 + \omega^2 + \omega^3 + \omega^4 = -1$.

   c Show that $\omega + \omega^4 = 2\cos\dfrac{2\pi}{5}$ and $\omega^2 + \omega^3 = 2\cos\dfrac{4\pi}{5}$.

   d Form a quadratic equation in $\cos\dfrac{2\pi}{5}$ and hence show that $\cos\dfrac{2\pi}{5} = \dfrac{\sqrt{5}-1}{4}$.

18 Let 1, ω, ω^2 be the solutions of the equation $z^3 = 1$.

   a Show that $1 + \omega + \omega^2 = 0$.

   b Find the value of

     i $(1 + \omega)(1 + \omega^2)$ **ii** $\dfrac{1}{1+\omega} + \dfrac{1}{1+\omega^2}$.

   c Hence find a cubic equation with integer coefficients and roots 3, $\dfrac{1}{1+\omega}$ and $\dfrac{1}{1+\omega^2}$.

19 Point A has coordinates $(1, 2)$. Triangle OAB has $OB = 2OA$ and angle $AOB = \dfrac{\pi}{6}$.

   a Write down the complex number corresponding to the point A.

   b Find the two possible pairs of coordinates of B.

20 Let Z and A be points on an Argand diagram representing complex numbers z and a, respectively. The complex number z_1 represents the point obtained by translating Z using the vector $\overrightarrow{OA}$ and then rotating the image through angle θ anticlockwise about the origin. The complex number z_2 corresponds to the point obtained by first rotating Z anticlockwise through angle θ about the origin and then translating Z by vector $\overrightarrow{OA}$.

Show that the distance between the points represented by z_1 and z_2 is independent of z.

21 **i** Show that $(z - e^{i\phi})(z - e^{-i\phi}) \equiv z^2 - (2\cos\phi)z + 1$.

   ii Write down the seven roots of the equation $z^7 - 1$ in the form $e^{i\theta}$ and show their positions in an Argand diagram.

   iii Hence express $z^7 - 1$ as the product of one real linear factor and three real quadratic factors.

© **OCR A Level Mathematics, Unit 4727/01 Further Pure Mathematics 3, June 2007**

22 Point A represents the complex number $3 + i$ on an Argand diagram. Point A is rotated through $\dfrac{\pi}{3}$ radians anticlockwise about the origin to point B. Point B is then translated by $\begin{pmatrix} -2 \\ 1 \end{pmatrix}$ to obtain point C.

a Find, in Cartesian form, the complex number corresponding to B.

b Find the distance AC.

23 **a** Points P and Q on an Argand diagram correspond to complex numbers $z_1 = x_1 + iy_1$ and $z_2 = x_2 + iy_2$. Show that $PQ = |z_1 - z_2|$.

b The diagram shows a triangle with one vertex at the origin, one vertex at the point $A(a, 0)$ and one vertex at the point B such that $OB = b$ and $\angle AOB = \theta$.

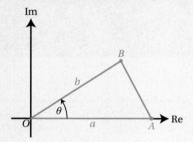

i Write down the complex number corresponding to point A.

ii Write down the complex number corresponding to point B in modulus–argument form.

iii Write down an expression for the length of AB in terms of a, b and θ.

iv Hence prove the cosine rule for the triangle AOB:

$$AB^2 = OA^2 + OB^2 - 2(OA)(OB)\cos AOB.$$

3 Complex numbers and trigonometry

In this chapter you will learn how to:

- use de Moivre's theorem to derive trigonometric identities
- find sums of some trigonometric series.

Before you start…

Chapter 2, Section 1	You should be able to use de Moivre's theorem to raise a complex number to a power.	1 Find $\left(2\left(\cos\dfrac{\pi}{7}+\mathrm{i}\sin\dfrac{\pi}{7}\right)\right)^5$ in modulus–argument form.
Chapter 2, Section 2	You should be able to use the exponential form of a complex number.	2 a Write $4\mathrm{e}^{-\frac{\mathrm{i}\pi}{3}}$ in exact Cartesian form. b Write down the complex conjugate of $2+\mathrm{e}^{3\mathrm{i}}$.
A Level Mathematics Student Book 1, Chapter 9	You should be able to use the binomial expansion for positive integer powers.	3 Expand and simplify $(x-2y)^5$.
Chapter 2, Section 2, Pure Core Student Book 1, Chapter 4	You should know how to divide complex numbers.	4 Find the real and imaginary part of $\dfrac{1-\mathrm{e}^{\mathrm{i}x}}{1+\mathrm{e}^{\mathrm{i}x}}$.
A Level Mathematics Student Book 2, Chapter 4	You should be able to use the formulae for the sum of a geometric series.	5 a Find an expression for the sum of the first n terms of the geometric series $\mathrm{e}^x+\mathrm{e}^{2x}+\mathrm{e}^{3x}+\ldots$ b For which values of x does the series in part a have a sum to infinity?

Using complex numbers to derive trigonometric identities

The modulus–argument form of a complex number provides a link between complex numbers and trigonometry. This is a powerful tool for deriving new trigonometric identities.

These trigonometric identities are one example of the use of complex numbers to establish facts about real numbers and functions. Other such applications include a formula for cubic equations, calculations involving alternating current, and analysing the motion of waves. The fact that complex numbers proved correct results in a concise way was a major factor in convincing mathematicians that they should be accepted.

Section 1: Deriving multiple angle formulae

You can raise a complex number to a power in two different ways. You can either use the Cartesian form and multiply out the brackets, or you can write the complex number in modulus–argument form and use de Moivre's theorem. Equating these two answers allows you to derive formulae for trigonometric ratios of multiple angles.

 Rewind

You have already met double angle formulae, such as $\cos 2\theta = 2\cos^2\theta - 1$, in A Level Mathematics Student Book 2, Chapter 8.

WORKED EXAMPLE 3.1

Derive a formula for $\cos 4\theta$ in terms of $\cos\theta$.

Let $z = \cos\theta + i\sin\theta$.

Then $z^4 = (\cos\theta + i\sin\theta)^4$.

First using the binomial theorem:

Start with an expression for a complex number involving $\cos\theta$, and find z^4 in two different ways.

$$z^4 = \cos^4\theta + 4\cos^3\theta(i\sin\theta) + 6\cos^2\theta(i\sin\theta)^2$$
$$+ 4\cos\theta(i\sin\theta)^3 + (i\sin\theta)^4$$

$$= \cos^4\theta + 4i\cos^3\theta\sin\theta$$
$$- 6\cos^2\theta\sin^2\theta - 4i\cos\theta\sin^3\theta + \sin^4\theta$$

$i^2 = -1$, $i^3 = -i$, $i^4 = 1$.

Now using de Moivre's theorem:

$$z^4 = \cos 4\theta + i\sin 4\theta$$

Equating real parts:

$$\cos 4\theta = \cos^4\theta - 6\cos^2\theta\sin^2\theta + \sin^4\theta$$

The two expressions for z^4 must have equal real parts and equal imaginary parts.

$$= \cos^4\theta - 6\cos^2\theta(1 - \cos^2\theta)$$
$$+ (1 - \cos^2\theta)^2$$

You want the answer in terms of $\cos\theta$ only, so use $\sin^2\theta = 1 - \cos^2\theta$.

$$\therefore \cos 4\theta = 8\cos^4\theta - 8\cos^2\theta + 1$$

Simplify the final expression.

▶▶ **Fast forward**

By equating imaginary parts of the two expressions in Worked example 3.1, you can obtain a similar expression for $\sin 4\theta$ (see question 1 in Exercise 3A).

ⓘ **Did you know?**

These expressions for sines and cosines of multiple angles can also be derived through repeated application of compound angle identities. However, the calculations become increasingly long.

EXERCISE 3A

1　**a**　Find the imaginary part of $(\cos\theta + i\sin\theta)^4$.

　　b　Hence show that $\sin 4\theta = 4\cos\theta(\sin\theta - 2\sin^3\theta)$.

2　Use the binomial expansion to find the real and imaginary parts of $(\cos\theta + i\sin\theta)^3$. Hence find an expression for $\sin 3\theta$ in terms of $\sin\theta$.

3　**a**　Expand $(\cos\theta + i\sin\theta)^5$.

　　b　Hence or otherwise express $\sin 5\theta$ in terms of $\sin\theta$.

4 **a** Show that $\cos 5\theta = 16\cos^5\theta - 20\cos^3\theta + 5\cos\theta$.

  b Hence solve the equation $\cos 5\theta = 5\cos\theta$ for $\theta \in [0, 2\pi]$.

5 **a** Find the values of A, B and C such that $\sin 5\theta = A\sin^5\theta - B\sin^3\theta + C\sin\theta$.

  b Given that $4\sin^5\theta + \sin 5\theta = 0$, find the possible values of $\sin\theta$.

6 **a** Find the real and imaginary parts of $(\cos\theta + i\sin\theta)^4$.

  b Hence express $\tan 4\theta$ in terms of $\tan\theta$.

7 **a** Show that $\tan 6\theta = \dfrac{6\tan\theta - 20\tan^3\theta + 6\tan^5\theta}{1 - 15\tan^2\theta + 15\tan^4\theta - \tan^6\theta}$.

  b Hence solve the equation:
  $$\tan^6\theta + 6\tan^5\theta - 15\tan^4\theta - 20\tan^3\theta + 15\tan^2\theta + 6\tan\theta - 1 = 0$$
  for $\theta \in \left[0, \dfrac{\pi}{2}\right]$.

8 **a** Use the binomial expansion to find the real and imaginary parts of $(\cos\theta + i\sin\theta)^5$.

  b Hence show that $\dfrac{\sin 5\theta}{\sin\theta} = 16\cos^4\theta - 12\cos^2\theta + 1$.

  c Assuming that θ is small enough that the terms in θ^4 and higher can be ignored, find an approximate expression, in increasing powers of θ, for $\dfrac{\sin 5\theta}{\sin\theta}$.

Section 2: Application to polynomial equations

In Section 1 you learnt how to express $\sin n\theta$ and $\cos n\theta$ as a polynomial in $\sin\theta$ or $\cos\theta$. For example, $\cos 4\theta = 8\cos^4\theta - 8\cos^2\theta + 1$. You can now use the roots of the polynomial and the solutions of $\cos 4\theta = 0$ to find the values of $\cos\theta$.

WORKED EXAMPLE 3.2

a Find all the values of $\theta \in [0, 2\pi)$ for which $\cos 4\theta = 0$.
You are given that $\cos 4\theta = 8\cos^4\theta - 8\cos^2\theta + 1$.

b Write down the roots of the equation $8c^2 - 8c^4 = 1$ in the form $\cos\theta$, where $\theta \in [0, \pi)$.

c Hence find the exact value of $\cos\dfrac{3\pi}{8}$.

a $\theta \in [0, 2\pi) \Rightarrow 4\theta \in [0, 8\pi)$

$4\theta = \dfrac{\pi}{2}, \dfrac{3\pi}{2}, \dfrac{5\pi}{2}, \dfrac{7\pi}{2}, \dfrac{9\pi}{2}, \dfrac{11\pi}{2}, \dfrac{13\pi}{2}, \dfrac{15\pi}{2}$

$\theta = \dfrac{\pi}{8}, \dfrac{3\pi}{8}, \dfrac{5\pi}{8}, \dfrac{7\pi}{8}, \dfrac{9\pi}{8}, \dfrac{11\pi}{8}, \dfrac{13\pi}{8}, \dfrac{15\pi}{8}$

b Write $c = \cos\theta$.

Then

$8c^2 - 8c^4 = 1$

$\Leftrightarrow 8c^4 - 8c^2 + 1 = 0$

$\Leftrightarrow \cos 4\theta = 0$

Making the substitution relates the equations from parts **a** and **b**.

Continues on next page ...

Hence

$c = \cos\theta$

$= \cos\dfrac{\pi}{8}, \cos\dfrac{3\pi}{8}, \cos\dfrac{5\pi}{8}, \cos\dfrac{7\pi}{8}$

The equation from part **a** has eight solutions but the equation from part **b** should only have four (since it is a degree 4 polynomial). This is because, for example,

$\cos\dfrac{\pi}{8} = \cos\dfrac{15\pi}{8}$.

c $8c^4 - 8c^2 + 1 = 0$

$c^2 = \dfrac{2 \pm \sqrt{2}}{4}$

$c = \pm\sqrt{\dfrac{2 \pm \sqrt{2}}{4}}$

You can actually solve the equation from part **b** exactly, as it is a quadratic in c^2.

$\cos\dfrac{3\pi}{8}$ is the smallest positive one of the four solutions from part **b**.

$\cos\dfrac{3\pi}{8}$ is one of these four solutions. You can see from the cos graph that it is the smallest positive one of the four numbers.

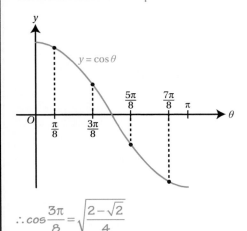

$\therefore \cos\dfrac{3\pi}{8} = \sqrt{\dfrac{2 - \sqrt{2}}{4}}$

Sometimes you can't solve the polynomial equation, but you can still use the results about sums and products of roots to derive expressions involving combinations of trigonometric ratios.

 Rewind

See Pure Core Student Book 1, Chapter 5, for a reminder about roots of polynomials.

WORKED EXAMPLE 3.3

a Show that $\tan 3\theta = \dfrac{3\tan\theta - \tan^3\theta}{1 - 3\tan^2\theta}$.

b Show that the equation $t^3 - 3t^2 - 3t + 1 = 0$ can be written as $\tan 3\theta = k$, where $t = \tan\theta$, and state the value of k.

c Hence find the exact value of $\tan\dfrac{\pi}{12} + \tan\dfrac{5\pi}{12}$.

Continues on next page ...

a Write $c = \cos\theta$ and $s = \sin\theta$.

Then

$\cos 3\theta + i\sin 3\theta = (\cos\theta + i\sin\theta)^3$

$\qquad = c^3 + 3ic^2 s - 3cs^2 - is^3$

> Use de Moivre's theorem.

Hence

$\tan 3\theta = \dfrac{\sin 3\theta}{\cos 3\theta} = \dfrac{3c^2 s - s^3}{c^3 - 3cs^2}$

> Separate real and imaginary parts to find sin and cos.

$\qquad = \dfrac{3t - t^3}{1 - 3t^2}$

> Divide top and bottom by c^3 and use $\dfrac{s}{c} = \tan\theta$.

where $t = \tan\theta$.

b $t^3 - 3t^2 - 3t + 1 = 0$

$\Leftrightarrow 1 - 3t^2 = 3t - t^3$

> Rearrange the equation into the form from part **a**.

$\Leftrightarrow \dfrac{3t - t^3}{1 - 3t^2} = 1$

$\Leftrightarrow \tan 3\theta = 1$

(so $k = 1$)

c $\tan 3\theta = 1$

$3\theta = \dfrac{\pi}{4}, \dfrac{5\pi}{4}, \dfrac{9\pi}{4} \ldots$

$\theta = \dfrac{\pi}{12}, \dfrac{5\pi}{12}, \dfrac{9\pi}{12} \ldots$

> Solve the cubic equation by solving $\tan 3\theta = 1$.

$t = \tan\theta = \tan\dfrac{\pi}{12}, \tan\dfrac{5\pi}{12}$ or $\tan\dfrac{9\pi}{12}$

> Although there are infinitely many values of θ, they only give three different values of $\tan\theta$ (since tan is a periodic function).

Hence

$\tan\dfrac{\pi}{12} + \tan\dfrac{5\pi}{12} + \tan\dfrac{9\pi}{12} = -\dfrac{-3}{1} = 3$

> Use the result about the sum of the roots of a cubic polynomial:
> $$p + q + r = -\dfrac{b}{a}$$

$\Rightarrow \tan\dfrac{\pi}{12} + \tan\dfrac{5\pi}{12} + (-1) = 3$

> $\tan\dfrac{9\pi}{12} = \tan\dfrac{3\pi}{4} = -1$

$\Rightarrow \tan\dfrac{\pi}{12} + \tan\dfrac{5\pi}{12} = 4$

EXERCISE 3B

 a Write down an expression for $\cos 2\theta$ in terms of $\cos\theta$.

b Given that $\cos 2\theta = \dfrac{\sqrt{3}}{2}$, find a quadratic equation in c, where $c = \cos\theta$.

c Hence find the exact value of $\cos\dfrac{\pi}{12}$.

2 **a** Given that $\tan 2\theta = 1$, show that $t^2 + 2t - 1 = 0$, where $t = \tan\theta$.

b Solve the equation $\tan 2\theta = 1$ for $\theta \in (0, \pi)$.

c Hence find the exact value of $\tan\dfrac{5\pi}{8}$.

3 You are given that $\cos 5\theta = 16\cos^5\theta - 20\cos^3\theta + 5\cos\theta$.

a Find the possible values of $\theta \in [0, \pi]$ for which $16\cos^4\theta - 20\cos^2\theta + 5 = 0$.

b Hence show that $\cos\dfrac{\pi}{10}\cos\dfrac{3\pi}{10} = \dfrac{\sqrt{5}}{4}$.

4 **a** Show that $\sin 3\theta = 3\sin\theta - 4\sin^3\theta$.

b Given that $\theta \in [0, 2\pi]$ and that $\sin 3\theta = \dfrac{1}{2}$, find the possible values of θ.

c Hence show that $\sin\dfrac{\pi}{18}$ is a root of the equation $8x^3 - 6x + 1 = 0$ and find, in a similar form, the other two roots.

5 You are given that $\tan 4\theta + \tan 3\theta = 0$.

a Show that $\tan 7\theta = 0$.

b Let $t = \tan\theta$. Express $\tan 4\theta$ and $\tan 3\theta$ in terms of t. Hence show that $t^7 - 21t^5 + 35t^3 - 7t = 0$.

6 You are given that $\sin 7\theta = 7\sin\theta - 56\sin^3\theta + 112\sin^5\theta - 64\sin^7\theta$.

a Show that the equation $64s^6 - 112s^4 + 56s^2 - 7 = 0$ has roots $\sin\left(\pm\dfrac{\pi}{7}\right)$, $\sin\left(\pm\dfrac{3\pi}{7}\right)$ and $\sin\left(\pm\dfrac{5\pi}{7}\right)$.

b Hence find the exact value of $\sin\dfrac{\pi}{7}\sin\dfrac{3\pi}{7}\sin\dfrac{5\pi}{7}$.

Section 3: Powers of trigonometric functions

Another important link with trigonometry comes from considering the exponential form of complex numbers:

$$e^{i\theta} = \cos\theta + i\sin\theta$$

and

$$e^{-i\theta} = \cos(-\theta) + i\sin(-\theta)$$
$$= \cos\theta - i\sin\theta$$

By adding and subtracting these two equations you can establish two very useful identities.

Key point 3.1

$$\cos\theta = \frac{e^{i\theta} + e^{-i\theta}}{2}$$

$$\sin\theta = \frac{e^{i\theta} - e^{-i\theta}}{2i}$$

You can further generalise this result.

 Key point 3.2

If $z = e^{i\theta}$, then

$$z^n + \frac{1}{z^n} = 2\cos n\theta$$

$$z^n - \frac{1}{z^n} = 2i\sin n\theta$$

PROOF 2

Using de Moivre's theorem for positive
and negative integers:

$z^n = \cos n\theta + i\sin n\theta$

$\dfrac{1}{z^n} = z^{-n} = \cos n\theta - i\sin n\theta$

Adding the two equations:

$z^n + \dfrac{1}{z^n} = 2\cos n\theta$

Subtracting the two equations:

$z^n - \dfrac{1}{z^n} = 2i\sin n\theta$

Remember that $\cos(-x) = \cos(x)$ and $\sin(-x) = -\sin x$.

You can use these results to derive another class of trigonometric identities, expressing powers of trigonometric functions in terms of functions of multiple angles. For example: $\cos^2\theta = \dfrac{1}{2}(\cos 2\theta + 1)$.

WORKED EXAMPLE 3.4

Show that $\sin^5\theta = \dfrac{1}{16}\sin 5\theta - \dfrac{5}{16}\sin 3\theta + \dfrac{5}{8}\sin\theta$.

Let $z = \cos\theta + i\sin\theta$.
Using the binomial expansion:

$\left(z - \dfrac{1}{z}\right)^5 = z^5 + 5z^4\left(-\dfrac{1}{z}\right) + 10z^3\left(-\dfrac{1}{z}\right)^2 + 10z^2\left(-\dfrac{1}{z}\right)^3 + 5z\left(-\dfrac{1}{z}\right)^4 + \left(-\dfrac{1}{z}\right)^5$

$= z^5 - 5z^3 + 10z - \dfrac{10}{z} + \dfrac{5}{z^3} - \dfrac{1}{z^5}$

$= \left(z^5 - \dfrac{1}{z^5}\right) - 5\left(z^3 - \dfrac{1}{z^3}\right) + 10\left(z - \dfrac{1}{z}\right)$

Simplify the fractions, taking care with negative signs.

Group the terms to get expressions of the form $z^n - \dfrac{1}{z^n}$.

Continues on next page ...

So

$$\left(2i\sin\theta\right)^5 = 2i\sin5\theta - 10i\sin3\theta + 20i\sin\theta$$

$$32i\sin^5\theta = 2i\sin5\theta - 10i\sin3\theta + 20i\sin\theta$$

$$\therefore \sin^5\theta = \frac{1}{16}\sin5\theta - \frac{5}{16}\sin3\theta + \frac{5}{8}\sin\theta$$

On both sides of the equation, use the result from Key point 3.2:

$$z^n - \frac{1}{z^n} = 2i\sin n\theta$$

Trigonometric identities such as these are very useful when integrating powers of trigonometric functions.

 Rewind

In A Level Mathematics Student Book 2, Chapter 11, you used the identity $\cos^2\theta = \frac{1}{2}(\cos2\theta+1)$ to find $\int\cos^2 x \, dx$.

WORKED EXAMPLE 3.5

a Expand and simplify $\left(z+\dfrac{1}{z}\right)^6$.

b Show that $\cos^6 x = \dfrac{1}{32}\cos6x + \dfrac{3}{16}\cos4x + \dfrac{15}{32}\cos2x + \dfrac{5}{16}$.

c Hence find $\int\cos^6 x \, dx$.

a Using the binomial expansion:

$$\left(z+\frac{1}{z}\right)^6 = z^6 + 6z^5\left(\frac{1}{z}\right) + 15z^4\left(\frac{1}{z}\right)^2 + 20z^3\left(\frac{1}{z}\right)^3 + 15z^2\left(\frac{1}{z}\right)^4 + 6z\left(\frac{1}{z}\right)^5 + \left(\frac{1}{z}\right)^6$$

$$= z^6 + 6z^4 + 15z^2 + 20 + \frac{15}{z^2} + \frac{6}{z^4} + \frac{1}{z^6}$$

b Let $z = \cos x + i\sin x$.

$$\left(z+\frac{1}{z}\right)^6 = \left(z^6 + \frac{1}{z^6}\right) + 6\left(z^4 + \frac{1}{z^4}\right) + 15\left(z^2 + \frac{1}{z^2}\right) + 20$$

$$\Rightarrow (2\cos x)^6 = (2\cos6x) + 6(2\cos4x) + 15(2\cos2x) + 20$$

$$\Rightarrow \cos^6 x = \frac{1}{32}\cos6x + \frac{3}{16}\cos4x + \frac{15}{32}\cos2x + \frac{5}{16}$$

Group the terms on the right so that you can use the result from Key point 3.2.

Divide by $2^6 = 64$.

c Using the result from part **a**:

$$\int\cos^6 x \, dx = \int\left(\frac{1}{32}\cos6x + \frac{3}{16}\cos4x + \frac{15}{32}\cos2x + \frac{5}{16}\right)dx$$

$$= \frac{1}{192}\sin6x + \frac{3}{64}\sin4x + \frac{15}{64}\sin2x + \frac{5}{16}x + c$$

Don't forget to divide by the coefficient of x.

EXERCISE 3C

1 Let $z = \cos\theta + i\sin\theta$. Express each of these as a sum of terms of the form $\cos k\theta$ or $\sin k\theta$.

  a **i** $\left(z + \dfrac{1}{z}\right)^3$ **ii** $\left(z + \dfrac{1}{z}\right)^4$

  b **i** $\left(z - \dfrac{1}{z}\right)^4$ **ii** $\left(z - \dfrac{1}{z}\right)^5$

2 Let $z = \cos\theta + i\sin\theta$.

  a Show that $z^n + z^{-n} = 2\cos n\theta$.

  b Hence show that $32\cos^5\theta = A\cos 5\theta + B\cos 3\theta + C\cos\theta$ where A, B and C are constants to be found.

3 **a** Use the expansion of $\left(z - \dfrac{1}{z}\right)^6$, where $z = e^{i\theta}$, to show that $32\sin^6\theta = 10 - 15\cos 2\theta + 6\cos 4\theta - \cos 6\theta$.

  b Hence find the exact value of $\int_0^{\frac{\pi}{3}} \sin^6\theta \, d\theta$.

4 A complex number is defined by $z = \cos\theta + i\sin\theta$.

  a **i** Show that $\dfrac{1}{z} = \cos\theta - i\sin\theta$.

    ii Use de Moivre's theorem to deduce that $z^n - \dfrac{1}{z^n} = 2i\sin n\theta$.

  b **i** Expand $\left(z - \dfrac{1}{z}\right)^5$.

    ii Hence find integers a, b and c such that
    $16\sin^5\theta = a\sin 5\theta + b\sin 3\theta + c\sin\theta$.

  c Find $\int \sin^5 2x \, dx$.

5 Let $z = \cos\theta + i\sin\theta$.

  a Show that $z^n - z^{-n} = 2i\sin n\theta$.

  b Expand $\left(z + z^{-1}\right)^6$ and $\left(z - z^{-1}\right)^6$.

  c Hence show that $\cos^6\theta + \sin^6\theta = \dfrac{1}{8}(3\cos 4\theta + 5)$.

6 **a** Write down expressions for $\sin x$ and $\cos x$ in terms of e^{ix}.

  b Hence evaluate $\int_0^\pi \sin^3 x \cos^4 x \, dx$, clearly showing your working.

Section 4: Trigonometric series

In Section 1 you learnt about expressions for sine and cosine of multiple angles. What happens if you add several such expressions together? For example, is it possible to simplify a sum such as $\sin x + \sin 2x + \sin 3x + \sin 4x$?

> 🔍 **Explore**
>
> Sums like these come up when combining waves (interference). They are also used in Fourier series, which is a way of writing other functions in terms of sines and cosines.

You can simplify certain sums of this type using the exponential form of complex numbers and the formula for the sum of geometric series. This is because $\sin kx$ is the imaginary part of e^{ikx}, and the numbers e^{ix}, e^{2ix}, e^{3ix}, e^{4ix} form a geometric series.

 Rewind

You met geometric series in A Level Mathematics Student Book 2, Chapter 4.

WORKED EXAMPLE 3.6

a Find an expression for $e^{ix} + e^{2ix} + e^{3ix} + \ldots + e^{nix}$.

b Hence show that $\sin x + \sin 2x + \sin 3x + \ldots + \sin 10x = \dfrac{\sin x + \sin 10x - \sin 11x}{4\sin^2\left(\dfrac{x}{2}\right)}$.

a Geometric series with $a = e^{ix}$, $r = e^{ix}$.

$$\therefore e^{ix} + e^{2ix} + e^{3ix} + \ldots + e^{nix} = \frac{e^{ix}\left(1 - e^{nix}\right)}{1 - e^{ix}}$$

This is a geometric series with common ratio e^{ix}. Use $S_n = \dfrac{a\left(1 - r^n\right)}{1 - r}$ for the sum of the first n terms.

b $\sin x + \sin 2x + \ldots + \sin 10x = \text{Im}\left(e^{ix} + e^{2ix} + \ldots + e^{10ix}\right)$

$$= \text{Im}\left(\frac{e^{ix}\left(1 - e^{10ix}\right)}{1 - e^{ix}}\right)$$

This is the imaginary part of the series from part **a**, with $n = 10$.

$$= \text{Im}\left(\frac{e^{ix}\left(1 - e^{10ix}\right)}{1 - e^{ix}} \times \frac{1 - e^{-ix}}{1 - e^{-ix}}\right)$$

$$= \text{Im}\left(\frac{e^{ix} - 1 - e^{11ix} + e^{10ix}}{1 - e^{ix} - e^{-ix} + 1}\right)$$

Multiply top and bottom by the complex conjugate of the denominator in order to separate real and imaginary parts.

$$= \text{Im}\left(\frac{e^{ix} - 1 - e^{11ix} + e^{10ix}}{2 - 2\cos x}\right)$$

Use $e^{ix} + e^{-ix} = 2\cos x$ in the denominator.

The imaginary part is:

$$\frac{\sin x - \sin 11x + \sin 10x}{2 - 2\cos x}$$

Now the denominator is real, so you just need to take the imaginary part of the numerator.

$$= \frac{\sin x + \sin 10x - \sin 11x}{4\sin^2\left(\dfrac{x}{2}\right)}$$

Use the double angle formula in the denominator: $2\cos x = 2\left(1 - 2\sin^2\left(\dfrac{x}{2}\right)\right)$.

If the modulus of the common ratio is smaller than 1, a geometric series also has a sum to infinity.

WORKED EXAMPLE 3.7

a Show that the geometric series $1+\dfrac{1}{2}e^{i\theta}+\dfrac{1}{4}e^{2i\theta}+\ldots$ converges, and find an expression for its sum to infinity.

b Hence evaluate $\displaystyle\sum_{k=0}^{\infty}\dfrac{1}{2^k}\cos k\theta$.

a The geometric series has $|r|=\left|\dfrac{1}{2}e^{i\theta}\right|=\dfrac{1}{2}<1$, hence it converges.

> The common ratio is $\dfrac{1}{2}e^{i\theta}$.

Using $S_{\infty}=\dfrac{a}{1-r}$:

$$S_{\infty}=\dfrac{1}{1-\frac{1}{2}e^{i\theta}}=\dfrac{2}{2-e^{i\theta}}$$

b $\displaystyle\sum_{k=0}^{\infty}\dfrac{1}{2^k}\cos k\theta=\operatorname{Re}\left(1+\dfrac{1}{2}e^{i\theta}+\dfrac{1}{4}e^{2i\theta}+\ldots\right)$

> The required sum is the real part of the sum from part **a**.

$$=\operatorname{Re}\left(\dfrac{2}{2-e^{i\theta}}\right)$$

$$=\operatorname{Re}\left(\dfrac{2}{2-e^{i\theta}}\times\dfrac{2-e^{-i\theta}}{2-e^{-i\theta}}\right)$$

> Multiply top and bottom by the complex conjugate of the denominator to separate real and imaginary parts.

$$=\operatorname{Re}\left(\dfrac{4-2e^{-i\theta}}{4-2e^{i\theta}-2e^{-i\theta}+1}\right)$$

$$=\operatorname{Re}\left(\dfrac{4-2e^{-i\theta}}{5-4\cos\theta}\right)$$

> Use $e^{i\theta}+e^{-i\theta}=2\cos\theta$.

$$=\dfrac{4-2\cos\theta}{5-4\cos\theta}$$

> Now take the real part of the numerator, using $e^{-i\theta}=\cos\theta-i\sin\theta$.

Another series you know how to sum is the binomial expansion.

WORKED EXAMPLE 3.8

By considering the expansion of $\left(e^{i\theta}+1\right)^5$, or otherwise, show that

$$\sin 5\theta+5\sin 4\theta+10\sin 3\theta+10\sin 2\theta+5\sin\theta=32\cos^5\dfrac{\theta}{2}\sin\dfrac{5\theta}{2}.$$

Using the binomial expansion:

$$\left(e^{i\theta}+1\right)^5=e^{5i\theta}+5e^{4i\theta}+10e^{3i\theta}+10e^{2i\theta}+5e^{i\theta}+1$$

$$\sin 5\theta+5\sin 4\theta+10\sin 3\theta+10\sin 2\theta+5\sin\theta=\operatorname{Im}\left(\left(e^{i\theta}+1\right)^5\right)$$

> The required series is the imaginary part of this.

Continues on next page ...

$e^{i\theta} + 1 = (\cos\theta + 1) + i\sin\theta$ ....

Use the double angle formulae.

$$= 2\cos^2\frac{\theta}{2} + 2i\sin\frac{\theta}{2}\cos\frac{\theta}{2}$$

$$= 2\cos\frac{\theta}{2}\left(\cos\frac{\theta}{2} + i\sin\frac{\theta}{2}\right)$$

$$= \left(2\cos\frac{\theta}{2}\right)e^{\frac{i\theta}{2}}$$

Hence

$$\left(e^{i\theta} + 1\right)^5 = \left(2\cos\frac{\theta}{2}\right)^5 e^{\frac{i5\theta}{2}}$$

so

$$\text{Im}\left(\left(e^{i\theta} + 1\right)^5\right) = \left(2\cos\frac{\theta}{2}\right)^5 \sin\frac{5\theta}{2}$$

Therefore, the sum of the series equals $32\cos^5\frac{\theta}{2}\sin\frac{5\theta}{2}$.

EXERCISE 3D

1 **a** Find an expression for the sum to infinity of the geometric series $1 + \frac{1}{3}e^{i\theta} + \frac{1}{9}e^{2i\theta} + \dots$.

   b Hence evaluate $\displaystyle\sum_{k=0}^{\infty}\frac{1}{3^k}\cos k$.

2 **a** Show that the geometric series $1 + \frac{1}{2}e^{i\theta} + \frac{1}{4}e^{2i\theta} + \dots$ converges and find an expression for its sum to infinity.

   b Hence show that $\frac{1}{2}\sin\theta + \frac{1}{4}\sin 2\theta + \frac{1}{8}\sin 3\theta + \dots = \frac{2\sin\theta}{5 - 4\cos\theta}$.

3 Use the geometric series $e^{ix} - \frac{1}{2}e^{3ix} + \frac{1}{4}e^{5ix} - \dots$ to evaluate $\sin 1 - \frac{1}{2}\sin 3 + \frac{1}{4}\sin 5 - \dots$.

4 Use the expansion of $\left(e^{i\theta} + 1\right)^4$ to show that $\cos 4\theta + 4\cos 3\theta + 6\cos 2\theta + 4\cos\theta + 1 = 16\cos^4\left(\frac{\theta}{2}\right)\cos 2\theta$.

5 By considering $\left(e^{i\theta} - 1\right)^5$ or otherwise, show that $\sin 5\theta - 5\sin 4\theta + 10\sin 3\theta - 10\sin 2\theta + 5\sin\theta = 32\sin^5\left(\frac{\theta}{2}\right)\cos\left(\frac{5\theta}{2}\right)$.

6 **a** Find an expression for the sum of the series $e^{i\theta} + e^{3i\theta} + e^{5i\theta} \dots + e^{(2n-1)i\theta}$.

   b Hence prove that $\cos\theta + \cos 3\theta + \cos 5\theta \dots + \cos(2n-1)\theta = \frac{\sin(2n\theta)}{2\sin\theta}$.

   c Find all the solutions to the equation $\cos\theta + \cos 3\theta + \cos 5\theta = 0$ for $0 < \theta < \pi$.

Checklist of learning and understanding

- By expanding $(\cos\theta + i\sin\theta)^n$ and comparing the real and imaginary parts to $\cos n\theta + i\sin n\theta$ you can derive expressions for $\sin n\theta$ and $\cos n\theta$ in terms of powers of $\sin\theta$ and $\cos\theta$.
  - Considering these expressions as polynomials in $\sin\theta$ or $\cos\theta$ you can find some exact values of trigonometric functions.
- If $z = e^{i\theta}$, then $z^n + \dfrac{1}{z^n} = 2\cos n\theta$ and $z^n - \dfrac{1}{z^n} = 2i\sin n\theta$.
  - In particular, $\cos\theta = \dfrac{e^{i\theta} + e^{-i\theta}}{2}$ and $\sin\theta = \dfrac{e^{i\theta} - e^{-i\theta}}{2i}$.
  - You can use these expressions, together with the binomial expansion, to express powers of $\sin\theta$ and $\cos\theta$ in terms of sin and cos of multiples of θ.
- By considering real and imaginary parts of geometric or binomial series involving $e^{i\theta}$ you can derive expressions for sums of trigonometric series.

Mixed practice 3

1 **a** Expand and simplify $(\cos\theta + i\sin\theta)^4$.

    b Hence find constants A and B such that $\dfrac{\sin 4\theta}{\cos\theta} = A\sin\theta - B\sin^3\theta$.

2 Use de Moivre's theorem to show that $\cos 5\theta = 16\cos^5\theta - 20\cos^3\theta + 5\cos\theta$. Hence find the largest and smallest values of $\cos\theta - 4\cos^3\theta + \dfrac{16}{5}\cos^5\theta$.

3 **a** By considering $\left(z + \dfrac{1}{z}\right)^5$, where $z = \cos\theta + i\sin\theta$, find the values of constants A, B and C such that

       $\cos^5\theta = A\cos 5\theta + B\cos 3\theta + C\cos\theta$.

    b Hence find the exact value of $\int_0^{\frac{\pi}{2}}\cos^5\theta\,d\theta$.

4 Show that $\sin 5\theta = 16\sin^5\theta - 20\sin^3\theta + 5\sin\theta$. Hence show that $\sin\dfrac{13\pi}{30}$ is a root of the equation $32x^5 - 40x^3 + 10x - 1 = 0$.

5 By considering the expansion of $(1+i)^{10}$, show that $\dbinom{10}{1} - \dbinom{10}{3} + \dbinom{10}{5} - \dbinom{10}{7} + \dbinom{10}{9} = 32$.

6 Show that $1 + 4\cos 2\theta + 6\cos 4\theta + 4\cos 6\theta + \cos 8\theta = 16\cos 4\theta\cos^4\theta$.

7 **i** By expressing $\cos\theta$ in terms of $e^{i\theta}$ and $e^{-i\theta}$, show that

       $\cos^5\theta \equiv \dfrac{1}{16}(\cos 5\theta + 5\cos 3\theta + 10\cos\theta)$.

    ii Hence solve the equation $\cos 5\theta + 5\cos 3\theta + 9\cos\theta = 0$ for $0 \leqslant \theta \leqslant \pi$.

© OCR A Level Mathematics, Unit 4727/01 Further Pure Mathematics 3, June 2008

8 Let $z = \cos\theta + i\sin\theta$.

    a Show that $2\cos\theta = z + \dfrac{1}{z}$.

    b Show that $2\cos n\theta = z^n + \dfrac{1}{z^n}$.

    c Consider the equation $3z^4 - z^3 + 2z^2 - z + 3 = 0$.

       i Show that the equation can be written as $6\cos 2\theta - 2\cos\theta + 2 = 0$.

       ii Find all four complex roots of the original equation.

9 **a** By considering $(\cos\theta + i\sin\theta)^3$, find expressions for $\cos 3\theta$ and $\sin 3\theta$.

    b Show that $\tan 3\theta = \dfrac{3\tan\theta - \tan^3\theta}{1 - 3\tan^2\theta}$.

    c Hence show that $\tan\dfrac{\pi}{12}$ is a root of the equation $x^3 - 3x^2 - 3x + 1 = 0$.

    d Show that $(x+1)$ is a factor of $x^3 - 3x^2 - 3x + 1$ and hence find the exact solutions of the equation $x^3 - 3x^2 - 3x + 1 = 0$.

    e By considering $\tan\dfrac{\pi}{4}$, explain why $\tan\dfrac{\pi}{12} < 1$.

    f Hence state the exact value of $\tan\dfrac{\pi}{12}$.

10 **i** Use de Moivre's theorem to prove that

$$\cos 6\theta = 32\cos^6\theta - 48\cos^4\theta + 18\cos^2\theta - 1.$$

ii Hence find the largest positive root of the equation

$$64x^6 - 96x^4 + 36x^2 - 3 = 0,$$

giving your answer in trigonometrical form.

© OCR A Level Mathematics, Unit 4727/01 Further Pure Mathematics 3, June 2007

11 Convergent infinite series C and S are defined by

$$C = 1 + \frac{1}{2}\cos\theta + \frac{1}{4}\cos 2\theta + \frac{1}{8}\cos 3\theta + \dots,$$

$$S = \frac{1}{2}\sin\theta + \frac{1}{4}\sin 2\theta + \frac{1}{8}\sin 3\theta + \dots.$$

i Show that $C + iS = \dfrac{2}{2 - e^{i\theta}}$.

ii Hence show that $C = \dfrac{4 - 2\cos\theta}{5 - 4\cos\theta}$, and find a similar expression for S.

© OCR A Level Mathematics, Unit 4727 Further Pure Mathematics 3, June 2010

In this chapter you will learn how to:

- find the equation of a plane in several different forms
- find intersections between lines and planes
- calculate angles between lines and planes
- calculate the distances between objects in three-dimensional space.

Before you start...

Pure Core Student Book 1, Chapter 2	You should be able to find the vector and Cartesian equation of a line in three dimensions.	1 A line passes through the points $(3, -1, 2)$ and $(5, 1, 8)$.
		  a Find a vector equation of the line.
		  b Write down a Cartesian equation of the line.

Pure Core Student Book 1, Chapter 2	You should be able to find the point of intersection of two lines.	2 Find the point of intersection of the line from question **1** and the line $\mathbf{r} = \begin{pmatrix} 2 \\ 2 \\ 9 \end{pmatrix} + \mu \begin{pmatrix} -1 \\ 1 \\ 2 \end{pmatrix}$.
Pure Core Student Book 1, Chapter 2	You should know how to calculate the scalar product of two vectors and use it to calculate an angle between two lines.	3 Find the acute angle between the two lines from question **2**.
Pure Core Student Book 1, Chapter 2	You should know how to calculate the vector product of two vectors and use it to find a vector perpendicular to two given vectors.	4 Find a vector perpendicular to both of the lines from question **2**.

Introduction

In Pure Core Student Book 1, Chapter 2, you learnt about equations of lines in three dimensions, and how to find intersections and angles between lines. You know that two lines might be skew (not intersecting but not parallel). In this chapter you will learn how to find the distance between two skew lines, as well as between two parallel lines.

You will also learn how to describe planes (flat surfaces) in three-dimensional space.

Section 1: Equation of a plane

You are already used to describing positions of points in the x-y plane using unit vectors parallel to the x- and y-axes: for example, the position vector of the point $P(3, 2)$ is $\mathbf{r}_p = 3\mathbf{i} + 2\mathbf{j}$.

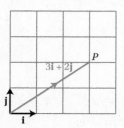

However, you can also use two directions other than those of $\mathbf{i}$ and $\mathbf{j}$. In the second diagram, the same point P is reached from the origin by moving 2 units in the direction of vector $\mathbf{d}_1$ and 2 units in the direction of vector $\mathbf{d}_2$. Hence its position vector is $\mathbf{r}_p = 2\mathbf{d}_1 + 2\mathbf{d}_2$. In the same way, every point in the x-y plane has a position vector of the form $\lambda\mathbf{d}_1 + \mu\mathbf{d}_2$, where λ and μ are scalars.

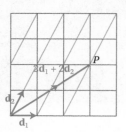

Consider now a plane that does not pass through the origin. To reach a point R in the plane starting from the origin, you can go to some other point in the plane first, and then move along two directions which lie in the plane, as shown.

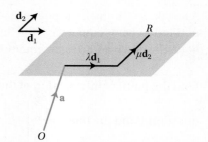

> **Tip**
>
> A **plane** is a flat surface in three-dimensional space. It extends indefinitely in all directions.

🔑 Key point 4.1

The vector equation of the plane containing a point with position vector $\mathbf{a}$ and parallel to the directions of vectors $\mathbf{d}_1$ and $\mathbf{d}_2$ is $\mathbf{r} = \mathbf{a} + \lambda\mathbf{d}_1 + \mu\mathbf{d}_2$.

WORKED EXAMPLE 4.1

Find a vector equation of the plane containing points $M(3, 4, -2)$, $N(1, -1, 3)$ and $P(5, 0, 2)$.

$\mathbf{r} = \mathbf{a} + \lambda\mathbf{d}_1 + \mu\mathbf{d}_2$

You need one point and two vectors parallel to the plane. Draw a diagram to see which vectors to use.

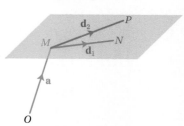

$a = \begin{pmatrix} 3 \\ 4 \\ -2 \end{pmatrix}$

You can choose any of the three given points to find $\mathbf{a}$, as they all lie in the plane.

Continues on next page ...

$$\underline{d}_1 = \overrightarrow{MN} = \begin{pmatrix} 1 \\ -1 \\ 3 \end{pmatrix} - \begin{pmatrix} 3 \\ 4 \\ -2 \end{pmatrix} = \begin{pmatrix} -2 \\ -5 \\ 5 \end{pmatrix}$$

Vectors $\overrightarrow{MN}$ and $\overrightarrow{MP}$ are parallel to the plane.

$$\underline{d}_2 = \overrightarrow{MP} = \begin{pmatrix} 5 \\ 0 \\ 2 \end{pmatrix} - \begin{pmatrix} 3 \\ 4 \\ -2 \end{pmatrix} = \begin{pmatrix} 2 \\ -4 \\ 4 \end{pmatrix}$$

$$\underline{r} = \begin{pmatrix} 3 \\ 4 \\ -2 \end{pmatrix} + \lambda \begin{pmatrix} -2 \\ -5 \\ 5 \end{pmatrix} + \mu \begin{pmatrix} 2 \\ -4 \\ 4 \end{pmatrix}$$

Use $\mathbf{r} = \mathbf{a} + \lambda \mathbf{d}_1 + \mu \mathbf{d}_2$.

In Worked example 4.1, the plane was determined by three points. Two points do not determine a plane: there is more than one plane containing the line determined by points A and B as shown in this diagram.

You can pick out one of these planes by requiring that it also passes through a third point, point C for example, which is not on the line AB, as illustrated here. This suggests that a plane can also be determined by a line and a point outside of that line.

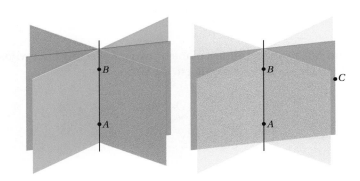

WORKED EXAMPLE 4.2

Find a vector equation of the plane containing the line $\mathbf{r} = \begin{pmatrix} -2 \\ 1 \\ 2 \end{pmatrix} + t \begin{pmatrix} -3 \\ 1 \\ 1 \end{pmatrix}$ and point A (4, −1, 2).

$$\underline{a} = \begin{pmatrix} 4 \\ -1 \\ 2 \end{pmatrix}$$

Point A lies in the plane.

$$\underline{d}_1 = \begin{pmatrix} -3 \\ 1 \\ 1 \end{pmatrix}$$

The direction vector of the line is parallel to the plane.

Continues on next page ...

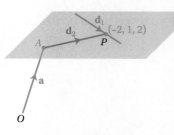

You need another vector parallel to the plane. You can use any vector between two points in the plane. One point in the plane is A. For the second point, you can pick any point on the line, for example $P(-2, 1, 2)$.

$$\underline{d}_2 = \begin{pmatrix} -2 \\ 1 \\ 2 \end{pmatrix} - \begin{pmatrix} 4 \\ -1 \\ 2 \end{pmatrix} = \begin{pmatrix} -6 \\ 2 \\ 0 \end{pmatrix}$$

$$\underline{r} = \begin{pmatrix} 4 \\ -1 \\ 2 \end{pmatrix} + \lambda \begin{pmatrix} -3 \\ 1 \\ 1 \end{pmatrix} + \mu \begin{pmatrix} -6 \\ 2 \\ 0 \end{pmatrix}$$

Now use $\mathbf{r} = \mathbf{a} + \lambda \mathbf{d}_1 + \mu \mathbf{d}_2$.

You can also determine a plane by two intersecting lines whose two direction vectors are parallel to the plane.

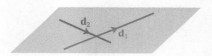

WORKED EXAMPLE 4.3

Find a vector equation of the plane containing the lines $\mathbf{r} = \begin{pmatrix} 3 \\ -1 \\ 2 \end{pmatrix} + \lambda \begin{pmatrix} -1 \\ 1 \\ 2 \end{pmatrix}$ and $\mathbf{r} = \begin{pmatrix} 3 \\ -1 \\ 2 \end{pmatrix} + \mu \begin{pmatrix} 3 \\ 0 \\ 2 \end{pmatrix}$.

$$\underline{r} = \begin{pmatrix} 3 \\ -1 \\ 2 \end{pmatrix} + \lambda \begin{pmatrix} -1 \\ 1 \\ 2 \end{pmatrix} + \mu \begin{pmatrix} 3 \\ 0 \\ 2 \end{pmatrix}$$

You can tell that the two lines intersect at the point $(3, -1, 2)$, so you can take that as one point in the plane. The two lines' direction vectors give two different directions in the plane.

If you have four points, they don't all necessarily lie in the same plane.

WORKED EXAMPLE 4.4

Determine whether points $A(2, -1, 3)$, $B(4, 1, 1)$, $C(3, 3, 2)$, and $D(-3, 1, 5)$ lie in the same plane.

Plane containing A, B, C:

$\mathbf{r} = \overrightarrow{OA} + \lambda\overrightarrow{AB} + \mu\overrightarrow{AC}$

The plan is to find the equation of the plane containing points A, B and C (as in Worked example 4.1) and then check whether the point D lies in that plane.

$\mathbf{r} = \begin{pmatrix} 2 \\ -1 \\ 3 \end{pmatrix} + \lambda\begin{pmatrix} 2 \\ 2 \\ -2 \end{pmatrix} + \mu\begin{pmatrix} 1 \\ 4 \\ -1 \end{pmatrix}$

$\mathbf{r} = \overrightarrow{OD}$:

For D to lie in the plane, you need values of λ and μ which make $\mathbf{r}$ equal to the position vector of D.

$\begin{cases} 2 + 2\lambda + \mu = -3 \\ -1 + 2\lambda + 4\mu = 1 \\ 3 - 2\lambda - \mu = 5 \end{cases}$

$\begin{cases} 2\lambda + \mu = -5 \\ 2\lambda + 4\mu = 2 \end{cases}$

You can solve the first two equations, and then check whether the solutions satisfy the third equation.

$\lambda = -\dfrac{11}{3}, \mu = \dfrac{7}{3}$

$3 - 2\times\left(-\dfrac{11}{3}\right) - \dfrac{7}{3} = 8 \neq 5$

D does not lie in the same plane as A, B and C.

There are no values of λ and μ that satisfy all three equations.

You can now summarise all possible ways to determine a plane.

Key point 4.2

A plane is uniquely determined by:

- three points, not on the same line, or
- a line and a point outside that line, or
- two intersecting lines.

Cartesian equation of a plane

The vector equation of the plane can be a little difficult to work with, as it contains two parameters. It is also difficult to see whether two equations represent the same plane, because the two vectors parallel to the plane are not unique.

Now you will look at the question: is there a way to describe the 'direction' of the plane using just one direction vector?

The diagram shows a plane and a vector **n** perpendicular to it. This vector is perpendicular to every line in the plane, and it is called the **normal vector** of the plane.

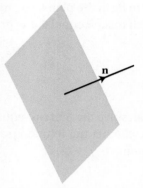

Suppose A is a fixed point in the plane and let P be any other point in the plane. The normal vector is perpendicular to the line AP, so $\overrightarrow{AP} \cdot \mathbf{n} = 0$. This means that $(\mathbf{r} - \mathbf{a}) \cdot \mathbf{n} = 0$, which gives another form of an equation of the plane.

 Key point 4.3

The **scalar product equation** of the plane is:

$$\mathbf{r} \cdot \mathbf{n} = \mathbf{a} \cdot \mathbf{n}$$

where **n** is the normal to the plane and **a** is the position vector of a point in the plane.

Remember that the position vector of a point is related to its coordinates. This means that you can use the scalar product equation to write the Cartesian equation of a plane.

Write $\mathbf{n} = \begin{pmatrix} n_1 \\ n_2 \\ n_3 \end{pmatrix}$ and $\mathbf{r} = \begin{pmatrix} x \\ y \\ z \end{pmatrix}$. The scalar product $\mathbf{a} \cdot \mathbf{n}$ is a constant, denoted d in Key point 4.4, and the scalar product $\mathbf{r} \cdot \mathbf{n}$ can be expanded to get an expression in terms of x, y and z.

 Key point 4.4

The Cartesian equation of a plane can be written in the form $n_1 x + n_2 y + n_3 z = d$.

WORKED EXAMPLE 4.5

Vector $\mathbf{n} = \begin{pmatrix} 2 \\ 4 \\ -1 \end{pmatrix}$ is perpendicular to the plane Π which contains point $A(3, -5, 1)$.

a Write an equation for Π in the form $\mathbf{r} \cdot \mathbf{n} = p$.

b Find the Cartesian equation of the plane.

> **Tip**
>
> The letter Π (capital π) is often used as the name for a plane.

a $\underline{r} \cdot \underline{n} = \begin{pmatrix} 3 \\ -5 \\ 1 \end{pmatrix} \cdot \begin{pmatrix} 2 \\ 4 \\ -1 \end{pmatrix} = 6 - 20 - 1$

The equation of the plane is $\mathbf{r} \cdot \mathbf{n} = \mathbf{a} \cdot \mathbf{n}$.

$\therefore \underline{r} \cdot \underline{n} = -15$

b $\begin{pmatrix} x \\ y \\ z \end{pmatrix} \cdot \begin{pmatrix} 2 \\ 4 \\ -1 \end{pmatrix} = -15$

$2x + 4y - z = -15$

The Cartesian equation involves x, y, and z (the coordinates of P), which are the components of the position vector $\mathbf{r}$.

You can convert from a vector to a Cartesian equation of the plane. This involves using the **vector product** to find the normal. The Cartesian equation is very convenient for checking whether a point lies in the plane: you just need to check that the coordinates of the point satisfy the equation.

> **Rewind**
>
> You met the vector product in Pure Core Student Book 1, Chapter 2.

WORKED EXAMPLE 4.6

a Find the Cartesian equation of the plane with vector equation $\mathbf{r} = \begin{pmatrix} 1 \\ -2 \\ 5 \end{pmatrix} + \lambda \begin{pmatrix} 1 \\ 1 \\ 3 \end{pmatrix} + \mu \begin{pmatrix} 2 \\ -3 \\ 5 \end{pmatrix}$.

b Show that the point $(2, 9, 10)$ lies in the plane.

a $\underline{r} \cdot \underline{n} = \underline{a} \cdot \underline{n}$

To find the Cartesian equation you need the normal vector and one point.

$\underline{a} = \begin{pmatrix} 1 \\ -2 \\ 5 \end{pmatrix}$

Point $(1, -2, 5)$ lies in the plane.

Continues on next page ...

$$\underline{n} = \begin{pmatrix} 1 \\ 1 \\ 3 \end{pmatrix} \times \begin{pmatrix} 2 \\ -3 \\ 5 \end{pmatrix} = \begin{pmatrix} 14 \\ 1 \\ -5 \end{pmatrix}$$

n is perpendicular to all lines in the plane, so it is perpendicular to the direction vectors $\begin{pmatrix} 1 \\ 1 \\ 3 \end{pmatrix}$ and $\begin{pmatrix} 2 \\ -3 \\ 5 \end{pmatrix}$.

The vector product of two vectors is perpendicular to both of them.

$$\underline{r} \cdot \begin{pmatrix} 14 \\ 1 \\ -5 \end{pmatrix} = \begin{pmatrix} 1 \\ -2 \\ 5 \end{pmatrix} \cdot \begin{pmatrix} 14 \\ 1 \\ -5 \end{pmatrix}$$

To get the Cartesian equation, write **r** as $\begin{pmatrix} x \\ y \\ z \end{pmatrix}$.

$$14x + y - 5z = -13$$

b $14(2) + 9 - 5(10) = -13$

Hence the point lies in the plane.

A point lies in the plane if its coordinates satisfy the Cartesian equation.

You can also convert from a Cartesian to a vector equation by finding two vectors that are perpendicular to the normal.

WORKED EXAMPLE 4.7

Find a vector equation of the plane with Cartesian equation $2x - 5y + z = 15$.

Vector equation:

$$\underline{r} = \underline{a} + \lambda \underline{d}_1 + \mu \underline{d}_2$$

In the vector equation of the plane, **a** is the position vector of one point in the plane and $\mathbf{d}_1$ and $\mathbf{d}_2$ are two direction vectors parallel to the plane.

Finding $\underline{a}$:

$$2x - 5y + z = 15$$

When $x = y = 0$:

$$2(0) - 5(0) + z = 15 \Rightarrow z = 15$$

The coordinates of A satisfy the Cartesian equation of the plane. You can choose any three numbers (x, y, z) that satisfy this equation. For example, you can set $x = y = 0$ and then find z.

Hence a possible position vector is $\underline{a} = \begin{pmatrix} 0 \\ 0 \\ 15 \end{pmatrix}$.

Finding $\underline{d}_1$ and $\underline{d}_2$:

Write $\underline{d}_1 = \begin{pmatrix} s \\ t \\ u \end{pmatrix}$. Then $\underline{d}_1 \cdot \underline{n} = 0$ so:

$$2s - 5t + u = 0.$$

The two direction vectors parallel to the plane must be perpendicular to the normal, which is $\mathbf{n} = \begin{pmatrix} 2 \\ -5 \\ 1 \end{pmatrix}$.

Continues on next page ...

When $s = 0$ and $t = 1$:

$$2(0)-5(1)+u=0 \Rightarrow u=5$$

As before, you can choose values for s and t and then find u. To make the calculation simple, take $s=0$ and $t=1$.

(Notice that, in this case, you can't set $s=t=0$ because that would make $u=0$ as well.)

Write $\underline{d}_2 = \begin{pmatrix} 1 \\ 0 \\ u \end{pmatrix}$. Then:

Repeat for $\mathbf{d}_2$, but this time take $s=1$ and $t=0$.

$$2(1)-5(0)+u=0 \Rightarrow u=-2$$

Hence the two direction vectors are

$$\underline{d}_1 = \begin{pmatrix} 0 \\ 1 \\ 5 \end{pmatrix} \text{ and } \underline{d}_2 = \begin{pmatrix} 1 \\ 0 \\ -2 \end{pmatrix}$$

A possible vector equation of the plane is

$$\underline{r} = \begin{pmatrix} 0 \\ 0 \\ 15 \end{pmatrix} + \lambda \begin{pmatrix} 0 \\ 1 \\ 5 \end{pmatrix} + \mu \begin{pmatrix} 1 \\ 0 \\ -2 \end{pmatrix}$$

Put all this together into the vector equation,

$$\mathbf{r} = \mathbf{a} + \lambda \mathbf{d}_1 + \mu \mathbf{d}_2$$

You should remember that the vector equation you found in Worked example 4.7 is not unique. You could have chosen any other point that satisfies the Cartesian equation, and there are infinitely many choices for pairs of direction vectors that are parallel to the normal.

EXERCISE 4A

1 Write down the vector equation of the plane parallel to vectors **a** and **b** and containing point P.

a i $\mathbf{a} = \begin{pmatrix} -1 \\ 5 \\ 2 \end{pmatrix}, \mathbf{b} = \begin{pmatrix} 1 \\ -2 \\ 3 \end{pmatrix}, P(1, 0, 2)$

ii $\mathbf{a} = \begin{pmatrix} 0 \\ 4 \\ -1 \end{pmatrix}, \mathbf{b} = \begin{pmatrix} 5 \\ 3 \\ 0 \end{pmatrix}, P(0, 2, 0)$

b i $\mathbf{a} = 3\mathbf{i} + \mathbf{j} - 3\mathbf{k}, \mathbf{b} = \mathbf{i} - 3\mathbf{j}, \mathbf{p} = \mathbf{j} + \mathbf{k}$

ii $\mathbf{a} = 5\mathbf{i} - 6\mathbf{j}, \mathbf{b} = -\mathbf{i} + 3\mathbf{j} - \mathbf{k}, P(1, -6, 2)$

2 Find a vector equation of the plane containing points A, B and C.

a i $A(3, -1, 3), B(1, 1, 2), C(4, -1, 2)$

ii $A(-1, -1, 5), B(4, 1, 2), C(-7, 1, 1)$

b i $A(9, 0, 0), B(-2, 1, 0), C(1, -1, 2)$

ii $A(11, -7, 3), B(1, 14, 2), C(-5, 10, 0)$

3 Find a vector equation of the plane containing line l and point P.

a i $l : \mathbf{r} = \begin{pmatrix} -3 \\ 5 \\ 1 \end{pmatrix} + t \begin{pmatrix} 4 \\ 1 \\ 2 \end{pmatrix}, P(-1, 4, 3)$

ii $l : \mathbf{r} = \begin{pmatrix} 9 \\ -3 \\ 7 \end{pmatrix} + t \begin{pmatrix} 6 \\ -3 \\ 1 \end{pmatrix}, P(11, 12, 13)$

b i $l : \mathbf{r} = \begin{pmatrix} 4 \\ 4 \\ 1 \end{pmatrix} + t \begin{pmatrix} 0 \\ 0 \\ 1 \end{pmatrix}, P(-3, 1, 0)$

ii $l : \mathbf{r} = t \begin{pmatrix} 2 \\ 1 \\ 1 \end{pmatrix}, P(4, 0, 2)$

4 A plane has normal vector **n** and contains point A. Find the equation of the plane in the form $\mathbf{r} \cdot \mathbf{n} = d$, and the Cartesian equation of the plane.

a i $\mathbf{n} = \begin{pmatrix} 3 \\ -5 \\ 2 \end{pmatrix}$, $A(3,3,1)$ 　　　 ii $\mathbf{n} = \begin{pmatrix} 6 \\ -1 \\ 2 \end{pmatrix}$, $A(4,3,-1)$

b i $\mathbf{n} = \begin{pmatrix} 3 \\ -1 \\ 0 \end{pmatrix}$, $A(-3,0,2)$ 　　　 ii $\mathbf{n} = \begin{pmatrix} 4 \\ 0 \\ -5 \end{pmatrix}$, $A(0,0,2)$

5 Find a normal vector to the plane given by the vector equation:

a i $\mathbf{r} = \begin{pmatrix} 5 \\ 0 \\ 1 \end{pmatrix} + \lambda \begin{pmatrix} 1 \\ 2 \\ 3 \end{pmatrix} + \mu \begin{pmatrix} 5 \\ -2 \\ 2 \end{pmatrix}$ 　　　 ii $\mathbf{r} = \begin{pmatrix} 0 \\ 0 \\ 1 \end{pmatrix} + \lambda \begin{pmatrix} -3 \\ 6 \\ 2 \end{pmatrix} + \mu \begin{pmatrix} -1 \\ 1 \\ 2 \end{pmatrix}$

b i $\mathbf{r} = \begin{pmatrix} 7 \\ 3 \\ 5 \end{pmatrix} + \lambda \begin{pmatrix} -5 \\ 1 \\ 2 \end{pmatrix} + \mu \begin{pmatrix} 0 \\ 0 \\ 1 \end{pmatrix}$ 　　　 ii $\mathbf{r} = \begin{pmatrix} 3 \\ 5 \\ 7 \end{pmatrix} + \lambda \begin{pmatrix} 6 \\ -1 \\ 2 \end{pmatrix} + \mu \begin{pmatrix} -1 \\ -1 \\ 3 \end{pmatrix}$

6 Find the equations of the planes from question **5** in the form $\mathbf{r} \cdot \mathbf{n} = p$.

7 Find the Cartesian equations of the planes from question **5**.

8 Find the Cartesian equation of the plane containing points A, B and C.

a i $A(7,1,2), B(-1,4,7), C(5,2,3)$

　ii $A(1,1,2), B(4,-6,2), C(12,12,2)$

b i $A(12,4,10), B(13,4,5), C(15,-4,0)$

　ii $A(1,0,0), B(0,1,0), C(0,0,1)$

9 In each of the following show that point P lies in the given plane Π.

a $P(-4,8,13)$, $\Pi : \mathbf{r} = \begin{pmatrix} 2 \\ 1 \\ 1 \end{pmatrix} + \lambda \begin{pmatrix} 4 \\ 1 \\ 2 \end{pmatrix} + \mu \begin{pmatrix} -1 \\ 4 \\ 7 \end{pmatrix}$

b $P(4,7,5)$, $\Pi : \mathbf{r} \cdot \begin{pmatrix} 4 \\ -1 \\ 2 \end{pmatrix} = 19$

c $P(1, 1, -2), \Pi : 2x - 3y - 7z = 13$

10 A plane contains the point $(3, -2, 5)$. The vector $6\mathbf{i} + \mathbf{j} - 3\mathbf{k}$ is perpendicular to the plane. Find the Cartesian equation of the plane.

11 A plane contains points $A(5, 1, 5)$, $B(-3, 1, 2)$ and $C(0, 1, 5)$.

Find the vector equation of the plane in the form $\mathbf{r} = \mathbf{a} + \lambda \mathbf{d}_1 + \mu \mathbf{d}_2$.

12 A plane contains points $P(3, 0, 2)$, $Q(-1, 1, 2)$ and $R(0, 5, 1)$.

    a Find $\overrightarrow{PQ} \times \overrightarrow{PR}$.

    b Hence find the Cartesian equation of the plane.

13 A plane is determined by the points $A(3, 1, 5)$, $B(-1, 4, 0)$ and $C(0, 0, 3)$.

    a Find the equation of the plane in the form $\mathbf{r} \cdot \mathbf{n} = k$.

    b Determine whether the point $D(1, 1, 4)$ lies in the same plane.

14 **a** Calculate $\begin{pmatrix} 4 \\ 4 \\ 1 \end{pmatrix} \times \begin{pmatrix} 1 \\ -1 \\ 3 \end{pmatrix}$.

    b Hence find the Cartesian equation of the plane with vector equation $\mathbf{r} = \begin{pmatrix} 1 \\ 1 \\ 5 \end{pmatrix} + \lambda \begin{pmatrix} 4 \\ 4 \\ 1 \end{pmatrix} + \mu \begin{pmatrix} 1 \\ -1 \\ 3 \end{pmatrix}$.

15 **a** Calculate $\begin{pmatrix} -1 \\ 0 \\ 2 \end{pmatrix} \times \begin{pmatrix} 0 \\ 1 \\ 3 \end{pmatrix}$.

    b Two lines have equations

$$l_1 : \mathbf{r} = \begin{pmatrix} 7 \\ -3 \\ 2 \end{pmatrix} + t \begin{pmatrix} -1 \\ 0 \\ 2 \end{pmatrix} \text{ and } l_2 : \mathbf{r} = \begin{pmatrix} 1 \\ 1 \\ 26 \end{pmatrix} + s \begin{pmatrix} 0 \\ 1 \\ 3 \end{pmatrix}$$

      i Show that l_1 and l_2 intersect.

      ii Find the coordinates of the point of intersection.

    c Plane Π contains lines l_1 and l_2. Find the Cartesian equation of Π.

16 Determine whether the points $(0, 3, 1)$, $(1, 1, 5)$, $(1, 0, 4)$ and $(3, 8, 5)$ lie in the same plane.

17 A plane has Cartesian equation $x - 3y + 4z = 16$.

    a Write down the normal vector, $\mathbf{n}$, of the plane.

    b Find the values of p and q such that the vectors $\begin{pmatrix} 1 \\ 0 \\ p \end{pmatrix}$ and $\begin{pmatrix} 0 \\ 1 \\ q \end{pmatrix}$ are perpendicular to $\mathbf{n}$.

    c Hence find a vector equation of the plane in the form $\mathbf{r} = \mathbf{a} + \lambda \mathbf{d}_1 + \mu \mathbf{d}_2$.

18 **a** Find the Cartesian equation of the plane with vector equation $\mathbf{r} = \begin{pmatrix} 0 \\ 1 \\ 5 \end{pmatrix} + \lambda \begin{pmatrix} -3 \\ 1 \\ 2 \end{pmatrix} + \mu \begin{pmatrix} 2 \\ 5 \\ 2 \end{pmatrix}$.

    b Another plane has Cartesian equation $x - 3y + z = 7$. Find a vector equation of this plane in the form $\mathbf{r} = \mathbf{a} + \lambda \mathbf{d}_1 + \mu \mathbf{d}_2$.

19 Find, in the form $\mathbf{r} = \mathbf{a} + \lambda \mathbf{d}_1 + \mu \mathbf{d}_2$, a vector equation of the plane $3y - z = 5$.

Section 2: Intersection between a line and a plane

The method introduced in this section requires equations of planes to be in Cartesian form and equations of lines to be in vector form. If in a question they are given in a different form, you will need to convert them first.

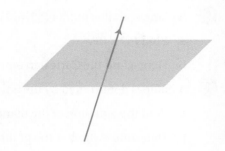

The coordinates of the intersection point (if there is one) must satisfy both the equation of the line and the equation of the plane.

WORKED EXAMPLE 4.8

Find the intersection between the given line and plane, or show that they do not intersect.

a $\quad r = \begin{pmatrix} 4 \\ -3 \\ 1 \end{pmatrix} + \lambda \begin{pmatrix} 3 \\ 0 \\ -2 \end{pmatrix}$ and $2x - y + 2z = 5$

b $\quad \dfrac{x-1}{-1} = \dfrac{y}{-3} = \dfrac{z+4}{2}$ and $x - 3y - 4z = 12$

a $\quad 2(4+3\lambda)-(-3)+2(1-2\lambda)=5$

$\qquad\qquad\qquad\qquad 2\lambda = -8$

$\qquad\qquad\qquad\qquad \lambda = -4$

> Any point on the line has coordinates $(4 + 3\lambda, -3, 1 - 2\lambda)$. The intersection point must also satisfy the equation of the plane, so substitute $x = 4 + 3\lambda$, $y = -3$, $z = 1 - 2\lambda$ into the equation of the plane.

$\quad r = \begin{pmatrix} 4 \\ -3 \\ 1 \end{pmatrix} - 4 \begin{pmatrix} 3 \\ 0 \\ -2 \end{pmatrix} = \begin{pmatrix} -8 \\ -3 \\ 9 \end{pmatrix}$

> Now use this value of λ to find the coordinates.

The intersection point is $(-8, -3, 9)$.

b $\quad \begin{cases} x - 1 = -\mu \\ y = -3\mu \\ z + 4 = 2\mu \end{cases}$

> Change the equation of the line into the vector form and then follow the same procedure as in part **a**.

$\quad \begin{pmatrix} x \\ y \\ z \end{pmatrix} = \begin{pmatrix} 1 - \mu \\ -3\mu \\ -4 + 2\mu \end{pmatrix}$

$\quad (1 - \mu) - 3(-3\mu) - 4(-4 + 2\mu) = 12$

$\qquad\qquad\qquad\qquad 17 = 12$

> Substitute the coordinates of a point on the line into the equation of the plane.

Impossible to find μ.

> It is impossible to find a value of μ for a point that satisfies both equations. This means that the line and the plane have no common points.

The line and plane do not intersect.

Notice that if a line and a plane do not intersect, this means that they are parallel. For example, in part **b** of Worked example 4.8, the direction vector of the line is perpendicular to the normal of the plane: $(-i - 3j + 2k) \cdot (i - 3j - 4k) = 0$; this shows that the line is parallel to the plane. By contrast, in part **a**, the direction of the line and the normal of the plane are not perpendicular: $(3i - 2k) \cdot (2i - j + 2k) = 2$.

It is possible for a line to lie entirely in a given plane.

WORKED EXAMPLE 4.9

Show that the line $\mathbf{r} = \begin{pmatrix} 3 \\ -1 \\ 1 \end{pmatrix} + t \begin{pmatrix} 3 \\ 1 \\ 0 \end{pmatrix}$ lies in the plane $x - 3y = 6$.

$(3+3t)-3(-1+t)=6$ .... A point on the line has coordinates $(3+3t, -1+t, 1)$.

$6=6$

You need to show that every such point satisfies the equation of the plane.

Every t is a solution. .... The equation is satisfied for all values of t. This means that every point on the line also lies in the plane.

So the line lies in the plane.

EXERCISE 4B

1 Find the coordinates of the point of intersection of line l and plane Π.

a i $l : \mathbf{r} = \begin{pmatrix} 2 \\ 1 \\ 2 \end{pmatrix} + \lambda \begin{pmatrix} 5 \\ 0 \\ -1 \end{pmatrix}$, $\Pi : 4x + 2y - z = 29$

ii $l : \mathbf{r} = \begin{pmatrix} -5 \\ 1 \\ 1 \end{pmatrix} + \lambda \begin{pmatrix} 7 \\ 3 \\ -3 \end{pmatrix}$, $\Pi : x + y + 5z = 11$

b i $l : \dfrac{x-2}{5} = \dfrac{y+1}{2} = \dfrac{z}{6}$, $\Pi : \mathbf{r} \cdot \begin{pmatrix} 1 \\ -4 \\ 1 \end{pmatrix} = 4$

ii $l : \dfrac{x-5}{-1} = \dfrac{y-3}{2} = \dfrac{z-5}{1}$, $\Pi : \mathbf{r} \cdot \begin{pmatrix} 2 \\ -1 \\ 1 \end{pmatrix} = 21$

2 Show that plane Π contains line l.

a $\Pi : x + 6y + 2z = 7$, $l : \mathbf{r} = \begin{pmatrix} 5 \\ 0 \\ 1 \end{pmatrix} + t \begin{pmatrix} 2 \\ -1 \\ 2 \end{pmatrix}$

b $\Pi : 5x + y - 2z = 15$, $l : \dfrac{x-4}{1} = \dfrac{y+1}{1} = \dfrac{z-2}{3}$

c $\Pi : \mathbf{r} \cdot \begin{pmatrix} 1 \\ 0 \\ -4 \end{pmatrix} = -5, l : \mathbf{r} = \begin{pmatrix} -1 \\ 0 \\ 1 \end{pmatrix} + t \begin{pmatrix} 8 \\ 3 \\ 2 \end{pmatrix}$

d $\Pi : \mathbf{r} \cdot \begin{pmatrix} -2 \\ -2 \\ 5 \end{pmatrix} = \begin{pmatrix} 5 \\ 3 \\ 1 \end{pmatrix} \cdot \begin{pmatrix} -2 \\ -2 \\ 5 \end{pmatrix}, l : \dfrac{x-3}{2} = \dfrac{y}{3} = \dfrac{z+1}{2}$

3 Find the point of intersection of the line $\mathbf{r} = \begin{pmatrix} 3 \\ -1 \\ 2 \end{pmatrix} + \lambda \begin{pmatrix} 2 \\ 1 \\ 1 \end{pmatrix}$ and the plane $x - y + z = 18$.

4 A line has equation $\dfrac{x-2}{-1} = \dfrac{y+1}{2} = \dfrac{z-2}{1}$.

   a Write down the direction vector of the line.

   b Find the coordinates of the point where the line intersects the plane with equation $\mathbf{r} \cdot \begin{pmatrix} 3 \\ 3 \\ 2 \end{pmatrix} = 16$.

5 Find the coordinates of the point of intersection of the line $\dfrac{x-2}{3} = \dfrac{y-1}{2} = z+1$ with the plane $2x - y - 2z = 7$.

6 The plane with equation $12x - 3y + 5z = 60$ intersects the x-, y-, and z-axes at points P, Q and R, respectively.

   a Find the coordinates of P, Q and R.

   b Find the area of the triangle PQR.

Section 3: Angles between lines and planes

The angle between a line l and a plane Π is the smallest possible angle that l makes with any of the lines in Π. In the diagram, this is the angle labelled θ between l and the line AP, where PR is perpendicular to the plane (so that $\overrightarrow{PR}$ is in the direction of the normal). Drawing a two-dimensional diagram of triangle APR makes the angles clearer.

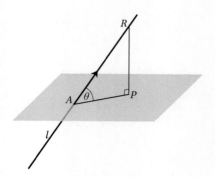
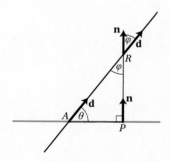

Key point 4.5

The angle between the line with direction vector **d** and the plane with normal **n** is $90° - \phi$, where ϕ is the acute angle between **d** and **n**.

 Rewind

You found the angle between two vectors using the scalar product in Pure Core Student Book 1, Chapter 2.

WORKED EXAMPLE 4.10

Find the angle between the line with equation $\mathbf{r} = \begin{pmatrix} 4 \\ 0 \\ 7 \end{pmatrix} + \lambda \begin{pmatrix} 3 \\ 3 \\ 2 \end{pmatrix}$ and the plane with equation $5x - y + z = 7$.

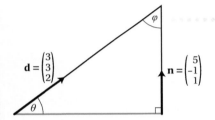

Draw a diagram, labelling vectors and angles as in Key point 4.5.

$$\cos\phi = \frac{\mathbf{d} \cdot \mathbf{n}}{|\mathbf{d}||\mathbf{n}|}$$

$$= \frac{\begin{pmatrix} 3 \\ 3 \\ 2 \end{pmatrix} \cdot \begin{pmatrix} 5 \\ -1 \\ 1 \end{pmatrix}}{\sqrt{9+9+4}\sqrt{25+1+1}}$$

$$= \frac{14}{\sqrt{22}\sqrt{27}}$$

$\therefore \phi = 54.9°$

The angle between the line and the plane is

The angle between a line and a plane is $90°$ − (angle between the line's direction vector and the plane's normal).

$\theta = 90° - \phi = 35.1°$

You can use a similar method to find the angle between two planes. Again, a diagram is helpful so you can see where the relevant angle is. The sum of angles in a quadrilateral is 360°, so the two angles marked θ are equal.

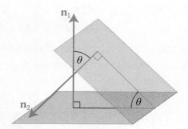

 Key point 4.6

The angle between two planes is equal to the angle between their normals.

WORKED EXAMPLE 4.11

Find the acute angle between the planes with equations $4x - y + 5z = 11$ and $x + y - 3z = 3$.

$$\cos\theta = \frac{\mathbf{n}_1 \cdot \mathbf{n}_2}{|\mathbf{n}_1||\mathbf{n}_2|}$$

You need to find the angle between the normals.

The components of the normal vector are the coefficients in the Cartesian equation.

$$= \frac{\begin{pmatrix} 4 \\ -1 \\ 5 \end{pmatrix} \cdot \begin{pmatrix} 1 \\ 1 \\ -3 \end{pmatrix}}{\sqrt{16+1+25}\sqrt{1+1+9}}$$

$$= \frac{-12}{\sqrt{42}\sqrt{11}}$$

$$\therefore \theta = 123.9°$$

$$180° - 123.9° = 56.1°$$

You need the acute angle.

The angle between the planes is 56.1°.

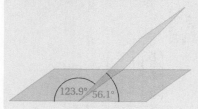

EXERCISE 4C

1 Find the acute angle between line l and plane Π, correct to the nearest 0.1°.

a i $l : \mathbf{r} = \begin{pmatrix} 4 \\ -1 \\ 2 \end{pmatrix} + \lambda \begin{pmatrix} 1 \\ -1 \\ 3 \end{pmatrix}, \Pi : \mathbf{r} \cdot \begin{pmatrix} 4 \\ -1 \\ 2 \end{pmatrix} = 7$

ii $l : \mathbf{r} = \begin{pmatrix} 2 \\ -3 \\ 1 \end{pmatrix} + \lambda \begin{pmatrix} -3 \\ 1 \\ 1 \end{pmatrix}, \Pi : \mathbf{r} \cdot \begin{pmatrix} -1 \\ -2 \\ 2 \end{pmatrix} = 1$

b **i** $l : \dfrac{x}{2} = \dfrac{y-1}{5} = \dfrac{z-2}{5}, \ \Pi : x - y - 3z = 1$

 ii $l : \dfrac{x+1}{-1} = \dfrac{y-3}{3} = \dfrac{z+2}{-3}, \ \Pi : 2x + y + z = 14$

2 Find the acute angle between each pair of planes.

a $3x - 7y + z = 4$ and $x + y - 4z = 5$

b $x - z = 4$ and $y + z = 1$

3 Line l has Cartesian equation $\dfrac{x-3}{2} = \dfrac{y+1}{3} = \dfrac{z-5}{-1}$.

a Write down the direction vector of l.

b Find the angle between l and the plane with equation $x - 3y + 5z = 7$.

4 Plane Π_1 has Cartesian equation $3x - y + z = 7$.

a Write down a normal vector of Π_1.

Plane Π_2 has equation $x - 5y + 5z = 11$.

b Find, correct to the nearest degree, the acute angle between Π_1 and Π_2.

5 Line l has equation $\dfrac{x-5}{4} = \dfrac{y+1}{2} = \dfrac{z-2}{3}$.

a Write down the direction vector of l.

b Find the acute angle that l makes with the plane $\mathbf{r} \cdot \begin{pmatrix} -1 \\ 4 \\ 3 \end{pmatrix} = 7$.

6 A plane has vector equation $\mathbf{r} = \begin{pmatrix} 3 \\ 7 \\ 1 \end{pmatrix} + \lambda \begin{pmatrix} -1 \\ 3 \\ 1 \end{pmatrix} + \mu \begin{pmatrix} 2 \\ 2 \\ 5 \end{pmatrix}$.

a Find the normal vector of the plane.

b Find the angle that the plane makes with the line $\mathbf{r} = \begin{pmatrix} 1 \\ 2 \\ -1 \end{pmatrix} + \lambda \begin{pmatrix} 3 \\ 1 \\ 5 \end{pmatrix}$.

7 Show that the planes with equations $3x + y + 4z = 7$ and $x + 9y - 3z = 8$ are perpendicular to each other.

8 Line l has Cartesian equation $\dfrac{4-x}{5} = z + 1, \ y = -3$.

a Find the direction vector of l.

b Find the acute angle that l makes with the plane $4x - 3z = 0$.

9 Plane Π has equation $5x - 3y - z = 1$.

   a Show that point $P(2,1,6)$ lies in the plane Π.

   b Point Q has coordinates $(7, -1, 2)$. Find the exact value of the sine of the angle between PQ and Π.

   c Find the exact distance PQ.

   d Hence find the exact distance of Q from Π.

 Fast forward

In Section 4 you will meet a formula for the distance from a point to a plane.

Section 4: Distances between points, lines and planes

Distance between a point and a plane

Given a plane with equation $\mathbf{r} \cdot \mathbf{n} = p$ and a point M outside of the plane, the shortest distance from M to the plane is equal to the distance MP, where the line MP is perpendicular to the plane. This means that the direction of PM is $\mathbf{n}$. (Point P is called the foot of the perpendicular from the point to the plane.)

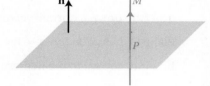

To find the distance MP:

* write down the vector equation of the line with direction $\mathbf{n}$ through point M
* find the intersection, P, between the line and the plane
* calculate the distance MP.

This procedure leads to the formula in Key point 4.7, which you can use unless the question explicitly asks you to carry out the three steps listed here (see questions 14 and 15 in Exercise 4D).

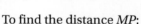 **Key point 4.7**

The shortest distance between the point with position vector $\mathbf{b}$ and the plane with equation $\mathbf{r} \cdot \mathbf{n} = p$ is given by

$$D = \frac{|\mathbf{b} \cdot \mathbf{n} - p|}{|\mathbf{n}|}$$

This will be given in your formula book.

WORKED EXAMPLE 4.12

Plane Π has Cartesian equation $3x - y + z = 8$. Find the shortest distance between Π and the point $M(13, -3, 10)$.

Π has equation $\underline{r} \cdot \underline{n} = 8$ with $\underline{n} = \begin{pmatrix} 3 \\ -1 \\ 1 \end{pmatrix}$.

To use the formula you need to identify the normal vector.

$\underline{b} \cdot \underline{n} = \begin{pmatrix} 13 \\ -3 \\ 10 \end{pmatrix} \cdot \begin{pmatrix} 3 \\ -1 \\ 1 \end{pmatrix} = 52$

and $|\underline{n}| = \sqrt{3^2 + (-1)^2 + 1^2} = \sqrt{11}$

The distance is

Now use the formula from Key point 4.7.

$D = \dfrac{|\underline{b} \cdot \underline{n} - p|}{|\underline{n}|}$

$= \dfrac{|52 - 8|}{\sqrt{11}} = 4\sqrt{11}$

Distance between a point and a line

Given a line with direction vector **d** and a point M not on the line, the shortest distance between M and the line is the distance from M to the point P on the line such that MP is perpendicular to **d**.

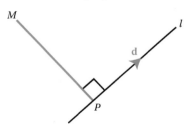

◀◀ Rewind

In Pure Core Student Book 1, Focus on ... Problem solving 1, you explored various methods for finding the shortest distance between a point and a line in three dimensions. For a reminder, see question 16 in Exercise 4D.

In this course you only need to find this distance in two dimensions. In that case the equation of the line can be written as $ax + by = c$ and you can use the formula in Key point 4.8.

🔑 Key point 4.8

The shortest distance between the point with coordinates (x_1, y_1) and the line with equation $ax + by = c$ is given by

$$D = \frac{|ax_1 + by_1 - c|}{\sqrt{a^2 + b^2}}$$

This will be given in your formula book.

WORKED EXAMPLE 4.13

Line l passes through the points $(-2, 5)$ and $(1, 9)$. Find the shortest distance between l and the point $(-4, 7)$.

Gradient of l:

$$m = \frac{1+2}{9-5} = \frac{3}{4}$$

> To use the formula you need to write the equation of l in the form $ax + by = c$. First you need the gradient.

Equation of l:

$$y - 5 = \frac{3}{4}(x+2)$$

$$\Leftrightarrow 4y - 20 = 3x + 6$$

$$\Leftrightarrow 3x - 4y = -26$$

> Use $y - y_1 = m(x - x_1)$.

$$D = \frac{|ax_1 + by_1 - c|}{\sqrt{a^2 + b^2}}$$

$$= \frac{|3(-4) - 4(7) - (-26)|}{\sqrt{3^2 + 4^2}}$$

$$= \frac{|-14|}{5} = \frac{14}{5}$$

> Now use the formula from Key point 4.8.

Distance between two skew lines

Consider points M and N moving along two skew lines. The distance between them is the minimum possible when MN is perpendicular to both lines. It may not be immediately obvious that such a position of M and N always exists, but it does. In sketching a diagram of this situation, it is useful to envisage a cuboid, where one line runs along an upper edge, and the other runs along the diagonal of the base, as shown in the diagram. The shortest distance between the two lines is then the height of the cuboid.

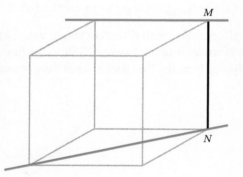

You can find the position of the points M and N by using the fact that MN is perpendicular to both lines' direction vector (see question 18 in Exercise 4D). However, in most questions you can use the following formula.

🔑 Key point 4.9

The shortest distance between two skew lines with equations $\mathbf{r} = \mathbf{a} + \lambda \mathbf{d}_1$ and $\mathbf{r} = \mathbf{b} + \mu \mathbf{d}_2$ is given by

$$D = \frac{|(\mathbf{b} - \mathbf{a}) \cdot \mathbf{n}|}{|\mathbf{n}|} \text{ where } \mathbf{n} = \mathbf{d}_1 \times \mathbf{d}_2$$

This will be given in your formula book.

You may need to use the equations of the lines to identify **a** and **b** and then calculate **n**.

WORKED EXAMPLE 4.14

Find the shortest distance between the lines with equations $\dfrac{x-1}{3}=\dfrac{y+1}{4}=\dfrac{3-z}{3}$ and $\dfrac{x+2}{1}=\dfrac{y-1}{-1}=\dfrac{z}{4}$.

The direction vectors are:

The components of the direction vectors are given by the denominators in the Cartesian equation when written in the form $\dfrac{x-a}{p}=\dfrac{y-b}{q}=\dfrac{z-c}{r}$.

For the first line, the last numerator is $3-z$ rather than $z-3$, so the corresponding component of the direction vector is -3.

$$\underline{d}_1=\begin{pmatrix}3\\4\\-3\end{pmatrix}, \underline{d}_2=\begin{pmatrix}1\\-1\\4\end{pmatrix}$$

$$\underline{n}=\begin{pmatrix}3\\4\\-3\end{pmatrix}\times\begin{pmatrix}1\\-1\\4\end{pmatrix}=\begin{pmatrix}13\\-15\\-7\end{pmatrix}$$

Use the vector product to calculate **n**.

$$D=\frac{|(\underline{b}-\underline{a})\cdot\underline{n}|}{|\underline{n}|}$$

Now use the formula from Key point 4.9 with $\mathbf{a}=\begin{pmatrix}1\\-1\\3\end{pmatrix}$ and $\mathbf{b}=\begin{pmatrix}-2\\1\\0\end{pmatrix}$.

$$=\frac{\left|\begin{pmatrix}-3\\2\\-3\end{pmatrix}\cdot\begin{pmatrix}13\\-15\\-7\end{pmatrix}\right|}{\sqrt{169+225+49}}$$

$$=\frac{48}{\sqrt{443}}=2.28\ (3\text{ s.f.})$$

Distance between two parallel lines

Consider two parallel lines, both with a direction vector **d**. You can measure the distance between them from any point A on the first line: it is the distance AP, where P is the point on the second line such that AP is perpendicular to **d**.

As you can see from the diagram, you can actually find the distance without finding the position vector of P. It equals $|\mathbf{a}-\mathbf{b}|\sin\theta$, where B is any point on the second line and θ is the angle between AB and **d**.

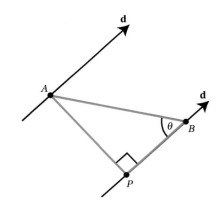

Key point 4.10

The distance between parallel lines with equations $\mathbf{r} = \mathbf{a} + \lambda\mathbf{d}$ and $\mathbf{r} = \mathbf{b} + \mu\mathbf{d}$ is given by

$$D = |\mathbf{a} - \mathbf{b}|\sin\theta \text{ where } \cos\theta = \frac{(\mathbf{a} - \mathbf{b}) \cdot \mathbf{d}}{|\mathbf{a} - \mathbf{b}||\mathbf{d}|}$$

 Fast forward

You can also find the distance from point A to the second line by using the fact that AP is perpendicular to the direction vector. See question 17 in Exercise 4D for an example.

The formula in Key point 4.10 will not be given in the formula book, so it is a good idea to draw a diagram to make sure you get it right.

WORKED EXAMPLE 4.15

Show that the lines with equations $\dfrac{x-2}{\frac{5}{2}} = \dfrac{y-1}{3} = \dfrac{z-5}{-2}$ and $\dfrac{2x-6}{10} = \dfrac{y+3}{6} = \dfrac{4-z}{4}$ are parallel and

find the distance between them.

The first line has direction vector

$$\underline{d} = \begin{pmatrix} 2.5 \\ 3 \\ -2 \end{pmatrix}$$

> You need to identify the direction vectors of the two lines.

Second line:

$$\frac{x-3}{5} = \frac{y+3}{6} = \frac{z-4}{-4}$$

> For the second line you need to write each term in the form, $\dfrac{x-a}{p}$.

has the direction vector

$$\begin{pmatrix} 5 \\ 6 \\ -4 \end{pmatrix} = 2\underline{d}$$

The two lines have parallel direction vectors so they are parallel.

> The second direction vector is a multiple of the first direction vector.

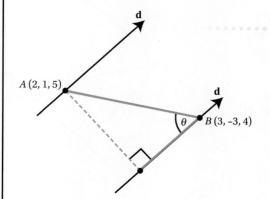

> Draw a diagram to identify the required distance.
>
> You can see from the equation that the point $A(2, 1, 5)$ lies on the first line and the point $B(3, -3, 4)$ lies on the second line.

Continues on next page ...

$$\overrightarrow{AB} = \begin{pmatrix} 1 \\ -4 \\ -1 \end{pmatrix}, \underline{d} = \begin{pmatrix} 2.5 \\ 3 \\ -2 \end{pmatrix}$$

The distance is $AB \sin\theta$ where θ is the angle between AB and $\mathbf{d}$.

$$\cos\theta = \frac{\overrightarrow{AB} \cdot \underline{d}}{|\overrightarrow{AB}||\underline{d}|}$$

$$= \frac{\frac{5}{2} - 12 + 2}{\sqrt{18}\sqrt{\frac{77}{4}}} = -0.403\ldots$$

$$\Rightarrow \sin\theta = 0.915\ldots$$

$$D = |\overrightarrow{AB}|\sin\theta$$

$$= \sqrt{18} \times 0.915 = 3.88 \, (3 \text{ s.f.})$$

EXERCISE 4D

1 Find the distance from the point M to the plane Π.

a i $M(1, -1, 3)$, $\Pi: \mathbf{r} \cdot \begin{pmatrix} 2 \\ 1 \\ 1 \end{pmatrix} = 23$

ii $M(3, 5, 10)$, $\Pi: \mathbf{r} \cdot \begin{pmatrix} 6 \\ -1 \\ 0 \end{pmatrix} = 1$

b i $M(4, 1, 2)$, $\Pi: 3x - y + 2z = 17$

ii $M(0, 3, -5)$, $\Pi: x - 4z = 8$

2 Find the distance between the point M and the line l.

a i $M(1, -3)$, $l: 3x + 8y = 6$

ii $M(0, 4)$, $l: x - 3y = 12$

b i $M(5, 2)$, $l: y = 4x + 5$

ii $M(-6, 1)$, $l: y = -3x + 2$

3 Find the distance between the lines l_1 and l_2.

a i $l_1: \mathbf{r} = \begin{pmatrix} 1 \\ 2 \\ 3 \end{pmatrix} + t\begin{pmatrix} -1 \\ 1 \\ 2 \end{pmatrix}$ and $l_2: \mathbf{r} = \begin{pmatrix} -4 \\ -4 \\ -11 \end{pmatrix} + s\begin{pmatrix} 5 \\ 1 \\ 2 \end{pmatrix}$

ii $l_1: \mathbf{r} = \begin{pmatrix} 4 \\ 0 \\ 2 \end{pmatrix} + t\begin{pmatrix} 2 \\ 0 \\ 1 \end{pmatrix}$ and $l_2: \mathbf{r} = \begin{pmatrix} -1 \\ 2 \\ 3 \end{pmatrix} + s\begin{pmatrix} 1 \\ -2 \\ -2 \end{pmatrix}$

b i $l_1: \frac{x-2}{-3} = \frac{y+1}{2} = \frac{z-1}{2}$ and $l_2: \frac{x+1}{1} = \frac{y}{6} = \frac{z-1}{3}$

ii $l_1: \frac{x+1}{2} = \frac{y-6}{-2} = \frac{z+7}{1}$ and $l_2: \frac{x-2}{-1} = \frac{y+1}{3} = \frac{z}{5}$

4 Show that the lines l_1 and l_2 are parallel and find the distance between them.

a i $l_1: \mathbf{r} = \begin{pmatrix} 0 \\ 0 \\ 5 \end{pmatrix} + t\begin{pmatrix} 1/2 \\ -1/3 \\ 2 \end{pmatrix}$ and $l_2: \mathbf{r} = \begin{pmatrix} 1 \\ 0 \\ 1 \end{pmatrix} + t\begin{pmatrix} -3 \\ 2 \\ -12 \end{pmatrix}$

ii $l_1: \mathbf{r} = \begin{pmatrix} 1 \\ 1 \\ 2 \end{pmatrix} + t\begin{pmatrix} 0.6 \\ 0.4 \\ -1 \end{pmatrix}$ and $l_2: \mathbf{r} = \begin{pmatrix} 3 \\ 0 \\ -1 \end{pmatrix} + t\begin{pmatrix} 3 \\ 2 \\ -5 \end{pmatrix}$

b **i** $l_1: \mathbf{r} = \begin{pmatrix} 1 \\ -7 \\ 1 \end{pmatrix} + t \begin{pmatrix} 2 \\ -3 \\ -2/3 \end{pmatrix}$ and $l_2: \dfrac{2x-1}{4} = \dfrac{y-2}{-3} = \dfrac{6-3z}{2}$

ii $l_1: \mathbf{r} = \begin{pmatrix} 1 \\ 1 \\ 2 \end{pmatrix} + t \begin{pmatrix} 3 \\ 1/2 \\ -2 \end{pmatrix}$ and $l_2: \dfrac{2-3x}{18} = \dfrac{1-y}{1} = \dfrac{2z+3}{8}$

5 Find the shortest distance between the lines with equations $\mathbf{r} = (2\mathbf{i} - \mathbf{k}) + t(4\mathbf{i} - \mathbf{j} + 3\mathbf{k})$ and $\mathbf{r} = (4\mathbf{j}) + t(\mathbf{i} - 5\mathbf{j})$.

6 Find the shortest distance between the point $(3, -1, 5)$ and the plane with equation $3x + y - z = 11$.

7 Find the exact distance of the plane $x - 4y + z = 6$ from the origin.

8 Find the perpendicular distance between the point with coordinates $(-3, 4)$ and the line passing through the points $(1, 3)$ and $(5, -2)$.

9 Show that the lines with equations $\dfrac{x-2}{3} = y+1 = \dfrac{z}{5}$ and $\dfrac{x+1}{3} = \dfrac{y-3}{4} = \dfrac{2-z}{2}$ do not intersect and find the shortest distance between them.

10 Points $A(5, -1)$, $B(1, 2)$ and $C(0, -9)$ form a triangle. Find the height of the triangle corresponding to the side BC and hence find the exact area of the triangle.

11 Show that the lines $\dfrac{x+1}{3} = \dfrac{4-y}{5} = \dfrac{-z}{2}$ and $\dfrac{2x-5}{6} = \dfrac{y+2}{-5} = \dfrac{1-3z}{6}$ are parallel and find the distance between them.

12 Two planes have equations:

$\Pi_1 : x - 3y + z = 6$, and $\Pi_2 : 3x - 9y + 3z = 0$.

a Show that Π_1 and Π_2 are parallel.

b Show that Π_2 passes through the origin.

c Hence find the distance between the planes Π_1 and Π_2.

13 **a** Show that the planes $\Pi_1 : x - z = 4$ and $\Pi_2 : z - x = 8$ are parallel.

b Given that the point $(4, -1, p)$ lies in Π_1 find the value of p.

c Use your answer from part **b** to find the exact distance between the two planes.

14 Plane Π has equation $2x + 2y - z = 11$. Line l is perpendicular to Π and passes through the point $P(-3, -3, 4)$.

a Find the equation of l.

b Find the coordinates of the point Q where l intersects Π.

c Find the shortest distance from P to Π.

15 Plane Π has equation $6x - 2y + z = 16$. Line l is perpendicular to Π and passes through the origin.

a Find the coordinates of the point of intersection of l and Π.

b Find the shortest distance of Π from the origin, giving your answer in exact form.

16 Line l has equation $\mathbf{r} = \begin{pmatrix} 4 \\ 2 \\ -1 \end{pmatrix} + \lambda \begin{pmatrix} 2 \\ -1 \\ 2 \end{pmatrix}$ and point P has coordinates $(7, 2, 3)$. Point C lies on l and PC is

perpendicular to l. Find the coordinates of C.

Hence find the shortest distance of P from l.

17 Two lines are given by Cartesian equations:

$$l_1: \frac{x-2}{3} = \frac{y+1}{-1} = \frac{z-2}{1}$$

$$l_2: \frac{x-5}{3} = 1 - y = z + 4$$

  a Show that l_1 and l_2 are parallel.

  b Show that the point $A(14, -5, 6)$ lies on l_1.

  c Find the coordinates of the point B on l_2 such that AB is perpendicular to the two lines.

  d Hence find the distance between l_1 and l_2, giving your answer to 3 significant figures.

18 Two lines have vector equations $l_1: \mathbf{r} = \begin{pmatrix} 1 \\ 3 \\ 1 \end{pmatrix} + \lambda \begin{pmatrix} 1 \\ -1 \\ 2 \end{pmatrix}$ and $l_2: \mathbf{r} = \begin{pmatrix} 5 \\ -1 \\ -6 \end{pmatrix} + \mu \begin{pmatrix} 1 \\ 1 \\ 3 \end{pmatrix}$.

The point A on l_1 and the point B on l_2 are such that AB is perpendicular to both lines.

  a Show that $\mu - \lambda = 1$.

  b Find a second equation linking λ and μ.

  c Hence find the shortest distance between l_1 and l_2, giving your answer as an exact value.

Checklist of learning and understanding

- The vector equation of a plane is $\mathbf{r} = \mathbf{a} + \lambda \mathbf{d}_1 + \mu \mathbf{d}_2$, where $\mathbf{d}_1$ and $\mathbf{d}_2$ are two vectors parallel to the plane and $\mathbf{a}$ is the position vector of one point in the plane.
- The Cartesian equation of a plane has the form $n_1 x + n_2 y + n_3 z = k$. This can also be written in the scalar product form $\mathbf{r} \cdot \mathbf{n} = \mathbf{a} \cdot \mathbf{n}$, where $\mathbf{n} = \begin{pmatrix} n_1 \\ n_2 \\ n_3 \end{pmatrix}$ is the normal vector of the plane, which is perpendicular to every line in the plane. To derive the Cartesian equation from a vector equation, use $\mathbf{n} = \mathbf{d}_1 \times \mathbf{d}_2$.
- The angle between two planes is the angle between their normals.
- The angle between a line and a plane is $90° -$ (angle between line's direction vector and plane's normal).
- To find the intersection between a line and a plane, express x, y, z for the line in terms of λ and substitute into the Cartesian equation of the plane.
- The shortest distance between the point with position vector $\mathbf{b}$ and the plane with equation $\mathbf{r} \cdot \mathbf{n} = p$ is given by $D = \dfrac{|\mathbf{b} \cdot \mathbf{n} - p|}{|\mathbf{n}|}$.
- The shortest distance between the point with coordinates (x_1, y_1) and the line with equation $ax + by = c$ is given by $D = \dfrac{|ax_1 + by_1 - c|}{\sqrt{a^2 + b^2}}$.
- The shortest distance between two skew lines with equations $\mathbf{r} = \mathbf{a} + \lambda \mathbf{d}_1$ and $\mathbf{r} = \mathbf{b} + \mu \mathbf{d}_2$ is given by $D = \dfrac{|(\mathbf{b} - \mathbf{a}) \cdot \mathbf{n}|}{|\mathbf{n}|}$ where $\mathbf{n} = \mathbf{d}_1 \times \mathbf{d}_2$.
- To find the distance between two parallel lines, find the perpendicular distance from a point on one line to the other line. (A diagram will help you see how to find this distance).

Mixed practice 4

1. Find the exact perpendicular distance from the point $(-4, 1)$ to the line with equation $y = 1 - 3x$.

2. Find the shortest distance of the point $(3, -5, 0)$ from the plane $3x - y + 3z = 16$.

3. The vector $\mathbf{n} = 3\mathbf{i} + \mathbf{j} - \mathbf{k}$ is normal to a plane which contains the point $(3, -1, 2)$.

   a Find an equation for the plane.

   b Find a if the point $(a, 2a, a-1)$ lies on the plane.

4. a Calculate $\begin{pmatrix} 2 \\ -1 \\ 1 \end{pmatrix} \times \begin{pmatrix} 3 \\ 1 \\ -1 \end{pmatrix}$.

   b Plane Π_1 has normal vector $\begin{pmatrix} 2 \\ -1 \\ 1 \end{pmatrix}$ and contains point A $(3, 4, -2)$. Find the Cartesian equation of the plane.

   c Plane Π_2 has equation $3x + y - z = 15$. Show that Π_2 contains point A.

   d A third plane, Π_3, has equation $\mathbf{r} \cdot \begin{pmatrix} 2 \\ 1 \\ 2 \end{pmatrix} = 12$. Find the angle between Π_1 and Π_3 in degrees.

5. The plane Π passes through the points with coordinates $(1, 6, 2)$, $(5, 2, 1)$ and $(1, 0, -2)$.

   i Find a vector equation of Π in the form $\mathbf{r} = \mathbf{a} + \lambda\mathbf{b} + \mu\mathbf{c}$.

   ii Find a cartesian equation of Π.

   © OCR A Level Mathematics, Unit 4727/01 Further Pure Mathematics 3, June 2013

6. Two skew lines have equations

   $$\frac{x}{2} = \frac{y+3}{1} = \frac{z-6}{3} \text{ and } \frac{x-5}{3} = \frac{y+1}{1} = \frac{z-7}{5}.$$

   i Find the direction of the common perpendicular to the lines.

   ii Find the shortest distance between the lines.

   © OCR A Level Mathematics, Unit 4727 Further Pure Mathematics 3, January 2009

7. Line l_1 has equation $\mathbf{r} = \begin{pmatrix} 5 \\ 1 \\ 2 \end{pmatrix} + t\begin{pmatrix} -1 \\ 1 \\ 3 \end{pmatrix}$ and line l_2 has equation $\mathbf{r} = \begin{pmatrix} 5 \\ 4 \\ 9 \end{pmatrix} + s\begin{pmatrix} 2 \\ 1 \\ 1 \end{pmatrix}$.

   a Find $\begin{pmatrix} -1 \\ 1 \\ 3 \end{pmatrix} \times \begin{pmatrix} 2 \\ 1 \\ 1 \end{pmatrix}$.

   b Find the coordinates of the point of intersection of the two lines.

   c Write down a vector perpendicular to the plane containing the two lines.

   d Hence find the Cartesian equation of the plane containing the two lines.

8. The plane Π has equation $x - 2y + z = 20$ and the point A has coordinates $(4, -1, 2)$.

   a Write down the vector equation of the line l through A which is perpendicular to Π.

   b Find the coordinates of the point of intersection of line l and plane Π.

   c Hence find the shortest distance from point A to plane Π.

9 Plane Π has equation $x - 4y + 2z = 7$ and point P has coordinates $(9, -7, 6)$.

   a Show that point $R(5, 1, 3)$ lies in the plane Π.

   b Find the vector equation of the line PR.

   c Write down the vector equation of the line through P perpendicular to Π.

   d N is the foot of the perpendicular from P to Π. Find the coordinates of N.

   e Find the exact distance of point P from the plane Π.

10 Find the shortest distance between the skew lines with equations

   $\mathbf{r} = -3\mathbf{i} + 3\mathbf{j} + 18\mathbf{k} + s(2\mathbf{i} - \mathbf{j} - 8\mathbf{k})$ and $\mathbf{r} = 5\mathbf{i} + 2\mathbf{k} + t(\mathbf{i} + \mathbf{j} - \mathbf{k})$.

11 Consider the four points $A(4, -1, 3)$, $B(1, 1, 2)$, $C(3, 0, 1)$ and $D(6, p, q)$.

   a Given that $ABCD$ is a parallelogram find the values of p and q.

   b Find the distance between the lines AB and DC.

   c Hence find the area of $ABCD$.

12 **a** Find the coordinates of the point of intersection of lines

     $l_1 : \dfrac{x-1}{3} = \dfrac{y+1}{4} = \dfrac{3-z}{3}$ and $l_2 : \dfrac{x+12}{2} = \dfrac{y}{1} = \dfrac{z+17}{1}$.

   b Find a vector perpendicular to both lines.

   c Hence find the Cartesian equation of the plane containing l_1 and l_2.

13 Point $A(3, 1, -4)$ lies on line l which is perpendicular to plane $\Pi : 3x - y - z = 1$.

   a Find the Cartesian equation of l.

   b Find the point of intersection of the line l and the plane Π.

   c Point A is reflected in Π. Find the coordinates of the image of A.

   d Point B has coordinates $(1, 1, 1)$. Show that B lies in Π.

   e Find the distance between B and l.

14 A line l has equation $\dfrac{x-6}{-4} = \dfrac{y+7}{8} = \dfrac{z+10}{7}$ and a plane p has equation $3x - 4y - 2z = 8$.

   i Find the point of intersection of l and p.

   ii Find the equation of the plane which contains l and is perpendicular to p, giving your answer in the form $ax + by + cz = d$.

© OCR A Level Mathematics, Unit 4727 Further Pure Mathematics 3, June 2009

15 A tetrahedron $ABCD$ is such that AB is perpendicular to the base BCD. The coordinates of the points A, C and D are $(-1, -7, 2)$, $(5, 0, 3)$ and $(-1, 3, 3)$ respectively, and the equation of the plane BCD is $x + 2y - 2z = -1$.

   i Find, in either order, the coordinates of B and the length of AB.

   ii Find the acute angle between the planes ACD and BCD.

© OCR A Level Mathematics, Unit 4727/01 Further Pure Mathematics 3, January 2008

16 Line l passes through point $A(-1,1,4)$ and has direction vector $\mathbf{d} = \begin{pmatrix} 6 \\ 1 \\ 5 \end{pmatrix}$. Point B has coordinates $(3,3,1)$.

Plane Π has normal vector $\mathbf{n}$, and contains the line l and the point B.

  a Write down a vector equation for l.

  b Explain why $\overrightarrow{AB}$ and $\mathbf{d}$ are both perpendicular to $\mathbf{n}$.

  c Hence find one possible vector $\mathbf{n}$.

  d Find the Cartesian equation of plane Π.

17 The plane $3x + 2y - z = 2$ contains the line $x - 3 = \dfrac{2y+2}{5} = \dfrac{z-5}{k}$. Find k.

18 Find the Cartesian equation of the plane containing the lines
$x = \dfrac{3-y}{2} = z - 1$ and $\dfrac{x-2}{3} = \dfrac{y+1}{-3} = \dfrac{z-3}{5}$.

19 Two planes have equations $\Pi_1 : 3x - y + z = 17$ and $\Pi_2 : x + 2y - z = 4$.

  a Calculate $\begin{pmatrix} 3 \\ -1 \\ 1 \end{pmatrix} \times \begin{pmatrix} 1 \\ 2 \\ -1 \end{pmatrix}$.

  b Show that Π_1 and Π_2 are perpendicular.

  c Show that the point $M(1,1,2)$ does not lie in either of the two planes.

  d Find a vector equation of the line through M which is parallel to both planes.

20 Four points have coordinates $A(7,0,1), B(8,-1,4), C(9,0,2), D(6,5,3)$.

  a Show that $\overrightarrow{AD}$ is perpendicular to both $\overrightarrow{AB}$ and $\overrightarrow{AC}$.

  b Write down the equation of the plane Π containing the points A, B and C in the form $\mathbf{r} \cdot \mathbf{n} = k$.

  c Find the exact distance of point D from plane Π.

  d Point D_1 is the reflection of D in Π. Find the coordinates of D_1.

21 Points $A(8,0,4)$, $B(12,-1,5)$ and $C(10,0,7)$ lie in the plane Π.

  a Find $\overrightarrow{AB} \times \overrightarrow{AC}$.

  b Find the area of the triangle ABC, correct to 3 significant figures.

  c Find the Cartesian equation of Π.

Point D has coordinates $(-7, -28, 11)$.

  d Find a vector equation of the line through D perpendicular to the plane.

  e Find the intersection of this line with Π, and hence find the perpendicular distance of D from Π.

  f Find the volume of the pyramid $ABCD$.

22 A regular tetrahedron has vertices at the points

$$A\left(0,0,\frac{2}{3}\sqrt{6}\right),\ B\left(\frac{2}{3}\sqrt{3},0,0\right),\ C\left(-\frac{1}{3}\sqrt{3},1,0\right),\ D\left(-\frac{1}{3}\sqrt{3},-1,0\right).$$

i Obtain the equation of the face *ABC* in the form

$$x+\sqrt{3}y+\left(\frac{1}{2}\sqrt{2}\right)z=\frac{2}{3}\sqrt{3}$$

(Answers which only verify the given equation will not receive full credit.)

ii Give a geometrical reason why the equation of the face *ABD* can be expressed as

$$x-\sqrt{3}y+\left(\frac{1}{2}\sqrt{2}\right)z=\frac{2}{3}\sqrt{3}$$

iii Hence find the cosine of the angle between two faces of the tetrahedron.

© OCR A Level Mathematics, Unit 4727 Further Pure Mathematics 3, January 2010

 23 With respect to the origin *O*, the position vectors of the points *U*, *V* and *W* are **u**, **v** and **w** respectively. The mid points of the sides *VW*, *WU* and *UV* of the triangle *UVW* are *M*, *N* and *P* respectively.

i Show that $\overrightarrow{UM}=\frac{1}{2}(\mathbf{v}+\mathbf{w}-2\mathbf{u})$.

ii Verify that the point *G* with position vector $\frac{1}{3}(\mathbf{u}+\mathbf{v}+\mathbf{w})$ lies on *UM*, and deduce that the lines *UM*, *VN* and *WP* intersect at *G*.

iii Write down, in the form $\mathbf{r}=\mathbf{a}+t\mathbf{b}$, an equation of the line through *G* which is perpendicular to the plane *UVW*. (It is not necessary to simplify the expression for **b**.)

iv It is now given that $\mathbf{u}=\begin{pmatrix}1\\0\\0\end{pmatrix}, \mathbf{v}=\begin{pmatrix}0\\1\\0\end{pmatrix}$ and $\mathbf{w}=\begin{pmatrix}0\\0\\1\end{pmatrix}$. Find the perpendicular distance from *O* to the plane *UVW*.

© OCR A Level Mathematics, Unit 4727 Further Pure Mathematics 3, June 2012

5 Simultaneous equations and planes

In this chapter you will learn how to:

- identify different geometrical configurations of two or three planes
- determine whether a set of simultaneous equations has a unique solution, no solutions or infinitely many solutions
- use simultaneous equations to determine the geometrical configuration of three planes.

Before you start…

Pure Core Student Book 1, Chapter 1	You should be able to find the determinant of a 2×2 and a 3×3 matrix and understand what is meant by a singular matrix.	1 Find the value of a for which the matrix $\begin{pmatrix} 1 & 1 & -2 \\ a & 1 & 1 \\ 0 & -2 & 3 \end{pmatrix}$ is singular.
Pure Core Student Book 1, Chapter 3	You should be able to use matrices to solve simultaneous equations in two and three unknowns.	2 Express simultaneous equations $\begin{cases} 2x - 3y = 2 \\ 5x - 8y = 3 \end{cases}$ in the form $\mathbf{M}\begin{pmatrix} x \\ y \end{pmatrix} = \begin{pmatrix} a \\ b \end{pmatrix}$. Find $\mathbf{M}^{-1}$ and hence find x and y.
Pure Core Student Book 1, Chapter 3	You should be able to determine when simultaneous equations do not have a unique solution.	3 Find the value of a for which the simultaneous equations $\begin{cases} x + y - 2z = 2 \\ ax + y + z = b \\ -2y + 3z = 1 \end{cases}$ do not have a unique solution.
GCSE	You should be able to use elimination to solve simultaneous equations.	4 Use elimination to solve the simultaneous equations $\begin{cases} 2x - 3y = 2 \\ 5x - 8y = 3 \end{cases}$
Chapter 4	You should know how to find the Cartesian equation of a plane, and to identify the normal vector of a plane with a given equation.	5 a Find the Cartesian equation of the plane with the normal vector $4\mathbf{i} - \mathbf{j} + 2\mathbf{k}$ which contains the point $(0, -1, 1)$. b Write down the normal vector of the plane with equation $3x - 4z = 1$.

In Chapter 4 you learnt about equations of planes in three dimensions. A Cartesian equation of a plane is a linear equation with three unknowns. In Pure Core Student Book 1, Chapter 3, you learnt how to solve three simultaneous equations with three unknowns by using an inverse matrix, and also how to tell when the solution is not unique.

In this chapter you will learn how to distinguish between different situations with non-unique solutions. You will then use simultaneous equations to find the intersection of three planes, and to determine the geometric configuration of the planes in the case when the intersection is not a single point.

> **📷 Focus on …**
>
> Matrices have applications in many other situations. You can explore one of them in Focus on … Modelling 1.

Section 1: Linear simultaneous equations

In Pure Core Student Book 1, Chapter 3, you learnt how to recast a system of two or three simultaneous equations into a matrix problem, and to use an inverse matrix to solve it. This method only works when the corresponding matrix is non-singular, and it leads to a unique solution of the system (a single pair of (x, y) values or a single triple of (x, y, z) values).

> **💡 Tip**
>
> A non-singular matrix has an inverse and its determinant is not zero.

If the matrix is singular (has a zero determinant) you need to use a different method, such as elimination, to determine whether there are any solutions.

The three possible cases for two equations with two unknowns can be illustrated by the examples in this table.

Unique solution	Infinitely many solutions	No solutions
$\begin{cases} 6x + 12y = 30 & (1) \\ 3x + 8y = 19 & (2) \end{cases}$	$\begin{cases} 6x + 12y = 30 & (1) \\ 4x + 8y = 20 & (2) \end{cases}$	$\begin{cases} 6x + 12y = 30 & (1) \\ 4x + 8y = 19 & (2) \end{cases}$
$\begin{vmatrix} 6 & 12 \\ 3 & 8 \end{vmatrix} = 12 \neq 0$	$\begin{vmatrix} 6 & 12 \\ 4 & 8 \end{vmatrix} = 0$	$\begin{vmatrix} 6 & 12 \\ 4 & 8 \end{vmatrix} = 0$
Non-singular matrix	Singular matrix	
$4 \times (1) - 6 \times (2): 6x = 6$	$4 \times (1) - 6 \times (2): 0x = 0$	$4 \times (1) - 6 \times (2): 0x = 6$
Unique solution: $x = 1, y = 2$	Infinitely many solutions: any (x, y) with $6x + 12y = 30$	No solutions
Consistent system		**Inconsistent** system

> **🔑 Key point 5.1**
>
> For a system of simultaneous equations in matrix form, $\mathbf{Mr} = \mathbf{a}$:
>
> - If $\det \mathbf{M} \neq 0$ the equations have a unique solution.
> - If $\det \mathbf{M} = 0$ there is no unique solution. Use elimination to distinguish between two cases:
>   - Consistent equations: there are infinitely many solutions.
>   - Inconsistent equations: there are no solutions.

WORKED EXAMPLE 5.1

Consider simultaneous equations

$$\begin{cases} 4x + 10y = 23 \\ 10x + ay = b \end{cases}$$

a Find the value of a for which the equations do not have a unique solution.

b For this value of a, find the value of b for which the equations are consistent.

a $\begin{vmatrix} 4 & 10 \\ 10 & a \end{vmatrix} = 0$ .... The solution is not unique when the determinant is zero.

$$\Leftrightarrow 4a - 100 = 0$$
$$\Leftrightarrow a = 25$$

b $\begin{cases} 4x + 10y = 23 \quad (1) \\ 10x + 25y = b \quad (2) \end{cases}$ .... Using $a = 25$, try to solve the equations by elimination; eliminate y.

$$5 \times (1) - 2 \times (2) : 0x = 115 - 2b$$

For solutions: .... For the system to be consistent, the RHS of the last
$$115 - 2b = 0$$ equation must be zero.

$$b = \frac{115}{2}$$

You can apply the same method to a system of three equations with three unknowns.

WORKED EXAMPLE 5.2

For the system of simultaneous equations

$$\begin{cases} x + y - 2z = 2 \\ ax + y + z = b \\ -2y + 3z = 1 \end{cases}$$

where a and b are constants:

a find the value of a for which there is not a unique solution

b for the value of a found in part **a**, find the value of b such that the equations are consistent.

a $\begin{pmatrix} 1 & 1 & -2 \\ a & 1 & 1 \\ 0 & -2 & 3 \end{pmatrix} \begin{pmatrix} x \\ y \\ z \end{pmatrix} = \begin{pmatrix} 2 \\ b \\ 1 \end{pmatrix}$ .... Recast the problem in matrix form as

$$\mathbf{M} \begin{pmatrix} x \\ y \\ z \end{pmatrix} = \begin{pmatrix} p \\ q \\ r \end{pmatrix}.$$

Continues on next page ...

$$\begin{vmatrix} 1 & 1 & -2 \\ a & 1 & 1 \\ 0 & -2 & 3 \end{vmatrix} = 1\begin{vmatrix} 1 & 1 \\ -2 & 3 \end{vmatrix} - 1\begin{vmatrix} a & 1 \\ 0 & 3 \end{vmatrix} - 2\begin{vmatrix} a & 1 \\ 0 & -2 \end{vmatrix}$$

The determinant tells you whether there is a unique solution.

$$= 5 - 3a - 2(-2a)$$
$$= 5 + a$$

$\therefore a = -5$

No unique solution when det $\mathbf{M} = 0$.

b Using elimination:
$$\begin{cases} x + y - 2z = 2 & (1) \\ -5x + y + z = b & (2) \\ -2y + 3z = 1 & (3) \end{cases}$$

Use elimination to determine when the equations are consistent.

$$\begin{cases} (2) + 5(1) : 6y - 9z = 10 + b & (4) \\ (3) : \quad -2y + 3z = 1 & (5) \end{cases}$$

Eliminate x from two equations.

$$(4) + 3(5) : 0 = 13 + b \quad (6)$$

Eliminate y from the final equation.

For a consistent solution,
$13 + b = 0$, so $b = -13$

Equation (6) says $0x + 0y + 0z = 13 + b$, which is only possible if $13 + b = 0$.

EXERCISE 5A

1 For each pair of simultaneous equations, determine whether there is a unique solution, no solutions or infinitely many solutions.

a i $\begin{cases} 2x + y = -3 \\ 3x - 6y = 4 \end{cases}$ 　　**b i** $\begin{cases} 3x + 2y = -3 \\ 9x + 6y = 4 \end{cases}$ 　　**c i** $\begin{cases} 10x + 5y = 15 \\ 6x + 3y = 9 \end{cases}$

ii $\begin{cases} x - 4y = 5 \\ 2x + y = -1 \end{cases}$ 　　**ii** $\begin{cases} 5x - 3y = 3 \\ 10x - 6y = 6 \end{cases}$ 　　**ii** $\begin{cases} 2x - 4y = -3 \\ 3x - 6y = 5 \end{cases}$

2 For each set of simultaneous equations determine whether or not there is a unique solution. Where there is a unique solution, use the inverse matrix to find it. Where there is no unique solution, determine whether the system is consistent or inconsistent.

a i $\begin{cases} 2x + y - z = -3 \\ 3x - 6y + z = 4 \\ 4x + 3y - 2z = 1 \end{cases}$ 　　**b i** $\begin{cases} 3x + y + z = 8 \\ -7x + 3y + z = 2 \\ x + y + 3z = 0 \end{cases}$ 　　**c i** $\begin{cases} 3x - y + z = 17 \\ x + 2y - z = 8 \\ 2x - 3y + 2z = 9 \end{cases}$

ii $\begin{cases} 2x + y - 5z = 15 \\ 5x + 6y + z = 7 \\ x - 8y + 5z = 1 \end{cases}$ 　　**ii** $\begin{cases} 3x - y + z = 17 \\ x + 2y - z = 8 \\ 2x - 3y + 2z = 3 \end{cases}$ 　　**ii** $\begin{cases} 2x + y - 2z = 0 \\ x - 2y - z = 2 \\ 3x + 4y - 3z = -2 \end{cases}$

3 Show that the system of equations

$$\begin{cases} 2x+3y-2z=2 \\ 3x+2y+z=5 \\ 3x+7y-7z=3 \end{cases}$$

does not have a unique solution.

4 **a** For what values of k does the system of equations

$$\begin{cases} -x+(2k-5)y-2z=2 \\ (1+k)x-y+(k-1)z=5 \\ x+y+2z=1 \end{cases}$$

have no unique solution?

b For each value of k found in part **a**, determine whether the equations have no solutions or infinitely many solutions.

5 **a** Show that the system of equations

$$\begin{cases} kx+3y-z=-2 \\ -3x+(k+4)y+z=-8 \\ x+3y+(k-2)z=4 \end{cases}$$

has no unique solution for $k=1$.

b Find the other values of k for which there is no unique solution.

c For $k=3$, find x, y and z.

d For $k=1$, determine whether the equations are consistent or inconsistent.

6 **a** Show that, for all values of a, the simultaneous equations

$$\begin{cases} 6x+3y+9z=p \\ 2x+ay+3z=q \\ 2x+y+3z=r \end{cases}$$

do not have a unique solution.

b Given that the equations have infinitely many solutions, show that $p=3r$.

7 Find the value of k and the value of c for which the system of equations

$$\begin{cases} 2x+3y-2z=2 \\ 3x+ky+z=5 \\ 3x+7y-7z=c \end{cases}$$

has infinitely many solutions.

Section 2: Intersections of planes

Simultaneous equations in two variables describe lines. If there is a unique solution, it represents the intersection of the lines, and if there is no unique solution this arises because the lines are parallel (no solution) or identical (infinitely many solutions).

Equations in three variables describe planes. Two distinct planes can either intersect (planes intersect in a line) or be parallel.

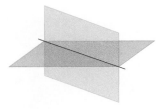

planes intersecting in a line   parallel planes

🔑 **Key point 5.2**

Two planes are parallel if their normal vectors are multiples of each other.

WORKED EXAMPLE 5.3

Five planes have these equations:

$\Pi_1 : 3x - y + z = 17$ $\qquad$ $\Pi_2 : x + 2y - z = 8$ $\qquad\qquad$ $\Pi_3 : -6x + 2y - 2z = 17$

$\Pi_4 : x - 2y + z = 6$ $\qquad$ $\Pi_5 : 3x + 6y - 3z = 2$

a Identify pairs of parallel planes.
b Which of the five plane(s) are identical to the plane $\Pi_6 : 2x + 4y - 2z - 16 = 0$?

a Π_1 and Π_3 are parallel. $\qquad$ · · · · · · · · · Parallel planes have normals in the same direction. This
$\quad$ Π_2 and Π_5 are parallel. $\qquad\qquad\qquad\qquad$ means that the LHS of the equations are multiples of
$\qquad\qquad\qquad\qquad\qquad\qquad\qquad\qquad\qquad$ each other.

b Π_2 and Π_5 are parallel to Π_6. $\qquad$ · · · · · First identify the plane(s) with the normals in the same
$\qquad\qquad\qquad\qquad\qquad\qquad\qquad\qquad\qquad$ direction.

$\quad$ $\Pi_2 : 2x + 4y - 2z = 16$ $\qquad$ · · · · · · · · Check whether the RHS is also the same.
$\quad$ $\Pi_5 : 2x + 4y - 2z = \dfrac{4}{3}$
$\quad$ Π_2 is identical to Π_6.

With three distinct planes there are several possibilities; altogether, there
are five different arrangements, but these fit into three cases:

1 Consistent system: unique solution
The three planes meet at a single point.

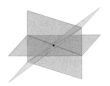

three distinct planes intersecting at a point

2 Consistent system: infinitely many solutions
The three planes intersect in a line (the planes form a sheaf).

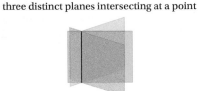

three distinct planes intersecting in a line

3 **Inconsistent** system: no solutions
   There is no point common to all three planes.
   a All three planes are parallel.

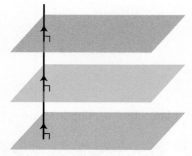

three distinct parallel planes

   b Two of the planes are parallel.

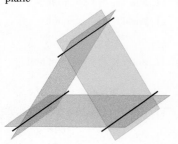

two parallel planes and one non-parallel plane

   c The planes enclose a triangular prism, so that each pair of planes intersects in a line, with the three distinct lines running parallel to each other.

three planes forming a triangular prism

You can distinguish between the different cases by using the methods from Section 1.

 Key point 5.3

To determine the geometrical arrangement of three planes described by a set of simultaneous equations, use $\mathbf{Mr} = \mathbf{a}$:

- If det $\mathbf{M} \neq 0$ the three planes meet at a single point.
- If det $\mathbf{M} = 0$ then:
  - If the equations are consistent the planes meet in a line (form a sheaf).
  - If the equations are inconsistent then either some of the planes are parallel, or the three planes form a prism.

 Tip

Remember that two planes are parallel if their normals are multiples of each other. If whole equations are multiples of each other then they describe the same plane.

WORKED EXAMPLE 5.4

The simultaneous equations $\begin{cases} kx - y + 3z = -2 \\ x + 6y - z = 3 \\ 3x - 8y + 7z = 6 \end{cases}$ describe three planes.

a Show that when $k = -4.5$ the planes intersect at a single point and find its coordinates.

b Find the value of k for which there is no unique solution, and describe the configuration of the three planes in that case.

$$\begin{pmatrix} k & -1 & 3 \\ 1 & 6 & -1 \\ 3 & -8 & 7 \end{pmatrix} \begin{pmatrix} x \\ y \\ z \end{pmatrix} = \begin{pmatrix} -2 \\ 3 \\ 6 \end{pmatrix}$$

Recast the problem in matrix form as

$$\mathbf{M} \begin{pmatrix} x \\ y \\ z \end{pmatrix} = \begin{pmatrix} p \\ q \\ r \end{pmatrix}.$$

a Setting $k = -4.5$:

$$\det \begin{pmatrix} -4.5 & -1 & 3 \\ 1 & 6 & -1 \\ 3 & -8 & 7 \end{pmatrix} = -221 \text{ (from calculator)}$$

Show that $\det \mathbf{M} \neq 0$ to establish the existence of a unique solution.

The matrix is non-singular for $k = -4.5$ and therefore there will be a unique solution.

$$\begin{pmatrix} x \\ y \\ z \end{pmatrix} = \begin{pmatrix} -4.5 & -1 & 3 \\ 1 & 6 & -1 \\ 3 & -8 & 7 \end{pmatrix}^{-1} \begin{pmatrix} -2 \\ 3 \\ 6 \end{pmatrix} = \begin{pmatrix} 1 \\ 0.5 \\ 1 \end{pmatrix}$$

Find the solution by using the inverse matrix.

The intersection point is $(1, 0.5, 1)$.

b $\det \begin{pmatrix} k & -1 & 3 \\ 1 & 6 & -1 \\ 3 & -8 & 7 \end{pmatrix} = k \begin{vmatrix} 6 & -1 \\ -8 & 7 \end{vmatrix} + 1 \begin{vmatrix} 1 & -1 \\ 3 & 7 \end{vmatrix} + 3 \begin{vmatrix} 1 & 6 \\ 3 & -8 \end{vmatrix}$

No unique solution when $\det \mathbf{M} = 0$.

$$= 34k + 10 - 78$$
$$= 34(k - 2)$$

There is no unique solution when $k = 2$.

Using elimination:

$$\begin{cases} 2x - y + 3z = -2 & (1) \\ x + 6y - z = 3 & (2) \\ 3x - 8y + 7z = 6 & (3) \end{cases}$$

You now need to use elimination to determine whether the equations are consistent.

$$\begin{cases} (1) - 2(2): -13y + 5z = -8 & (4) \\ 3(1) - 2(3): 13y - 5z = -18 & (5) \end{cases}$$

Eliminate x from two equations.

$(4) + (5): 0 = -26 \quad (6)$

Eliminate y from the final equation.

The equations are inconsistent, so the three planes do not intersect.

The resulting equation has no solutions.

No row of the 3×3 matrix is a multiple of another, so there are no parallel planes.

Check whether any of the planes are parallel.

Therefore the three planes form a triangular prism.

WORKED EXAMPLE 5.5

Planes Π_1, Π_2 and Π_3 are given by the equations:

$\Pi_1 : 3x - y + z = 17$

$\Pi_2 : x + 2y - z = 8$

$\Pi_3 : 2x + py + qz = k$

a Describe the geometric configuration of the three planes in the case when $p = 4$, $q = -2$, $k = 7$.

b In the case $p = -3$ find the value of q and the value of k for which the three planes intersect along a line.

a $\Pi_1 : 3x - y + z = 17$

$\Pi_2 : x + 2y - z = 8$

$\Pi_3 : 2x + 4y - 2z = 7$

$\Pi_2 : 2x + 4y - 2z = 16$

so Π_2 and Π_3 are parallel.

Π_1 is not parallel to them.

There are two parallel planes, with a third plane intersecting them.

> It is a good idea to first check whether any of the planes are parallel, as that is easily seen from the equations.

> Describe the geometric configuration. A sketch might help you visualise it.

b $\begin{vmatrix} 3 & -1 & 1 \\ 1 & 2 & -1 \\ 2 & -3 & q \end{vmatrix}$

> If the three planes intersect along a line then the equations don't have any unique solutions. This means that the determinant is 0.

$= 3 \begin{vmatrix} 2 & -1 \\ -3 & q \end{vmatrix} + 1 \begin{vmatrix} 1 & -1 \\ 2 & q \end{vmatrix} + 1 \begin{vmatrix} 1 & 2 \\ 2 & -3 \end{vmatrix}$

$= 7q - 14$

$= 0$ when $q = 2$.

Using elimination:

$\begin{cases} 3x - y + z = 17 & (1) \\ x + 2y - z = 8 & (2) \\ 2x - 3y + 2z = k & (3) \end{cases}$

> You now need to use elimination to determine when the equations are consistent.

$\begin{cases} 3(2) - (1) : 7y - 4z = 7 & (4) \\ 3(3) - 2(1) : -7y + 4z = 3k - 34 & (5) \end{cases}$

> Eliminate x from two equations.

$(4) + (5) : 0 = 3k - 27 \quad (6)$

> Eliminate y from the final equation.

Consistent equations, so

$3k - 27 = 0 \therefore k = 9$

> If the planes intersect along a line, the equations must be consistent.

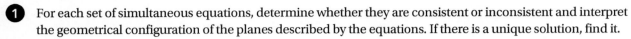

EXERCISE 5B

1 For each set of simultaneous equations, determine whether they are consistent or inconsistent and interpret the geometrical configuration of the planes described by the equations. If there is a unique solution, find it.

a i $\begin{cases} 2x+y-z=6 \\ -x+2y+z=3 \\ 3x-5y+2z=3 \end{cases}$ b i $\begin{cases} x+y-2z=6 \\ -x+2y+z=5 \\ 3x+3y-6z=2 \end{cases}$ c i $\begin{cases} 9x-3y+3z=5 \\ 4x-2y+z=1 \\ x+5y+2z=6 \end{cases}$ d i $\begin{cases} 2x+3y+z=2 \\ 5x-6y+z=1 \\ x+3y+2z=3 \end{cases}$

ii $\begin{cases} 4x+2y-z=2 \\ 2x-y+z=5 \\ 3x-3y+2z=8 \end{cases}$ ii $\begin{cases} 5x-3y+2z=4 \\ 2x-2y+z=2 \\ x+5y-z=-2 \end{cases}$ ii $\begin{cases} 4x+2y-6z=6 \\ -x-2y+3z=-3 \\ 6x+3y-9z=-9 \end{cases}$ ii $\begin{cases} 4x+2y-z=-1 \\ -x+3y+z=5 \\ 3x-5y+2z=7 \end{cases}$

2 Consider a set of simultaneous equations $\begin{cases} 3x+y+z=8 \\ -7x+3y+z=2 \\ x+y+3z=0 \end{cases}$

a Show that the equations have a unique solution and find this solution.

b The three equations represent planes. Describe the configuration of the three planes.

3 A system of equations is given by $\begin{cases} x=2 \\ x+y-z=7 \\ 2x+y+z=3 \end{cases}$

a Show that the system has a unique solution.

b The three equations represent planes. Describe the configuration of the three planes.

4 Find the intersection of the planes
$\begin{cases} x-2y+z=5 \\ 2x+y+z=1 \\ x+2y-z=-2 \end{cases}$

5 a Show that there is no unique solution to the simultaneous equations given by $\begin{cases} 2x-y+z=6 \\ 3x+y+5z=-7 \\ x-3y-3z=8 \end{cases}$

b Show that the equations are inconsistent.

c Interpret this situation geometrically.

6 Describe the configuration of these three planes:

$\Pi_1 : 6x-10y+2z=17$

$\Pi_2 : x+2y-z=8$

$\Pi_3 : 15x-25y+5z=7$

7 a Find the value of k such that the planes $\Pi_1 : 3x-y+5z=10$ and $\Pi_2 : 15x-5y+kz=11$ are parallel.

b Now let $k=2$. Describe the configuration of the planes Π_1, Π_2 and $\Pi_3 : 9x-3y-2z=8$.

8 Consider this system of equations:

$$\begin{cases} 2x+y-2z=0 \\ x-2y-z=2 \\ 3x+4y-3z=d \end{cases}$$

    a Show that the system does not have a unique solution.

    b Find the value of d for which the system is consistent.

    c The three equations represent planes. For the value of d found in part **b**, describe the configuration of the three planes.

9 **a** Show that the system of equations $\begin{cases} x+y=0 \\ x-4y-2z=0 \\ \dfrac{1}{2}x+3y+z=0 \end{cases}$ is consistent.

The three equations in part **a** represent three planes.

    b Describe the geometrical configuration of the planes.

10 **a** Find the inverse of the matrix $\begin{pmatrix} 1 & -1 & 0 \\ 0 & 1 & 1 \\ 1 & 0 & -1 \end{pmatrix}$.

    b Hence find, in terms of d, the coordinates of the point of intersection of the planes $x-y=4$, $y+z=1$ and $x-z=d$.

11 Consider the system of equations $\begin{cases} x-2y-z=-2 \\ 2x+y-3z=9 \\ x+3y-az=3 \end{cases}$

    a Find the value of a for which the system does not have a unique solution.

    b For the value of a found in part **a**, determine whether the system is consistent, and describe the geometric configuration of the three planes represented by the equations.

12 **a** Find the value of p for which the system of equations $\begin{cases} x-y-z=-2 \\ 2x+3y-7z=a+4 \\ x+2y+pz=a^2 \end{cases}$ does not have a unique solution.

    b For the value of p found in part **a**, find the two values of a for which the system is consistent.

    c For the value of p from part **a** and the values of a from part **b**, describe the geometric configuration of the three planes represented by the three equations.

13 Find the values of a and b for which the intersection of the planes $\Pi_1 : x+y-2z=7$, $\Pi_2 : x-2y-z=8$ and $\Pi_3 : 2x-y+az=b$ is a line.

Checklist of learning and understanding

- Three different planes could:
  - intersect at a single point
  - intersect along a line (form a sheaf)
  - not intersect because the line of intersection of two of the planes is parallel to the third plane (form a triangular prism)
  - not intersect because two of the planes are parallel or all three planes are parallel.
- Two planes are parallel if their normals are parallel.
- You can represent a system of three linear simultaneous equations in three unknowns in matrix form as

$$\mathbf{Mr} = \mathbf{a} \text{ where } \mathbf{r} = \begin{pmatrix} x \\ y \\ z \end{pmatrix}.$$

  Each row of matrix $\mathbf{M}$ contains the coefficients of x, y and z in the planes described.
- If $\det \mathbf{M} \neq 0$ there is a unique solution representing the point of intersection of the three planes.

$$\mathbf{r} = \mathbf{M}^{-1}\mathbf{a}$$

- If $\det \mathbf{M} = 0$ then the three planes do not intersect at a single point and could be
  - inconsistent (no common intersection: parallel planes or a triangular prism)
  - consistent (a line or a plane as the common intersection).
- When $\det \mathbf{M} = 0$, you can determine the geometrical interpretation using elimination.
  - If you get $0 = 0$ the three planes are identical or intersect along a line.
  - If you get $0 = k \neq 0$ then either at least two of the planes are parallel and distinct, or they form a triangular prism.

Mixed practice 5

1 The planes Π_1, Π_2 and Π_3 are given by the equations:

$\Pi_1 : 3x - y + z = 17$

$\Pi_2 : x + 2y - z = 8$

$\Pi_3 : 3x + y + 2z = 19$

Find the point of intersection of all three planes.

2 By using the determinant of an appropriate matrix, find the values of k for which the simultaneous equations

$$\begin{cases} kx + 8y = 1, \\ 2x + ky = 3, \end{cases}$$

do not have a unique solution.

© OCR A Level Mathematics, Unit 4725 Further Pure Mathematics 1, June 2011

3 The planes Π_1, Π_2 and Π_3 are given by the equations:

$\Pi_1 : 3x - y + z = 17$

$\Pi_2 : x + 2y - z = 8$

$\Pi_3 : 2x - 3y + 2z = k$

a Show that, when $k = 3$, the three planes form a triangular prism.

b Find the value of k for which the three planes intersect along a line.

4 Consider this system of equations, where a and b are real:

$$\begin{cases} ax + 9y + 6z = 6 \\ ay - z = b \\ x + 6y + z = 4 \end{cases}$$

a Given that the system has no unique solution, find all possible values of a.

b When the system has a unique solution, find that solution in terms of a when $b = -1$.

c Find k such that the system is always consistent when $a = kb$.

5 The matrix $\mathbf{M}$ is given by $\mathbf{M} = \begin{pmatrix} a & -a & 1 \\ 3 & a & 1 \\ 4 & 2 & 1 \end{pmatrix}$.

i Find, in terms of a, the determinant of $\mathbf{M}$.

ii Hence find the values of a for which $\mathbf{M}^{-1}$ does not exist.

iii Determine whether the simultaneous equations

$$\begin{cases} 6x - 6y + z = 3k, \\ 3x + 6y + z = 0, \\ 4x + 2y + z = k, \end{cases}$$

where k is a non-zero constant, have a unique solution, no solution or an infinite number of solutions, justifying your answer.

© OCR A Level Mathematics, Unit 4725 Further Pure Mathematics 1, January 2011

6 The matrix **D** is given by $\mathbf{D} = \begin{pmatrix} a & 2 & -1 \\ 2 & a & 1 \\ 1 & 1 & a \end{pmatrix}$.

i Find the determinant of **D** in terms of a.

ii Three simultaneous equations are shown below.

$$\begin{cases} ax + 2y - z = 0 \\ 2x + ay + z = a \\ x + y + az = a \end{cases}$$

For each of the following values of a, determine whether or not there is a unique solution. If the solution is not unique, determine whether the equations are consistent or inconsistent.

a $a = 3$

b $a = 2$

c $a = 0$

© **OCR A Level Mathematics, Unit 4725 Further Pure Mathematics 1, June 2012**

Extending the proof of de Moivre's theorem

De Moivre's theorem states that

$$\left(r(\cos\theta + i\sin\theta)\right)^n = r^n(\cos n\theta + i\sin n\theta)$$

In Chapter 2, Section 1, you saw how to prove this result for integer values of n. However, the result extends, with some careful consideration of conventions, to rational values.

Proving the result for rational numbers

You have to be a little careful when raising a number to a rational power. For example, if you write z as $r(\cos\theta + i\sin\theta)$, then you can also write it as $r(\cos(\theta + 2k\pi)) + i\sin(\theta + 2k\pi)$. If you could apply de Moivre's theorem with a rational power $\dfrac{a}{b}$, where a and b are integers with no common factors, then $z^{\frac{a}{b}}$ would equal

$$r^{\frac{a}{b}}\left(\cos\left(\frac{a}{b}\theta + \frac{2ka\pi}{b}\right) + i\sin\left(\frac{a}{b}\theta + \frac{2ka\pi}{b}\right)\right).$$

This has b different values, corresponding to $k = 0, 1, \ldots, b-1$. Multi-valued expressions are usually considered inconvenient, so you need to apply a convention that, when raising to a rational power, you choose θ to be the smallest positive value and $k = 0$. This is called the principal root.

 Tip

Notice that when the power is an integer (for example $b = 1$) then there is no problem: there is only one possible answer.

Question

1 By considering $\left(r(\cos\theta + i\sin\theta)\right)^{\frac{a}{b}} = r^n(\cos m\theta + i\sin m\theta)$,

prove that one possible value for m and n is $\dfrac{a}{b}$.

You can assume de Moivre's theorem for integer powers and that the normal rules for indices hold.

Not proving the result for irrational numbers

It is tempting to think that if de Moivre's theorem can be proved for all rational numbers, then it must hold for irrational numbers. However, this turns out to be difficult to define. For example: consider 1^π.

You could write $1 = \cos 2k\pi + i\sin 2k\pi$. Then, if de Moivre's theorem did extend to irrational numbers, you would have

$$1^\pi = \cos 2k\pi^2 + i\sin 2k\pi^2.$$

Unlike in the rational case there is no period to this expression.

Each different value of k therefore produces a different value for the expression. There are therefore infinitely many values (all lying on the circle with modulus 1), which makes this expression very hard to work with.

Question

 Use proof by contradiction to prove that if

$$\cos 2m\pi^2 + i\sin 2m\pi^2 = \cos 2p\pi^2 + i\sin 2p\pi^2,$$

then $m = p$.

You can assume that the period of the $\cos\theta + i\sin\theta$ function is 2π and that π is an irrational number.

Using complex numbers to describe rotations

You know two different ways to describe rotations in a plane. The first method is using matrices. You can find the image of a point with position vector $\begin{pmatrix} x \\ y \end{pmatrix}$ after a rotation through an angle θ about the origin by multiplying it by the rotation matrix:

$$\begin{pmatrix} \cos\theta & -\sin\theta \\ \sin\theta & \cos\theta \end{pmatrix}\begin{pmatrix} x \\ y \end{pmatrix} = \begin{pmatrix} x\cos\theta - y\sin\theta \\ x\sin\theta + y\cos\theta \end{pmatrix}$$

> **Rewind**
>
> You met the rotation matrix in Pure Core Student Book 1, Chapter 3.

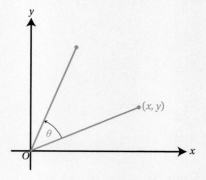

The second method is using complex numbers. When a point corresponding to a complex number $z = x + iy$ is rotated through an angle θ about the origin, you can find the complex number corresponding to the image point by multiplying z by $e^{i\theta}$:

$$(x+iy)(\cos\theta + i\sin\theta) = (x\cos\theta - y\sin\theta) + i(x\sin\theta + y\cos\theta)$$

> **Rewind**
>
> You met the idea of multiplication by $e^{i\theta}$ representing a rotation in Chapter 2, Section 6.

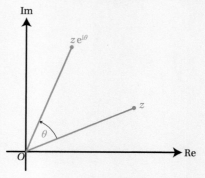

You can see that the two methods give the same coordinates for the image point. The advantage of the complex numbers method is that it results in a single equation, whereas the matrix method results in two equations (one for each component).

Here you will compare the two methods when solving the following problem

Three snails start at the vertices of an equilateral triangle. Each snail moves with the same constant speed towards an adjacent snail: S_1 towards S_2, S_2 towards S_3, and S_3 towards S_1. Describe the path followed by each snail. After how long (if at all) do the snails meet?

First you need to specify the problem a little more precisely. Set up the coordinate axes so that the origin is at the centre of the equilateral triangle and let the initial position of S_1 be at $(1, 0)$. Let v be the speed of each snail.

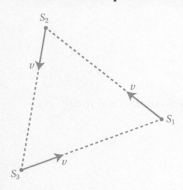

Because of the symmetry of the situation, the three snails will always form an equilateral triangle. You only need to find the path followed by S_1. You can find the position of S_2 by rotating S_1 120° anticlockwise about the origin, and you can find the position of S_3 by rotating S_2 by the same amount.

You will first approach the problem using position vectors and matrices.

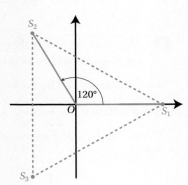

Questions

Let $\mathbf{r} = \begin{pmatrix} x \\ y \end{pmatrix}$ be the position vector of S_1 at time t.

1 Use a rotation matrix to write down the position vector of S_2 in terms of x and y.

2 Explain why $\dfrac{d\mathbf{r}}{dt} = k \begin{pmatrix} -\dfrac{3}{2}x - \dfrac{\sqrt{3}}{2}y \\ \dfrac{\sqrt{3}}{2}x - \dfrac{3}{2}y \end{pmatrix}$ for some constant k. Show that $k = \dfrac{v}{\sqrt{3}\sqrt{x^2+y^2}}$.

3 Hence show that x and y satisfy the system of differential equations

$$\begin{cases} 2\sqrt{x^2+y^2}\,\dfrac{dx}{dt} = -v\sqrt{3}x - vy \\ 2\sqrt{x^2+y^2}\,\dfrac{dy}{dt} = vx - v\sqrt{3}y \end{cases}$$

Although you will learn in Chapter 11 how to solve some systems of differential equations, these equations are non-linear so the methods from that chapter won't work here. You will return to this system of equations later, but for now you will consider a different approach.

Now, let z be the complex number corresponding to the position of S_1 at time t. Then the position of S_2 is given by $ze^{i\frac{2\pi}{3}}$.

Questions

4 Show that $\dfrac{dz}{dt} = \dfrac{v}{\sqrt{3}}\left(e^{i\frac{2\pi}{3}} - 1\right)\dfrac{z}{|z|}$.

5 Write $z = re^{i\theta}$. (Remember that both r and θ vary with time.) Show that

$$\frac{dr}{dt} + ir\frac{d\theta}{dt} = \frac{v}{\sqrt{3}}\left(e^{i\frac{2\pi}{3}} - 1\right).$$

6 By equating real and imaginary parts, obtain this system of differential equations for r and θ:

$$\frac{dr}{dt} = -\frac{\sqrt{3}v}{2}, \quad \frac{d\theta}{dt} = \frac{v}{2r}.$$

7 Given that initially $r = 1$ and $\theta = 0$, show that

$$r = 1 - \frac{\sqrt{3}v}{2}t, \quad \theta = -\frac{1}{\sqrt{3}}\ln\left(1 - \frac{\sqrt{3}v}{2}t\right).$$

8 The position of S_1 is then given by $z = re^{i\theta}$, S_2 by $re^{i\left(\theta + \frac{2\pi}{3}\right)}$ and S_3 by $re^{i\left(\theta + \frac{4\pi}{3}\right)}$. At what time do the snails meet at the origin? What happens to the value of θ as t approaches this value?

The curve described by the equations in question **7** is called a logarithmic spiral. Although each snail travels a finite distance $\left(v\dfrac{2}{\sqrt{3}v} = \dfrac{2}{\sqrt{3}}\right)$, it performs an infinite number of rotations. This diagram shows the paths of all three snails, and their positions when $t = 0$ and $t \approx \dfrac{0.7}{v}$.

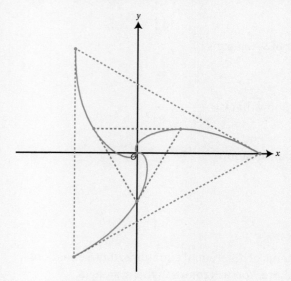

In this problem, using complex numbers resulted in equations you could solve, while this was not the case when using position vectors and matrices.

You should read the rest of this section after you have studied Chapter 9 on polar coordinates.

In question **6** you derived two separate differential equations for r and θ, the modulus and the argument of the complex number representing the position of S_1. This suggests that you might also be able to solve this problem using polar coordinates, which are basically the same as the modulus and argument of a complex number.

Look again at the system of equations from question **3**:

$$\begin{cases} 2\sqrt{x^2+y^2}\,\dfrac{\mathrm{d}x}{\mathrm{d}t} = -v\sqrt{3}x - vy \\[2mm] 2\sqrt{x^2+y^2}\,\dfrac{\mathrm{d}y}{\mathrm{d}t} = vx - v\sqrt{3}y \end{cases}$$

Let r and θ be the polar coordinates of the point (x, y). Then the 'problem' term in the equations, $\sqrt{x^2+y^2}$, is simply r. You can rewrite the equations in terms of r and θ.

⏪ Rewind

Remember that $x = r\cos\theta$ and $y = r\sin\theta$.

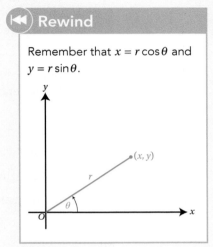

Questions

9 Show that $\dfrac{\mathrm{d}x}{\mathrm{d}t} = \dfrac{\mathrm{d}r}{\mathrm{d}t}\cos\theta - r\dfrac{\mathrm{d}\theta}{\mathrm{d}t}\sin\theta$ and obtain a similar expression for $\dfrac{\mathrm{d}y}{\mathrm{d}t}$.

10 Rewrite the system of equations in terms of r and θ. Combine the two equations to show that

$$\frac{\mathrm{d}r}{\mathrm{d}t} = -\frac{v\sqrt{3}}{2}, \quad \frac{\mathrm{d}\theta}{\mathrm{d}t} = \frac{v}{2r}$$

11 Obtain an expression for $\dfrac{\mathrm{d}r}{\mathrm{d}\theta}$ and hence show that $r = \mathrm{e}^{-\sqrt{3}\,\theta}$.

The final equation in question **11** is the polar equation of a logarithmic spiral, the path followed by each snail.

💡 Tip

Notice that these are the same equations you derived in question **6**.

Leslie matrices

Matrices are applied in many different real-life situations. Leslie matrices are a particular application to a biological population structured into different groups such as adults and juveniles.

Imagine a group of rabbits. Each adult on average produces three juvenile rabbits each year. Each year 10% of adult rabbits die and 20% of juvenile rabbits die. Those juveniles who do not die become adults.

The number of adult rabbits in year n is denoted by a_n and the number of juvenile rabbits is denoted by j_n.

Questions

1 Explain why $a_{n+1} = 0.9a_n + 0.8j_n$.

2 Find an expression for j_{n+1} in terms of a_n.

3 The equations found in questions **1** and **2** can be written in a matrix form as

$$\begin{pmatrix} a_{n+1} \\ j_{n+1} \end{pmatrix} = \mathbf{M} \begin{pmatrix} a_n \\ j_n \end{pmatrix}$$

Write down the matrix $\mathbf{M}$.

4 An uninhabited island is populated with 200 adult rabbits in year 0. Use technology to find the number of adult rabbits in:

a year 1   **b** year 10.

5 By investigating the sequence formed, find the long-term growth rate of the population.

6 Find the long-term ratio of juveniles to adults.

7 The population of rabbits is infected with a disease which decreases the average number of juvenile rabbits produced per adult rabbit each year to α. Find the smallest value of α so that the population will not become extinct.

8 Describe the assumptions made in creating this model.

9 In an alternative model each adult rabbit produces exactly one juvenile each year and there is no death. If the population starts with one (presumably pregnant) adult, investigate the number of adult rabbits after n years. Can you form a conjecture and prove it by induction?

Explore

The situation in question **9** was described by Fibonacci, leading to his eponymous sequence.

Rewind

For a reminder of proof by induction see Chapter 1.

CROSS-TOPIC REVIEW EXERCISE 1

1   **a**   Show that $\cos z = \dfrac{e^{iz} + e^{-iz}}{2}$.

     b   Hence find the value of $\cos 2i$ correct to 3 significant figures.

2   **a**   Express $-8i$ in the form $re^{i\theta}$, where $r > 0$ and $-\pi < \theta \leqslant \pi$.

     b   Solve the equation $z^6 + 8i = 0$, giving your answers in the form $re^{i\theta}$, where $r > 0$ and $-\pi < \theta \leqslant \pi$.

3   **a**   Find the Cartesian equation of the plane Π_1 containing the points $(1, 1, 0)$, $(0, -2, 0)$ and $(0, 1, 2)$.

     The plane Π_2 has Cartesian equation $2x + 3y - 4z = 5$.

     b   Find, to 3 significant figures, the acute angle between the planes Π_1 and Π_2.

4   Given that $\displaystyle\sum_{r=1}^{n}(ar^3 + br) = n(n-1)(n+1)(n+2)$, find the values of the constants a and b.

          © **OCR AS Level Mathematics, Unit 4725 Further Pure Mathematics 1, January 2011**

5   Find $\displaystyle\sum_{r=1}^{n}(4r^3 - 3r^2 + r)$, giving your answer in a fully factorised form.

          © **OCR AS Level Mathematics, Unit 4725/01 Further Pure Mathematics 1, June 2013**

6   **i**   Show that $(z^n - e^{i\theta})(z^n - e^{-i\theta}) \equiv z^{2n} - (2\cos\theta)z^n + 1$.

     ii   Express $z^4 - z^2 + 1$ as the product of four factors of the form $(z - e^{i\alpha})$, where $0 \leqslant \alpha < 2\pi$.

          © **OCR A Level Mathematics, Unit 4727 Further Pure Mathematics 3, January 2012**

7   **i**   Solve the equation $z^4 = 2(1 + i\sqrt{3})$, giving the roots exactly in the form $r(\cos\theta + i\sin\theta)$, where $r > 0$ and $0 \leqslant \theta < 2\pi$.

     ii   Sketch an Argand diagram to show the lines from the origin to the point representing $2(1 + i\sqrt{3})$ and from the origin to the points which represent the roots of the equation in part **i**.

          © **OCR A Level Mathematics, Unit 4727 Further Pure Mathematics 3, June 2012**

8   The line l_1 passes through the points $(0, 0, 10)$ and $(7, 0, 0)$ and the line l_2 passes through the points $(4, 6, 0)$ and $(3, 3, 1)$. Find the shortest distance between l_1 and l_2.

          © **OCR A Level Mathematics, Unit 4727 Further Pure Mathematics 3, June 2010**

9   By using the determinant of an appropriate matrix, find the values of λ for which the simultaneous equations

$$3x + 2y + 4z = 5,$$
$$\lambda y + z = 1,$$
$$x + \lambda y + \lambda z = 4,$$

     do not have a unique solution for x, y and z.

          © **OCR AS Level Mathematics, Unit 4725/01 Further Pure Mathematics 1, January 2013**

10   **a**   Given that a and $(a + i)^5$ are both real, with $a > 0$, show that $a^2 = \dfrac{5 \pm 2\sqrt{5}}{5}$.

     b   Find, in terms of a, the argument of $(a + i)^5$.

     c   Hence show that $\cot\dfrac{\pi}{5} = \sqrt{\dfrac{5 + 2\sqrt{5}}{5}}$.

11 i Show that $\dfrac{1}{\sqrt{r+2}+\sqrt{r}} \equiv \dfrac{\sqrt{r+2}-\sqrt{r}}{2}$.

ii Hence find an expression, in terms of n, for

$$\sum_{r=1}^{n} \dfrac{1}{\sqrt{r+2}+\sqrt{r}}.$$

iii State, giving a brief reason, whether the series $\displaystyle\sum_{r=1}^{n} \dfrac{1}{\sqrt{r+2}+\sqrt{r}}$ converges.

© OCR AS Level Mathematics, Unit 4725 Further Pure Mathematics 1, June 2010

12 i Show that $\dfrac{1}{r} - \dfrac{1}{r+2} \equiv \dfrac{2}{r(r+2)}$.

ii Hence find an expression, in terms of n, for $\displaystyle\sum_{r=1}^{n} \dfrac{2}{r(r+2)}$.

iii Given that $\displaystyle\sum_{r=N+1}^{\infty} \dfrac{2}{r(r+2)} = \dfrac{11}{30}$, find the value of N.

© OCR AS Level Mathematics, Unit 4725 Further Pure Mathematics 1, June 2012

13 i Show that $\dfrac{1}{r^2} - \dfrac{1}{(r+2)^2} \equiv \dfrac{4(r+1)}{r^2(r+2)^2}$.

ii Hence find an expression, in terms of n, for $\displaystyle\sum_{r=1}^{n} \dfrac{4(r+1)}{r^2(r+2)^2}$.

iii Find $\displaystyle\sum_{r=5}^{\infty} \dfrac{4(r+1)}{r^2(r+2)^2}$, giving your answer in the form $\dfrac{p}{q}$ where p and q are integers.

© OCR AS Level Mathematics, Unit 4725/01 Further Pure Mathematics 1, June 2014

14 The sequence $u_1, u_2, u_3, \ldots$ is defined by $u_1 = 2$ and $u_{n+1} = \dfrac{u_n}{1+u_n}$ for $n \geqslant 1$.

i Find u_2 and u_3, and show that $u_4 = \dfrac{2}{7}$.

ii Hence suggest an expression for u_n.

iii Use induction to prove that your answer to part **ii** is correct.

© OCR AS Level Mathematics, Unit 4725/01 Further Pure Mathematics 1, January 2013

15 The roots of the equation $z^3 - 1 = 0$ are denoted by 1, ω and ω^2.

i Sketch an Argand diagram to show these roots.

ii Show that $1 + \omega + \omega^2 = 0$.

iii Hence evaluate

a $(2+\omega)(2+\omega^2)$,

b $\dfrac{1}{2+\omega} + \dfrac{1}{2+\omega^2}$.

iv Hence find a cubic equation, with integer coefficients, which has roots 2, $\dfrac{1}{2+\omega}$ and $\dfrac{1}{2+\omega^2}$.

© OCR A Level Mathematics, Unit 4727/01 Further Pure Mathematics 3, June 2008

16 i Write down, in Cartesian form, the roots of the equation $z^4 = 16$.

ii Hence solve the equation $w^4 = 16(1-w)^4$, giving your answers in Cartesian form.

© OCR A Level Mathematics, Unit 4727 Further Pure Mathematics 3, January 2010

17 The cube roots of 1 are denoted by 1, ω and ω^2, where the imaginary part of ω is positive.

i Show that $1+\omega+\omega^2=0$.

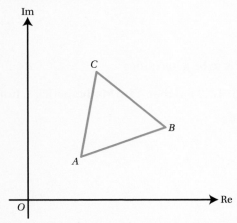

In the diagram, ABC is an equilateral triangle, labelled anticlockwise. The points A, B and C represent the complex numbers z_1, z_2 and z_3 respectively.

ii State the geometrical effect of multiplication by ω and hence explain why
$z_1 - z_3 = \omega(z_3 - z_2)$.

iii Hence show that $z_1 + \omega z_2 + \omega^2 z_3 = 0$.

© **OCR A Level Mathematics, Unit 4727 Further Pure Mathematics 3, January 2011**

  18 **i** Solve the equation $z^5=1$, giving your answers in polar form.

ii Hence, by considering the equation $(z+1)^5 = z^5$, show that the roots of

$$5z^4 + 10z^3 + 10z^2 + 5z + 1 = 0$$

can be expressed in the form $\dfrac{1}{e^{i\theta}-1}$, stating the values of θ.

© **OCR A Level Mathematics, Unit 4727/01 Further Pure Mathematics 3, January 2013**

  19 In an Argand diagram, the complex numbers 0, z and $ze^{\frac{1}{6}i\pi}$ are represented by the points O, A and B respectively.

i Sketch a possible Argand diagram showing the triangle OAB. Show that the triangle is isosceles and state the size of angle AOB.

The complex numbers $1 + i$ and $5 + 2i$ are represented by the points C and D respectively. The complex number w is represented by the point E, such that $CD = CE$ and angle $DCE = \dfrac{1}{6}\pi$.

ii Calculate the possible values of w, giving your answers exactly in the form $a + bi$.

© **OCR A Level Mathematics, Unit 4727/01 Further Pure Mathematics 3, June 2015**

20 i By expressing $\sin\theta$ and $\cos\theta$ in terms of $e^{i\theta}$ and $e^{-i\theta}$, prove that

$$\sin^3\theta\cos^2\theta \equiv -\frac{1}{16}(\sin 5\theta - \sin 3\theta - 2\sin\theta).$$

ii Hence show that all the roots of the equation

$$\sin 5\theta = \sin 3\theta + 2\sin\theta$$

are of the form $\theta = \dfrac{n\pi}{k}$, where n is any integer and k is to be determined.

© OCR A Level Mathematics, Unit 4727 Further Pure Mathematics 3, June 2012

 21 i By expressing $\sin\theta$ in terms of $e^{i\theta}$ and $e^{-i\theta}$, show that

$$\sin^5\theta \equiv \frac{1}{16}(\sin 5\theta - 5\sin 3\theta + 10\sin\theta).$$

ii Hence solve the equation

$$\sin 5\theta + 4\sin\theta = 5\sin 3\theta$$

for $-\dfrac{1}{2}\pi \leqslant \theta \leqslant \dfrac{1}{2}\pi$.

© OCR A Level Mathematics, Unit 4727/01 Further Pure Mathematics 3, June 2014

 22 The line l has equations $\dfrac{x-1}{2} = \dfrac{y-1}{3} = \dfrac{z+1}{2}$ and the point A is $(7, 3, 7)$. M is the point where the perpendicular from A meets l.

i Find, in either order, the coordinates of M and the perpendicular distance from A to l.

ii Find the coordinates of the point B on AM such that $\overrightarrow{AB} = 3\overrightarrow{BM}$.

© OCR A Level Mathematics, Unit 4727 Further Pure Mathematics 3, January 2012

23 The plane Π has equation $\mathbf{r} = \begin{pmatrix} 1 \\ 6 \\ 7 \end{pmatrix} + \lambda\begin{pmatrix} 2 \\ -1 \\ -1 \end{pmatrix} + \mu\begin{pmatrix} 2 \\ -3 \\ -5 \end{pmatrix}$ and the line l has equation $\mathbf{r} = \begin{pmatrix} 7 \\ 4 \\ 1 \end{pmatrix} + t\begin{pmatrix} 3 \\ 0 \\ -1 \end{pmatrix}$.

i Express the equation of Π in the form $\mathbf{r} \cdot \mathbf{n} = p$.

ii Find the point of intersection of l and Π.

iii The equation of Π may be expressed in the form $\mathbf{r} = \begin{pmatrix} 1 \\ 6 \\ 7 \end{pmatrix} + \lambda\begin{pmatrix} 2 \\ -1 \\ -1 \end{pmatrix} + \mu\mathbf{c}$, where $\mathbf{c}$ is perpendicular

to $\begin{pmatrix} 2 \\ -1 \\ -1 \end{pmatrix}$. Find $\mathbf{c}$.

© OCR A Level Mathematics, Unit 4727 Further Pure Mathematics 3, January 2012

 24 The plane p has equation $\mathbf{r} \cdot (\mathbf{i} - 3\mathbf{j} + 4\mathbf{k}) = 4$ and the line l_1 has equation $\mathbf{r} = 2\mathbf{j} - \mathbf{k} + t(3\mathbf{i} + \mathbf{j} + 2\mathbf{k})$. The line l_2 is parallel to p and perpendicular to l_1, and passes through the point with position vector $\mathbf{i} + 4\mathbf{j} + 2\mathbf{k}$. Find the equation of l_2, giving your answer in the form $\mathbf{r} = \mathbf{a} + t\mathbf{b}$.

© OCR A Level Mathematics, Unit 4727 Further Pure Mathematics 3, June 2012

25 The lines l_1 and l_2 have equations

$$\mathbf{r} = \begin{pmatrix} 1 \\ 2 \\ 1 \end{pmatrix} + \lambda \begin{pmatrix} 2 \\ 3 \\ -1 \end{pmatrix} \text{ and } \mathbf{r} = \begin{pmatrix} 3 \\ 0 \\ 1 \end{pmatrix} + \mu \begin{pmatrix} 4 \\ -1 \\ -1 \end{pmatrix}$$

respectively.

i Find the shortest distance between the lines.

ii Find a Cartesian equation of the plane which contains l_1 and which is parallel to l_2.

© OCR A Level Mathematics, Unit 4727/01 Further Pure Mathematics 3, January 2013

 26 **a** Integrate e^{kx} with respect to x.

b Show that, for $x \in \mathbb{R}$, the imaginary part of $e^{(1+3i)x}$ is $e^x \sin 3x$.

c Hence find the exact value of $\int_0^{\frac{\pi}{2}} e^x \sin 3x \, dx$.

© OCR A Level Mathematics, Unit 4727 Further Pure Mathematics 3, June 2012

 27 **a** Show that $\cos z = \dfrac{e^{iz} + e^{-iz}}{2}$.

b Hence find possible complex numbers z for which $\cos z = 2$.

© OCR A Level Mathematics, Unit 4727 Further Pure Mathematics 3, June 2012

 28 **a** If $z = \dfrac{1}{2} \cos \theta + \dfrac{i}{2} \sin \theta$, show that $|z| < 1$.

b Find an expression for $1 + \dfrac{1}{2} e^{i\theta} + \dfrac{1}{4} e^{2i\theta} + \dfrac{1}{8} e^{3i\theta} + \dots$.

c Hence show that $\dfrac{1}{2} \sin \theta + \dfrac{1}{4} \sin 2\theta + \dfrac{1}{8} \sin 3\theta + \dots = \dfrac{2 \sin \theta}{5 - 4 \cos \theta}$.

© OCR A Level Mathematics, Unit 4727 Further Pure Mathematics 3, June 2012

29 **a** Find the smallest positive integer N for which $N! > 2^N$.

b Prove that $n! > 2^n$ for all $n \geq N$.

30 **a** Prove using induction that

$$\sin \theta + \sin 3\theta + \dots + \sin(2n-1)\theta = \frac{\sin^2 n\theta}{\sin \theta} \text{ for integer } n \geq 1.$$

b Hence find the exact value of $\sin \dfrac{\pi}{7} + \sin \dfrac{3\pi}{7} + \dots + \sin \dfrac{13\pi}{7}$.

31 Prove, using induction, that for positive integer n,

$$\cos x \times \cos 2x \times \cos 4x \times \cos 8x \ \dots \ \times \cos(2^n x) = \frac{\sin(2^{n+1} x)}{2^{n+1} \sin x}$$

32 **i** Show that $\dfrac{1}{r} - \dfrac{2}{r+1} + \dfrac{1}{r+2} = \dfrac{2}{r(r+1)(r+2)}$.

ii Hence find an expression, in terms of n, for

$$\sum_{r=1}^{n} \frac{2}{r(r+1)(r+2)}.$$

iii Show that $\displaystyle\sum_{r=n+1}^{\infty} \frac{2}{r(r+1)(r+2)} = \frac{1}{(n+1)(n+2)}$.

© OCR AS Level Mathematics, Unit 4725 Further Pure Mathematics 1, January 2011

33 The integrals C and S are defined by

$$C = \int_{0}^{\frac{1}{2}\pi} e^{2x}\cos 3x \, dx \qquad \text{and} \qquad S = \int_{0}^{\frac{1}{2}\pi} e^{2x}\sin 3x \, dx.$$

By considering $C + iS$ as a single integral, show that

$$C = -\frac{1}{13}\left(2 + 3e^{\pi}\right),$$

and obtain a similar expression for S.

(You may assume that the standard result for $\int e^{kx} \, dx$ remains true when k is a complex constant,

so that $\int e^{(a+ib)x} dx = \dfrac{1}{a+ib} e^{(a+ib)x}$.)

© OCR A Level Mathematics, Unit 4727/01 Further Pure Mathematics 3, January 2008

34 **i** Use de Moivre's theorem to prove that

$$\tan 3\theta \equiv \frac{\tan\theta\left(3 - \tan^2\theta\right)}{1 - 3\tan^2\theta}.$$

ii a By putting $\theta = \dfrac{1}{12}\pi$ in the identity in part **i**, show that $\tan\dfrac{1}{12}\pi$ is a solution of the equation

$t^3 - 3t^2 - 3t + 1 = 0$.

b Hence show that $\tan\dfrac{1}{12}\pi = 2 - \sqrt{3}$.

iii Use the substitution $t = \tan\theta$ show that

$$\int_{0}^{2-\sqrt{3}} \frac{t(3-t^2)}{(1-3t^2)(1+t^2)} \, dt = a\ln b,$$

where a and b are positive constants to be determined.

© OCR A Level Mathematics, Unit 4727 Further Pure Mathematics 3, June 2009

35 **i** Solve the equation $\cos 6\theta = 0$, for $0 < \theta < \pi$.

ii By using de Moivre's theorem, show that

$$\cos 6\theta \equiv \left(2\cos^2\theta - 1\right)\left(16\cos^4\theta - 16\cos^2\theta + 1\right).$$

iii Hence find the exact value of

$$\cos\left(\frac{1}{12}\pi\right)\cos\left(\frac{5}{12}\pi\right)\cos\left(\frac{7}{12}\pi\right)\cos\left(\frac{11}{12}\pi\right),$$

justifying your answer.

© OCR A Level Mathematics, Unit 4727 Further Pure Mathematics 3, January 2010

36 i Use de Moivre's theorem to express $\cos 4\theta$ as a polynomial in $\cos\theta$.

ii Hence prove that $\cos 4\theta \cos 2\theta \equiv 16\cos^6\theta - 24\cos^4\theta + 10\cos^2\theta - 1$.

iii Use part **ii** to show that the only roots of the equation $\cos 4\theta \cos 2\theta = 1$ are $\theta = n\pi$, where n is an integer.

iv Show that $\cos 4\theta \cos 2\theta = -1$ only when $\cos\theta = 0$.

© **OCR A Level Mathematics, Unit 4727 Further Pure Mathematics 3, June 2011**

  37 i Use de Moivre's theorem to prove that

$$\tan 5\theta = \frac{5\tan\theta - 10\tan^3\theta + \tan^5\theta}{1 - 10\tan^2\theta + 5\tan^4\theta}.$$

ii Solve the equation $\tan 5\theta = 1$, for $0 \leqslant \theta < \pi$.

iii Show that the roots of the equation

$$t^4 - 4t^3 - 14t^2 - 4t + 1 = 0$$

may be expressed in the form $\tan\alpha$, stating the exact values of α, where $0 \leqslant \alpha < \pi$.

© **OCR A Level Mathematics, Unit 4727 Further Pure Mathematics 3, January 2012**

  38 Let $S = e^{i\theta} + e^{2i\theta} + e^{3i\theta} + \ldots + e^{10i\theta}$.

i a Show that, for $\theta \neq 2n\pi$, where n is an integer,

$$S = \frac{e^{\frac{1}{2}i\theta}\left(e^{10i\theta} - 1\right)}{2i\sin\left(\frac{1}{2}\theta\right)}.$$

b State the value of S for $\theta = 2n\pi$, where n is an integer.

ii Hence show that, for $\theta \neq 2n\pi$, where n is an integer,

$$\cos\theta + \cos 2\theta + \cos 3\theta + \ldots + \cos 10\theta = \frac{\sin\left(\frac{21}{2}\theta\right)}{2\sin\left(\frac{1}{2}\theta\right)} - \frac{1}{2}.$$

iii Hence show that $\theta = \frac{1}{11}\pi$ is a root of $\cos\theta + \cos 2\theta + \cos 3\theta + \ldots + \cos 10\theta = 0$ and find

another root in the interval $0 < \theta < \frac{1}{4}\pi$.

© **OCR A Level Mathematics, Unit 4727/01 Further Pure Mathematics 3, January 2013**

6 Hyperbolic functions

In this chapter you will learn how to:

- define the hyperbolic functions $\sinh x$, $\cosh x$ and $\tanh x$
- draw the graphs of hyperbolic functions, showing their domains and ranges
- write the inverse hyperbolic functions in terms of logarithms
- define the reciprocal hyperbolic functions $\operatorname{sech} x$, $\operatorname{cosec} x$ and $\coth x$
- solve equations and prove identities involving hyperbolic functions
- differentiate hyperbolic functions.

Before you start…

A Level Mathematics Student Book 2, Chapter 2	You should understand the terms domain and range of a function.	1 For the function $f(x) = \sqrt{x-3}$, state: 　a　the largest possible domain 　b　the corresponding range.
A Level Mathematics Student Book 2, Chapter 3	You should be able to draw a graph after two (or more) transformations.	2 The graph of $y = f(x)$ is shown. Sketch the graph of $y = 3 - f(2x)$, giving the new coordinates of the three points labelled on the original graph.
A Level Mathematics Student Book 2, Chapter 9	You should know how to differentiate and integrate the exponential function.	3 Find: 　a　$\dfrac{d}{dx}\left(e^{2x}\right)$ 　b　$\int e^{-x} dx.$
A Level Mathematics Student Book 2, Chapter 9	You should know how to differentiate and integrate trigonometric functions.	4 Find: 　a　$\dfrac{d}{dx}(\tan x)$ 　b　$\int \cos x\, dx.$
A Level Mathematics Student Book 2, Chapter 10	You should know how to use the chain rule, product rule and quotient rule for differentiation.	5 Find $f'(x)$ for these functions: 　a　$f(x) = \sin^2 3x$ 　b　$f(x) = x\cos x$ 　c　$f(x) = \dfrac{\tan 2x}{x}$

What are hyperbolic functions?

Trigonometric functions are sometimes called **circular functions**. This is because of the definition that states: a point on the unit circle (with equation $x^2 + y^2 = 1$) defining a radius at an angle θ to the positive x-axis, has coordinates $(\cos\theta, \sin\theta)$.

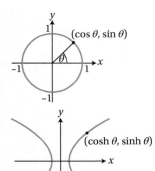

Related to the circle is a curve with equation $x^2 - y^2 = 1$, called a **hyperbola**. Points on this hyperbola have coordinates $(\cosh\theta, \sinh\theta)$, although θ can no longer be interpreted as an angle.

Section 1: Defining hyperbolic functions

Although the geometric definition of **hyperbolic functions** gives some helpful insight, a more useful definition is related to the number e.

 Key point 6.1

- $\sinh x = \dfrac{e^x - e^{-x}}{2}$

- $\cosh x = \dfrac{e^x + e^{-x}}{2}$

Tip

Cosh is pronounced as it reads, sinh is pronounced either 'sinch' or 'shine' and tanh is pronounced 'tanch' or 'than'.

You can define $\tanh x$ by analogy with the trigonometric definition of $\tan x$.

 Key point 6.2

$$\tanh x \equiv \frac{\sinh x}{\cosh x} \equiv \frac{e^x - e^{-x}}{e^x + e^{-x}}$$

Did you know?

The tanh function is frequently used in physics, particularly in the context of special relativity and the study of entropy.

There are not many special values of these functions that you need to know, but, from Key points 6.1 and 6.2, you should be able to see that $\cosh 0 = 1$, $\sinh 0 = 0$ and $\tanh 0 = 0$.

As for trigonometric functions, you need to know the graphs of hyperbolic functions.

 Key point 6.3

The graphs of $\sinh x$, $\cosh x$ and $\tanh x$ look like this.

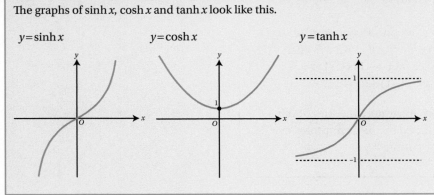

ⓘ Did you know?

You may think that the graph of $\cosh x$ looks like a parabola, but it is slightly flatter. It is called a **catenary**, which is the shape formed by a hanging chain.

You can establish the domains and ranges of the hyperbolic functions from their graphs.

🔑 Key point 6.4

The domains and ranges of the hyperbolic functions $\sinh x$, $\cosh x$ and $\tanh x$ are:

Function	Domain	Range
$\sinh x$	$x \in \mathbb{R}$	$f(x) \in \mathbb{R}$
$\cosh x$	$x \in \mathbb{R}$	$f(x) \geqslant 1$
$\tanh x$	$x \in \mathbb{R}$	$-1 < f(x) < 1$

 Rewind

You met the domain and range of a function in A Level Mathematics Student Book 2, Chapter 2.

WORKED EXAMPLE 6.1

Given that $f(x) = 3\tanh x + 2$ for $x \in \mathbb{R}$,

a sketch the graph of $y = f(x)$
b state the range of f.

a

 Rewind

You learnt about transformations of graphs in A Level Mathematics Student Book 1, Chapter 5.

You need to apply two transformations to the graph of $y = \tanh x$:

Stretch by scale factor 3 parallel to the y-axis.

Translation by $\begin{pmatrix} 0 \\ 2 \end{pmatrix}$.

The horizontal asymptote at $y = 1$ moves to $y = 3(1) + 2 = 5$, and the one at $y = -1$ is still at -1 ($y = 3(-1) + 2 = -1$).

b $-1 < f(x) < 5$

From the graph, the function is bounded by the asymptotes at $y = -1$ and $y = 5$.

EXERCISE 6A

1 For each hyperbolic function, sketch the graph of $y = f(x)$ and state the largest possible domain and the corresponding range.

a $f(x) = 3 - \sinh\left(\dfrac{x}{2}\right)$

b $f(x) = 2\sinh(x-1)$

c $f(x) = \cosh(2x+3)$

d $f(x) = 4 - \cosh x$

e $f(x) = 5 + 2\tanh x$

f $f(x) = 4\tanh(-x)$

2 The diagram shows the graph of $y = a\cosh(x+b) - 5$, where a and b are integers.

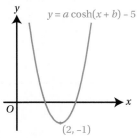

Find the values of a and b.

3 The diagram shows the graph of $y = a\tanh(2x+b)$, where a and b are integers.

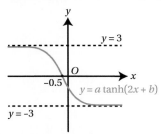

Find the values of a and b.

> **Rewind**
>
> You saw in A Level Mathematics Student Book 2, Chapter 2, how to form the graphs of inverse functions from their original function by reflection in the line $y = x$.

Section 2: Inverse hyperbolic functions

The **inverse functions** of the hyperbolic functions are called $\operatorname{arsinh} x$, $\operatorname{arcosh} x$ and $\operatorname{artanh} x$.

The graphs of these functions look like this.

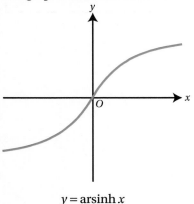

$y = \operatorname{arsinh} x$

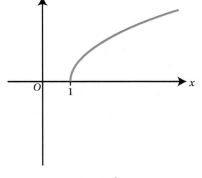

$y = \operatorname{arcosh} x$

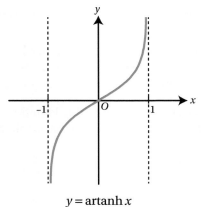

$y = \operatorname{artanh} x$

You need to know the domain and range of each function.

Key point 6.5

The domains and ranges of the inverse hyperbolic functions $\sinh^{-1}x$, $\cosh^{-1}x$ and $\tanh^{-1}x$ are:

Function	Domain	Range
$\sinh^{-1}x$	$x \in \mathbb{R}$	$f(x) \in \mathbb{R}$
$\cosh^{-1}x$	$x \geqslant 1$	$f(x) \geqslant 0$
$\tanh^{-1}x$	$-1 < x < 1$	$f(x) \in \mathbb{R}$

Tip

$\sinh^{-1}x$, $\cosh^{-1}x$ and $\tanh^{-1}x$ are alternative notations for $\operatorname{arsinh}x$, $\operatorname{arcosh}x$ and $\operatorname{artanh}x$.

WORKED EXAMPLE 6.2

Let $f(x) = 1 - \cosh^{-1}\left(\dfrac{x}{3}\right)$.

a State the largest possible domain of f.
b For the domain in part **a**, find the range of f.

a Domain: $x \geqslant 3$

> The domain of $\cosh^{-1}x$ is $x \geqslant 1$,
>
> so $\dfrac{x}{3} \geqslant 1 \Rightarrow x \geqslant 3$.

b

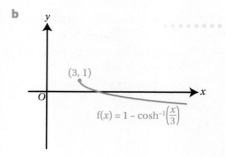

$$f(x) = 1 - \cosh^{-1}\left(\tfrac{x}{3}\right)$$

> It is always a good idea to sketch the graph when finding the range.
>
> You need to apply three transformations to the graph of $y = \cosh^{-1}x$:
>
> Stretch by scale factor 3 parallel to the x-axis.
>
> Reflection in the x-axis.
>
> Translation by $\begin{pmatrix} 0 \\ 1 \end{pmatrix}$.

Range: $f(x) \leqslant 1$

You can use the inverse hyperbolic functions to solve simple equations involving hyperbolic functions. For example, if $\sinh x = 2$ then $x = \operatorname{arsinh}2$, which you can evaluate, on a calculator, as $1.4436\ldots$.

However, you can use the definition of $\sinh x$ to derive a logarithmic form of this result. You can do this for all three inverse hyperbolic functions.

Key point 6.6

- $\text{arsinh}\, x = \ln\left(x + \sqrt{x^2 + 1}\right)$
- $\text{arcosh}\, x = \ln\left(x + \sqrt{x^2 - 1}\right)$
- $\text{artanh}\, x = \frac{1}{2}\ln\left(\frac{1+x}{1-x}\right)$

These will be given in your formula book.

These results can all be proved in the same way. The proof for $\text{arcosh}\, x$ is given here.

PROOF 3

Prove that $\text{arcosh}\, x = \ln\left(x + \sqrt{x^2 - 1}\right)$.

Let $y = \text{arcosh}\, x$	Let $y = \text{arcosh}\, x$ and then look to find an expression for y.
Then $\cosh y = x$	Take cosh of both sides.
$\dfrac{e^y + e^{-y}}{2} = x$	Use the definition of $\cosh y$.
$e^y + e^{-y} = 2x$	Rearrange into a disguised quadratic in e^y.
$e^y + \dfrac{1}{e^y} = 2x$	
$(e^y)^2 + 1 = 2xe^y$	
$(e^y)^2 - 2xe^y + 1 = 0$	Use the quadratic formula.
So	
$e^y = \dfrac{2x \pm \sqrt{(2x)^2 - 4}}{2}$	
$= \dfrac{2x \pm \sqrt{4x^2 - 4}}{2}$	
$= \dfrac{2x \pm \sqrt{4(x^2 - 1)}}{2}$	
$= \dfrac{2x \pm \sqrt{4}\sqrt{x^2 - 1}}{2}$	Use the algebra of surds to simplify the expression.
$= x \pm \sqrt{x^2 - 1}$	
But $\text{arcosh}\, x$ is a function so it can only take one value.	Conventionally, you take the positive root, so this makes $e^y > 1$ and $y > 0$.
$\therefore e^y = x + \sqrt{x^2 - 1}$	
$y = \ln\left(x + \sqrt{x^2 - 1}\right)$	
But $y = \text{arcosh}\, x$	
So $\text{arcosh}\, x = \ln\left(x + \sqrt{x^2 - 1}\right)$	

WORKED EXAMPLE 6.3

Solve $\sinh x = 7$, giving your answer in the form $\ln\left(a + \sqrt{b}\right)$ for integers a and b.

$\sinh x = 7$

$\quad x = \text{arsinh}\,7$ — Apply the inverse sinh function to find x.

$\quad = \ln\left(7 + \sqrt{7^2 + 1}\right)$ — Use the logarithmic form $\text{arsinh}\,x = \ln\left(x + \sqrt{x^2 + 1}\right)$.

$\quad = \ln\left(7 + 5\sqrt{2}\right)$

When you are trying to solve equations involving hyperbolic cosines, using the inverse function does not give all the solutions: it just gives the positive one. This is because the cosh function is not one-to-one. As can be seen from the graph, there is a second, negative solution. (This is analogous to solving an equation like $x^2 = 6$, where taking the square root of both sides gives $x = \sqrt{6}$, but there are in fact two solutions, $x = \pm\sqrt{6}$.).

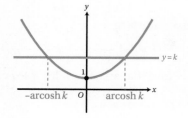

WORKED EXAMPLE 6.4

Given that $\cosh^2 x - \cosh x = 2$, express x in the form $\ln\left(a + \sqrt{b}\right)$ or $\ln\left(a - \sqrt{b}\right)$.

$\quad \cosh^2 x - \cosh x - 2 = 0$ — The expression is a disguised quadratic, so rearrange it to make one side zero and then factorise it. You could also have used the quadratic formula.

$\quad (\cosh x - 2)(\cosh x + 1) = 0$

$\quad \cosh x = 2 \text{ or } \cosh x = -1$

But $\cosh x \geqslant 0$ so $\cosh x = -1$ has no solutions. — Use the inverse cosh function to find x. Remember that you need a plus or minus ($\pm$).

$x = \pm \, \text{arcosh}\, 2$

$\quad = \pm \ln\left(2 + \sqrt{2^2 - 1}\right)$ — Use the logarithmic form $\text{arcosh}\,x = \ln\left(x + \sqrt{x^2 - 1}\right)$.

$\quad = \pm \ln\left(2 + \sqrt{3}\right)$

So

$x = \ln\left(2 + \sqrt{3}\right) \text{ or } \ln\left(\dfrac{1}{2 + \sqrt{3}}\right)$ — Use the fact that $-\ln x \equiv \ln(x^{-1}) \equiv \ln\left(\dfrac{1}{x}\right)$.

$\ln\left(\dfrac{1}{2 + \sqrt{3}}\right) = \ln\left(\dfrac{2 - \sqrt{3}}{(2 + \sqrt{3})(2 - \sqrt{3})}\right)$ — Simplify the second solution by rationalising the denominator to produce the required form.

$\quad = \ln\left(\dfrac{2 - \sqrt{3}}{1}\right)$

So $x = \ln\left(2 + \sqrt{3}\right)$ or $x = \ln\left(2 - \sqrt{3}\right)$

You can generalise the method used at the end of Worked example 6.4 to write $-\ln\left(2 + \sqrt{3}\right)$ as $\ln\left(2 - \sqrt{3}\right)$, so the two solutions to $\cosh x = k$ for $k > 1$ can always be written as $x = \ln\left(k \pm \sqrt{k^2 - 1}\right)$.

EXERCISE 6B

1 For each inverse hyperbolic function, sketch the graph of $y = f(x)$ and state the largest possible domain and the corresponding range.

    a **i** $f(x) = 3\sinh^{-1} x + 2$ **ii** $f(x) = 2 + \sinh^{-1}(-x)$

    b **i** $f(x) = 1 + \cosh^{-1} 2x$ **ii** $f(x) = 2\cosh^{-1}\left(\dfrac{x}{3}\right)$

    c **i** $f(x) = 2\tanh^{-1}(x+1) + 1$ **ii** $f(x) = 3\tanh^{-1}(x-2) + 1$

2 Use your calculator to evaluate each expression where possible.

    a **i** $\cosh(-1)$ **ii** $\sinh 3$ **b** **i** $\tanh^2 1$ **ii** $\cosh^2 3$

    c **i** $3\sinh(0.2) + 1$ **ii** $5\tanh\left(\dfrac{1}{2}\right) + 8$ **d** **i** $\sinh^{-1} 0.5$ **ii** $\cosh^{-1} 2$

    e **i** $\tanh^{-1} 2$ **ii** $\cosh^{-1} 0$

3 Solve each equation, giving your answers to 3 significant figures.

    a **i** $\sinh x = -2$ **ii** $\sinh x = 0.1$ **b** **i** $2\cosh x = 5$ **ii** $\cosh x = 4$

    c **i** $4\tanh x = 3$ **ii** $\tanh x = 0.4$ **d** **i** $3\tanh x = 4$ **ii** $3\cosh x = 1$

    e **i** $\sinh^{-1} x = 5$ **ii** $\cosh^{-1} x = 4$

4 Without using your calculator, find the exact value of each expression.

    a **i** $\operatorname{arsinh} 1$ **ii** $\operatorname{arsinh} 2$ **b** **i** $\cosh^{-1} 2$ **ii** $\cosh^{-1} 3$

    c **i** $\operatorname{artanh}\dfrac{1}{3}$ **ii** $\operatorname{artanh}\dfrac{1}{4}$ **d** **i** $\operatorname{arcosh}(-3)$ **ii** $\operatorname{artanh}(-2)$

    e **i** $\sinh^{-1}\sqrt{2}$ **ii** $\tanh^{-1}\dfrac{1}{\sqrt{3}}$

5 Solve the equation $3\cosh(x-1) = 5$.

6 Find and simplify the exact value of $\cosh(\ln 2)$.

7 Find and simplify a rational expression for $\tanh(\ln 3)$.

8 The function f is given by $f(x) = \cosh^{-1}(x+a) + \tanh^{-1}(x+b)$, where a and b are constants.

    Find, in terms of a, the set of values of the constant b so that $f(x)$ has the largest domain possible.

9 Solve the equation $\sinh^2 3x = 5$.

10 Solve the equation $2\tanh^2 x + 2 = 5\tanh x$.

11 Find and simplify an expression for $\cosh(\sinh^{-1} x)$.

12 Prove that $\sinh^{-1} x = \ln(x + \sqrt{x^2 + 1})$.

13 Prove that $\tanh^{-1} x = \dfrac{1}{2}\ln\left(\dfrac{1+x}{1-x}\right)$.

14 In the derivation of $\cosh^{-1} x$ you found that two possible expressions were $\ln(x + \sqrt{x^2 - 1})$ and $\ln(x - \sqrt{x^2 - 1})$. Show that their sum is zero and hence explain why the expression chosen in Proof 3 is non-negative.

Section 3: Hyperbolic identities

Just as there is the identity $\sin^2 x + \cos^2 x \equiv 1$ linking the trigonometric functions $\sin^2 x$ and $\cos^2 x$, there is also an identity linking the hyperbolic functions $\sinh^2 x$ and $\cosh^2 x$.

 Key point 6.7

$$\cosh^2 x - \sinh^2 x \equiv 1$$

This will be given in your formula book.

 Rewind

The result in Key point 6.7 proves that $(\cosh x, \sinh x)$ lies on the hyperbola $x^2 - y^2 = 1$, as described in the introduction to this chapter.

You can prove the identity in Key point 6.7 by using the definitions of sinh and cosh given in Key point 6.1.

WORKED EXAMPLE 6.5

Prove that $\cosh^2 x - \sinh^2 x \equiv 1$.

$$\cosh^2 x = \left(\frac{e^x + e^{-x}}{2}\right)^2$$

Start from the definition of one of the hyperbolic functions. It doesn't matter which one. It is squared in the expression so square it and simplify.

$$= \frac{e^{2x} + 2e^x e^{-x} + e^{-2x}}{4}$$

$$= \frac{e^{2x} + 2 + e^{-2x}}{4}$$

Since $e^x e^{-x} = 1$.

$$\sinh^2 x = \left(\frac{e^x - e^{-x}}{2}\right)^2$$

Repeat with the $\sinh^2 x$ term.

$$= \frac{e^{2x} - 2e^x e^{-x} + e^{-2x}}{4}$$

$$= \frac{e^{2x} - 2 + e^{-2x}}{4}$$

$e^x e^{-x} = 1$ again.

$$\cosh^2 x - \sinh^2 x \equiv \frac{e^{2x} + 2 + e^{-2x}}{4} - \frac{e^{2x} - 2 + e^{-2x}}{4}$$

Combine the two terms and simplify.

$$\equiv \frac{e^{2x} + 2 + e^{-2x} - (e^{2x} - 2 + e^{-2x})}{4}$$

$$\equiv \frac{e^{2x} + 2 + e^{-2x} - e^{2x} + 2 - e^{-2x}}{4}$$

$$\equiv \frac{4}{4}$$

$$\equiv 1$$

You might be asked to prove other unfamiliar hyperbolic identities. To do this, always return to the definitions of the functions and follow a process similar to that in Worked examples 6.5 and 6.6.

WORKED EXAMPLE 6.6

Prove that $\sinh 2x = 2\sinh x \cosh x$.

$\text{LHS} \equiv \dfrac{e^{2x} - e^{-2x}}{2}$

On the LHS use the definition of $\sinh x$ and replace each x with $2x$.

$\text{RHS} \equiv 2 \times \dfrac{e^x - e^{-x}}{2} \times \dfrac{e^x + e^{-x}}{2}$

Then work from the RHS. Substitute the definitions of $\sinh x$ and $\cosh x$.

$\equiv \dfrac{(e^x - e^{-x}) \times (e^x + e^{-x})}{2}$

$\equiv \dfrac{(e^x)^2 - (e^{-x})^2}{2}$

Multiply out the brackets, using the difference of two squares.

$\equiv \dfrac{e^{2x} - e^{-2x}}{2}$

Using the rules of indices.

$\equiv \text{LHS}$

EXERCISE 6C

1 Prove that $\cosh x - \sinh x \equiv e^{-x}$.

2 Simplify $\sqrt{1 + \sinh^2 x}$.

3 Prove that $\cosh 2x \equiv \cosh^2 x + \sinh^2 x$.

4 Prove that $1 - \tanh^2 x \equiv \dfrac{1}{\cosh^2 x}$.

5 Prove that $\tanh 2x \equiv \dfrac{2\tanh x}{1 + \tanh^2 x}$.

6 Prove that $\cosh x - 1 \equiv \dfrac{1}{2}\left(e^{0.5x} - e^{-0.5x}\right)^2$. Hence prove that $\cosh x \geqslant 1$.

7 Prove that $\cosh A + \cosh B \equiv 2\cosh\left(\dfrac{A+B}{2}\right)\cosh\left(\dfrac{A-B}{2}\right)$.

8 Use the binomial theorem to show that $\sinh^3 x \equiv \dfrac{1}{4}\sinh 3x - \dfrac{3}{4}\sinh x$.

9 **a** Explain why $(\cosh x + \sinh x)^3 \equiv \cosh 3x + \sinh 3x$ and $(\cosh x - \sinh x)^3 \equiv \cosh 3x - \sinh 3x$.

   b Hence show that $\cosh 3x \equiv \cosh^3 x + 3\cosh x \sinh^2 x$.

   c Write $\cosh 3x$ in terms of $\cosh x$.

10 Given that $\tan y = \sinh x$ show that $\sin y = \pm\tanh x$.

Section 4: Solving harder hyperbolic equations

When you are solving equations involving hyperbolic functions you have several options:

- Rearrange to get a hyperbolic function that is equal to a constant and use inverse hyperbolic functions.
- Use the definition of hyperbolic functions to get an exponential function that is equal to a constant and use logarithms.
- Use an identity for hyperbolic functions to simplify the situation to one of the two preceding options.

It is only with experience that you will develop an instinct about which method will be most efficient.

WORKED EXAMPLE 6.7

Solve $\sinh x + \cosh x = 4$.

$$\sinh x + \cosh x = 4$$

$$\frac{e^x - e^{-x}}{2} + \frac{e^x + e^{-x}}{2} = 4$$

Use the definitions of $\sinh x$ and $\cosh x$.

$$\frac{2e^x}{2} = 4$$

$$e^x = 4$$

$$x = \ln 4$$

> **Tip**
>
> When you are dealing with the sum or difference of two hyperbolic functions, it is often useful to use the exponential form.

WORKED EXAMPLE 6.8

Solve $5\sinh x - 4\cosh x = 0$, giving your answer in the form $\ln a$.

$$5\sinh x = 4\cosh x$$

$$\frac{\sinh x}{\cosh x} = \frac{4}{5}$$

You could use the definitions of sinh and cosh, but it is easier to use the identity $\tanh x \equiv \dfrac{\sinh x}{\cosh x}$.

$$\tanh x = \frac{4}{5}$$

$$x = \operatorname{artanh} x$$

Then use the logarithmic form of artanh.

$$= \frac{1}{2}\ln\left(\frac{1 + \frac{4}{5}}{1 - \frac{4}{5}}\right)$$

$$= \frac{1}{2}\ln 9$$

$$= \ln 3$$

$$\frac{1}{2}\ln 9 = \ln 9^{\frac{1}{2}} = \ln 3$$

WORKED EXAMPLE 6.9

Solve $\cosh^2 x + 1 = 3\sinh x$, giving your answer in logarithmic form.

$$\cosh^2 x + 1 = 3\sinh x$$

The equation involves two types of function. You can use the identity $\cosh^2 x - \sinh^2 x \equiv 1$ to replace the $\cosh^2 x$ term.

$$(1+\sinh^2 x) + 1 = 3\sinh x$$

$$\sinh^2 x - 3\sinh x + 2 = 0$$

Solve the resulting quadratic.

$$(\sinh x - 1)(\sinh x - 2) = 0$$

$$\sinh x = 1$$
$$x = \text{arsinh } 1$$
$$x = \ln(1+\sqrt{2})$$

Use the logarithmic form of arsinh.

or
$$\sinh x = 2$$
$$x = \text{arsinh } 2$$
$$x = \ln(2+\sqrt{5})$$

WORK IT OUT 6.1

Solve $\sinh 2x \cosh 2x = 6\sinh 2x$.

Which is the correct solution? Identify the errors made in the incorrect solutions.

Solution 1	Solution 2	Solution 3
Dividing by 2:	Dividing by $\sinh 2x$:	$\sinh 2x \cosh 2x = 6\sinh 2x$
$\sinh x \cosh x = 3\sinh x$	$\cosh 2x = 6$	$\sinh 2x \cosh 2x - 6\sinh 2x = 0$
$\sinh x \cosh x - 3\sinh x = 0$	$2x = \cosh^{-1} 6$	$\sinh 2x(\cosh 2x - 6) = 0$
$\sinh x(\cosh x - 3) = 0$	$= \ln(6+\sqrt{35})$	$\sinh 2x = 0$ or $\cosh 2x = 6$
$\sinh x = 0$ or $\cosh x = 3$	$x = \frac{1}{2}\ln(6+\sqrt{35})$	$2x = \sinh^{-1} 0$ or $2x = \pm\cosh^{-1} 6$
$x = \sinh^{-1} 0$ or $x = \cosh^{-1} 3$		$x = 0$ or $x = \pm 1.24$
$x = 0$ or $x = 1.76$		

139

WORKED EXAMPLE 6.10

a Prove that $1 - \tanh^2 x \equiv \dfrac{1}{\cosh^2 x}$.

b Solve the equation $\dfrac{3}{\cosh^2 x} + 4\tanh x + 1 = 0$.

a $1 - \tanh^2 x \equiv 1 - \dfrac{\sinh^2 x}{\cosh^2 x}$

Since the RHS of the required identity contains cosh, it is easiest to start from the definition of tanh in terms of sinh and cosh.

$\equiv \dfrac{\cosh^2 x - \sinh^2 x}{\cosh^2 x}$

Write as a single fraction.

$\equiv \dfrac{1}{\cosh^2 x}$

Use the identity from Key Point 6.7.

b $3 - 3\tanh^2 x + 4\tanh x + 1 = 0$

From **a**, $\dfrac{3}{\cosh^2 x} = 3(1 - \tanh^2 x)$.

$3\tanh^2 x - 4\tanh x - 4 = 0$

This is a quadratic equation in tanh x.

$(3\tanh x + 2)(\tanh x - 2) = 0$

$\tanh x = -\dfrac{2}{3}$ or 2

$\therefore x = \operatorname{artanh}\left(-\dfrac{2}{3}\right)$

The range of tanh x is $(-1, 1)$, so $\tanh x = 2$ is not possible.

$\therefore x = \dfrac{1}{2}\ln\left(\dfrac{1 + \left(-\dfrac{2}{3}\right)}{1 - \left(-\dfrac{2}{3}\right)}\right)$

Then use $\operatorname{artanh} x = \dfrac{1}{2}\ln\left(\dfrac{1 + x}{1 - x}\right)$.

$= \dfrac{1}{2}\ln\left(\dfrac{\frac{1}{3}}{\frac{5}{3}}\right)$

$= \dfrac{1}{2}\ln\left(\dfrac{1}{5}\right)$

$= -\dfrac{1}{2}\ln 5$

EXERCISE 6D

1 Find the exact solution to $\cosh x = 5 - \sinh x$.

2 Solve $\cosh x - \sinh x = 2$, giving your answer in the form $\ln k$.

3 Solve $3(2 \sinh x - 1)(\cosh x - 4) = 0$, giving your answers correct to 3 significant figures.

4 Solve $5 \sinh x + 3 \cosh x = 0$, giving your answer in the form $\ln k$, where k is a rational number.

5 Solve the equation $\dfrac{2}{\cosh x} = e^x$, giving your answer in the form $\ln k$.

6 Solve the equation $2 \sinh 2x = 9 \tanh x$, giving exact answers.

7 Find the exact solution to $2 \sinh x = 1 + \cosh x$.

8 Solve $6 \sinh x - 2 \cosh x = 7$, giving your answers in logarithmic form.

9 Solve $2 \cosh^2 x - 5 \sinh x = 5$, giving your answers in exact form.

10 Solve $\sinh^2 x = \cosh x + 1$, giving your answer in logarithmic form.

11 Solve $\tanh x = \dfrac{1}{\cosh x}$, giving your answer in logarithmic form.

12 Solve the equation $6 \tanh x - \dfrac{7}{\cosh x} = 2$, giving your answer in the form $\ln k$, where k is a rational number.

13 Using the identity $\dfrac{1}{\cosh^2 x} \equiv 1 - \tanh^2 x$, solve the equation $2 \tanh^2 x = 4 - \dfrac{5}{\cosh x}$, giving your answers in the form $\ln k$.

14 $\sinh x + \sinh y = \dfrac{21}{8}$

$\cosh x + \cosh y = \dfrac{27}{8}$

   a Show that $e^x = 6 - e^y$ and $e^{-x} = 0.75 - e^{-y}$.

   b Hence find the exact solutions to the simultaneous equations.

15 Find a sufficient condition on p, q and r for $p^2 \cosh x + q^2 \sinh x = r^2$ to have at least one solution.

16 **a** Prove that $\sinh 3x \equiv 4 \sinh^3 x + 3 \sinh x$.

   b Hence solve the equation $\sinh 6x = 6 + \sinh 2x$, giving your answer in the form $a \ln b$.

17 **a** Show that, for any real number k,

$(\cosh x + \sinh x)^k + (\cosh x - \sinh x)^k \equiv 2 \cosh kx$.

   b Hence solve the equation

$(\cosh x + \sinh x)^6 + (\cosh x - \sinh x)^6 = 6$

giving your answers in the form $a \ln b$.

Section 5: Differentiation

 Key point 6.8

- $\dfrac{d}{dx}(\sinh x) = \cosh x$

- $\dfrac{d}{dx}(\cosh x) = \sinh x$

- $\dfrac{d}{dx}(\tanh x) = \dfrac{1}{\cosh^2 x}$

Only the final one of these will be given in your formula book.

 Tip

The first two of these formulae will *not* be given in your formula book.

You can derive the results for $\sinh x$ and $\cosh x$ by returning to the definitions of these functions.

WORKED EXAMPLE 6.11

Show that $\dfrac{d}{dx}(\sinh x) = \cosh x$.

$y = \sinh x$

$ = \dfrac{e^x - e^{-x}}{2}$ .... Use the definition of $\sinh x$.

Differentiating:

$\dfrac{dy}{dx} = \dfrac{e^x - \left(-e^{-x}\right)}{2}$

$\phantom{\dfrac{dy}{dx}} = \dfrac{e^x + e^{-x}}{2}$

$\phantom{\dfrac{dy}{dx}} = \cosh x$

You can show the result for $\tanh x$ either from the definition again or by using $\tanh x \equiv \dfrac{\sinh x}{\cosh x}$ and the quotient rule.

WORKED EXAMPLE 6.12

Use the derivatives of $\sinh x$ and $\cosh x$ to show that $\dfrac{d}{dx}(\tanh x) = \dfrac{1}{\cosh^2 x}$.

$y = \tanh x$

$ = \dfrac{\sinh x}{\cosh x}$ .... Use $\tanh x \equiv \dfrac{\sinh x}{\cosh x}$.

Differentiating using the quotient rule:

$\dfrac{dy}{dx} = \dfrac{\cosh x \cosh x - \sinh x \sinh x}{\cosh^2 x}$

$\phantom{\dfrac{dy}{dx}} = \dfrac{\cosh^2 x - \sinh^2 x}{\cosh^2 x}$

$\phantom{\dfrac{dy}{dx}} = \dfrac{1}{\cosh^2 x}$ .... Use $\cosh^2 x - \sinh^2 x \equiv 1$.

WORKED EXAMPLE 6.13

Given that $y = x\tanh(x^2)$, find $\dfrac{dy}{dx}$.

Let $u = x$ and $v = \tanh(x^2)$ Use the product rule.

Then $u' = 1$

and v is a composite function so use the chain rule to

$v' = \dfrac{1}{\cosh^2 x} \times 2x$ differentiate.

$\quad = \dfrac{2x}{\cosh^2 x}$

$\dfrac{dy}{dx} = 1 \times \tanh(x^2) + x \times \dfrac{2x}{\cosh^2 x}$ Now apply the product rule formula.

$\quad = \tanh(x^2) + \dfrac{2x^2}{\cosh^2 x}$

EXERCISE 6E

1   Differentiate each function with respect to x.

    a   **i** $f(x) = \sinh 3x$ **ii** $f(x) = \sinh \dfrac{1}{2} x$

    b   **i** $f(x) = \cosh(4x+1)$ **ii** $f(x) = \cosh \dfrac{1}{3} x$

    c   **i** $f(x) = \tanh \dfrac{2}{3} x$ **ii** $f(x) = \tanh(1-2x)$

2   Differentiate each function with respect to x.

    a $f(x) = x^2 \tanh 3x$ **b** $f(x) = \dfrac{1}{\tanh^2 5x}$

3   Find the exact coordinates of the turning point on the curve $y = e^{\cosh x} - \cosh x$.

4   Find the exact coordinates of the minimum point on the curve $y = 3\sinh x + 5\cosh x$.

5   Show that the equation of the tangent to the curve $y = \tanh x$ at $x = \ln 2$ is $16x - 25y + 15 - 16\ln 2 = 0$.

6   Find the equation of the normal to the curve $y = 2\sinh x - \cosh x$ at $x = \ln 3$, giving your answer in the form $ax + by + c = 0$.

7   **a**   Find the exact values of the x-coordinates of the turning points on the curve $y = \tanh 2x - x$.

      b   Show that the maximum point has y-coordinate $\dfrac{\sqrt{2} - \ln(\sqrt{2} + 1)}{2}$.

8   Find the coordinates of the stationary point on the curve $y = e^{-x} \sinh \dfrac{1}{2} x$.

9   Show that the two points of inflection on the curve $y = \dfrac{1}{\cosh x}$ have x-coordinates $\pm \ln k$, stating the value of k.

10   **a**   Find the exact value of the x-coordinates of the stationary points on the curve with equation
        $y = 8\sinh x - 27\tanh x$.

      b   Prove that one of the stationary points from part **a** is a local maximum and that one is a local minimum point.

Section 6: Integration

Key point 6.9

- $\int \sinh x \, dx = \cosh x + c$

- $\int \cosh x \, dx = \sinh x + c$

- $\int \tanh x \, dx = \ln \cosh x + c$

Tip

These results will *not* be given in your formula book.

As with differentiation, you can derive the results for the integrals of $\sinh x$ and $\cosh x$ by returning to the definitions of these functions.

WORKED EXAMPLE 6.14

a Show that $\int \sinh x \, dx = \cosh x + c$.

b Hence find the exact value of $\int_0^{\ln 5} \sinh 3x \, dx$.

a $\int \sinh x \, dx = \int \dfrac{e^x - e^{-x}}{2} \, dx$ .... Use the definition of $\sinh x$.

$\qquad = \dfrac{e^x - (-e^{-x})}{2} + c$

$\qquad = \dfrac{e^x + e^{-x}}{2} + c$

$\qquad = \cosh x + c$

b $\int_0^{\ln 5} \sinh 3x \, dx = \left[\dfrac{1}{3} \cosh 3x \right]_0^{\ln 5}$ .... Use the result from part **a** together with the reverse chain rule.

$\qquad = \dfrac{1}{3} \cosh(3\ln 5) - \dfrac{1}{3} \cosh(0)$

$\qquad = \dfrac{1}{3} \dfrac{\left(e^{3\ln 5} + e^{-3\ln 5} \right)}{2} - \dfrac{1}{3}$ .... Use the definition of $\cosh$ in terms of e, and the fact that $\cosh(0) = 1$.

$\qquad = \dfrac{125 + \frac{1}{125}}{6} - \dfrac{1}{3}$ .... $e^{3\ln 5} = e^{\ln(5^3)} = 125$

$\qquad = \dfrac{7688}{375}$

You can now find the integral of $\tanh x$ either from the definition again or by using $\tanh x \equiv \dfrac{\sinh x}{\cosh x}$ and applying the reverse chain rule.

WORKED EXAMPLE 6.15

Show that $\int \tanh x \, dx = \ln \cosh x + c$.

$\int \tanh x \, dx = \int \dfrac{\sinh x}{\cosh x} \, dx$ Use $\tanh x \equiv \dfrac{\sinh x}{\cosh x}$.

$\qquad\qquad = \ln \cosh x + c$

This is of the form $\int \dfrac{f'(x)}{f(x)} \, dx$, so you can integrate it directly.

 Tip

Look out for integrals of the form $\int f'(x)[f(x)]^n \, dx$ or $\int \dfrac{f'(x)}{f(x)} \, dx$ as you can integrate these without need for a substitution, by reversing the chain rule.

 Rewind

See A Level Mathematics Student Book 2, Chapter 11, for a reminder of integrating trigonometric functions using the reverse chain rule, trigonometric identities and integration by parts.

Often you will need to use a hyperbolic identity before integrating.

Tip

When integrating hyperbolic functions, you can often use the same approach as with the corresponding trigonometric function.

WORKED EXAMPLE 6.16

Find $\int \cosh^2 x \, dx$.

$\cosh 2x \equiv 2\cosh^2 x - 1$ Use the identity for $\cosh 2x$ in terms of $\cosh^2 x$.

$\Rightarrow \cosh^2 x \equiv \dfrac{\cosh 2x + 1}{2}$

$\therefore \int \cosh^2 x \, dx = \int \dfrac{\cosh 2x + 1}{2} \, dx$

$\qquad\qquad\qquad = \dfrac{1}{2}\left(\dfrac{1}{2}\sinh 2x + x \right) + c$ Remember to divide by the coefficient of x when integrating $\cosh 2x$.

Sometimes it's better to use the definition of the hyperbolic function, rather than the method you would have used with the corresponding trigonometric function.

WORKED EXAMPLE 6.17

Find $\int e^x \cosh x \, dx$.

$$\int e^x \cosh x \, dx = \int e^x \left(\frac{e^x + e^{-x}}{2} \right) dx$$

$$= \int \frac{e^{2x} + 1}{2} dx$$

$$= \frac{1}{2} \left(\frac{1}{2} e^{2x} + x \right) + c$$

Use the definition of $\cosh x$.

▶ **Rewind**

If the integral in Worked example 6.17 had been $\int e^x \cos x \, dx$, you would have done integration by parts twice and rearranged.

EXERCISE 6F

1 Find:

a i $\int \sinh 3x \, dx$ **ii** $\int \sinh \dfrac{x}{2} \, dx$

b i $\int \cosh(2x+1) \, dx$ **ii** $\int \cosh 4x \, dx$

c i $\int \tanh(-2x) \, dx$ **ii** $\int \tanh(3x-2) \, dx$

2 Find the exact value of each integral.

a i $\int_0^2 \sinh x \, dx$ **ii** $\int_0^5 \cosh x \, dx$

b i $\int_0^1 \sinh 2x \, dx$ **ii** $\int_0^3 \cosh 2x \, dx$

c i $\int_{\ln 2}^{\ln 4} \cosh 3x \, dx$ **ii** $\int_{\ln 2}^{\ln 3} \sinh 2x \, dx$

3 Use an appropriate hyperbolic identity to find each integral.

a i $\int \sinh^2 2x \, dx$ **ii** $\int \cosh^2 3x \, dx$

b i $\int \tanh^2 \dfrac{x}{2} \, dx$ **ii** $\int \tanh^2 3x \, dx$

c i $\int \sinh x \cosh x \, dx$ **ii** $\int \sinh 3x \cosh 3x \, dx$

4 Use integration by parts to find each integral.

a i $\int x \sinh x \, dx$ **ii** $\int x \sinh 2x \, dx$

b i $\int 3x \cosh x \, dx$ **ii** $\int x \cosh \dfrac{x}{2} \, dx$

c i $\int x^2 \sinh x \, dx$ **ii** $\int x^2 \sinh 3x \, dx$

d i $\int x^2 \cosh 2x \, dx$ **ii** $\int 3x^2 \cosh x \, dx$

5 Use the definitions of $\sinh x$ and/or $\cosh x$ to find each integral.

a i $\int e^x \sinh 2x \, dx$ **ii** $\int e^{2x} \cosh x \, dx$

b i $\int \sinh x \sinh 4x \, dx$ **ii** $\int \cosh 2x \cosh 3x \, dx$

6 Find $\int \dfrac{\sinh x + \cosh x}{4 \cosh x} \, dx$.

7 By expressing $\sinh x$ and $\cosh x$ in terms of e^x, evaluate $\int_0^1 \dfrac{1}{\sinh x + \cosh x} \, dx$.

8 The diagram shows the region R, which is bounded by the curve $y = \sinh x$, the x-axis and the line $x = \ln 3$.

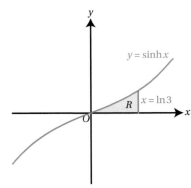

Show that the volume of the solid formed when the region R is rotated through 2π radians about the x-axis is given by $\dfrac{\pi}{18}(20 - 9\ln 3)$.

9 Find:

a $\displaystyle\int \cosh^3 x \sinh^2 x \, dx$

b $\displaystyle\int \frac{\cosh^3 x}{\sinh^2 x} \, dx.$

10 Find $\displaystyle\int \frac{x}{\cosh^2 x} \, dx.$

11 The diagram shows the region R bounded by curve $y = 4\cosh\dfrac{x}{2}$, for $x \geqslant 0$, the y-axis and the line $y = 3\sqrt{2}$.

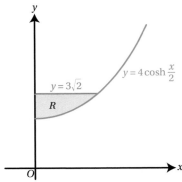

Find the exact volume of the solid formed when the region R is rotated through 2 radians about the x-axis.

12 Using the substitution $u = \cosh x$, show that $\displaystyle\int_0^{\ln 2} \frac{\sinh^3 x}{\cosh x + 1} \, dx = \frac{1}{32}.$

13 Show that $\displaystyle\int_0^{\frac{\pi}{4}} \sin x \, \text{artanh}(\sin x) \, dx = \frac{\pi - \sqrt{2}\ln(3 + 2\sqrt{2})}{4}$

14 **a** Given that $u = \text{arsinh}\, x$, write down an expression for $\dfrac{du}{dx}$.

b Use integration by parts to show that
$$\int \text{arsinh}\, x \, dx = x\,\text{arsinh}\, x - \sqrt{x^2 + 1} + c.$$

Checklist of learning and understanding

- Definitions of hyperbolic functions:

  - $\sinh x = \dfrac{e^x - e^{-x}}{2}$

  - $\cosh x = \dfrac{e^x + e^{-x}}{2}$

  - $\tanh x \equiv \dfrac{\sinh x}{\cosh x} \equiv \dfrac{e^x - e^{-x}}{e^x + e^{-x}}$

- Graphs of hyperbolic functions:

  - $y = \sinh x$
    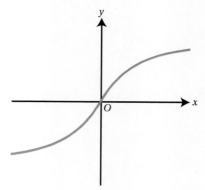

  - $y = \cosh x$
    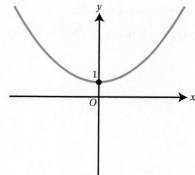

  - $y = \tanh x$
    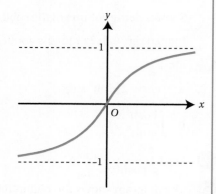

- Logarithmic form of inverse hyperbolic functions:

  - $\operatorname{arsinh} x = \ln\left(x + \sqrt{x^2 + 1}\right)$

  - $\operatorname{arcosh} x = \ln\left(x + \sqrt{x^2 - 1}\right)$

  - $\operatorname{artanh} x = \dfrac{1}{2}\ln\left(\dfrac{1 + x}{1 - x}\right)$

- Domain and range of hyperbolic, inverse hyperbolic, and reciprocal hyperbolic functions:

Function	Domain	Range
$\sinh x$	$x \in \mathbb{R}$	$f(x) \in \mathbb{R}$
$\cosh x$	$x \in \mathbb{R}$	$f(x) \geqslant 1$
$\tanh x$	$x \in \mathbb{R}$	$-1 < f(x) < 1$
$\sinh^{-1} x$	$x \in \mathbb{R}$	$f(x) \in \mathbb{R}$
$\cosh^{-1} x$	$x \geqslant 1$	$f(x) \geqslant 0$
$\tanh^{-1} x$	$-1 < x < 1$	$f(x) \in \mathbb{R}$

Continues on next page ...

- Identities:
  - $\cosh^2 x - \sinh^2 x \equiv 1$
  - To prove other identities, return to the definitions of the functions involved.
- Derivatives of hyperbolic and reciprocal hyperbolic functions:
  - $\dfrac{d}{dx}(\sinh x) = \cosh x$
  - $\dfrac{d}{dx}(\cosh x) = \sinh x$
  - $\dfrac{d}{dx}(\tanh x) = \dfrac{1}{\cosh^2 x}$
- Integrals of hyperbolic functions:
  - $\int \sinh x = \cosh x + c$
  - $\int \cosh x = \sinh x + c$
  - $\int \tanh x = \ln \cosh x + c$
- Many hyperbolic integrals can be done by using the same method that you would use for the corresponding trigonometric integral.

Mixed practice 6

1 Given that $f(x) = 3\tanh^2 x + 1$ for $x \in \mathbb{R}$,

   a sketch the graph of $y = f(x)$

   b state the range of f.

2 Solve $\sinh x + \cosh x = k$, giving your answer in terms of k.

3 Simplify $\tanh(1 + \ln p)$.

4 Solve $\cosh(x + 1) = 3$, giving your answer in terms of logarithms.

5 Solve $4\sinh 2x = \cosh 2x$, giving your answer correct to 3 significant figures.

6 Find the exact solutions to $16\cosh^2 x + 8\cosh x = 35$.

7 Solve the equation $\sinh x = \dfrac{1}{\cosh x}$, giving your answer in the form $a\ln b$.

8 Given $f(x) = \sinh^2 3x$, find $f''(x)$.

9 Show that the curve $y = e^x \cosh 2x$ has no points of inflection.

10 Given that $y = a\sinh nx + b\cosh nx$, show that $\dfrac{d^2 y}{dx^2} = n^2 y$.

11 By first expressing $\cosh x$ and $\sinh x$ in terms of exponentials, solve the equation $3\cosh x - 4\sinh x = 7$ giving your answer in an exact logarithmic form.

© OCR A Level Mathematics, Unit 4726/01 Further Pure Mathematics 2, January 2013

12 Find $\displaystyle\int \dfrac{\tanh 3x}{\cosh 3x}\,dx$.

13 Show that $\displaystyle\int_0^{\ln\sqrt{2}} e^{\cosh 4x}\sinh 4x\,dx = \dfrac{e}{4}\left(e^{\frac{9}{8}} - 1\right)$.

14 Solve the equation $\sinh 3x\cosh^2 3x = 5\sinh 3x$, giving your answers in exact form.

15 Solve $3\sinh^2 x - 13\cosh x + 7 = 0$, giving your answers in terms of natural logarithms.

16 Prove that $\cosh x > \sinh x$ for all x.

17 Find and simplify an expression for $\tanh(\operatorname{arsinh} x)$.

18 Use the binomial theorem to show that $\cosh^4 x \equiv \dfrac{1}{8}\cosh 4x + \dfrac{1}{2}\cosh 2x + \dfrac{3}{8}$.

19 **a** Sketch the graph of $y = \tanh x$.

   b Given that $u = \tanh x$, use the definitions of $\sinh x$ and $\cosh x$ in terms of e^x and e^{-x} to show that
$$x = \dfrac{1}{2}\ln\left(\dfrac{1+u}{1-u}\right).$$

   c **i** Show that the equation $\dfrac{3}{\cosh^2 x} + 7\tanh x = 5$ can be written as $3\tanh^2 x - 7\tanh x + 2 = 0$.

     ii Show that the equation $3\tanh^2 x - 7\tanh x + 2 = 0$ has only one solution for x.

     Find this solution in the form $\dfrac{1}{2}\ln a$ where a is an integer.

20 **a** Prove that $\dfrac{1}{\cosh^2 x} \equiv 1 - \tanh^2 x$.

   b Hence solve the equation $\dfrac{1}{\cosh^2 x} = 4 + \tanh x$, giving your answers in terms of natural logarithms.

21 **i** Given that $y = \sinh^{-1} x$, prove that $y = \ln\left(x + \sqrt{x^2 + 1}\right)$.

ii It is given that x satisfies the equation $\sinh^{-1} x - \cosh^{-1} x = \ln 2$. Use the logarithmic forms for $\sinh^{-1} x$ and $\cosh^{-1} x$ to show that $\sqrt{x^2 + 1} - 2\sqrt{x^2 - 1} = x$.

Hence, by squaring this equation, find the exact value of x.

© **OCR A Level Mathematics, Unit 4726 Further Pure Mathematics 2, January 2012**

22 Using the substitution $u = e^x$, find $\displaystyle\int \frac{1}{4\sinh x + 5\cosh x} \, dx$.

23 The diagram shows the graphs of $y = 5\cosh x$ and $y = \sinh x = 7$.

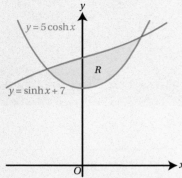

Find the exact value of the area of the shaded region.

24 **a** Prove the identity $\cosh 3x = 4\cosh^3 x - 3\cosh x$.

b If $48u^3 - 36u - 13 = 0$ and $u = \cosh x$ find the value of x.

c Hence find the exact real solution to $48u^3 - 36u - 13 = 0$, giving your answer in a form without logarithms.

25 Solve these simultaneous equations, giving your answers in exact logarithmic form.
$$\begin{cases} \sinh x + \sinh y = 3.15 \\ \cosh x + \cosh y = 3.85 \end{cases}$$

26 Using the logarithmic definition, prove that $\operatorname{arsinh}(-x) = -\operatorname{arsinh} x$.

27 Given that $\operatorname{artanh} x + \operatorname{artanh} y = \ln\sqrt{5}$, show that $y = \dfrac{3x - 2}{2x - 3}$.

28 Prove that $\dfrac{\sinh x + \cosh x - 1}{\sinh x + \cosh x + 1} = \tanh\left(\dfrac{1}{2}x\right)$.

7 Further calculus techniques

In this chapter you will learn how to:

- differentiate inverse trigonometric and inverse hyperbolic functions
- reverse those results to find integrals of the form $(a^2+x^2)^{-1}, (a^2-x^2)^{-\frac{1}{2}}$, $(a^2+x^2)^{-\frac{1}{2}}$ and $(x^2-a^2)^{-\frac{1}{2}}$
- use trigonometric and hyperbolic substitutions to find similar integrals
- integrate using partial fractions with a quadratic expression in the denominator.

Before you start...

A Level Mathematics Student Book 2, Chapter 10	You should know how to differentiate functions defined implicitly.	1 Given that $x^2 - y^3 = 5x$, find an expression for $\dfrac{dy}{dx}$.
A Level Mathematics Student Book 2, Chapter 11	You should be able to integrate using a substitution.	2 Use a suitable substitution to evaluate $\int_0^1 x^2 \sqrt{1+2x^3}\, dx$.
A Level Mathematics Student Book 2, Chapter 11	You should know how to integrate rational functions by splitting them into partial fractions.	3 Find $\int \dfrac{2x^2 - 9x + 8}{(x-1)(x-2)^2}\, dx$.

Introduction

In this chapter you will extend your range of integration methods and the variety of functions you can integrate. Differentiation of inverse trigonometric functions leads to rules for integrating functions of the form $\dfrac{1}{a^2+x^2}$ and $\dfrac{1}{\sqrt{a^2-x^2}}$ and suggests that you can use trigonometric substitution to find other similar integrals. Likewise, differentiation of inverse hyperbolic functions leads to rules for integrating $\dfrac{1}{\sqrt{a^2+x^2}}$ and $\dfrac{1}{\sqrt{x^2-a^2}}$. You can use these results in combination with partial fractions to integrate many rational functions.

Section 1: Differentiation of inverse trigonometric functions

You already know how to differentiate $\sin x$, $\cos x$ and $\tan x$. To differentiate their inverse functions, you can use implicit differentiation.

⏪ **Rewind**

You met implicit differentiation in A Level Mathematics Student Book 2, Chapter 10.

WORKED EXAMPLE 7.1

Given that $y = \sin^{-1} x$, and that $|x| < 1$, find $\dfrac{dy}{dx}$ in terms of x.

$y = \sin^{-1} x$

$\Rightarrow \sin y = x$

You know how to differentiate sin, so express x in terms of y.

Differentiating each term with respect to x:

$\cos y \dfrac{dy}{dx} = 1$

$\dfrac{dy}{dx} = \dfrac{1}{\cos y}$

Remember the chain rule.

$= \dfrac{1}{\sqrt{1 - \sin^2 y}}$

$= \dfrac{1}{\sqrt{1 - x^2}}$

You want the answer in terms of x, so you need to change cos to sin.

You should notice two important details in the derivation of the derivative of $\sin^{-1} x$ shown in Worked example 7.1. First, the $\sin^{-1} x$ function is defined for $|x| \leqslant 1$. However, you can see from the graph that the gradient at $x = \pm 1$ is not finite, so the condition $|x| < 1$ is required for the derivative to exist. (You can also see that the expression for $\dfrac{dy}{dx}$ is not defined when $x = \pm 1$.)

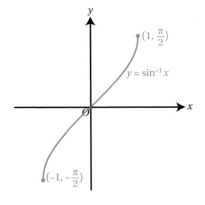

Second, you used $\cos^2 y = 1 - \sin^2 y$ to write $\cos y = \sqrt{1 - \sin^2 y}$. When taking a square root, you need to ask whether it should be positive or negative (or both). In this case, the range of the $\sin^{-1} x$ function is $-\dfrac{\pi}{2} \leqslant y \leqslant \dfrac{\pi}{2}$ and in this range, $\cos y > 0$; this justifies taking the positive square root.

You can establish the results for the inverse cos and tan functions similarly.

🔑 **Key point 7.1**

- $\dfrac{d}{dx}(\sin^{-1} x) = \dfrac{1}{\sqrt{1 - x^2}}, |x| < 1$

- $\dfrac{d}{dx}(\cos^{-1} x) = \dfrac{-1}{\sqrt{1 - x^2}}, |x| < 1$

- $\dfrac{d}{dx}(\tan^{-1} x) = \dfrac{1}{1 + x^2}$

These will be given in your formula book.

Notice that the $\tan^{-1} x$ function is defined for all $x \in \mathbb{R}$, so there is no restriction on the domain of its derivative.

You can combine these results with other rules of differentiation.

WORKED EXAMPLE 7.2

Differentiate:

a $y = x^2 \tan^{-1} 4x$

b $y = \arccos\sqrt{x-3}$ and state the values for which the derivative is valid.

 Tip

Remember that arccos x is alternative notation for $\cos^{-1} x$.

a Using the product rule:

$u = x^2, v = \tan^{-1} 4x$

$\dfrac{du}{dx} = 2x$

$\dfrac{dv}{dx} = \dfrac{1}{1+(4x)^2} \times 4$ .... Multiply by 4 (the derivative of $4x$) due to the chain rule.

$= \dfrac{4}{1+16x^2}$

$\therefore \dfrac{dy}{dx} = 2x\tan^{-1} 4x + \dfrac{4x^2}{1+16x^2}$ ..... Use $\dfrac{dy}{dx} = \dfrac{du}{dx}v + u\dfrac{dv}{dx}$.

b Using the chain rule:

$\dfrac{dy}{dx} = \dfrac{-1}{\sqrt{1-\left(\sqrt{x-3}\right)^2}} \times \dfrac{1}{2}(x-3)^{-\frac{1}{2}}$ ..... Multiply by $\dfrac{1}{2}(x-3)^{-\frac{1}{2}}$ (the derivative of $\sqrt{x-3}$).

$= \dfrac{-1}{\sqrt{1-(x-3)}} \times \dfrac{1}{2\sqrt{x-3}}$

$= \dfrac{-1}{2\sqrt{(4-x)(x-3)}}$

The derivative is valid when

$|x-3| < 1$ and $x \geqslant 3$ .... The derivative of $\arccos x$ is only defined for $|x| < 1$ and the square root is only defined when $x - 3 \geqslant 0$.

$3 \leqslant x < 4$

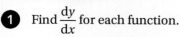 **EXERCISE 7A**

---

1 Find $\dfrac{dy}{dx}$ for each function.

a i $y = \cos^{-1} 3x$ **ii** $y = \cos^{-1} 2x$

b i $y = \tan^{-1}\left(\dfrac{x}{2}\right)$ **ii** $y = \tan^{-1}\left(\dfrac{2x}{5}\right)$

c i $y = x\arcsin x$ **ii** $y = x^2\arcsin x$

d i $y = \arctan(x^2 + 1)$ **ii** $y = \arcsin(1 - x^2)$

2 Find the exact value of the gradient of the graph of $y = \cos^{-1}\left(\dfrac{x}{2}\right)$ at the point where $x = \dfrac{1}{3}$.

3 Find the exact value of the gradient of the graph of $y = x\arctan 3x$ at the point where $x = -\dfrac{1}{3}$.

4 Differentiate $\arctan(3x+2)$, simplifying your answer as far as possible.

5 Find the derivative of $\arcsin(x^2 - 3)$, stating the range of values of x for which your answer is valid.

6 **a** Given that $y = \tan^{-1} x$, show that $\dfrac{dy}{dx} = \dfrac{1}{1+x^2}$.

    b Hence differentiate $\tan^{-1}\dfrac{1}{x}$ with respect to x.

7 Given that $y = \sin^{-1}\left(\dfrac{3x}{2}\right)$, show that $\dfrac{dy}{dx} = \dfrac{3}{\sqrt{4-9x^2}}$ and state the values of x for which the derivative is valid.

8 Given that $x\arctan y = 1$, find an expression for $\dfrac{dy}{dx}$.

9 **a** Find $\dfrac{d}{dx}(x\sin^{-1} x)$.

    b Hence find $\int \sin^{-1} x \, dx$.

10 Show that the graph of $y = \arcsin(x^2)$ has no points of inflection.

Section 2: Differentiation of inverse hyperbolic functions

You know how to differentiate hyperbolic functions, and so again you can use implicit differentiation to differentiate their inverse functions.

> **Rewind**
>
> See Chapter 6, Section 5, for differentiation of hyperbolic functions.

WORKED EXAMPLE 7.3

$y = \sinh^{-1} x$ Rewrite in terms of $\sinh y$.

$\Rightarrow \sinh y = x$

Differentiating with respect to y:

$\dfrac{dx}{dy} = \cosh y$

$\dfrac{dy}{dx} = \dfrac{1}{\cosh y}$ $\dfrac{dy}{dx} = \dfrac{1}{\left(\dfrac{dx}{dy}\right)}$, so take the reciprocal of both sides.

$= \dfrac{1}{\sqrt{\sinh^2 y + 1}}$ Use $\cosh^2 x - \sinh^2 x \equiv 1$.

$= \dfrac{1}{\sqrt{x^2 + 1}}$

You can establish the results for the inverse cosh and tanh functions similarly.

> ### 🔑 Key point 7.2
>
> - $\dfrac{d}{dx}\left(\sinh^{-1} x\right) = \dfrac{1}{\sqrt{x^2+1}}$
>
> - $\dfrac{d}{dx}\left(\cosh^{-1} x\right) = \dfrac{1}{\sqrt{x^2-1}}, \ x>1$
>
> - $\dfrac{d}{dx}\left(\tanh^{-1} x\right) = \dfrac{1}{1-x^2}, \ |x|<1$
>
> **These will be given in your formula book.**

WORKED EXAMPLE 7.4

Find the value of the x-coordinate of the point on the curve $y = \operatorname{arcosh}\left(\dfrac{x}{2}\right)$ at which the tangent is parallel to the line $y = x$.

Differentiating using the chain rule:

$$y' = \frac{1}{\sqrt{\left(\dfrac{x}{2}\right)^2 - 1}} \times \frac{1}{2}$$

Remember to multiply by the derivative of $\dfrac{x}{2}$.

$$= \frac{1}{2\sqrt{\dfrac{x^2}{4} - 1}}$$

Simplify the denominator.

$$= \frac{1}{2\sqrt{\dfrac{x^2-4}{4}}}$$

$$= \frac{1}{\sqrt{x^2-4}}$$

So

$$\frac{1}{\sqrt{x^2-4}} = 1$$

$y = x$ has gradient 1, so set $y' = 1$ and solve for x.

$$\sqrt{x^2-4} = 1$$

$$x^2 - 4 = 1$$

$$x^2 = 5$$

$$\therefore x = \sqrt{5}$$

The domain of $y = \cosh^{-1}\left(\dfrac{x}{2}\right)$ is $x \geqslant 2$ so take the positive square root.

EXERCISE 7B

1 Differentiate each function with respect to x.

   a **i** $f(x) = \operatorname{arsinh} 2x$ **ii** $f(x) = \operatorname{arsinh}(x+2)$

   b **i** $f(x) = \operatorname{arcosh}(-x)$ **ii** $f(x) = \operatorname{arcosh} 3x$

   c **i** $f(x) = \operatorname{artanh} 4x$ **ii** $f(x) = \operatorname{artanh}(1-2x)$

2 Given that $f(x) = \operatorname{arsinh}(\cosh x)$, find $f'(x)$.

3 Given that $f(x) = x \operatorname{arcosh}(x^2)$, find $f'(x)$.

4 Given that $y = \operatorname{artanh}\left(\dfrac{2}{x}\right)$ for $x > 2$, show that

$$\frac{\mathrm{d}y}{\mathrm{d}x} = \frac{a}{b - x^2}$$

   where a and b are integers to be found.

5 Find the equation of the tangent to the curve $y = \operatorname{artanh} x$ at the point where $x = \dfrac{3}{5}$, giving your answer in the form $ax + by + c = 0$.

6 The tangents at $x = 0$ and $x = 1$ to the curve $y = \operatorname{arsinh} x$ intersect at the point P. Show that the x-coordinate of P is $(2 + \sqrt{2}) \ln(1 + \sqrt{2}) - (1 + \sqrt{2})$.

7 Find the coordinates of the point of inflection on the curve $y = \operatorname{arsinh}(x+1)$.

8 Show that $y = (\operatorname{arcosh} x)^2$ satisfies $(x^2 - 1)\dfrac{\mathrm{d}^2 y}{\mathrm{d}x^2} + x\dfrac{\mathrm{d}y}{\mathrm{d}x} = 2$.

9 Prove that the x-coordinate of the point on the curve $y = \operatorname{artanh}(\mathrm{e}^x)$ at which the gradient is $\sqrt{2}$ is $x = a \ln 2$, where a is a value to be found.

Section 3: Using inverse trigonometric and hyperbolic functions in integration

You can reverse the derivatives from Sections 1 and 2 to derive four more integration results:

$$\int \frac{1}{\sqrt{1 - x^2}}\,\mathrm{d}x = \sin^{-1} x + c$$

$$\int \frac{1}{1 + x^2}\,\mathrm{d}x = \tan^{-1} x + c$$

$$\int \frac{1}{\sqrt{1 + x^2}}\,\mathrm{d}x = \sinh^{-1} x + c$$

$$\int \frac{1}{\sqrt{x^2 - 1}}\,\mathrm{d}x = \cosh^{-1} x + c$$

> 💡 **Tip**
>
> Notice that the results
> $\int \dfrac{-1}{\sqrt{1 - x^2}}\,\mathrm{d}x = \cos^{-1} x + c$ and
>
> $\int \dfrac{1}{1 - x^2}\,\mathrm{d}x = \tanh^{-1} x + c$ are not included in this list, as the first is just the negative of $\sin^{-1} x$ and the second can be done by partial fractions.

These results can be generalised slightly by making a linear substitution.

Focus on ...

See Focus on ... Problem solving 2 for an example of using one of these integrals.

Key point 7.3

- $\int \dfrac{1}{\sqrt{a^2 - x^2}}\, dx = \sin^{-1}\left(\dfrac{x}{a}\right) + c, \ |x| < a$

- $\int \dfrac{1}{a^2 + x^2}\, dx = \dfrac{1}{a}\tan^{-1}\left(\dfrac{x}{a}\right) + c$

- $\int \dfrac{1}{\sqrt{a^2 + x^2}}\, dx = \sinh^{-1}\left(\dfrac{x}{a}\right) + c$

- $\int \dfrac{1}{\sqrt{x^2 - a^2}}\, dx = \cosh^{-1}\left(\dfrac{x}{a}\right) + c, \ x > a$

These will be given in your formula book.

You also need to know how to derive these results using trigonometric or hyperbolic substitutions.

WORKED EXAMPLE 7.5

Use the substitution $x = a\sin u$ to prove the result $\int \dfrac{1}{\sqrt{a^2 - x^2}}\, dx = \sin^{-1}\left(\dfrac{x}{a}\right) + c$ when $|x| < a$.

$\dfrac{dx}{du} = a\cos u$

$\Rightarrow dx = a\cos u\, du$

> Differentiate the substitution and express dx in terms of du.

$\dfrac{1}{\sqrt{a^2 - x^2}} = \dfrac{1}{\sqrt{a^2 - a^2\sin^2 u}}$

$= \dfrac{1}{\sqrt{a^2(1 - \sin^2 u)}}$

> Express the integrand in terms of u.

$= \dfrac{1}{\sqrt{a^2\cos^2 u}}$

> Use $\sin^2 u + \cos^2 u \equiv 1$.

$= \dfrac{1}{a\cos u}$

> Since you are choosing the substitution, you can choose $a > 0$. For a given value of $\sin u$ there are two possible values of $\cos u$. You can choose the u that gives the positive value.

$\therefore \int \dfrac{1}{\sqrt{a^2 - x^2}}\, dx = \int \dfrac{1}{a\cos u}\, a\cos u\, du$

> Make the substitution and integrate.

$= \int 1\, du = u + c$

$= \sin^{-1}\left(\dfrac{x}{a}\right) + c$

> Write the answer in terms of x:
>
> $x = a\sin u \Rightarrow u = \sin^{-1}\left(\dfrac{x}{a}\right).$

You can derive the result $\int \dfrac{1}{a^2 + x^2}\,dx = \dfrac{1}{a}\tan^{-1}\left(\dfrac{x}{a}\right) + c$ similarly, using the substitution $x = a\tan u$ and the identity $1 + \tan^2 u \equiv \sec^2 u$.

 **Fast forward**

You will be asked to derive this result in Question 8 in Exercise 7C.

WORKED EXAMPLE 7.6

Use the substitution $x = a\sinh u$ to prove the result $\int \dfrac{1}{\sqrt{a^2 + x^2}}\,dx = \sinh^{-1}\left(\dfrac{x}{a}\right) + c$.

$\dfrac{dx}{du} = a\cosh u$

$\Rightarrow dx = a\cosh u\,du$

> Differentiate the substitution and express dx in terms of du.

$\dfrac{1}{\sqrt{a^2 + x^2}} = \dfrac{1}{\sqrt{a^2 + a^2\sinh^2 u}}$

$= \dfrac{1}{\sqrt{a^2\left(1 + \sinh^2 u\right)}}$

> Express the integrand in terms of u.

$= \dfrac{1}{\sqrt{a^2\cosh^2 u}}$

> Use $\cosh^2 u - \sinh^2 u \equiv 1$.

$= \dfrac{1}{a\cosh u}$

> Since you are choosing the substitution, you can choose $a > 0$.

$\therefore \int \dfrac{1}{\sqrt{a^2 + x^2}}\,dx = \int \dfrac{1}{a\cosh u}\,a\cosh u\,du$

> Make the substitution and integrate.

$= \int 1\,du = u + c$

$= \sinh^{-1}\left(\dfrac{x}{a}\right) + c$

> Write the answer in terms of x:
> $$x = a\sinh u \Rightarrow u = \sinh^{-1}\left(\dfrac{x}{a}\right).$$

You can derive the result $\int \dfrac{1}{\sqrt{x^2 - a^2}}\,dx = \cosh^{-1}\left(\dfrac{x}{a}\right) + c$ similarly, using the substitution $x = a\cosh u$ and the identity $\cosh^2 u - \sinh^2 u \equiv 1$.

You can combine these results with algebraic manipulation to integrate an even wider variety of functions.

▶▶ **Fast forward**

You will be asked to derive this result in Question 9 in Exercise 7C.

WORKED EXAMPLE 7.7

Find $\displaystyle\int \frac{3}{9x^2+5}\,dx$.

$$\int \frac{3}{9x^2+5}\,dx = \int \frac{3}{(3x)^2+\left(\sqrt{5}\right)^2}\,dx$$

You can turn the integrand into the form $\dfrac{1}{u^2+a^2}$ (with $a=\sqrt{5}$) by making a substitution $u=3x$.

$$=\frac{1}{3}\frac{3}{\sqrt{5}}\tan^{-1}\left(\frac{x}{\sqrt{5}}\right)+c$$

Since the substitution is linear, you can simply divide by the coefficient of x.

$$=\frac{1}{\sqrt{5}}\tan^{-1}\left(\frac{x}{\sqrt{5}}\right)+c$$

If the denominator is not in the form x^2+a^2 or $\sqrt{a^2-x^2}$, you might need to complete the square to write it in this form.

WORKED EXAMPLE 7.8

Find $\displaystyle\int \frac{1}{\sqrt{4x^2-12x-7}}\,dx$.

$$4x^2-12x-7=\left(4x^2-12x\right)-7$$

The expression in the denominator is quadratic, so you should check whether you can complete the square to write it in the form u^2-a^2.

$$=(2x-3)^2-9-7$$

$$=(2x-3)^2-16$$

Hence

$$\int \frac{1}{\sqrt{4x^2-12x-7}}\,dx = \int \frac{1}{\sqrt{(2x-3)^2-16}}\,dx$$

$$=\frac{1}{2}\cosh^{-1}\left(\frac{2x-3}{4}\right)+c$$

The integrand is of the form $\dfrac{1}{\sqrt{u^2-a^2}}$ with $u=2x-3$ and $a=4$. Remember to divide by the coefficient of x when integrating.

EXERCISE 7C

1 Find each indefinite integral.

a i $\displaystyle\int \frac{3}{x^2+4}\,dx$ ii $\displaystyle\int \frac{5}{x^2+36}\,dx$

b i $\displaystyle\int \frac{1}{9x^2+4}\,dx$ ii $\displaystyle\int \frac{4}{4x^2+25}\,dx$

c i $\displaystyle\int \frac{6}{2x^2+3}\,dx$ ii $\displaystyle\int \frac{10}{5x^2+2}\,dx$

d **i** $\displaystyle\int \frac{2}{\sqrt{9-x^2}}\,dx$ **ii** $\displaystyle\int \frac{5}{\sqrt{4-x^2}}\,dx$

e **i** $\displaystyle\int \frac{1}{\sqrt{9-4x^2}}\,dx$ **ii** $\displaystyle\int \frac{3}{\sqrt{25-9x^2}}\,dx$

f **i** $\displaystyle\int \frac{15}{\sqrt{5-3x^2}}\,dx$ **ii** $\displaystyle\int \frac{6}{\sqrt{7-12x^2}}\,dx$

2 Find each indefinite integral.

a **i** $\displaystyle\int \frac{3}{\sqrt{16+x^2}}\,dx$ **ii** $\displaystyle\int \frac{5}{\sqrt{25+x^2}}\,dx$

b **i** $\displaystyle\int \frac{10}{\sqrt{25+9x^2}}\,dx$ **ii** $\displaystyle\int \frac{3}{\sqrt{9+4x^2}}\,dx$

c **i** $\displaystyle\int \frac{4}{\sqrt{3+2x^2}}\,dx$ **ii** $\displaystyle\int \frac{6}{\sqrt{5+7x^2}}\,dx$

d **i** $\displaystyle\int \frac{2}{\sqrt{x^2-49}}\,dx$ **ii** $\displaystyle\int \frac{7}{\sqrt{x^2-36}}\,dx$

e **i** $\displaystyle\int \frac{1}{\sqrt{9x^2-16}}\,dx$ **ii** $\displaystyle\int \frac{15}{\sqrt{25x^2-36}}\,dx$

f **i** $\displaystyle\int \frac{5}{\sqrt{3x^2-7}}\,dx$ **ii** $\displaystyle\int \frac{2}{\sqrt{7x^2-11}}\,dx$

3 By first completing the square, find:

a **i** $\displaystyle\int \frac{1}{x^2+4x+5}\,dx$ **ii** $\displaystyle\int \frac{1}{x^2-6x+10}\,dx$

b **i** $\displaystyle\int \frac{1}{\sqrt{8x-x^2-15}}\,dx$ **ii** $\displaystyle\int \frac{1}{\sqrt{2x-x^2}}\,dx$

c **i** $\displaystyle\int \frac{6}{x^2+10x+27}\,dx$ **ii** $\displaystyle\int \frac{5}{\sqrt{-4x^2-12x}}\,dx$

d **i** $\displaystyle\int \frac{1}{\sqrt{x^2+6x+10}}\,dx$ **ii** $\displaystyle\int \frac{1}{\sqrt{x^2+4x+5}}\,dx$

e **i** $\displaystyle\int \frac{1}{\sqrt{x^2-4x-12}}\,dx$ **ii** $\displaystyle\int \frac{1}{\sqrt{x^2-2x}}\,dx$

f **i** $\displaystyle\int \frac{6}{\sqrt{4x^2-12x+4}}\,dx$ **ii** $\displaystyle\int \frac{3}{\sqrt{x^2+2x+5}}\,dx$

4 Find the exact value of $\displaystyle\int_0^4 \frac{1}{\sqrt{x^2+16}}\,dx$.

5 Find the exact value of $\displaystyle\int_0^{\frac{\sqrt{3}}{2}} \frac{3}{1+4x^2}\,dx$.

6 Find the exact value of $\displaystyle\int_{\frac{1}{\sqrt{3}}}^1 \frac{1}{\sqrt{4-3x^2}}\,dx$.

7 Find:

a $\displaystyle\int \frac{1}{1+9x^2}\,dx$ **b** $\displaystyle\int \frac{16}{16+x^2}\,dx$

8 **a** Use a trigonometric substitution to prove that $\int \dfrac{1}{a^2+x^2}\,dx = \dfrac{1}{a}\tan^{-1}\left(\dfrac{x}{a}\right)+c.$

    b Hence evaluate $\displaystyle\int_0^2 \dfrac{5}{4+x^2}\,dx.$

9 **a** Use a hyperbolic substitution to prove that $\int \dfrac{1}{\sqrt{x^2-a^2}}\,dx = \cosh^{-1}\left(\dfrac{x}{a}\right)+c, \quad x>a.$

    b Hence evaluate $\displaystyle\int_3^6 \dfrac{2}{\sqrt{x^2-9}}\,dx$, giving your answer in terms of a natural logarithm.

10 **a** Write $2x^2+4x+11$ in the form $2(x+p)^2+q.$

    b Hence find $\int \dfrac{3}{2x^2+4x+11}\,dx.$

11 **a** Write $1+6x-3x^2$ in the form $a^2-3(x-b)^2.$

    b Hence find the exact value of $\displaystyle\int_1^2 \dfrac{1}{\sqrt{1+6x-3x^2}}\,dx.$

12 **a** Using a suitable substitution prove that, when $|x|<a$,

$$\int \dfrac{1}{\sqrt{a^2-x^2}}\,dx = \sin^{-1}\left(\dfrac{x}{a}\right)+c.$$

    b Find $\int \dfrac{3}{\sqrt{-4x^2-4x+8}}\,dx.$

13 Use a suitable trigonometric substitution to show that

$$\int_{\frac{2}{5}}^{\frac{2\sqrt{3}}{5}} \dfrac{20}{25x^2+4}\,dx = \dfrac{\pi}{6}.$$

14 Find $\int \dfrac{1}{x^2+2x+2}\,dx.$

15 Show that $\displaystyle\int_3^{5.5} \dfrac{10}{4x^2-24x+61}\,dx = \dfrac{\pi}{4}.$

16 Find $\int \dfrac{4x+5}{\sqrt{1-x^2}}\,dx.$

17 Find $\int \dfrac{x+1}{\sqrt{x^2-1}}\,dx.$

18 Find $\int \dfrac{6x-5}{x^2+9}\,dx.$

19 **a** Write $2x^2-8x+17$ in the form $a(x-p)^2+q.$

    b Hence find $\int \dfrac{2x+8}{2x^2-8x+17}\,dx.$

20 Use a suitable hyperbolic substitution to show that

$$\int \sqrt{x^2-9}\,dx = \dfrac{x}{2}\sqrt{x^2-9} - \dfrac{9}{2}\cosh^{-1}\left(\dfrac{x}{3}\right)+c.$$

21 Use a suitable trigonometric substitution to show that

$$\int \sqrt{4-9x^2}\,dx = \dfrac{x}{2}\sqrt{4-9x^2} + \dfrac{2}{3}\sin^{-1}\left(\dfrac{3x}{2}\right)+c.$$

22 a Given that $\tan u = x$ express $\cos u$ and $\sin u$ in terms of x.

b Use a suitable trigonometric substitution to show that

$$\int \frac{1}{1+2x^2+x^4}\,dx = \frac{x}{2(1+x^2)} + \frac{1}{2}\arctan x + c.$$

Section 4: Using partial fractions in integration

You have already used partial fractions to integrate rational expressions with linear and repeated linear factors in the denominator, such as

$\int \frac{2x+1}{(x-1)(x+2)^2}\,dx$. You can now use the results from Section 3 to extend the range of rational functions you can integrate to include those with denominators of the form $(x^2 + q^2)$.

In general, when there is a quadratic factor in the denominator, there are three possibilities:

 Rewind

You met partial fractions in A Level Mathematics Student Book 2, Chapter 5, and then used them in integration in Chapter 11.

- The quadratic factorises into two different linear factors, $(x-p)(x-q)$. The corresponding partial fractions are $\dfrac{A}{x-p} + \dfrac{B}{x-q}$.

- The quadratic is a perfect square, $(x-p)^2$. The corresponding partial fractions are $\dfrac{A}{x-p} + \dfrac{B}{(x-p)^2}$.

- The quadratic does not factorise (the quadratic factor is **irreducible**). For example, (x^2+1) or (x^2+2x+5). Then there is only one corresponding partial fraction, with a numerator of the form $Bx+C$.

> 🔑 **Key point 7.4**
>
> If f(x) is a polynomial of order less than or equal to 2, then
>
> $$\frac{f(x)}{(x-p)(x^2+q^2)} = \frac{A}{x-p} + \frac{Bx+C}{x^2+q^2}$$

WORKED EXAMPLE 7.9

a Express $\dfrac{3x}{(x-1)(x^2+2)}$ in partial fractions.

b Hence find $\displaystyle\int \frac{3x}{(x-1)(x^2+2)}\,dx$.

a $\dfrac{3x}{(x-1)(x^2+2)} = \dfrac{A}{x-1} + \dfrac{Bx+C}{x^2+2}$ ..... Use the form from Key point 7.4.

$3x = A(x^2+2) + (Bx+C)(x-1)$ ..... Multiply through by the common denominator.

Continues on next page ...

$x = 1: 3 = A(1+2) + 0 \Rightarrow A = 1$

$x = 0: 0 = 1(0+2) + (C)(0-1) \Rightarrow C = 2$

Comparing coefficients of x^2:

$0 = 1 + B$

$B = -1$

Hence

$$\frac{3x}{(x-1)(x^2+2)} = \frac{1}{x-1} + \frac{-x+2}{x^2+2}$$

> Substitute in the values of x which make some of the terms zero.

> Look at the coefficient of x^2 to find B.

b $\displaystyle\int \frac{3x}{(x-1)(x^2+2)}\,dx = \int \left(\frac{1}{x-1} + \frac{-x}{x^2+2} + \frac{2}{x^2+2} \right) dx$

$$\int \frac{1}{x-1}\,dx = \ln|x-1|$$

> Integrate each term separately before applying limits. You need to split the second integral into two in order to apply standard results.

$$\int -\frac{x}{x^2+2}\,dx = -\frac{1}{2}\ln|x^2+2|$$

> Here you can use a substitution $u = x^2 + 2$, or the reverse chain rule, as x is half the derivative of $x^2 + 2$.

$$\int \frac{2}{x^2+2}\,dx = \frac{2}{\sqrt{2}}\arctan\left(\frac{x}{\sqrt{2}}\right)$$

> Use $\displaystyle\int \frac{1}{x^2+a^2}\,dx = \frac{1}{a}\arctan\left(\frac{x}{a}\right)$ with $a = \sqrt{2}$.

Hence

$$\int \frac{3x}{(x-1)(x^2+2)}\,dx = \ln|x-1| - \frac{1}{2}\ln|x^2+2| + \sqrt{2}\arctan\left(\frac{x}{\sqrt{2}}\right) + c$$

If there is a quadratic factor in the denominator, you first need to check whether it is irreducible or whether it can be factorised. If a quadratic factor is irreducible, you need to write it in completed square form before you can apply standard integration results.

WORKED EXAMPLE 7.10

Given that $\dfrac{dy}{dx} = \dfrac{16x+36}{(x^2-4)(x^2+4x+5)}$, find an expression for y in terms of x.

The denominator is

$(x-2)(x+2)(x^2+4x+5)$.

> You need to split the function into partial fractions before integrating.

Hence

$$\frac{16x+36}{(x^2-4)(x^2+4x+5)} = \frac{A}{x-2} + \frac{B}{x+2} + \frac{(Cx+D)}{x^2+4x+5}$$

> Check whether the quadratic factors factorise. The second one has the discriminant $4^2 - 20 < 0$ so it is irreducible.

Continues on next page ...

$$16x+36=A(x+2)(x^2+4x+5)+B(x-2)(x^2+4x+5)$$

$$+(Cx+D)(x-2)(x+2)$$

Multiply through by the denominator.

$$x=2:68=A(4)(17)\Rightarrow A=1$$

Substitute in suitable values of x.

$$x=-2:4=B(-4)(1)\Rightarrow B=-1$$

$$x=0:36=1(2)(5)-1(-2)(5)+D(-2)(2)\Rightarrow D=-4$$

$$x=1:52=1(3)(10)-1(-1)(10)+(C-4)(-1)(3)\Rightarrow C=0$$

$$y=\int\left(\frac{1}{x-2}-\frac{1}{x+2}-\frac{4}{x^2+4x+5}\right)dx$$

$$\int\frac{4}{(x+2)^2+1}\,dx=4\arctan(x+2)$$

For the third integral, you need to complete the square and then use $\int\dfrac{1}{x^2+a^2}\,dx=\arctan\left(\dfrac{x}{a}\right)$.

$$\therefore y=\ln\left|\frac{x-2}{x+2}\right|-4\arctan(x+2)+c$$

EXERCISE 7D

1 Use partial fractions to find each integral.

a **i** $\displaystyle\int\frac{2x^2+x+7}{(x^2+2)(x+3)}\,dx$ **ii** $\displaystyle\int\frac{-x^2+2x-5}{(x^2+1)(x-2)}\,dx$

b **i** $\displaystyle\int\frac{2x^2+13x+21}{(x+1)(x^2+6x+10)}\,dx$ **ii** $\displaystyle\int\frac{x^2-2x+13}{(x-2)(x^2+2x+5)}\,dx$

c **i** $\displaystyle\int\frac{-x^2+3x-2}{(x^2+1)(x+1)}\,dx$ **ii** $\displaystyle\int\frac{-3x-2}{(x^2+4)(x-1)}\,dx$

d **i** $\displaystyle\int\frac{x^3+2x^2+x+8}{(x+1)^2(x^2+3)}\,dx$ **ii** $\displaystyle\int\frac{x^3+x^2-7x+7}{(x-2)^2(x^2+1)}\,dx$

2 Use partial fractions to find the exact value of $\displaystyle\int_0^1\frac{-2x^2+x-1}{(x+1)(x^2+1)}\,dx$

3 **a** Write $\dfrac{x^2-x+11}{(x-2)(x^2+9)}$ in partial fractions.

b Given that $\dfrac{dy}{dx}=\dfrac{x^2-x+11}{(x-2)(x^2+9)}$, and that $y=0$ when $x=0$, find y in terms of x.

4 Use partial fractions to integrate:

a $\dfrac{3x^2+x-5}{(x-2)(x^2+2x+1)}$ **b** $\dfrac{x^2+4x-2}{(x-2)(x^2+2x+2)}.$

5 Let $f(x) = \dfrac{2x^3 + x^2 + 8x - 4}{(x^2 - 4)(x^2 + 4)}$.

    a Write $f(x)$ in partial fractions.   **b** Hence find the exact value of $\displaystyle\int_0^{2\sqrt{3}} f(x)\,dx$.

6 Let $f(x) = \dfrac{x^3 + 4x^2 + 3x + 4}{(x+1)^2(x^2+1)}$. Use partial fractions to evaluate $\displaystyle\int_0^1 f(x)\,dx$.

7 Use partial fractions to find $\displaystyle\int \dfrac{2x^2 + 4x + 18}{(x^2 + 2x - 3)(x^2 + 2x + 3)}\,dx$.

8 Show that

$$\int \frac{2x^2 + 3x - 3}{(x^2 + 2x + 5)(x+1)}\,dx = P\ln(x^2 + 2x + 5) + Q\arctan\left(\frac{x+1}{2}\right) + R\ln|x+1| + c$$

where P, Q and R are constants to be found.

Checklist of learning and understanding

- Derivatives of inverse trigonometric functions:

  - $\dfrac{d}{dx}(\sin^{-1} x) = \dfrac{1}{\sqrt{1-x^2}}, \; |x| < 1$

  - $\dfrac{d}{dx}(\cos^{-1} x) = \dfrac{-1}{\sqrt{1-x^2}}, \; |x| < 1$

  - $\dfrac{d}{dx}(\tan^{-1} x) = \dfrac{1}{1+x^2}$

- Derivatives of inverse hyperbolic functions:

  - $\dfrac{d}{dx}(\sinh^{-1} x) = \dfrac{1}{\sqrt{x^2+1}}$

  - $\dfrac{d}{dx}(\cosh^{-1} x) = \dfrac{1}{\sqrt{x^2-1}}, \; x > 1$

  - $\dfrac{d}{dx}(\tanh^{-1} x) = \dfrac{1}{1-x^2}, \; |x| < 1$

- You can derive the corresponding integrals using a trigonometric substitution ($x = a\sin u$ or $x = a\tan u$) or a hyperbolic substitution ($x = a\sinh u$ or $x = a\cosh u$):

  - $\displaystyle\int \dfrac{1}{\sqrt{a^2 - x^2}}\,dx = \sin^{-1}\left(\dfrac{x}{a}\right) + c, \; |x| < a$

  - $\displaystyle\int \dfrac{1}{a^2 + x^2}\,dx = \dfrac{1}{a}\tan^{-1}\left(\dfrac{x}{a}\right) + c$

  - $\displaystyle\int \dfrac{1}{\sqrt{a^2 + x^2}}\,dx = \sinh^{-1}\left(\dfrac{x}{a}\right) + c$

  - $\displaystyle\int \dfrac{1}{\sqrt{x^2 - a^2}}\,dx = \cosh^{-1}\left(\dfrac{x}{a}\right) + c, \; x > a$

- You might need to write a quadratic expression in completed square form in order to apply one of the results shown.

- When splitting an expression into partial fractions, if the denominator has an irreducible quadratic factor $x^2 + px + q$, then the corresponding partial fraction is $\dfrac{Ax + B}{x^2 + px + q}$.

Mixed practice 7

1 Differentiate $f(x) = \arctan(e^x)$.

2 Find $\dfrac{dy}{dx}$ when $y = x^2 \sin^{-1} x$.

3 Differentiate $f(x) = \cos^{-1}(1 - x^2)$.

4 Find the x-coordinates of the points on the curve $y = \tanh^{-1}\left(\dfrac{x}{2}\right)$ where the gradient is 2.

5 By first completing the square, find the exact value of $\displaystyle\int_{\frac{1}{2}}^{1} \dfrac{1}{\sqrt{2x - x^2}}\, dx$.

© OCR A Level Mathematics, Unit 4726/01 Further Pure Mathematics 2, June 2015

6 It is given that $f(x) = \dfrac{x^2 + 9x}{(x-1)(x^2 + 9)}$.

   i Express $f(x)$ in partial fractions.

   ii Hence find $\int f(x)\, dx$.

© OCR A Level Mathematics, Unit 4726/01 Further Pure Mathematics 2, June 2007

7 Given that $y = \tan^{-1}(x^2)$, find $\dfrac{d^2 y}{dx^2}$.

8 Show that $y = (\operatorname{arsinh} x)^2$ satisfies $(1 + x^2)\dfrac{d^2 y}{dx^2} + x\dfrac{dy}{dx} - 2 = 0$.

9 Find $\displaystyle\int \dfrac{6x + 4}{x^2 + 4}\, dx$.

10 Find $\displaystyle\int \dfrac{1}{2 - 2x + x^2}\, dx$.

In questions 11 and 12 you must show detailed reasoning.

11 Given that

$$\int_0^1 \dfrac{1}{\sqrt{16 + 9x^2}}\, dx + \int_0^2 \dfrac{1}{\sqrt{9 + 4x^2}}\, dx = \ln a,$$

find the exact value of a.

© OCR A Level Mathematics, Unit 4726 Further Pure Mathematics 2, June 2009

> **Tip**
>
> Remember that 'show detailed reasoning' means that you need to show full algebraic working, rather than using your calculator to evaluate indefinite integrals.

12 **i** Given that

$$y = x\sqrt{1 - x^2} - \cos^{-1} x,$$

   find $\dfrac{dy}{dx}$ in a simplified form.

   ii Hence, or otherwise, find the exact value of $\displaystyle\int_0^1 2\sqrt{1 - x^2}\, dx$.

© OCR A Level Mathematics, Unit 4726/01 Further Pure Mathematics 2, June 2007

13 **i** Express $\dfrac{4}{(1-x)(1+x)(1+x^2)}$ in partial fractions.

   ii Show that $\displaystyle\int_0^{\frac{1}{\sqrt{3}}} \dfrac{4}{1 - x^4}\, dx = \ln\left(\dfrac{\sqrt{3} + 1}{\sqrt{3} - 1}\right) + \dfrac{1}{3}\pi$.

© OCR A Level Mathematics, Unit 4726/01 Further Pure Mathematics 2, January 2010

14 **a** Show that $\sqrt{\dfrac{1-3x}{1+3x}} = \dfrac{1-3x}{\sqrt{1-9x^2}}$.

b Hence find $\displaystyle\int \sqrt{\dfrac{1-3x}{1+3x}}\,dx$.

15 Use the substitution $x = 9\sinh^2\theta$ to show that

$$\int_0^1 \sqrt{\dfrac{x+9}{x}}\,dx = 9\sinh^{-1}\left(\dfrac{1}{3}\right) + \sqrt{A}$$

and state the value of the integer A.

16 **a** Split $\dfrac{4-3x}{(x+2)(x^2+1)}$ into partial fractions.

b Hence find $\displaystyle\int \dfrac{4-3x}{(x+2)(x^2+1)}\,dx$.

c Find the exact value of $\displaystyle\int_0^{\frac{\sqrt{3}}{2}} \dfrac{4-3x}{\sqrt{1-x^2}}\,dx$.

17 **a** Show that $\displaystyle\int \sqrt{k^2-x^2}\,dx = \dfrac{k^2}{2}\arcsin\left(\dfrac{x}{k}\right) + \dfrac{x}{2}\sqrt{k^2-x^2} + c$.

b Hence show that the area enclosed by the ellipse with equation $\dfrac{x^2}{a^2} + \dfrac{y^2}{b^2} = 1$ is πab.

18 **i** Prove that $\dfrac{d}{dx}\left(\cosh^{-1}x\right) = \dfrac{1}{\sqrt{x^2-1}}$.

ii Hence, or otherwise, find $\displaystyle\int \dfrac{1}{\sqrt{4x^2-1}}\,dx$.

iii By means of a suitable substitution, find $\displaystyle\int \sqrt{4x^2-1}\,dx$.

© **OCR A Level Mathematics, Unit 4726/01 Further Pure Mathematics 2, January 2008**

8 Applications of calculus

In this chapter you will learn how to:

- find infinite series expansions (called Maclaurin series) of functions
- use given results to find the Maclaurin series of more complicated functions
- understand for which values of x these series are valid
- find the value of definite integrals in certain cases where a limiting process is required (improper integrals)
- find the volume of a shape formed by rotating a curve around the x-axis or the y-axis
- find the mean value of a function.

Before you start…

A Level Mathematics Student Book 2, Chapter 10	You should know how to differentiate functions using the chain rule.	1 For $f(x) = \left(x^2 + 3\right)^5$, find $f'(x)$.
A Level Mathematics Student Book 2, Chapter 9	You should know how to differentiate exponential, logarithmic and trigonometric functions.	2 For each function, find: i $f'(x)$ ii $f''(x)$. a $f(x) = e^{-2x}$ b $f(x) = \ln x$ c $f(x) = \cos 3x$
Chapter 6	You should know how to differentiate hyperbolic functions.	3 For $f(x) = \tanh x$, find: a $f'(x)$ b $f''(x)$.
Chapter 6	You should know how to differentiate inverse hyperbolic functions.	4 For $f(x) = \cosh^{-1} x$, find: a $f'(x)$ b $f''(x)$.
Chapter 7	You should know how to differentiate inverse trigonometric functions.	5 For $f(x) = \sin^{-1} x$, find: a $f'(x)$ b $f''(x)$.

Introduction

In the first part of this chapter you will see that, with certain restrictions, you can write many functions as infinite series in ascending positive integer powers of x. Being able to take a number of terms of the infinite series as an approximation to a given function has many uses; for example, calculators and computers use these series to evaluate a function at a particular value or to produce an approximation for definite integrals of functions that can't be integrated using standard functions.

You will also look at definite integrals where either the integrand is not defined at one or more points in the range of integration or where the range of integration extends to infinity. These are known as improper integrals.

Finally, you will see two further applications of calculus: finding volumes and finding the mean value of a function.

Section 1: Maclaurin series

You know from A Level Mathematics Student Book 2, Chapter 6, that functions such as $(1-3x)^{-2}$ and $\sqrt{1+x}$ can be written as infinite series using the binomial expansion. In general, for some function f(x) such a series will be of the form

$f(x) = a_0 + a_1 x + a_2 x^2 + a_3 x^3 + \ldots$ where a_0, a_1, a_2, etc. are real constants.

Differentiating this series several times:

$$f'(x) = a_1 + 2a_2 x + 3a_3 x^2 + 4a_4 x^3 + \ldots$$
$$f''(x) = 2a_2 + (3 \times 2)a_3 x + (4 \times 3)a_4 x^2 + \ldots$$
$$f'''(x) = (3 \times 2)a_3 + (4 \times 3 \times 2)a_4 x + \ldots$$
$$\vdots$$

Substituting $x = 0$ into f(x) and each of its derivatives to find expressions for a_0, a_1, a_2, etc:

$$f(0) = a_0$$
$$f'(0) = a_1$$
$$f''(0) = 2!a_2$$
$$f'''(0) = 3!a_3$$
$$\vdots$$

Substituting these expressions for a_0, a_1, a_2, etc. back into the expression for f(x) gives the **Maclaurin series** formula for any function.

> ### ⓘ Did you know?
>
> Maclaurin series are named after the 18th-century mathematician Colin Maclaurin, who also developed some of Newton's work on calculus, algebra and gravitation theory.

You are assuming here that you can differentiate an infinite series term by term in the same way as a finite series. In fact, this is only possible for values of x within the interval of convergence of the series.

> ### Fast forward
>
> You will meet the interval of convergence for some standard functions in Section 2.

You can use Key point 8.1 to find the first few terms of a Maclaurin series. You can sometimes spot a pattern in the derivatives, which enables you to also write down the **general term**, $\dfrac{f^{(r)}(0)}{r!}x^r$.

Key point 8.1

The Maclaurin series of a function $f(x)$ is given by

$$f(x)=f(0)+f'(0)x+\frac{f''(0)}{2!}x^2+\ldots+\frac{f^{(r)}(0)}{r!}x^r+\ldots$$

WORKED EXAMPLE 8.1

a Find the first three non-zero terms in the Maclaurin series of $\sin x$.
b Write down a conjecture for the general term (you need not prove your conjecture).

a $f(x)=\sin x \Rightarrow f(0)=0$ — Find $f(0)$.

$f'(x)=\cos x \Rightarrow f'(0)=1$ — Then differentiate and evaluate each derivative at $x=0$.

$f''(x)=-\sin x \Rightarrow f''(0)=0$

$f'''(x)=-\cos x \Rightarrow f'''(0)=-1$ — Notice that you need to go as far as the fifth derivative to get three non-zero terms.

$f^{(4)}(x)=\sin x \Rightarrow f^{(4)}(0)=0$

$f^{(5)}(x)=\cos x \Rightarrow f^{(5)}(0)=1$

So

$f(x)=0+1x+\dfrac{0}{2!}x^2+\dfrac{-1}{3!}x^3+\dfrac{0}{4!}x^4+\dfrac{1}{5!}x^5\ldots$

Substitute these values into the Maclaurin series formula:

$\quad =x-\dfrac{x^3}{3!}+\dfrac{x^5}{5!}+\ldots$

$$f(x)=f(0)+f'(0)x+\frac{f''(0)}{2!}x^2+\ldots$$

b The general term is

$\dfrac{(-1)^n\cos(0)}{(2n+1)!}x^{2n+1}\ldots$

The series will only contain terms with odd powers because even derivatives are $\pm\sin x$, and $\sin(0)=0$.

$\quad =\dfrac{(-1)^n}{(2n+1)!}x^{2n+1}\ldots$

Because of the pattern of differentiating $\sin x$, the signs will alternate between $+$ and $-$.

Not every function has a Maclaurin series. For example, for $f(x)=\ln x$, $f(0)$ doesn't exist (nor do any of the derivatives of $\ln x$ at $x=0$). However, $f(x)=\ln(1+x)$ does have a Maclaurin series as now $f(0)$, and all the derivatives at $x=0$, do exist.

WORKED EXAMPLE 8.2

a Find the Maclaurin series of $\ln(1+x)$ up to and including the term in x^4.

b Prove by induction that the general term is $\dfrac{(-1)^{n-1}}{n}x^n$.

a $f(x)=\ln(1+x) \Rightarrow f(0)=0$ ··· Find f(0).

$f'(x)=(1+x)^{-1} \Rightarrow f'(0)=1$

$f''(x)=-(1+x)^{-2} \Rightarrow f''(0)=-1$ ··· Then differentiate and evaluate each derivative at $x=0$.

$f'''(x)=2(1+x)^{-3} \Rightarrow f'''(0)=2$

$f^{(4)}(x)=-6(1+x)^{-4} \Rightarrow f^{(4)}(0)=-6$

So

$f(x)=0+1x-\dfrac{1}{2!}x^2+\dfrac{2}{3!}x^3-\dfrac{6}{4!}x^4+\dots$ ···

Substitute these values into the Maclaurin series formula:

$f(x)=f(0)+f'(0)x+\dfrac{f''(0)}{2!}x^2+\dots$

$=x-\dfrac{x^2}{2}+\dfrac{x^3}{3}-\dfrac{x^4}{4}+\dots$

b To prove:

$f^{(n)}(x)=(-1)^{n-1}(n-1)!(1+x)^{-n}$ ···

To find the general term you need an expression for the nth derivative, which you then divide by $n!$ to get the coefficient of x_n. You can conjecture the expression by looking at the first four derivatives you found in part **a**.

When $n=1$:

$f'(x)=(1+x)^{-1}$

$=(-1)^0(0!)(1+x)^{-1}$ ···

Show that the expression is correct when $n=1$.

Hence the expression is correct for $n=1$.

Suppose that the expression is correct for the kth derivative: ···

Now suppose that the expression is correct for some k and show that it is still correct for $k+1$.

$f^{(k)}(x)=(-1)^{k-1}(k-1)!(1+x)^{-k}$

Then the $(k+1)$th derivative is: ···

Differentiate $f^{(k)}$ to get $f^{(k+1)}$.

$f^{(k+1)}(x)=(-1)^{k-1}(k-1)!(-k)(1+x)^{-(k+1)}$

$=(-1)^k k!(1+x)^{-(k+1)}$ ···

The negative sign in $-k$ changes the sign of the whole expression.

Hence the expression is correct for the $(k+1)$th derivative.

$(k-1)!\,k=k!$

The expression is correct for $n=1$ and, if it is correct for $n=k$, then it is also correct for $n=k+1$. It is therefore true for all $n \geqslant 1$, by the principle of mathematical induction. ···

Write a conclusion.

One use of Maclaurin series is to approximate definite integrals of functions that can't be integrated by standard methods.

> **Tip**
>
> The question will make it clear whether you are required to find the Maclaurin series of a function from first principles or whether you can use one of the standard results in the formula book to find the series you need.

> **▶▶) Fast forward**
>
> In Section 2 you will see how to use the Maclaurin series of certain standard functions to find the series of more complicated functions.

WORKED EXAMPLE 8.3

a Use the Maclaurin series of $\sin x$ to find the first three non-zero terms in the Maclaurin series of $\sin(x^2)$.

b Hence find an approximate value for $\int_0^{\frac{\pi}{3}} \sin(x^2)\,dx$, giving your answer to three decimal places.

a $\sin(x^2) = (x^2) - \dfrac{(x^2)^3}{3!} + \dfrac{(x^2)^5}{5!} - \cdots$ Substitute x^2 into the series for $\sin x$.

$= x^2 - \dfrac{x^6}{3!} + \dfrac{x^{10}}{5!} - \cdots$

b $\int_0^{\frac{\pi}{3}} \sin(x^2)\,dx \approx \int_0^{\frac{\pi}{3}} \left(x^2 - \dfrac{x^6}{3!} + \dfrac{x^{10}}{5!} \right) dx$

$= \left[\dfrac{x^3}{3} - \dfrac{x^7}{7 \times 3!} + \dfrac{x^{11}}{11 \times 5!} \right]_0^{\frac{\pi}{3}}$ Integrate the polynomial as usual.

≈ 0.351

EXERCISE 8A

1 Using Key point 8.1, find the first four non-zero terms of the Maclaurin series of these functions. Also conjecture the general term for each series (you need not prove your conjecture).

a i e^x **ii** e^{-3x}

b i $\sin(-x)$ **ii** $\sin 2x$

c i $\cos x$ **ii** $\cos 3x$

d i $\ln(1-x)$ **ii** $\ln(1+2x)$

e i $\sinh x$ **ii** $\sinh 2x$

f i $\cosh x$ **ii** $\cosh(-x)$

2 Find the Maclaurin series of $f(x) = \sqrt{3+e^x}$ up to and including the term in x^2.

3 a Show that the first two non-zero terms in the Maclaurin series of $\tan x$ are $x + \dfrac{1}{3}x^3$.

b Hence find, to three decimal places, an approximation to $\tan\dfrac{\pi}{10}$.

4 It is given that $f(x) = e^{-x^2}$.

a i Find the first four derivatives of $f(x)$.

ii Hence find the Maclaurin series of $f(x)$, up to and including the term in x^4.

b Use your result from part **a ii** to find an approximation to $\int_0^1 e^{-x^2}\,dx$.

Give your answer in the form $\dfrac{a}{b}$ where a and b are integers.

5 **a** Find the Maclaurin series of $\cos^2 x$ up to and including the term in x^6.

   b Hence state the Maclaurin series of $\sin^2 x$ up to and including the term in x^6.

6 It is given that $f(x)=\ln(1+\sin x)$, $-\dfrac{\pi}{2}<x<\dfrac{3\pi}{2}$.

   a **i** Show that $f'(x)=\dfrac{\cos x}{1+\sin x}$ and $f''(x)=-\dfrac{1}{1+\sin x}$

   ii Find the third and fourth derivatives of f.

   b Hence find the Maclaurin series of $\ln(1+\sin x)$ up to and including the term in x^4.

   c Use your series from part **b** to find an approximation to $\int_0^{\frac{\pi}{6}}\ln(1+\sin x)\,dx$, giving your answer to three decimal places.

7 The function f is defined by $f(x)=\ln\left(\dfrac{1}{1-x}\right)$, $-1<x<1$.

   a **i** Find the first three derivatives of $f(x)$.

   ii Hence show that the Maclaurin series for $f(x)$ up to and including the x^3 term is $x+\dfrac{x^2}{2}+\dfrac{x^3}{3}$.

   b Use the series from part **a ii** to find an approximate value for $\ln 3$. Give your answer in the form $\dfrac{a}{b}$, where a and b are integers.

8 **a** Given that $f(x)=x\,e^x$, use induction to show that $f^{(n)}(x)=(n+x)e^x$.

   b Hence find the general term in the Maclaurin series for $f(x)$.

9 **a** Given that $f(x)=\dfrac{1}{1-5x}$, prove by induction that $f^{(n)}(x)=\dfrac{5^n n!}{(1-5x)^{n+1}}$.

   b Hence find the general term in the Maclaurin series for $\dfrac{1}{1-5x}$.

10 **a** Find the first three non-zero terms in the Maclaurin series for $\arcsin x$.

   b **i** Let $f(x)=\arcsin x$ and $g(x)=\arccos x$. State the relationship between $f^{(n)}(x)$, the nth derivative of $f(x)$, and $g^{(n)}(x)$, the nth derivative of $g(x)$, for any integer $n>0$.

   ii Hence show that $\arcsin x+\arccos x=k$, where k is a constant to be determined.

11 The diagram shows part of the graph of $y=f(x)$.

Explain why neither of these can be Maclaurin series of the function $f(x)$:

a $\dfrac{1}{2}+\dfrac{x}{2}+\dfrac{x^2}{8}+\dots$ **b** $1-3x-\dfrac{x^2}{4}+\dots$

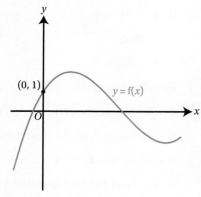

Section 2: Using standard Maclaurin series

The Maclaurin series of a few standard functions are given in your formula book. These can often be used, without needing to be derived, to find the series for more complicated functions.

> **🔑 Key point 8.2**
>
> Maclaurin series for some common functions and the values of x for which they are valid:
>
> - $e^x = \exp(x) = 1 + x + \dfrac{x^2}{2!} + \ldots + \dfrac{x^r}{r!} + \ldots$ for all x
>
> - $\ln(1+x) = x - \dfrac{x^2}{2} + \dfrac{x^3}{3} - \ldots + (-1)^{r+1}\dfrac{x^r}{r} + \ldots \; -1 < x \leqslant 1$
>
> - $\sin x = x - \dfrac{x^3}{3!} + \dfrac{x^5}{5!} - \ldots + (-1)^r \dfrac{x^{2r+1}}{(2r+1)!} + \ldots$ for all x
>
> - $\cos x = 1 - \dfrac{x^2}{2!} + \dfrac{x^4}{4!} - \ldots + (-1)^r \dfrac{x^{2r}}{(2r)!} + \ldots$ for all x
>
> - $(1+x)^n = 1 + nx + \dfrac{n(n-1)}{2!}x^2 + \ldots + \dfrac{n(n-1)\ldots(n-r+1)}{r!}x^r + \ldots |x| < 1, n \in \mathbb{R}$
>
> **These will be given in your formula book.**

> **💡 Tip**
>
> Don't overlook the information on the values of x for which these series are valid; this is a very important part of each result.

> **⏮ Rewind**
>
> Note that the last result in Key point 8.2 is the binomial expansion, which is covered in A Level Mathematics Student Book 2, Chapter 6.
>
> Note also that replacing x by $\mathrm{i}x$ in the series for e^x gives the same series as adding $\cos x + \mathrm{i}\sin x$, which agrees with Euler's formula from Chapter 2, Section 2.

> **WORKED EXAMPLE 8.4**
>
> **a** Use the Maclaurin series for $\cos x$ to find the first four terms in the series for $\cos(2x^3)$.
> **b** State the values of x for which the series is valid.
>
> **a** $\cos(2x^3) = 1 - \dfrac{(2x^3)^2}{2!} + \dfrac{(2x^3)^4}{4!} - \dfrac{(2x^3)^6}{6!} + \ldots$
>
> $\quad = 1 - \dfrac{4x^6}{2!} + \dfrac{16x^{12}}{4!} - \dfrac{64x^{18}}{6!} + \ldots$
>
> $\quad = 1 - 2x^6 + \dfrac{2}{3}x^{12} - \dfrac{4}{45}x^{18} + \ldots$
>
> *Substitute $2x^3$ into the series for $\cos x$:*
> $\cos x = 1 - \dfrac{x^2}{2!} + \dfrac{x^4}{4!} - \dfrac{x^6}{6!} + \ldots$
>
> *Expand and simplify.*
>
> **b** Valid for all $x \in \mathbb{R}$.
>
> *Both $2x^3$ and $\cos x$ are valid for all $x \in \mathbb{R}$.*

This process can be more complicated if it involves finding two separate Maclaurin series and then combining them.

WORKED EXAMPLE 8.5

a   Use the Maclaurin series for $\sin x$ and that for e^x to find the series for $e^{\sin x}$ as far as the term in x^4.

b   State the values of x for which your series is valid.

a $e^{\sin x} = e^{x - \frac{x^3}{3!} + \cdots}$

> Start by replacing $\sin x$ with its series.

$\approx e^x \times e^{-\frac{x^3}{3!}}$

> Now split this into a product of two terms.

$= \left(1 + x + \dfrac{x^2}{2!} + \dfrac{x^3}{3!} + \dfrac{x^4}{4!} + \cdots\right)\left(1 + \left(-\dfrac{x^3}{3!}\right) + \cdots\right)$

> Then form the series for each of them. For $e^{-\frac{x^3}{3!}}$ substitute $-\dfrac{x^3}{3!}$ into the series for e^x.

$= 1 + x + \dfrac{x^2}{2} + \dfrac{x^3}{6} + \dfrac{x^4}{24} - \dfrac{x^3}{6} - \dfrac{x^4}{6} + \cdots$

$= 1 + x + \dfrac{x^2}{2} - \dfrac{x^4}{8} + \cdots$

> Expand term by term and simplify.

b   Valid for all $x \in \mathbb{R}$.

> The series for both e^x and $\sin x$ are valid for all $x \in \mathbb{R}$.

WORKED EXAMPLE 8.6

a   Find the first three terms in the Maclaurin series for $\ln(2 - 3x)$.

b   Hence find the Maclaurin series up to the term in x^3 for $\ln\left(\dfrac{\sqrt{1+2x}}{2-3x}\right)$.

c   State the interval in which the expansion is valid.

a $\ln(2 - 3x) = \ln\left[2\left(1 - \dfrac{3x}{2}\right)\right]$

$= \ln\left[2\left(1 + \dfrac{-3x}{2}\right)\right]$

> You know the series expansion for $\ln(1 + x)$ so you need to write $\ln(2 - 3x)$ in this form. Start by factorising 2.

$= \ln 2 + \ln\left(1 + \dfrac{-3x}{2}\right)$

> Separate the 2, using $\ln(ab) = \ln a + \ln b$

$= \ln 2 + \left(\dfrac{-3x}{2}\right) - \dfrac{\left(\dfrac{-3x}{2}\right)^2}{2} + \dfrac{\left(\dfrac{-3x}{2}\right)^3}{3} + \cdots$

> Then substitute $\dfrac{-3x}{2}$ into the series of $\ln(1 + x)$:
>
> $\ln(1 + x) = x - \dfrac{x^2}{2} + \dfrac{x^3}{3} - \dfrac{x^4}{4} + \cdots$

$= \ln 2 + \dfrac{-3x}{2} - \dfrac{\dfrac{9x^2}{4}}{2} + \dfrac{\dfrac{-27x^3}{8}}{3} + \cdots$

> Expand and simplify.

$= \ln 2 - \dfrac{3x}{2} - \dfrac{9x^2}{8} - \dfrac{9x^3}{8} + \cdots$

Continues on next page

b $\ln\left(\dfrac{\sqrt{1+2x}}{2-3x}\right) = \ln(\sqrt{1+2x}) - \ln(2-3x)$

Again, you need everything in the form of $\ln(1+x)$. First, use the laws of logs.

$$= \frac{1}{2}\ln(1+2x) - \ln(2-3x)$$

$$\frac{1}{2}\ln(1+2x) = \frac{1}{2}\left((2x) - \frac{(2x)^2}{2} + \frac{(2x)^3}{3} + \cdots\right)$$

For the first term, substitute $2x$ into the series for $\ln(1+x)$.

$$= \frac{1}{2}\left(2x - 2x^2 + \frac{8x^3}{3} + \cdots\right)$$

$$= x - x^2 + \frac{4x^3}{3} + \cdots$$

So:

You know the series expansion for the second term from part **a**.

$$\ln\left(\frac{\sqrt{1+2x}}{2-3x}\right) = \left(x - x^2 + \frac{4x^3}{3} + \cdots\right)$$

Now put both series together.

$$-\left(\ln 2 - \frac{3x}{2} - \frac{9x^2}{8} - \frac{9x^3}{8} + \cdots\right)$$

$$= x - x^2 + \frac{4x^3}{3} + \cdots - \ln 2 + \frac{3x}{2} + \frac{9x^2}{8} + \frac{9x^3}{8} + \cdots$$

$$= -\ln 2 + \frac{5x}{2} + \frac{x^2}{8} + \frac{59x^3}{24} + \cdots$$

c Since $\ln(1+x)$ is valid when $-1 < x \leqslant 1$:

Find the interval of validity separately for each function.

- $\ln\left(1 + \dfrac{-3x}{2}\right)$ is valid when $-1 < \dfrac{-3x}{2} \leqslant 1$

  This is when $-\dfrac{2}{3} \leqslant x < \dfrac{2}{3}$.

- $\ln(1+2x)$ is valid when $-1 < 2x \leqslant 1$

  This is when $-\dfrac{1}{2} < x \leqslant \dfrac{1}{2}$.

Therefore, $\ln\left(\dfrac{\sqrt{1+2x}}{2-3x}\right)$ is valid

when $-\dfrac{1}{2} < x \leqslant \dfrac{1}{2}$.

For both to be valid, you need the smaller interval.

EXERCISE 8B

1 Find the first three non-zero terms and the general term of the Maclaurin series for each expression.

a **i** e^{-3x} **ii** e^{x^3} **b** **i** $\ln(1+3x)$ **ii** $\ln(1-2x)$

c **i** $\sin\left(-\dfrac{x}{2}\right)$ **ii** $\sin(3x^2)$ **d** **i** $\cos\left(\dfrac{x^2}{3}\right)$ **ii** $\cos(-2x)$

e **i** $(1-4x)^{\frac{1}{2}}$ **ii** $\left(1+\dfrac{x}{3}\right)^{-4}$

2 By first manipulating it into an appropriate form, find the first three non-zero terms of the Maclaurin series for each expression.

a **i** $\ln(3+x)$ **ii** $\ln\left(\dfrac{1}{2}-x\right)$

b **i** $(2-3x)^{-3}$ **ii** $\left(\dfrac{1}{4}+2x\right)^{-\frac{1}{2}}$

c **i** $(8x-27)^{\frac{1}{3}}$ **ii** $(3x-4)^{-2}$

3 By combining Maclaurin series of different functions, find the series expansion as far as the term in x^4 for each expression.

a **i** $\ln(1+x)\sin 2x$ **ii** $\ln(1-x)\cos 3x$

b **i** $\dfrac{e^x}{1+x}$ **ii** $\dfrac{\sin x}{1-2x}$

c **i** $\ln(1+\sin x)$ **ii** $\ln(\cos x)$

4 Find the Maclaurin series for $\ln(1+4x^2+4x)$ and state the interval in which the series is valid.

5 Find the Maclaurin series as far as the term in x^4 for $e^{3x}\sin 2x$.

6 Show that $\sqrt{1+x^2}\,e^{-x} = 1-x+x^2-\dfrac{2}{3}x^3+\dfrac{1}{6}x^4+\dots$.

7 **a** Find the first two non-zero terms of the Maclaurin series for $\tan x$.

    b Hence find the Maclaurin series of $e^{\tan x}$ up to and including the term in x^4.

8 **a** By using the Maclaurin series for $\cos x$, find the series expansion for $\ln(\cos x)$ up to the term in x^4.

    b Hence find the first two non-zero terms of the expansion of $\ln(\sec x)$.

    c Use your result from **b** to find the first two non-zero terms of the series for $\tan x$.

9 **a** Find the first four terms of the Maclaurin series for $f(x)=\ln[(2+x)^3(1-3x)]$.

    b Find the equation of the tangent to $f(x)$ at $x=0$.

10 **a** Find the Maclaurin series for $\ln\sqrt{\dfrac{1+x}{1-x}}$, stating the interval in which the series is valid.

    b Use the first three terms of this series to estimate the value of $\ln 2$, stating the value of x used.

Section 3: Improper integrals

Integrals where the range of integration extends to infinity

You are by now very familiar with evaluating definite integrals

$$\int_a^b f(x)dx = g(b) - g(a) \text{ where } g'(x) = f(x).$$

In the examples you have encountered so far, the limits were often convenient, relatively small numbers such as $0, 1, \pi$. However, there is nothing to stop them from being very large numbers; this would make no difference to the method for evaluating the integral.

If you continue along this line and let $b \to \infty$, you can still find a finite value for the integral in certain cases. In much the same way that you have seen that a sequence can either converge to a finite limit or diverge to infinity, so can an integral. Integrals of the form $\int_a^\infty f(x)dx$ are known as **improper integrals**.

To evaluate an improper integral, you need to replace the infinite limit by b, find the value of the integral in terms of b and then consider what happens when $b \to \infty$.

 Key point 8.3

The value of the improper integral $\int_a^\infty f(x)dx$ is

$$\lim_{b \to \infty} \int_a^b f(x)dx = \lim_{b \to \infty}\{I(b)\} - I(a),$$

if this limit exists and is finite.

If this limit is infinite you say that the improper integral diverges (does not have a value).

WORKED EXAMPLE 8.7

a Explain why $\int_0^\infty e^{-3x}\, dx$ is an improper integral.

b Evaluate $\int_0^\infty e^{-3x}\, dx$.

a The integral is improper because the range of integration extends to infinity.

b $\int_0^\infty e^{-3x}\, dx = \lim_{b \to \infty} \int_0^b e^{-3x}\, dx$

> Integrate as normal, but replace the upper limit with b and take the limit as $b \to \infty$ after you have completed the integration.

$$= \lim_{b \to \infty}\left[-\frac{1}{3}e^{-3x} \right]_0^b$$

$$= \lim_{b \to \infty}\left(-\frac{1}{3}e^{-3b} + \frac{1}{3} \right)$$

$$= \lim_{b \to \infty}\left(-\frac{1}{3}e^{-3b} \right) + \frac{1}{3}$$

$$= \frac{1}{3}$$

> As $b \to \infty$, $e^{-3b} \to 0$. Therefore the integral converges.

WORKED EXAMPLE 8.8

Explain why the improper integral $\int_2^\infty \frac{1}{x}\,dx$ diverges.

$\int_2^\infty \frac{1}{x}dx = \lim_{b\to\infty}\int_2^\infty \frac{1}{x}dx$ .... Integrate as normal, but replace the upper limit with b and consider the limit as $b\to\infty$ after you have completed the integration.

$= \lim_{b\to\infty}\left[\ln x\right]_2^b$

When $b\to\infty$, $\ln x$ tends to infinity.

Therefore the integral diverges.

When evaluating improper integrals, you might need to use some more complicated limits. These will be given in each question.

WORKED EXAMPLE 8.9

Evaluate $\int_0^\infty x e^{-x}\,dx$, showing clearly the limiting process used.

[You can use without proof the result $\lim_{x\to\infty} x^k e^{-x} = 0$, where $k>0$.]

$\int_0^\infty x e^{-x}\,dx = \lim_{b\to\infty}\int_0^b x e^{-x}\,dx$ .... Integrate as normal, but replace the upper limit with b and consider the limit as $b\to\infty$ after you have completed the integration.

$u = x, \dfrac{dv}{dx} = e^{-x}$ .... Use integration by parts.

$\Rightarrow \dfrac{du}{dx} = 1,\ v = -e^{-x}$

$\int_0^b x e^{-x}\,dx = \left[-x e^{-x}\right]_0^b - \int_0^b -e^{-x}\,dx$

$= \left[-x e^{-x} - e^{-x}\right]_0^b$

$= \left(-b e^{-b} - e^{-b}\right) - (0 - 1)$

$= -b e^{-b} - e^{-b} + 1$

$\lim_{b\to\infty}\int_0^b x e^{-x}\,dx = \lim_{b\to\infty}\left(-b e^{-b} - e^{-b} + 1\right)$ .... Now take the limit as $b\to\infty$.

$= 0 + 0 + 1$ Use the given result: $\lim_{x\to\infty} x^k e^{-x} = 0$, with $k = 1$.

$= 1$

$\therefore \int_0^\infty x e^{-x}\,dx = 1$

Integrals where the integrand is undefined at a point within the range of integration

There is another type of improper integral, where the range of integration is finite but the integrand is not defined at a point within the range of integration (which could be at an end point or inside the range).

Examples of such integrals are $\int_0^2 x^3 \ln x \, dx$, which isn't defined at $x = 0$,

and $\int_0^5 \frac{1}{\sqrt{x-3}} \, dx$, which isn't defined at $x = 3$.

To evaluate the first of these integrals, you need to replace 0 by b as the lower limit, find the value of the integral in terms of b and then consider the limit $b \to 0$.

 Key point 8.4

If $f(x)$ is not defined at $x = k$, then

$$\int_a^k f(x) \, dx = \lim_{b \to k} \int_a^b f(x) \, dx$$

and

$$\int_k^c f(x) \, dx = \lim_{b \to k} \int_b^c f(x) \, dx.$$

If the limit is not finite, then the improper integral diverges (does not have a value).

WORKED EXAMPLE 8.10

Evaluate $\int_0^2 x^3 \ln x \, dx$, showing clearly the limiting process used.

[You may use without proof the result $\lim_{x \to 0} x^k \ln x = 0$, where $k > 0$.]

$\int_0^2 x^3 \ln x \, dx = \lim_{b \to 0} \int_b^2 x^3 \ln x \, dx$

> $\ln x$ is not defined at $x = 0$. Integrate as normal, but replace the lower limit with b and consider the limit as $b \to 0$ after you have completed the integration.

$u = \ln x, \dfrac{dv}{dx} = x^3$

$\Rightarrow \dfrac{du}{dx} = \dfrac{1}{x}, v = \dfrac{1}{4} x^4$

> Use integration by parts.
>
> Remember that integrals with ln are an exception where you take $\ln x = u$.

$\int_b^2 x^3 \ln x \, dx = \left[\dfrac{1}{4} x^4 \ln x \right]_b^2 - \int_b^2 \dfrac{1}{4} x^3 \, dx$

$= \left[\dfrac{1}{4} x^4 \ln x - \dfrac{1}{16} x^4 \right]_b^2$

$= (4\ln 2 - 1) - \left(\dfrac{1}{4} b^4 \ln b - \dfrac{1}{16} b^4 \right)$

$\lim_{b \to 0} \int_b^2 x^3 \ln x \, dx = \lim_{b \to 0} \left(4\ln 2 - 1 - \dfrac{1}{4} b^4 \ln b + \dfrac{1}{16} b^4 \right)$

> Now take the limit as $b \to 0$.
>
> Use the given result: $\lim_{x \to 0} x^k \ln x = 0$, with $k = 4$.

$= 4\ln 2 - 1 - 0 + 0$

$= 4\ln 2 - 1$

$\therefore \int_0^2 x^3 \ln x \, dx = 4\ln 2 - 1$

If the point where the integrand is not defined is not an end point, you need to split the integral into two.

 Key point 8.5

If $f(x)$ is undefined at $x = k \in (a, c)$, then

$$\int_a^c f(x)\,dx = \lim_{b \to k} \int_a^b f(x)\,dx + \lim_{b \to k} \int_b^c f(x)\,dx.$$

If either limit is not finite, then the improper integral diverges (does not have a value).

WORKED EXAMPLE 8.11

Find the exact value of $\displaystyle\int_0^5 \frac{1}{\sqrt[3]{x-3}}\,dx$.

$\displaystyle\int_0^5 \frac{1}{\sqrt[3]{x-3}}\,dx = \int_0^3 \frac{1}{\sqrt[3]{x-3}}\,dx + \int_3^5 \frac{1}{\sqrt[3]{x-3}}\,dx$

The integrand is not defined at $x = 3$, so you need to split the integral in two.

$\displaystyle\int_0^3 \frac{1}{\sqrt[3]{x-3}}\,dx = \lim_{b \to 3} \int_0^b \frac{1}{\sqrt[3]{x-3}}\,dx$

For each integral replace 3 by b, evaluate the integral and then find the limit when $b \to 3$.

$\displaystyle = \lim_{b \to 3} \int_0^b (x-3)^{-\frac{1}{3}}\,dx$

$\displaystyle = \lim_{b \to 3}\left[\frac{3}{2}(x-3)^{\frac{2}{3}} \right]_0^b$

Integrate as usual.

$\displaystyle = \lim_{b \to 3}\left[\frac{3}{2}(b-3)^{\frac{2}{3}} - \frac{3}{2}(0-3)^{\frac{2}{3}} \right]$

$\displaystyle = -\frac{3}{2}\sqrt[3]{9}$

As $b \to 3$, $(b-3)^{\frac{2}{3}} \to 0$.

$\displaystyle\int_3^5 \frac{1}{\sqrt[3]{x-3}}\,dx = \lim_{b \to 3} \int_b^5 \frac{1}{\sqrt[3]{x-3}}\,dx$

$\displaystyle = \lim_{b \to 3}\left[\frac{3}{2}(5-3)^{\frac{2}{3}} - \frac{3}{2}(b-3)^{\frac{2}{3}} \right]$

Repeat the same process for the second integral.

$\displaystyle = \frac{3}{2}\sqrt[3]{4}$

$\displaystyle\therefore \int_0^5 \frac{1}{\sqrt[3]{x-3}}\,dx = \frac{3}{2}\left(\sqrt[3]{4} - \sqrt[3]{9} \right)$

EXERCISE 8C

1 Determine which of these improper integrals converge. Evaluate the ones that do converge.

a $\displaystyle\int_0^\infty \frac{1}{(1+x)^2}\,\mathrm{d}x$

b $\displaystyle\int_0^\infty e^{-\frac{x}{4}}\,\mathrm{d}x$

c $\displaystyle\int_0^\infty \frac{1}{\sqrt{1+x}}\,\mathrm{d}x$

d $\displaystyle\int_0^\infty x\,e^{-x^2}\,\mathrm{d}x$

2 For what values of p do each of these improper integrals converge?

a $\displaystyle\int_0^\infty e^{px}\,\mathrm{d}x$

b $\displaystyle\int_1^\infty \frac{\ln x}{x^p}\,\mathrm{d}x$

3 Explain why $\displaystyle\int_0^4 \frac{1}{\sqrt{x}}\,\mathrm{d}x$ is an improper integral and find its value.

4 Evaluate $\displaystyle\int_0^\infty e^{-x}\,\mathrm{d}x$.

5 Evaluate $\displaystyle\int_0^\infty \frac{1}{x^2+1}\,\mathrm{d}x$.

6 Evaluate the improper integral $\displaystyle\int_0^\infty \left(\frac{2x}{x^2+5} - \frac{6}{3x+2} \right)\mathrm{d}x$, giving your answer in the form $\ln k$, where k is a constant.

Section 4: Volumes of revolution

In A Level Mathematics Student Book 1, Chapter 15, you saw that the area between a curve and the x-axis from $x = a$ to $x = b$ is given by $\int_a^b y\,\mathrm{d}x$, as long as $y > 0$. In this section, you will use a similar formula to find the volume of a shape formed by rotating the curve about either the x-axis or the y-axis.

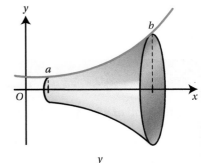

If a curve is rotated about the x-axis or the y-axis, the resulting shape is called a **solid of revolution** and the volume of that shape is referred to as the **volume of revolution**.

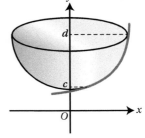

Key point 8.6

- When the curve $y = f(x)$ between $x = a$ and $x = b$ is rotated $360°$ about the x-axis, the volume of revolution is given by $V = \pi\displaystyle\int_a^b y^2\,\mathrm{d}x$.

- When the curve $y = f(x)$ between $y = c$ and $y = d$ is rotated $360°$ about the y-axis, the volume of revolution is given by $V = \pi\displaystyle\int_c^d x^2\,\mathrm{d}y$.

The proof of these results is very similar. The proof for rotation about the x-axis is given in Proof 4.

PROOF 4

The solid can be split into small cylinders.

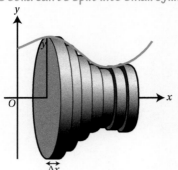

Draw an outline of a representative function to illustrate the argument.

The volume of each cylinder is $\pi y^2 \Delta x$.

The radius of each cylinder is the y-coordinate and the height is Δx.

The total volume is approximately:

$$V \approx \sum_a^b \pi y^2 \Delta x$$

You are starting at $x = a$ and stopping at $x = b$.
It is only approximate because the volume of revolution is not exactly the same as the total volume of the cylinders.

$$V = \lim_{\Delta x \to 0} \sum_a^b \pi y^2 \Delta x$$

$$= \int_a^b \pi y^2 \, dx$$

$$= \pi \int_a^b y^2 \, dx$$

However, as you make the cylinders smaller the volume gets more and more accurate. The sum then becomes an integral. You can leave π out of the integration and multiply by it at the end.

WORKED EXAMPLE 8.12

The graph of $y = \sqrt{x^2 + 1}$, $0 \leqslant x \leqslant 3$, is rotated $360°$ about the x-axis.

Find, in terms of π, the volume of the solid generated.

$$V = \pi \int_0^3 \left(x^2 + 1 \right) dx$$

Use the formula: $V = \pi \int_a^b y^2 \, dx$.

$$= \pi \left[\frac{x^3}{3} + x \right]_0^3$$

Evaluate the definite integral.

$$= \pi \left[\left(\frac{3^3}{3} + 3 \right) - 0 \right]$$

$$= 12\pi$$

To find the volume of revolution about the y-axis you will often have to rearrange the equation of the curve to find x in terms of y.

 Tip

Remember that the limits of the integration need to be in terms of y and not x.

WORKED EXAMPLE 8.13

The part of the curve $y = \dfrac{1}{x}$ between $x = 1$ and $x = 4$ is rotated $360°$ about the y-axis.
Find the exact value of the volume of the solid generated.

When $x = 1$, $y = \dfrac{1}{1} = 1$ · · · · · · · · · · · · · Find the limits in terms of y.

When $x = 4$, $y = \dfrac{1}{4}$

$y = \dfrac{1}{x} \Rightarrow x = \dfrac{1}{y}$ · · · · · · · · · · · · · Express x in terms of y.

$V = \pi \displaystyle\int_a^b x^2 \,\mathrm{d}y$ · · · · · · · · · · · · · Use the formula $V = \pi \displaystyle\int_a^b x^2 \,\mathrm{d}y$, substituting in $x = \dfrac{1}{y}$.

$\quad = \pi \displaystyle\int_{\frac{1}{4}}^{1} \left(\dfrac{1}{y}\right)^2 \mathrm{d}y$

$\quad = \pi \displaystyle\int_{\frac{1}{4}}^{1} y^{-2} \,\mathrm{d}y$

$\quad = \pi \left[-y^{-1} \right]_{\frac{1}{4}}^{1}$

$\quad = \pi \left[(-1) - (-4) \right]$

$\quad = 3\pi$

You might also be asked to find a volume of revolution of an area between two curves.

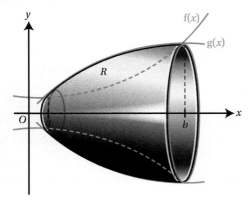

From the diagram you can see that the volume formed when the region R is rotated around the x-axis is given by the volume of revolution of $g(x)$ minus the volume of revolution of $f(x)$.

Key point 8.7

The volume of revolution of the region between curves g(x) and f(x) is:

$$V = \pi \int_a^b \left(g(x)^2 - f(x)^2 \right) dx$$

where the curve of g(x) is above f(x) and the curves intersect at $x = a$ and $x = b$.

 Tip

Make sure that you square each term within the brackets and do not make the mistake of squaring the whole expression inside the brackets: the formula is **not** $\pi \int_a^b \left(g(x) - f(x) \right)^2 dx$.

WORKED EXAMPLE 8.14

Find the volume formed when the region enclosed by $y = x^2 + 6$ and $y = 8x - x^2$ is rotated through $360°$ about the x-axis.

For points of intersection:

$$x^2 + 6 = 8x - x^2$$
$$2x^2 - 8x + 6 = 0$$
$$x^2 - 4x + 3 = 0$$
$$(x - 1)(x - 3) = 0$$
$$x = 1 \text{ or } x = 3$$

First find the x-coordinates of the points where the curves meet, by equating the RHS of both equations and solving. This will give you the limits of integration.

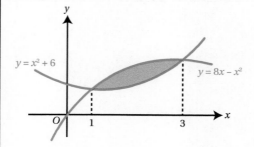

Sketch the graphs in the region concerned.

$y = 8x - x^2$ is above $y = x^2 + 6$.

$$V = \pi \int_1^3 \left((8x - x^2)^2 - (x^2 + 6)^2 \right) dx$$

$$= \frac{176}{3}\pi$$

Apply the formula

$$V = \pi \int_a^b \left(g(x)^2 - f(x)^2 \right) dx.$$

Use a calculator to evaluate the integral.

 Tip

Don't forget that you can use your calculator to evaluate definite integrals. However, look out for the instruction to 'show detailed reasoning' which means that you must show full integration and evaluation.

Did you know?

There are also formulae to find the surface area of a solid formed by rotating a region around an axis. Some particularly interesting examples arise if you allow one end of the region to tend to infinity; for example, rotating the region formed by the lines $y = \frac{1}{x}$, $x = 1$ and the x-axis results in a solid called Gabriel's horn or Torricelli's trumpet.

Areas and volumes can also be calculated using improper integrals, and it turns out that it is possible to have a solid of finite volume but infinite surface area!

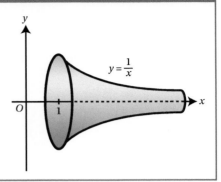

You can also use the formulae for the volume of revolution about the coordinate axes in the case where the curve is defined parametrically.

Rewind

You learnt how to find the area defined by a parametric curve in A Level Mathematics Student Book 2, Chapter 12.

Key point 8.8

When the part of a curve with parametric equations $x = f(t)$, $y = g(t)$, between points with parameter values t_1 and t_2, is rotated about one of the coordinate axes, the resulting volume of revolution is

$$\pi \int_{t_1}^{t_2} y^2 \frac{dx}{dt} \, dt \text{ for rotation about the } x\text{-axis}$$

$$\pi \int_{t_1}^{t_2} x^2 \frac{dy}{dt} \, dt \text{ for rotation about the } y\text{-axis.}$$

WORKED EXAMPLE 8.15

The curve shown in the diagram has parametric equations $x = 5t^2$, $y = 2t^3$ for $t \in \mathbb{R}$.

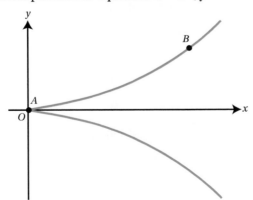

The part of the curve between the points $A(0, 0)$ and $B(20, 16)$ is rotated about the x-axis. Find the exact value of the resulting volume of revolution.

Continues on next page ...

When $x = 0, t = 0$.

When $x = 20, t = \pm 2$; but $y > 0$ so $t = 2$.

$V = \pi \displaystyle\int_{0}^{2} \left(2t^3\right)^2 (10t)\, dt$

$\qquad = \pi \displaystyle\int_{0}^{2} 40t^7\, dt$

$\qquad = 1280\pi$

Find the values of t corresponding to the end points.

Use the formula $\pi \displaystyle\int_{t_1}^{t_2} y^2 \dfrac{dx}{dt}\, dt$ for the volume of revolution about the x-axis.

You can use your calculator to evaluate the integral (unless the question asks you to 'show detailed reasoning').

EXERCISE 8D

In this exercise, whenever a question asks for an exact volume, you must show detailed reasoning.

1 The part of the curve $y = f(x)$ for $a \leqslant y \leqslant b$ is rotated $360°$ about the x-axis. Find the exact volume of revolution formed in each case.

  a **i** $f(x) = x^2$; $a = -1$, $b = 1$ **ii** $f(x) = x^3$; $a = 0$, $b = 2$

  b **i** $f(x) = x^2 + 6$; $a = -1$, $b = 3$ **ii** $f(x) = 2x^3 + 1$; $a = 0$, $b = 1$

  c **i** $f(x) = \dfrac{1}{x}$; $a = 1$, $b = 2$ **ii** $f(x) = \dfrac{1}{x^2}$; $a = 1$, $b = 4$

2 Find the exact volume of revolution formed when each curve, for $a \leqslant x \leqslant b$, is rotated through 2π radians about the x-axis.

  a **i** $y = e^x$; $a = 0$, $b = 1$ **ii** $y = e^{-x}$; $a = 0$, $b = 3$

  b **i** $y = e^{2x} + 1$; $a = 0$, $b = 1$ **ii** $y = e^{-x} + 2$; $a = 0$, $b = 2$

  c **i** $y = \sqrt{\sin x}$; $a = 0$, $b = \pi$ **ii** $y = \sqrt{\cos x}$; $a = 0$, $b = \dfrac{\pi}{2}$

3 The part of the curve for $a \leqslant y \leqslant b$ is rotated $360°$ about the y-axis.

Find the exact volume of revolution formed in each case.

  a **i** $y = 4x^2 + 1$; $a = 1$, $b = 17$ **ii** $y = \dfrac{x^2 - 1}{3}$; $a = 0$, $b = 5$

  b **i** $y = x^3$; $a = 0$, $b = 8$ **ii** $y = x^4$; $a = 2$, $b = 8$

  c **i** $y = \dfrac{1}{x^3}$; $a = 8$, $b = 27$ **ii** $y = \dfrac{1}{x^5}$; $a = 1$, $b = 32$

4 The part of the curve $y = f(x)$ for $a \leqslant y \leqslant b$ is rotated $360°$ about the y-axis.

Find the exact volume of revolution formed in each case.

  a **i** $f(x) = \ln x + 1$; $a = 1$, $b = 3$ **ii** $f(x) = \ln(2x - 1)$; $a = 0$, $b = 4$

  b **i** $f(x) = \dfrac{1}{x^2}$; $a = 1$, $b = 2$ **ii** $f(x) = \dfrac{1}{x^2} + 2$; $a = 3$, $b = 5$

  c **i** $f(x) = \arcsin x$; $a = -\dfrac{\pi}{2}$, $b = \dfrac{\pi}{2}$ **ii** $f(x) = \arcsin x$; $a = -\dfrac{\pi}{4}$, $b = \dfrac{\pi}{4}$

5 The part of the curve $x = f(t)$, $y = g(t)$ for $a \leqslant t \leqslant b$ is rotated through $360°$ about the x-axis. Find the exact volume of revolution formed in each case.

  a **i** $x = 4t^2, y = 3t^3; a = 0, b = 2$ **ii** $x = \dfrac{1}{2}t^2, y = 2t^3; a = 0, b = 1$

  b **i** $x = t^2 + 1, y = t + \dfrac{1}{t}; a = 1, b = 2$ **ii** $x = t^3 + 2, y = 2t + \dfrac{1}{t}; a = 1, b = 2$

  c **i** $x = \cos t, y = \sqrt{\sin t}; a = 0, b = \dfrac{\pi}{2}$ **ii** $x = \cos t, y = \dfrac{1}{\sqrt{\sin t}}; a = \dfrac{\pi}{6}, b = \dfrac{\pi}{2}$

6 The part of the curve $x = f(t)$, $y = g(t)$ for $a \leqslant t \leqslant b$ is rotated through $360°$ about the y-axis. Find the exact volume of revolution formed in each case.

  a **i** $x = 4t^2, y = 3t^3; a = 0, b = 2$ **ii** $x = \dfrac{1}{2}t^2, y = 2t^3; a = 0, b = 1$

  b **i** $x = t^2 + 1, y = t + \dfrac{1}{t}; a = \dfrac{1}{2}, b = 1$ **ii** $x = t^3 + 2, y = 2t + \dfrac{1}{t}; a = 1, b = 2$

  c **i** $x = \sqrt{\cos t}, y = \sin t; a = 0, b = \dfrac{\pi}{2}$ **ii** $x = \cos t, y = \sin^2 t; a = 0, b = \dfrac{\pi}{2}$

7 The diagram shows the region, R, bounded by the curve $y = \sqrt{x} - 2$, the x-axis and the line $x = 9$.

  a Find the coordinates of the point A where the curve crosses the x-axis.

This region is rotated $360°$ about the x-axis.

  b Find the exact volume of the solid generated.

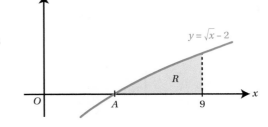

8 The curve $y = 3x^2 + 1$, for $0 \leqslant x \leqslant 2$, is rotated through $360°$ about the y-axis.

Find the volume of revolution generated, correct to 3 significant figures.

9 The part of the curve $y^2 = \sin x$ between $x = 0$ and $x = \dfrac{\pi}{2}$ is rotated through 2π radians about the x-axis.

Find the exact volume of the solid generated.

10 The curve $y = x^2$, for $0 < x < a$, is rotated through $180°$ about the x-axis.

The resulting volume is $\dfrac{16\pi}{5}$.

Find the value of a.

11 The region enclosed by the curve $y = x^2 - a^2$ and the x-axis is rotated $90°$ about the x-axis.

Find an expression, in terms of a, for the volume of revolution formed.

12 The part of the curve $y = \sqrt{\dfrac{3}{x}}$ between $x = 1$ and $x = a$ is rotated through 2π radians about the x-axis. The volume of the resulting solid is $\pi \ln \dfrac{64}{27}$.

Find the exact value of a.

13 **a** Find the coordinates of the points of intersection of curves $y = x^2 + 3$ and $y = 4x + 3$.

  b Find the volume of revolution generated when the region between the curves $y = x^2 + 3$ and $y = 4x + 3$ is rotated through $360°$ about the x-axis.

14 The region bounded by the curves $y = x^2 + 6$ and $y = 8x - x^2$ is rotated through $360°$ about the x-axis. Find the volume of the resulting solid.

15 **a** Find the coordinates of the points of intersection of the curves $y = 4\sqrt{x}$ and $y = x + 3$.

    b The region between the curves $y = 4\sqrt{x}$ and $y = x + 3$ is rotated through 360° about the y-axis. Find the volume of the solid generated.

16 By rotating the circle $x^2 + y^2 = r^2$ around the x-axis, prove that the volume of a sphere of radius r is given by $\frac{4}{3}\pi r^3$.

17 The part of the curve with parametric equations $x = t^2 + 3$, $y = 3t + 1$, between the points $(4, 4)$ and $(7, 7)$, is rotated through 360° about the x-axis. Find the exact volume generated.

18 The diagram shows a part of the curve with parametric equations
$x = \dfrac{1}{1+t}, y = t^2$.
The section of the curve between points $P\left(\dfrac{1}{2}, 1\right)$ and $Q\left(\dfrac{1}{3}, 4\right)$ is rotated a full turn about the y-axis. Find the exact volume of the resulting solid.

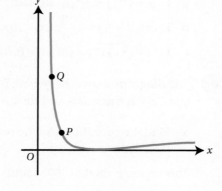

19 The diagram shows the curve with parametric equations
$x = \sin\theta, y = \sin 2\theta$.

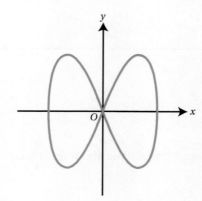

One of the loops of the curve is rotated 2π radians about the x-axis. Find the exact value of the volume of revolution.

20 By choosing a suitable function to rotate around the x-axis, prove that the volume of a circular cone with base radius r and height h is $\dfrac{\pi r^2 h}{3}$.

21 Find the volume of revolution when the region enclosed by the graphs of $y = e^x$, $y = 1$ and $x = 1$ is rotated through 360° about the line $y = 1$.

Section 5: Mean value of a function

Suppose an object travels between time $t = 0$ and $t = 3$ with a velocity given by $v = t$. Its velocity–time graph looks like this.

Its average velocity can be found from:

$$\frac{\text{initial velocity} + \text{final velocity}}{2} = \frac{0 + 3}{2}$$
$$= 1.5$$

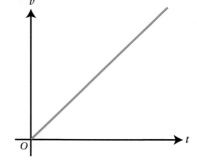

Suppose, instead, the object has velocity given by $v = \frac{t^2}{3}$. Then you can compare the two velocity–time graphs.

The formula $\frac{\text{initial velocity} + \text{final velocity}}{2}$ would give the same mean velocity for the two graphs, which can't be correct because the red curve is underneath the blue line everywhere other than at the end points.

You need a method of calculating the mean that takes into account the value of the function everywhere.

One possibility is to use $\frac{\text{total distance}}{\text{time taken}}$.

You can then use the fact that total distance is the integral of velocity with respect to time.

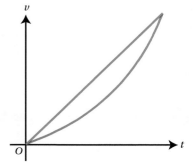

For the blue line this gives:

$$\text{average velocity} = \frac{\int_0^3 t\,dt}{3}$$
$$= \frac{1}{3}\left[\frac{t^2}{2}\right]_0^3$$
$$= 1.5$$

For the red curve this gives:

$$\text{average velocity} = \frac{\int_0^3 \frac{t^2}{3}\,dt}{3}$$
$$= \frac{1}{3}\left[\frac{t^3}{9}\right]_0^3$$
$$= 1$$

This process can be generalised for any function.

🔑 Key point 8.9

The mean value of a function $f(x)$ between a and b is:

$$\frac{1}{b-a}\int_a^b f(x)\,dx$$

WORKED EXAMPLE 8.16

You are given that $f(x) = x^2 - x$. Find the mean value of $f(x)$ between 3 and 4.

Mean value $= \dfrac{1}{4-3} \displaystyle\int_3^4 (x^2 - x)\,dx$ $\cdots\cdots$ Use the formula for the mean value of a function: $\dfrac{1}{b-a}\displaystyle\int_a^b f(x)\,dx$.

$= \dfrac{1}{4-3}\left[\dfrac{x^3}{3} - \dfrac{x^2}{2} \right]_3^4$

$= \dfrac{37}{3} - \dfrac{7}{2}$

$= \dfrac{53}{6}$ $\cdots\cdots\cdots\cdots\cdots\cdots$ Notice that $x^2 - x$ varies between 6 and 12, so a mean of around 9 seems reasonable.

EXERCISE 8E

1 Find the mean value of each function between the given values of x.

a i x^2 for $0 < x < 1$ **ii** x^2 for $1 < x < 3$

b i $\sqrt{x}$ for $0 < x < 4$ **ii** $\dfrac{1}{x^2}$ for $1 < x < 5$

c i $x^3 + 1$ for $0 < x < 4$ **ii** $x^4 - x$ for $0 < x < 10$

2 Find the mean value of each function over the domain given.

a i $\sin x$ for $0 < x < \pi$ **ii** $\cos x$ for $0 < x < \pi$

b i e^x for $0 < x < 1$ **ii** $\dfrac{1}{x}$ for $1 < x < e$

c i $\sqrt{x+1}$ for $3 < x < 8$ **ii** $x\sin(x^2)$ for $0 < x < \sqrt{\pi}$

3 The velocity of a rocket is given by $v = 30\sqrt{t}$ where t is time, in seconds, and v is velocity, in metres per second.

Find the mean velocity in the first T seconds.

4 The mean value of the function $f(x) = x^2 - x$ for $0 < x < a$ is zero.

Find the value of a.

5 $f(x) = x^2$ for $x \geq 0$.

a f_{mean} is the mean value of $f(x)$ between 0 and a. Find an expression for f_{mean} in terms of a.

b Given that $f(c) = f_{mean}$ find an expression for c in terms of a.

6 Show that the mean value of $\dfrac{1}{x^2}$ between 1 and a is inversely proportional to a.

7 An alternating current has time period 2. The power dissipated by the current through a resistor is given by $P = P_0 \sin^2(\pi t)$.

Find the ratio of the mean power of one complete period to the maximum power.

8 The mean value of $f(x)$ between a and b is F.

Prove that the mean value of $f(x) + 1$ between a and b is $F + 1$.

9 **a** Sketch the graph of $f(x) = \dfrac{1}{2\sqrt{x}}$.

b Use the graph to explain why the mean value of $f(x)$ between a and b is less than the mean of $f(a)$ and $f(b)$.

c Hence prove that, if $0 < a < b$, $\sqrt{b} - \sqrt{a} < \dfrac{1}{3}\left(\dfrac{b}{\sqrt{a}} - \dfrac{a}{\sqrt{b}}\right)$.

10 If f_{mean} is the mean value of $f(x)$ for $a < x < b$ and $f(a) < f(b)$, then $f(a) < f_{mean} < f(b)$.

Either prove this statement or disprove it using a counterexample.

Checklist of learning and understanding

- The Maclaurin series for a function $f(x)$ is given by

$$f(x) = f(0) + f'(0)x + \frac{f''(0)}{2!}x^2 + \ldots + \frac{f^{(r)}(0)}{r!}x^r + \ldots$$

- Maclaurin series for some common functions and the values of x for which they are valid:

  - $e^x = \exp(x) = 1 + x + \dfrac{x^2}{2!} + \ldots + \dfrac{x^r}{r!} + \ldots$ for all x

  - $\ln(1 + x) = x - \dfrac{x^2}{2} + \dfrac{x^3}{3} - \ldots + (-1)^{r+1}\dfrac{x^r}{r} + \ldots \quad -1 < x \leqslant 1$

  - $\sin x = x - \dfrac{x^3}{3!} + \dfrac{x^5}{5!} - \ldots + (-1)^r \dfrac{x^{2r+1}}{(2r+1)!} + \ldots$ for all x

  - $\cos x = 1 - \dfrac{x^2}{2!} + \dfrac{x^4}{4!} - \ldots + (-1)^r \dfrac{x^{2r}}{(2r)!} + \ldots$ for all x

  - $(1 + x)^n = 1 + nx + \dfrac{n(n-1)}{2!}x^2 + \ldots + \dfrac{n(n-1)\ldots(n-r+1)}{r!}x^r + \ldots \quad |x| < 1, n \in \mathbb{R}$

- Improper integrals are definite integrals where either:
  - the range of integration is infinite or
  - the integrand isn't defined at every point in the range of integration.
- The value of the improper integral $\displaystyle\int_a^\infty f(x)\,dx$ is

$$\lim_{b \to \infty} \int_a^b f(x)\,dx = \lim_{b \to \infty}\{I(b)\} - I(a)$$

if this limit exists and is finite.

- If $f(x)$ is not defined at $x = k$, then

$$\int_a^k f(x)\,dx = \lim_{b \to k}\int_a^b f(x)\,dx \quad \text{and} \quad \int_k^c f(x)\,dx = \lim_{b \to k}\int_b^c f(x)\,dx$$

if the limits exist and are finite.

Continues on next page …

- If $f(x)$ is undefined at $x = k \in (a,c)$, then

$$\int_a^c f(x)\,dx = \lim_{b \to k} \int_a^b f(x)\,dx + \lim_{b \to k} \int_b^c f(x)\,dx$$

if the limits exist and are finite.
- The volume of a shape formed by rotating a curve about the x-axis or the y-axis is known as the volume of revolution.
  - When the curve $y = f(x)$ between $x = a$ and $x = b$ is rotated $360°$ about the x-axis, the volume of revolution is given by

$$V = \pi \int_a^b y^2\,dx$$

  - When the curve $y = f(x)$ between $y = c$ and $y = d$ is rotated $360°$ about the y-axis, the volume of revolution is given by

$$V = \pi \int_c^d x^2\,dy$$

  - The volume of revolution of the region between curves $g(x)$ and $f(x)$ is:

$$V = \pi \int_a^b \left(g(x)^2 - f(x)^2 \right) dx$$

  where the curve of $g(x)$ is above $f(x)$ and the curves intersect at $x = a$ and $x = b$.

  - When the part of a curve with parametric equations $x = f(t)$, $y = g(t)$, between points with parameter values t_1 and t_2, is rotated about one of the coordinate axes, the resulting volume of revolution is

$$\pi \int_{t_1}^{t_2} y^2 \frac{dx}{dt}\,dt \text{ for rotation about the } x\text{-axis}$$

$$\pi \int_{t_1}^{t_2} x^2 \frac{dy}{dt}\,dt \text{ for rotation about the } y\text{-axis}$$

- The mean value of a function $f(x)$ between a and b is:

$$\frac{1}{b-a} \int_a^b f(x)\,dx$$

Mixed practice 8

1 **a** Show that the first four terms in the Maclaurin series of e^x are $1 + x + \dfrac{x^2}{2} + \dfrac{x^3}{6}$.

   b Use the series in part **a** to show that $\sqrt{e} \approx \dfrac{79}{48}$.

2 **a** Find the first four derivatives of $f(x) = \ln(1+x)$.

   b Hence find the first four non-zero terms of the Maclaurin series of $f(x)$.

   c Using this expansion, find the exact value of the infinite series $1 - \dfrac{1}{2} + \dfrac{1}{3} - \dfrac{1}{4} + \dots$.

3 **a** Explain why $\displaystyle\int_0^4 \dfrac{5-x}{\sqrt{x^3}}\,dt$ is an improper integral.

   b Either find the value of the integral $\displaystyle\int_0^4 \dfrac{5-x}{\sqrt{x^3}}\,dx$ or explain why it does not have a finite value.

4 Given that $f(x) = \ln(\cos 3x)$, find $f'(0)$ and $f''(0)$. Hence show that the first term in the Maclaurin series for $f(x)$ is ax^2, where the value of a is to be found.

© OCR A Level Mathematics, Unit 4726 Further Pure Mathematics 2, January 2012

5 The curve $y = \sqrt{x}$ between 0 and a is rotated through $360°$ about the x-axis. The resulting solid has a volume of 18π.

   Find the value of a.

6 The curve $x = \dfrac{y^2 - 1}{3}$, with $1 \leqslant y \leqslant 4$, is rotated through $360°$ about the y-axis.

   Find the volume of revolution generated, correct to 3 significant figures.

7 For $0 < x < a$, the mean value of x is equal to the mean value of x^2.

   Find the value of a.

8 The mean value of $\dfrac{1}{\sqrt{x}}$ from 0 to b is 1.

   Find the value of b.

9 Find the set of values of x for which the Maclaurin series of the function $f(x) = \sqrt{1 + e^x}$ is valid.

10 **a** Find the Maclaurin series of $\ln(\cos x)$ up to and including the term in x^4.

   b Hence show that $\ln 2 \approx \dfrac{\pi^2}{16}\left(1 + \dfrac{\pi^2}{96}\right)$.

11 It is given that $f(x) = \ln(1 + \sin x)$, $-\dfrac{\pi}{2} < x < \dfrac{3\pi}{2}$.

   a Find the first three derivatives of $f(x)$.

   b Hence find the Maclaurin series of $f(x)$ up to and including the term in x^3.

   c Hence find $\displaystyle\lim_{x \to 0} \dfrac{\ln(1 + \sin x) - x}{x^2}$.

12 You are given that $f(x) = e^{-x} \sin x$.

   i Find $f(0)$ and $f'(0)$.

   ii Show that $f''(x) = -2f'(x) - 2f(x)$ and hence, or otherwise, find $f''(0)$.

   iii Find a similar expression for $f'''(x)$ and hence, or otherwise, find $f'''(0)$.

   iv Find the Maclaurin series for $f(x)$ up to and including the term in x^3.

© OCR A Level Mathematics, Unit 4726/01 Further Pure Mathematics 2, January 2013

13 The region bounded by the curve $y = ax - x^2$ and the x-axis is rotated one full turn about the x-axis.

Find, in terms of a, the resulting volume of revolution.

In questions 14 to 20 you must show detailed reasoning.

14 The diagram shows the curve $y = \ln x$ and the line $y = -\dfrac{1}{e}x + 2$.

   a Show that the two graphs intersect at $(e, 1)$.

The shaded region is rotated through 360° about the y-axis.

   b Find the exact value of the volume of revolution.

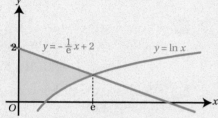

15 The region enclosed by $y = (x-1)(x-2) + 1$ and the line $y = 1$ is rotated through 180° about the line $y = 1$.

Find the exact value of the resulting volume.

16 The diagram shows the curve $y = \sqrt{\dfrac{3}{4x+1}}$ for $0 \leqslant x \leqslant 20$. The point

P on the curve has coordinates $\left(20, \dfrac{1}{9}\sqrt{3}\right)$. The shaded region R is

enclosed by the curve and the lines $x = 0$ and $y = \dfrac{1}{9}\sqrt{3}$.

   i Find the exact area of R.

   ii Find the exact volume of the solid obtained when R is rotated completely about the x-axis.

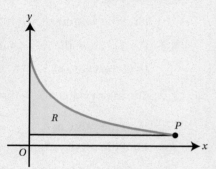

© OCR A Level Mathematics, Unit 4723/01 Core Mathematics 3, June 2014

17 **i** Show that the derivative with respect to y of

$$y\ln(2y) - y$$

   is $\ln(2y)$.

   ii The diagram shows the curve with equation $y = \dfrac{1}{2}e^{x^2}$. The point

$P\left(2, \dfrac{1}{2}e^4\right)$ lies on the curve. The shaded region is bounded

by the curve and the lines $x = 0$ and $y = \dfrac{1}{2}e^4$. Find the exact

volume of the solid produced when the shaded region is rotated completely about the y-axis.

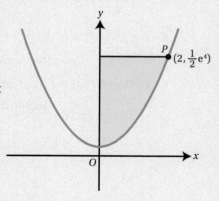

   iii Hence find the volume of the solid produced when the region bounded by the curve and the lines $x = 0$, $x = 2$ and $y = 0$ is rotated completely about the y-axis.

© OCR A Level Mathematics, Unit 4723 Core Mathematics 3, June 2012

18 The region bounded by the curves $y = \sqrt{x}$ and $y = 2\sqrt{x-3}$ is rotated one full turn, about the x-axis. Find the resulting volume of revolution.

19 The shape of a rugby ball can be modelled as a solid obtained by rotating an ellipse about one of its axes of symmetry.

An ellipse has parametric equations $x = a\cos\theta$, $y = b\sin\theta$. Find the volume of the solid generated when the ellipse is rotated through $360°$ about the x-axis.

20 The diagram shows a part of the curve with parametric equations $x = e^t$, $y = t^2 - 1$.

The part of the curve between points $A(1, -1)$ and $B\left(\dfrac{1}{e}, 0\right)$ is

rotated a full turn about the y-axis. Find the exact volume of the resulting solid.

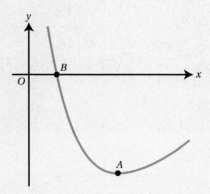

21 **a** Using the series for e^x, or otherwise, find the Maclaurin series of $x e^x$, stating the first four non-zero terms and the general term.

b Hence find a series expansion of $\displaystyle\int_0^x t e^t \, dt$.

c Hence show that $\dfrac{1}{2} + \dfrac{1}{3} + \dfrac{1}{4(2!)} + \dfrac{1}{5(3!)} + \ldots = 1$.

22 The part of the curve $y = x^2 + 3$ between $y = 3$ and $y = k$ $(k > 0)$ is rotated $360°$ about the y-axis. The volume of revolution formed is 25π.

Find the value of k.

23 Consider two curves with equations $y = x^2 - 8x + 12$ and $y = 12 + x - x^2$.

a Find the coordinates of the points of intersection of the two curves.

The region enclosed by the curves is rotated through $360°$ about the x-axis.

b Write down an integral expression for the volume of the solid generated.

c Evaluate the volume, giving your answer to the nearest integer.

24 The region enclosed by $y = x^2$ and $y = \sqrt{x}$ is to be labelled R.

a Draw a sketch showing R.

b Find the volume when R is rotated through $360°$ about the x-axis.

c Hence find the volume when R is rotated through $360°$ about the y-axis.

9 Polar coordinates

In this chapter you will learn how to:

- use polar coordinates to represent curves
- establish various properties of those curves
- convert between polar and Cartesian equations of a curve
- find the area enclosed by a polar curve, or between two curves.

Before you start…

A Level Mathematics Student Book 2, Chapter 7	You should be able to use radians.	1	**a** Express $\frac{7\pi}{6}$ radians in degrees. **b** State the exact value of $\sin \frac{4\pi}{3}$.
A Level Mathematics Student Book 1, Chapter 10	You should be familiar with graphs of trigonometric functions.	2	**a** Find the set of values of θ, between 0 and 2π, for which $\cos \theta < 0$. **b** State the greatest possible value of $5 - 2\cos\theta$.
A Level Mathematics Student Book 2, Chapter 11	You should be able to integrate trigonometric functions.	3	Evaluate: **a** $\int_0^{\frac{\pi}{6}} \cos 3\theta \, d\theta$ **b** $\int_0^{\frac{\pi}{2}} \sin^2 \theta \, d\theta$

What are polar coordinates?

You are familiar with describing positions of points in the plane by using Cartesian coordinates, which represent the distance of a point from the x- and y-axes. But you are also familiar with bearings, which determine a direction in terms of an angle from a fixed line. If you know that a point lies on a certain bearing, you can describe its exact position by also specifying the distance from the origin. For example, this diagram shows that P is 4 cm from O on a bearing of 250°.

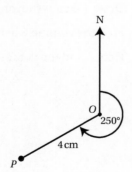

Polar coordinates use a similar idea: positions of points are described in terms of a direction and the distance from the origin. They can be used to describe curves that cannot easily be represented in Cartesian coordinates. In this chapter, you will learn about equations of curves such as these.

Because the distance from the origin explicitly features as a variable, polar coordinates are often used to describe quantities that vary with distance from a point, such as the strength of a gravitational field.

Section 1: Curves in polar coordinates

Polar coordinates describe the position of a point by specifying its distance from the origin (also called the **pole**) and the angle relative to a fixed line (called the **initial line**). By convention the initial line is drawn horizontally, in the direction of the positive x-axis, and the angle is measured anticlockwise.

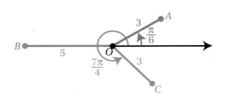

You write polar coordinates as (r, θ), where r is the distance from the pole and θ is the angle. For example, point A in the diagram has polar coordinates $\left(3, \dfrac{\pi}{6} \right)$, point $B\ (5, \pi)$ and point $C\left(3, \dfrac{7\pi}{4} \right)$.

Notice that polar coordinates of a point are not uniquely defined. For example, you could also say that the polar coordinates of B are $(5, -\pi)$ or $(5, 3\pi)$. Conventionally, θ is taken to be between 0 and 2π (i.e. $0 \leqslant \theta < 2\pi$).

WORKED EXAMPLE 9.1

Points M and N have polar coordinates $\left(12, \dfrac{\pi}{4} \right)$ and $\left(9, \dfrac{5\pi}{6} \right)$. Find:

a the length MN

b the area of the triangle MON, where O is the pole.

a

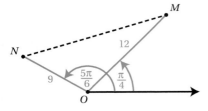

In triangle MON, $OM = 12$, $ON = 9$.	Polar coordinates give information about lengths and angles.

$\angle MON = \dfrac{5\pi}{6} - \dfrac{\pi}{4} = \dfrac{7\pi}{12}$

So:

You can use the cosine rule in triangle MON.

$$MN^2 = 12^2 + 9^2 - 2 \times 12 \times 9 \, \cos \dfrac{7\pi}{12}$$

$$MN = \sqrt{280.9} = 16.8$$

b Area $= \dfrac{1}{2} (12)(9) \sin \dfrac{7\pi}{12} = 52.2$

Use area of triangle $= \dfrac{1}{2} ab \sin C$.

In Cartesian coordinates, an equation of a curve gives a relationship between the x- and y-coordinate of any point on the curve. Similarly, a polar equation of a curve is a relationship between r and θ that holds for any point on the curve.

WORKED EXAMPLE 9.2

a Make a table of values for the curve with polar equation $r = \sqrt{\theta}$ for $0 \leqslant \theta < 2\pi$.

b Hence sketch the curve.

a

θ	0	$\dfrac{\pi}{4}$	$\dfrac{\pi}{2}$	$\dfrac{3\pi}{4}$	π	$\dfrac{5\pi}{4}$	$\dfrac{3\pi}{2}$	$\dfrac{7\pi}{4}$	2π
r	0	0.89	1.25	1.53	1.77	1.98	2.17	2.34	2.51

Use $r = \sqrt{\theta}$ to calculate r for various values of θ.

b

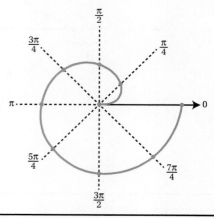

Plot the points and join them up.

There might be values of θ for which r is not defined. This happens when the expression for r has a negative value; r is a distance, so it must be

 Tip

If you use a graphical calculator or graphing software to plot polar curves, you will find that some of them allow negative values of r, showing parts of a curve where we claim the curve is not defined. In this course, we require that r takes non-negative values.

WORKED EXAMPLE 9.3

Sketch the curve with equation $r = \sin 2\theta$ for $0 \leqslant \theta < 2\pi$.

Finding disallowed values of θ:

$\sin 2\theta \geqslant 0$

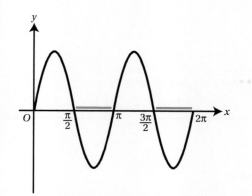

The curve is not defined when $\sin 2\theta < 0$. Sketch the graph of $y = \sin 2x$ to see where it is negative.

Continues on next page ...

r is not defined for:

$\dfrac{\pi}{2} < \theta < \pi$ or $\dfrac{3\pi}{2} < \theta < 2\pi$

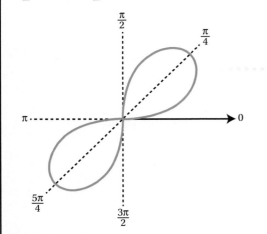

There should be no points in the sections $\dfrac{\pi}{2} < \theta < \pi$

and $\dfrac{3\pi}{2} < \theta < 2\pi$.

You can also see from the graph that *r* increases for

$0 < \theta < \dfrac{\pi}{4}$, then decreases for $\dfrac{\pi}{4} < \theta < \dfrac{\pi}{2}$, then repeats

the same values between π and $\dfrac{3\pi}{2}$.

non-negative. An effective way to identify such values is to sketch the graph of *r* against θ.

EXERCISE 9A

1 Plot the points with the given polar coordinates.

a i $\left(3, \dfrac{\pi}{4}\right)$ **ii** $\left(4, \dfrac{2\pi}{3}\right)$ **b i** $\left(5, \dfrac{7\pi}{6}\right)$ **ii** $\left(3, \dfrac{5\pi}{4}\right)$

c i $(2, \pi)$ **ii** $\left(1, \dfrac{3\pi}{2}\right)$

2 For points *A* and *B* with given polar coordinates, find the distance *AB* and the area of the triangle *AOB*.

a i $A\left(5, \dfrac{\pi}{6}\right), B\left(7, \dfrac{\pi}{4}\right)$ **ii** $A\left(2, \dfrac{\pi}{2}\right), B\left(5, \dfrac{2\pi}{3}\right)$

b i $A\left(10, \dfrac{\pi}{4}\right), B\left(8, \dfrac{7\pi}{6}\right)$ **ii** $A\left(4, \dfrac{3\pi}{4}\right), B\left(5, \dfrac{5\pi}{3}\right)$

c i $A\left(1, \dfrac{2\pi}{3}\right), B\left(2, \dfrac{11\pi}{6}\right)$ **ii** $A\left(6, \dfrac{7\pi}{4}\right), B\left(4, \dfrac{\pi}{4}\right)$

3 For each equation, make a table of values (for $0 \leqslant \theta < 2\pi$) and sketch the curve.

a i $r = 2\theta$ **ii** $r = \theta^2$

b i $r = \theta^2 - 5\theta + 6$ **ii** $r = \theta^2 - 2\theta$

c i $r = 2\cos 2\theta$ **ii** $r = \sin 3\theta$

4. Shade the region described by each inequality. They are given in polar coordinates.

   a $r \leqslant 2$ **b** $1 \leqslant r \leqslant 3$ **c** $\dfrac{\pi}{4} < \theta \leqslant \pi$

5. A curve has polar equation $r = \cos 2\theta$, $0 \leqslant \theta < 2\pi$.

   a State the values of θ for which the curve is not defined.

   b Hence sketch the curve.

6. A curve has polar equation $r = 4 \sin \theta$.

   a Find the set of values of θ for which r is not defined.

   b Show that the points A and B, with polar coordinates $\left(2, \dfrac{\pi}{6}\right)$ and $\left(4, \dfrac{\pi}{2}\right)$ lie on the curve.

   c Sketch the curve.

   d Find the exact length of AB.

Section 2: Some features of polar curves

When sketching curves in Cartesian coordinates you normally mark the axis intercepts, maximum and minimum points. For polar curves, there are similar features that you can deduce from the equation.

Minimum and maximum values of r

Since r is a function of θ, you can use differentiation to find its minimum and maximum values.

> **Key point 9.1**
>
> The minimum and maximum values of r occur where $\dfrac{dr}{d\theta} = 0$.

WORKED EXAMPLE 9.4

A curve has polar equation $r = 150 + 9\theta^2 - 2\theta^3$ for $0 \leqslant \theta < 2\pi$.

a Find the minimum and maximum values of r, and the values of θ for which they occur.

b Explain why there is a point on the curve corresponding to every value of θ.

c Sketch the curve.

a

$\dfrac{dr}{d\theta} = 18\theta - 6\theta^2$

When $\dfrac{dr}{d\theta} = 0$:

$18\theta - 6\theta^2 = 0$

$6\theta(3 - \theta) = 0$

$\theta = 0 \text{ or } \theta = 3$

The maximum and minimum values of r occur where $\dfrac{dr}{d\theta} = 0$.

Continues on next page ...

$$\frac{d^2r}{d\theta^2} = 18 - 12\theta$$

When $\theta = 0$:

$18 - 12(0) = 18 \, (> 0)$ so there is a minimum at $(150, 0)$.

> When $\theta = 0$, $r = 150$.

When $\theta = 3$:

$18 - 12(3) = -18 \, (< 0)$ so there is maximum at $(177, 3)$.

When $\theta = 2\pi$, $r = 9.21$.

> When $\theta = 3$, $r = 177$.

Hence the minimum value of $r = 9.21$ occurs when $\theta = 2\pi$.
The maximum value of $r = 177$ occurs when $\theta = 3$.

> The minimum value could occur at the end of the domain. You have already checked $\theta = 0$, so you just need to check $\theta = 2\pi$.

b r is always positive for $0 \leqslant \theta \leqslant 2\pi$, so the curve exists for all θ.

> For the curve to be defined, r needs to be positive.

c

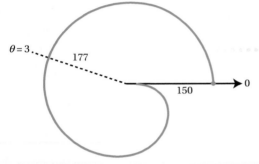

> As θ increases from 0 to 2π, r increases from 150 to 177 (when $\theta = 3$, which is just below π) and then decreases to 9.21.

Polar equations often involve trigonometric functions. You might be able to use trigonometric graphs, rather than differentiation, to find the maximum and minimum values of r.

WORKED EXAMPLE 9.5

A curve has polar equation $r = 5 - 2\cos\theta$ for $0 \leqslant \theta < 2\pi$.

a Find the largest and smallest values of r.
b Hence sketch the curve.

a $-1 \leqslant \cos\theta \leqslant 1$
so $3 \leqslant 5 - 2\cos\theta \leqslant 7$

> Start by considering the minimum and maximum values of $\cos\theta$: -1, when $\theta = \pi$, and 1, when $\theta = 0$ and 2π.

The largest value is $r = 7$ when $\theta = \pi$.
The smallest value is $r = 3$ when $\theta = 0, 2\pi$.

b

> Sketch the graph of $y = 5 - 2\cos x$:

> You can see that r increases from 3 to 7 and decreases to 3 again.

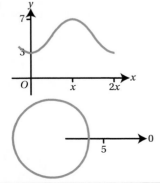

Tangents at the pole

In Worked example 9.3 you saw a curve ($r = \sin 2\theta$) that is only defined for certain values of θ. This happens because we do not allow negative values of r.

The value of $r = \sin 2\theta$ changes from positive to negative, or vice versa, when $\theta = 0, \dfrac{\pi}{2}, \pi, \dfrac{3\pi}{2}, 2\pi$. Each of those θ values corresponds to a half-line, shown in red in the diagram. As the curve approaches each of the lines, r gets closer to zero (so points on the curve get closer and closer to the pole). This means that each of the lines $\theta = 0, \dfrac{\pi}{2}, \pi, \dfrac{3\pi}{2}$ is a tangent to the curve at the pole.

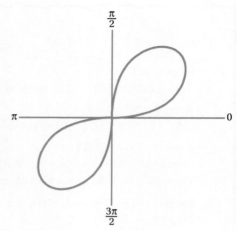

🔑 **Key point 9.2**

For a curve with polar equation $r = f(\theta)$, the line $\theta = \alpha$ is a **tangent at the pole** if $f(\alpha) = 0$ but $f(\alpha) > 0$ on one side of the line.

WORKED EXAMPLE 9.6

For the curve with polar equation $r = 2\cos 3\theta$, find the tangents at the pole and hence sketch the curve.

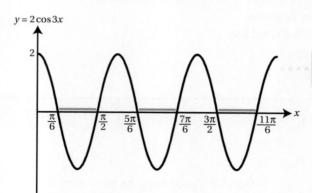

$y = 2\cos 3x$

Sketch the graph of $y = 2\cos 3x$ to see which values of θ would produce negative values of r.

The tangents at the pole are:

$\theta = \dfrac{\pi}{6}, \dfrac{\pi}{2}, \dfrac{5\pi}{6}, \dfrac{7\pi}{6}, \dfrac{3\pi}{2}$ and $\dfrac{11\pi}{6}$.

The value of $2\cos 3\theta$ passes through zero when $\theta = \dfrac{\pi}{6}, \dfrac{\pi}{2}, \dfrac{5\pi}{6}, \dfrac{7\pi}{6}, \dfrac{3\pi}{2}$ and $\dfrac{11\pi}{6}$.

Continues on next page ...

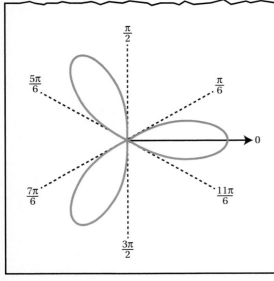

Between the tangents where the curve is defined, the value of r increases from 0 to the maximum value of 2 and then decreases back to 0.

1 For each curve, find the maximum and minimum possible value of r, and the corresponding values of θ. Hence sketch the curve. (In all cases, $0 \leqslant \theta < 2\pi$.)

    a   **i** $r = 3 + 2\sin\theta$ **ii** $r = 5 + \cos\theta$

    b   **i** $r = 7 - 3\cos 2\theta$ **ii** $r = 5 - 2\sin 2\theta$

2 Find the equations of the tangents at the pole for each curve. Hence sketch the curve. (In all cases, $0 \leqslant \theta < 2\pi$.)

    a   **i** $r = 2\sin 3\theta$ **ii** $r = 3\cos 2\theta$

    b   **i** $r = 2 + 4\cos 3\theta$ **ii** $r = \sqrt{2} - 2\sin 4\theta$

3 Consider the curve with polar equation $r = 3\cos 4\theta, r \geqslant 0$ for $0 \leqslant \theta < 2\pi$.

    a   Find the equations of the tangents at the pole.

    b   State the set of values of θ for which the curve is not defined.

    c   Hence sketch the curve.

4   **a**   Sketch the curve with polar equation $r = 3 - 2\cos^2\theta, 0 \leqslant \theta < 2\pi$.

    b   State the largest and smallest values of r.

5 Consider the curve with polar equation $r = 1 + 2\sin 2\theta, 0 \leqslant \theta < 2\pi$.

    a   Find the range of values of θ for which the curve exists.

    b   Sketch the curve, labelling the tangents at the pole and indicating the points where r has maximum value.

6 A curve has polar equation $r = \dfrac{3}{2-\sin\theta}$, $0 \leqslant \theta < 2\pi$.

   a Find the largest and smallest value of r and the values of θ at which they occur.

   b Hence sketch the graph.

7 **a** Sketch the graph of $y = x\left(x - \dfrac{2\pi}{3}\right)\left(x - \dfrac{3\pi}{2}\right)$ for $0 \leqslant x < 2\pi$.

   b Sketch the curve with polar equation $r = \theta\left(\theta - \dfrac{2\pi}{3}\right)\left(\theta - \dfrac{3\pi}{2}\right)$.

8 **a** Find the smallest and largest values of $y = 3x^2 - 6\pi x + 4\pi^2$ for $x \in [0, 2\pi]$.

   b Sketch the curve with the polar equation $r = 3\theta^2 - 6\pi\theta + 4\pi^2$, for $0 \leqslant x < 2\pi$.

9 Sketch the curve with equation $r = -\theta(\theta - \pi)^2(\theta - 2\pi)$ for $0 \leqslant \theta < 2\pi$.

10 Sketch the curve with equation $r = \tan\theta$ for $0 \leqslant \theta < 2\pi$.

Section 3: Changing between polar and Cartesian coordinates

You can use trigonometry to find the Cartesian coordinates of a point with given polar coordinates. Usually, the origin of the Cartesian coordinates is taken to be the pole, and the x-axis to be the initial line.

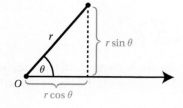

🔑 Key point 9.3

A point with polar coordinates (r, θ) has Cartesian coordinates $(r\cos\theta, r\sin\theta)$.

WORKED EXAMPLE 9.7

Points P and Q have polar coordinates $\left(4, \dfrac{\pi}{3}\right)$ and $\left(2, \dfrac{7\pi}{6}\right)$.

a Show points P and Q on the same diagram.

b Find the Cartesian coordinates of P and Q.

a

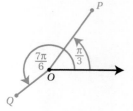

The first coordinate is the distance from the origin and the second coordinate is the angle.

$\dfrac{\pi}{3}$ is $60°$ and $\dfrac{7\pi}{6}$ is $210°$.

b For P:

$x = 4\cos\dfrac{\pi}{3} = 2$

$y = 4\sin\dfrac{\pi}{3} = 2\sqrt{3}$

So the Cartesian coordinates of P are $(2, 2\sqrt{3})$.

Use $x = r\cos\theta$ and $y = r\sin\theta$.

Continues on next page ...

For Q:

$x = 2 \cos \dfrac{7\pi}{6} = -\sqrt{3}$

$y = 2 \sin \dfrac{7\pi}{6} = -1$

So the Cartesian coordinates of Q are $(-\sqrt{3}, -1)$.

To change from Cartesian to polar coordinates, consider the same diagram again.

The value of r is the distance from the origin, so $r^2 = x^2 + y^2$. Remember that we require r to be positive. You need to be a little careful when finding the angle. Since $x = r \cos \theta$ and $y = r \sin \theta$, you can divide the two equations to get $\tan \theta = \dfrac{y}{x}$. However, there are two values $\theta \in [0, 2\pi)$ with the same value of $\tan \theta$; you need to consider the position of the point to decide which one is correct.

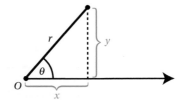

Key point 9.4

For a point with Cartesian coordinates (x, y) the polar coordinates satisfy:

- $r = \sqrt{x^2 + y^2}$
- $\tan \theta = \dfrac{y}{x}$

Rewind

This should remind you of the modulus and argument of a complex number – see Pure Core Student Book 1, Chapter 4, and Chapter 2 of this book.

WORKED EXAMPLE 9.8

Find the polar coordinates of the points $A(-3, 5)$ and $B(4, -1)$.

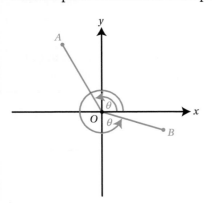

Start by plotting the points to see which angle to use.

For A:

Use $r = \sqrt{x^2 + y^2}$.

$r = \sqrt{(-3)^2 + 5^2}$

$= \sqrt{34}$

Continues on next page …

$$\tan\theta = \frac{5}{-3}$$

$$\Rightarrow \theta = 2.11 \text{ or } \theta = 5.25$$

> Find $\tan^{-1}\left(-\frac{5}{3}\right)$, then add π to get the two possible values between 0 and 2π.

Hence the polar coordinates of A are $(\sqrt{34}, 2.11)$.

> The angle for A is smaller than π.

For B:

$$r = \sqrt{4^2 + (-1)^2}$$

$$= \sqrt{17}$$

$$\tan\theta = -\frac{1}{4}$$

$$\Rightarrow \theta = 2.90 \text{ or } \theta = 6.04$$

Hence the polar coordinates of B are $(\sqrt{17}, 6.04)$.

> The angle for B is greater than π.

You can now convert equations of curves between polar and Cartesian forms.

WORKED EXAMPLE 9.9

Find the Cartesian equation of the curve with polar equation $r = 2\sin\theta$.

$$r = \sqrt{x^2 + y^2}$$

$$\sin\theta = \frac{y}{r}$$

$$\therefore \sin\theta = \frac{y}{\sqrt{x^2 + y^2}}$$

> Use $r^2 = x^2 + y^2$ and $y = r\sin\theta$.

Hence:

$$\sqrt{x^2 + y^2} = 2\left(\frac{y}{\sqrt{x^2 + y^2}}\right)$$

$$x^2 + y^2 = 2y$$

> Substitute for $\sin\theta$ in the equation of the curve.

> Simplify if possible. In this case, multiply both sides by the 'square root' term.

WORKED EXAMPLE 9.10

Find the polar equation of the curve $(x^2 + y^2)^3 = 3xy$.

$$(r^2)^3 = 3(r\cos\theta)(r\sin\theta)$$

$$r^6 = 3r^2 \sin\theta \cos\theta$$

$$r^4 = 3\sin\theta \cos\theta$$

> Use $x = r\cos\theta$ and $y = r\sin\theta$.

> You also know that $x^2 + y^2 = r^2$.

EXERCISE 9C

1 Each point is given in polar coordinates. Find the Cartesian coordinates.

   a **i** $\left(5, \dfrac{\pi}{4}\right)$ **ii** $\left(3, \dfrac{\pi}{3}\right)$

   b **i** $\left(\sqrt{2}, \dfrac{3\pi}{4}\right)$ **ii** $\left(\sqrt{3}, \dfrac{5\pi}{6}\right)$

   c **i** $(6, 4.1)$ **ii** $(3, 5.7)$

2 Each point is given in Cartesian coordinates. Find the polar coordinates. Take $\theta \in [0, 2\pi)$.

   a **i** $(5, 2)$ **ii** $(3, 4)$

   b **i** $(0, 2)$ **ii** $(0, -3)$

   c **i** $(-1, -5)$ **ii** $(4, -1)$

3 Find the polar equation of each curve.

   a **i** $x^2 + y^2 = 3xy$ **ii** $(x^2 + y^2)^2 = 2x^2 y$

   b **i** $\dfrac{1}{x} + \dfrac{1}{y} = \dfrac{1}{5}$ **ii** $x^3 + y^3 = 3$

   c **i** $y = 3x + 1$ **ii** $x^2 + y^2 = 6$

4 Find the Cartesian equation of each curve.

   a **i** $r = 2\theta$ **ii** $r = 3\theta^2$

   b **i** $r = 4\sin\theta$ **ii** $r = 2\cos\theta$

   c **i** $r = 2\tan\theta$ **ii** $r^2 = \tan\theta$

5 A curve has polar equation $r = 3\cos\theta$. Point Q, with polar coordinates $(2, \alpha)$ where $\pi < \alpha < 2\pi$, lies on the curve.

   a Find the value of α.

   b Find Cartesian coordinates of Q.

   c Find the Cartesian equation of the curve.

6 Find the polar equation of the circle $(x - 1)^2 + (y - 1)^2 = 2$, giving your answer in the form $r = f(\theta)$.

7 Find the Cartesian equation of the curve with polar equation $r = 3\tan\theta$.

8 A curve has polar equation $r = \dfrac{3}{2 + \cos\theta}$.

   Show that the Cartesian equation of the curve can be written as $3x^2 + 4y^2 + 6x = 9$.

9 Find the Cartesian equation of the curve with polar equation:

   a $r = \cos^3\theta$ **b** $r = \dfrac{1}{\cos^3\theta}$.

Section 4: Area enclosed by a polar curve

Finding the area bounded by a polar curve is similar to finding the area bounded by a Cartesian curve, except that rather than being the area between the curve, the x-axis and vertical lines $x = a$ and $x = b$, now it is the area between the curve, the pole and lines from the pole $\theta = \alpha$ and $\theta = \beta$.

 Key point 9.5

The area enclosed between a polar curve and the half-lines $\theta = \alpha$ and $\theta = \beta$ is

$$A = \int_\alpha^\beta \frac{1}{2} r^2 \, d\theta.$$

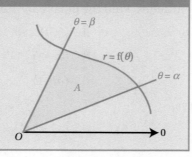

PROOF 5

Consider a curve $r = f(\theta)$, where $r \geqslant 0$ and $\alpha < \beta$.

You can split the region into small sectors of angle $\Delta\theta$ and area ΔA.

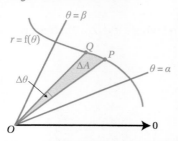

The polar coordinates of the point P are (r, θ) and the polar coordinates of the nearby point Q are $(r + \Delta r, \theta + \Delta\theta)$.

The area of each sector is approximately the same as the area of a sector of a circle with angle ΔA and radius r:

$$\Delta A = \frac{1}{2} r^2 \Delta\theta$$

The area of a sector of a circle is $A = \frac{1}{2} r^2 \theta$.

The total area is approximately:

$$A \approx \sum_{\theta=\alpha}^{\theta=\beta} \frac{1}{2} r^2 \Delta\theta$$

Summing all these sectors between $\theta = \alpha$ and $\theta = \beta$ gives the approximate total area.

$$A = \lim_{\Delta\theta \to 0} \sum_{\theta=\alpha}^{\theta=\beta} \frac{1}{2} r^2 \Delta\theta$$

The approximation becomes more and more accurate as the angle gets smaller.

$$= \int_\alpha^\beta \frac{1}{2} r^2 \, d\theta$$

In the limit as $\Delta\theta \to 0$ the sum becomes an integral.

WORKED EXAMPLE 9.11

In this question you must show detailed reasoning.

The diagram shows the curve with polar equation $r = 3 - 2\sin\theta$.

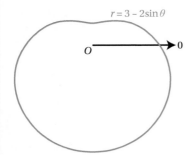

$r = 3 - 2\sin\theta$

Find the area enclosed by the curve.

$A = \int_0^{2\pi} \frac{1}{2}(3 - 2\sin\theta)^2 \, d\theta$ .... Use the formula $A = \int_\alpha^\beta \frac{1}{2}r^2 \, d\theta$.

$= \frac{1}{2}\int_0^{2\pi} (9 - 12\sin\theta + 4\sin^2\theta) \, d\theta$ .... Expand the brackets.

$= \frac{1}{2}\int_0^{2\pi} (9 - 12\sin\theta + 2 - 2\cos 2\theta) \, d\theta$ .... To integrate $\sin^2\theta$, use the $\cos 2\theta$ identity:
$4\sin^2\theta = 2 - 2\cos 2\theta$.

$= \frac{1}{2}\int_0^{2\pi} (11 - 12\sin\theta - 2\cos 2\theta) \, d\theta$

$= \frac{1}{2}\left[11\theta + 12\cos\theta - \sin 2\theta\right]_0^{2\pi}$

$= \frac{1}{2}\left[(22\pi + 12 - 0) - (0 + 12 - 0)\right]$

$= 11\pi$

EXERCISE 9D

1 Find the area enclosed between these polar curves and half-lines.

  a **i** $r^2 = \cos 2\theta,\ a = -\frac{\pi}{4},\ b = \frac{\pi}{4}$ **ii** $r^2 = \sin 3\theta,\ a = 0,\ b = \frac{\pi}{3}$

  b **i** $r = 2\theta,\ a = 0,\ b = \pi$ **ii** $r = \theta^2,\ a = 0,\ b = \pi$

  c **i** $r = 2e^\theta,\ a = 0,\ b = 2\pi$ **ii** $r = e^{\frac{\theta}{2}},\ a = 0,\ b = 2\pi$

  d **i** $r = \cos\theta,\ a = 0,\ b = \frac{\pi}{2}$ **ii** $r = \sin\theta,\ a = \frac{\pi}{4},\ b = \frac{\pi}{2}$

  e **i** $r = 1 + \sin\theta,\ a = -\frac{\pi}{2},\ b = \frac{\pi}{2}$ **ii** $r = 1 - \cos\theta,\ a = 0,\ b = 2\pi$

> **Focus on ...**
>
> Some areas can only be calculated exactly using polar coordinates. Focus on ... Proof 2 looks at one important example.

2 **a** Write down the polar equation of a circle of radius a with centre at the pole.

    b Using your answer to part **a**, show that the area of the circle is πa^2.

3 Find the exact value of the area enclosed between the curve $r = \tan\theta$, the initial line and the half-line $\theta = \dfrac{\pi}{4}$, clearly showing all your working.

4 The diagram shows the curve with polar equation $r = 2 + \cos\theta, 0 \leqslant \theta < 2\pi$.

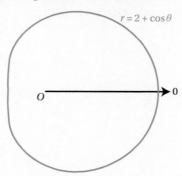

$r = 2 + \cos\theta$

Show that the exact area enclosed by the curve is $\dfrac{9\pi}{2}$.

5 The diagram shows the curve with polar equation $r = 5 + 2\sin\theta, 0 \leqslant \theta < 2\pi$.

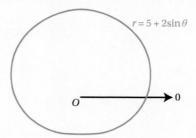

$r = 5 + 2\sin\theta$

Find the exact area enclosed by the curve, clearly showing all your working.

6 a Sketch the curve with polar equation $r = \theta^{-\frac{1}{2}}, 0 \leqslant \theta < 2\pi$.

b Show that the area enclosed between the lines $\theta = a$ and $\theta = 2a$, where $0 < a \leqslant \pi$, is independent of a.

7 a Sketch the curve C with polar equation $r = 3\sin 2\theta, 0 \leqslant \theta < 2\pi$.

b Find the total area of the region enclosed by C, clearly showing all your working.

8 The curve C has polar equation $r = a\cos 2\theta$, for $r \geqslant 0$ and $0 \leqslant \theta < 2\pi$.

a Sketch C, giving the equations of any tangents at the pole.

b Find, in terms of a, the total area of the region enclosed by C, clearly showing all your working.

9 The area of the region enclosed between the curve with polar equation $r = a(1 + \tan\theta)$, the initial line and the half-line $\theta = k$ is $a^2\left(\ln 2 + \dfrac{\sqrt{3}}{2}\right)$.

Find the value of the positive constant k.

10 The diagram shows the curve with polar equation $r = a\sin\theta\sin 2\theta, 0 \leqslant \theta < \dfrac{\pi}{2}$.

Show that the area of the region enclosed by the curve is $\dfrac{\pi a^2}{16}$.

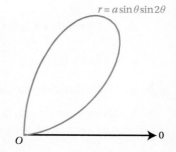

$r = a\sin\theta\sin 2\theta$

Section 5: Area between two curves

To find the area enclosed between two polar curves, find the intersection points of the curves and calculate the part of the area bounded by each curve separately.

WORKED EXAMPLE 9.12

Two curves have polar equations:

$$C_1 : r = 3 + \cos\theta$$

$$C_2 : r = 7\cos\theta$$

for $0 \leqslant \theta < 2\pi$.

a Find the polar coordinates of the points of intersection of C_1 and C_2.
b Find the exact value of the area of the finite region enclosed between C_1 and C_2.

a The curves intersect where

$$3 + \cos\theta = 7\cos\theta$$

$$\cos\theta = \frac{1}{2}$$

> Equate the equations of the two curves.

$$\theta = \frac{\pi}{3}, \frac{5\pi}{3}$$

> Solve for θ. There are two values between 0 and 2π.

From C_2: when $\cos\theta = \frac{1}{2}, r = \frac{7}{2}$.

> Find the corresponding values of r.

The points of intersection are $\left(\frac{7}{2}, \frac{\pi}{3}\right)$ and $\left(\frac{7}{2}, \frac{5\pi}{3}\right)$.

b Sketching the curves:

> It is a good idea to sketch the curves to see where the required region is.

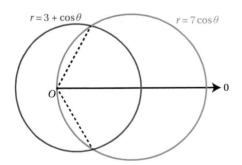

$$\text{Area} = 2\left[\int_0^{\frac{\pi}{3}} \frac{1}{2}(3 + \cos\theta)^2 \, d\theta + \int_{\frac{\pi}{3}}^{\frac{\pi}{2}} \frac{1}{2}(7\cos\theta)^2 \, d\theta\right]$$

> The required region above the initial line is made up of two parts: one bounded by C_1 between $\theta = 0$ and $\theta = \frac{\pi}{3}$ and one bounded by C_2 between $\theta = \frac{\pi}{3}$ and $\theta = \frac{\pi}{2}$.
>
> By symmetry about the initial line, the full area is double this.

Continues on next page …

$$= \int_0^{\frac{\pi}{3}} \left(9 + 6\cos\theta + \cos^2\theta\right) d\theta + \int_{\frac{\pi}{3}}^{\frac{\pi}{2}} 49\cos^2\theta \, d\theta$$

Expand and use $\cos^2\theta = \dfrac{\cos 2\theta + 1}{2}$.

$$= \int_0^{\frac{\pi}{3}} \left(9 + 6\cos\theta + \frac{\cos 2\theta + 1}{2}\right) d\theta + \int_{\frac{\pi}{3}}^{\frac{\pi}{2}} \frac{49}{2}\left(\cos 2\theta + 1\right) d\theta$$

$$= \left[9\theta + 6\sin\theta + \frac{1}{4}\sin 2\theta + \frac{1}{2}\theta\right]_0^{\frac{\pi}{3}} + \frac{49}{2}\left[\frac{1}{2}\sin 2\theta + \theta\right]_{\frac{\pi}{3}}^{\frac{\pi}{2}}$$

$$= \left[\left(\frac{19\pi}{6} + 3\sqrt{3} + \frac{\sqrt{3}}{8}\right) - (0)\right] + \frac{49}{2}\left[\left(\frac{\pi}{2}\right) - \left(\frac{\sqrt{3}}{4} + \frac{\pi}{3}\right)\right]$$

$$= \frac{29\pi}{4} - 3\sqrt{3}$$

Tip

In more complicated questions where the region is between two curves, remember that in polar coordinates you are finding the area of a sector bounded by the curve and two half-lines from the pole; not a region bounded by two vertical lines as in Cartesian coordinates.

EXERCISE 9E

1   The diagram shows the curve with polar equation $r = 2$ and the line with polar equation $r = \sqrt{3}\sec\theta$, both defined for $0 \leqslant \theta < \dfrac{\pi}{2}$.

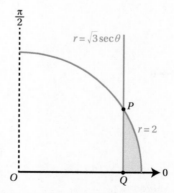

The line intersects the curve at the point P and the initial line at the point Q.

a   Find the polar coordinates of P.

b   i   Find the exact area of the triangle OPQ.
    ii   Hence show that the area of the shaded region is $\dfrac{2\pi - 3\sqrt{3}}{6}$.

2 The diagram shows the curve with polar equation $r = a(1 + \cos\theta)$, $0 \leqslant \theta < \pi$.

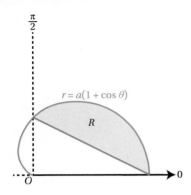

Find, in terms of a, the exact area of the shaded region R.

3 The diagram shows the curves with polar equations $r = a$ and $r = 2a\sin 2\theta$ for $0 \leqslant \theta < \dfrac{\pi}{2}$.

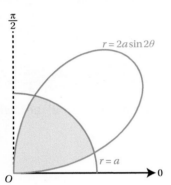

a Find the polar coordinates of the points of intersection of the two curves.

b Find the exact area of the shaded region enclosed within both curves.

4 The diagram shows the curves with polar equations $r = \dfrac{1}{2}$ and $r = 1 - \sin\theta$, $0 \leqslant \theta < 2\pi$.

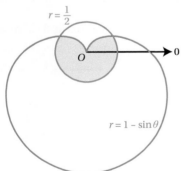

a Find the polar coordinates of the points of intersection of the two curves.

b Find the exact area enclosed inside both curves which is shaded on the diagram.

5 The diagram shows the curves C_1 and C_2 with polar equations $r = 6 - 6\cos\theta$ and $r = 2 + 2\cos\theta$, $0 \leqslant \theta < 2\pi$.

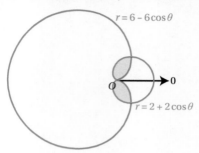

$r = 6 - 6\cos\theta$

$r = 2 + 2\cos\theta$

a Find the polar coordinates of the points of intersection of the two curves.

b Show that the area of the shaded region is $2\left(11\pi - 18\sqrt{3}\right)$.

6 a On the same axes, sketch the curves with polar equations $r = 2$ and $r = 3 - 2\cos\theta$ for $0 \leqslant \theta < 2\pi$.

b Show that the exact value of the area inside $r = 3 - 2\cos\theta$ but outside $r = 2$ is $\dfrac{33\sqrt{3} + 28\pi}{6}$.

Checklist of learning and understanding

- Polar coordinates (r, θ) describe the position of a point in terms of its distance from the pole and the angle measured anticlockwise from the initial line.
- The connection between polar and Cartesian coordinates is:
  - $x = r\cos\theta$, $y = r\sin\theta$
  - $r = \sqrt{x^2 + y^2}$, $\tan\theta = \dfrac{y}{x}$
- For a curve with equation given in polar coordinates:
  - r cannot be negative, so not all values of θ are possible
  - there might be one or more tangents at the pole, given by the values of θ for which $r = 0$.
- The area enclosed between a polar curve and the half-lines $\theta = \alpha$ and $\theta = \beta$ is $A = \displaystyle\int_\alpha^\beta \frac{1}{2} r^2 \, d\theta$.
- To find the area enclosed between two polar curves, find the intersection points of the curves and calculate the part of the area bounded by each curve separately.

Mixed practice 9

1 Find the greatest distance from the pole of any point on the curve $r = 2(5 - 3\sin\theta), 0 \leqslant \theta < 2\pi$.

2 Find the polar equation of the curve $x^2 + y^2 = a(x - y)$.

3 Points A and B have polar coordinates $\left(7, \dfrac{\pi}{4}\right)$ and $\left(4, \dfrac{5\pi}{6}\right)$. Find:

    a the distance AB

    b the area of the triangle AOB.

4 Sketch the curve with polar equation $r = 1 - \cos 2\theta, 0 \leqslant \theta < 2\pi$.

5 Find the area of the region enclosed between the initial line and the curve with polar equation $r = \sqrt{2a}\, e^{\frac{\theta}{2}}, 0 \leqslant \theta < 2\pi$.

6   **a** Sketch the curve with polar equation $r = \theta, 0 \leqslant \theta < 2\pi$.

    b Show that the area bounded by the curve and the initial line is $\dfrac{4\pi^3}{3}$.

7   **a** Sketch the curve with polar equation $r = 5 - 4\cos\theta, 0 \leqslant \theta < 2\pi$.

    b Find the exact area enclosed by the curve, clearly showing your working.

8 The Cartesian equation of a curve is $x^2 + y^2 - 2x = \sqrt{x^2 + y^2}, r \geqslant 0$.

    a Show that the polar equation of the curve is $r = 1 + 2\cos\theta$.

    b Find the equation of any tangents at the pole.

    c Hence sketch the curve for $0 \leqslant \theta < 2\pi$.

    d Show that the area enclosed by the curve is $2\pi + \dfrac{3\sqrt{3}}{2}$.

9 Find a Cartesian equation for the curve $r = 3\cos^2\theta, 0 \leqslant \theta < 2\pi$.

10 A curve has polar equation $r = 2 + 4\sin\theta, 0 \leqslant \theta < 2\pi$.

    a Find the equations of the tangents at the pole.

    b Sketch the curve.

    c Find the Cartesian equation of the curve.

11   **a** Sketch the curve with polar equation $r = 5 - 3\cos\theta, 0 \leqslant \theta < 2\pi$.

    b Find the Cartesian coordinates of the point that is furthest away from the pole.

12 A curve has polar equation $r = 2 - 4\sin 2\theta, 0 \leqslant \theta < 2\pi$.

    a Find the equations of the tangents at the pole.

    b State the polar coordinates of the points at greatest distance from the pole.

    c Hence sketch the graph.

13 A curve is defined by the polar equation $r = 3\theta$ for $0 \leqslant \theta < 2\pi$.

    a Sketch the curve.

    b Find the Cartesian coordinates of the point where the curve intersects the line $\theta = \dfrac{2\pi}{3}$.

14 Sketch the curve with polar equation $r = 5\cos 3\theta, 0 \leqslant \theta < 2\pi$. Indicate the equations of the tangents at the pole, and give the polar coordinates of the point where the curve crosses the initial line.

15 The diagram shows the curve with polar equation $r = 2 + 4\cos\theta, 0 \leqslant \theta < 2\pi$.

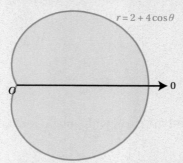

Find the exact value of the shaded area, clearly showing your working.

16 The diagram shows the curve C with polar equation $r = 10 - 10\cos\theta, 0 \leqslant \theta < 2\pi$.

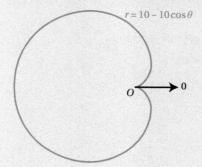

a Show that the area of the region bounded by C is 150π.

The circle $x^2 + y^2 = 25$ intersects C at the points A and B.

b Find the polar coordinates of A and B.

c Find the area enclosed between the circle and C.

17 The diagram shows the curve with polar equation $r = \cos\theta + \cos 3\theta, 0 \leqslant \theta < \pi$.

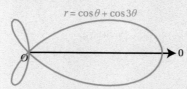

a i Show that $\cos 3\theta \equiv 4\cos^3\theta - 3\cos\theta$.

ii Hence find the equations of the tangents at the pole.

b Show that the area enclosed in the large loop is $\dfrac{3\pi + 8}{12}$.

18 The equation of a curve is $x^2 + y^2 - x = \sqrt{x^2 + y^2}$.

    i   Find the polar equation of this curve in the form $r = \mathrm{f}(\theta)$.

    ii Sketch the curve.

    iii The line $x + 2y = 2$ divides the region enclosed by the curve into two parts. Find the ratio of the two areas.

© OCR A Level Mathematics, Unit 4726/01 Further Pure Mathematics 2, June 2013

19

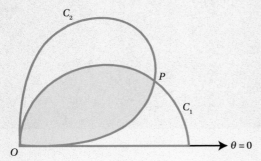

The diagram shows two curves, C_1 and C_2, which intersect at the pole O and at the point P. The polar equation of C_1 is $r = \sqrt{2}\cos\theta$ and the polar equation of C_2 is $r = \sqrt{2\sin 2\theta}$. For both curves, $0 \leqslant \theta \leqslant \frac{1}{2}\pi$. The value of θ at P is α.

    i   Show that $\tan\alpha = \frac{1}{2}$.

    ii Show that the area of the region common to C_1 and C_2, shaded in the diagram, is $\frac{1}{4}\pi - \frac{1}{2}\alpha$.

© OCR A Level Mathematics, Unit 4726 Further Pure Mathematics 2, January 2012

10 Differential equations

In this chapter you will learn how to:

- understand and use the language associated with differential equations
- solve differential equations of the form $\dfrac{dy}{dx} + P(x)y = Q(x)$
- solve differential equations of the form $a\dfrac{d^2y}{dx^2} + b\dfrac{dy}{dx} + cy = f(x)$
- use substitutions to turn differential equations into the required form.

Before you start…

A Level Mathematics Student Book 2, Chapter 13	You should know how to solve separable differential equations.	1 Solve $\dfrac{dy}{dx} = xy$.
A Level Mathematics Student Book 2, Chapter 10	You should know how to differentiate expressions, including using the product and chain rules.	2 Differentiate $y = x\,e^{3x}$ with respect to x.
A Level Mathematics Student Book 2, Chapter 11	You should be able to use various methods to integrate expressions.	3 Integrate $x\,e^x$ with respect to x.

Introduction

In many academic areas such as Physics and Economics it is important to describe situations in terms of rates of change. This produces differential equations. In this chapter you will extend the types of differential equations you can solve. You will then see in Chapter 11 how these methods can be applied in many real-life situations.

 Rewind

You met differential equations in A Level Mathematics Student Book 2, Chapter 13.

i Did you know?

If you read other books about differential equations you will see that the equations covered in this book are referred to as ordinary differential equations (ODEs). This is in contrast to another type of differential equation called partial differential equations (PDEs) which use a different type of differentiation.

Section 1: Terminology of differential equations

Differential equations have an **independent variable** (which is the variable on the bottom of the derivatives) and at least one **dependent variable** (which is the variable on the top of the derivatives). For example, in the equation $\dfrac{dy}{dx} = x^2 + y$ the independent variable is x and the dependent variable is y.

There are many different types of differential equation. To decide which technique to use when solving differential equations you need to be able to categorise them.

- The **order of a differential equation** is the largest number of times the dependent variable is differentiated. For example:
  $\dfrac{d^3 y}{dx^3} + 3\dfrac{dy}{dx} + y = x^2$ is a third-order differential equation.

- A **linear differential equation** is one in which the dependent variable (y in these examples) only appears to the power of 1 (or not at all) in any expression. For example: $x^2 \dfrac{dy}{dx} + 3\dfrac{d^2 y}{dx^2} + \sin x = 0$ is a linear differential equation, but any differential equation involving y^2, $\sin y$ or even $y\dfrac{dy}{dx}$ is non-linear.

- A **homogeneous differential equation** is one where every term involves the dependent variable. For example: $\dfrac{d^2 y}{dx^2} + x\dfrac{dy}{dx} + y^2 = 0$ is homogeneous, but $\dfrac{dy}{dx} = y + 2$ is a **non-homogeneous differential equation**. Every non-homogeneous differential equation has a homogeneous differential equation associated with it, formed by removing all the terms not involving the dependent variable.

> **Tip**
>
> In some books homogeneous is used to refer to a different property of differential equations. The definition given here is the only one relevant to this course.

WORKED EXAMPLE 10.1

Consider the differential equation $x\dfrac{dy}{dx} + 3y = \ln x$.

a State the order of the differential equation.

b Is the equation linear? Explain your answer.

c Explain why the equation is non-homogeneous, and write down the associated homogeneous equation.

a *The equation is first order.*

> The highest derivative of y in the equation is $\dfrac{dy}{dx}$, which is a first derivative.

b *The equation is linear because $3y$ and $\dfrac{dy}{dx}$ are both linear terms.*

> The only occurrences of the dependent variable are y and $\dfrac{dy}{dx}$, and they are both linear.
>
> (Note that it doesn't matter that $\dfrac{dy}{dx}$ is multiplied by x.)

Continues on next page …

c The equation is non-homogeneous because the term $\ln x$ does not contain y.

..... Non-homogeneous equations include terms which do not contain the dependent variable.

The associated homogeneous equation is

..... Remove all terms without y to get a homogeneous equation.

$$x\frac{dy}{dx}+3y=0$$

To solve a differential equation, you need to find y as a function of x (if y is the dependent variable and x is the independent variable). When solving a differential equation, because the process is effectively integration, there will be arbitrary constants involved. The solution containing all the arbitrary constants is called the **general solution**.

 Key point 10.1

The general solution to an nth-order differential equation has n arbitrary constants.

To fix the arbitrary constants you either use initial conditions (values of y, $\frac{dy}{dx}$, etc. at one value of x) or boundary conditions (values of y, $\frac{dy}{dx}$, etc. at several values of x). You need one piece of information for each arbitrary constant, and then you normally use simultaneous equation techniques to find the values of each constant. When the constants in the general solution have the values required to fit the conditions, the result is called the **particular solution**.

WORKED EXAMPLE 10.2

a Show that $y = Ax^3 + \dfrac{B}{x^2} + 3x^2$ is the general solution of the differential equation

$$x^2\frac{d^2y}{dx^2} - 6y + 12x^2 = 0.$$

b Find the particular solution that satisfies $y = 7$ and $\dfrac{dy}{dx} = 3$ when $x = 1$.

a $y = Ax^3 + \dfrac{B}{x^2} + 3x^2$

$\dfrac{dy}{dx} = 3Ax^2 - \dfrac{2B}{x^3} + 6x$

$\dfrac{d^2y}{dx^2} = 6Ax + \dfrac{6B}{x^4} + 6$

Continues on next page ...

Then:

$$x^2\frac{d^2y}{dx^2}-6y+12x^2$$

$$=\left(6Ax^3+\frac{6B}{x^2}+6x^2\right)-\left(6Ax^3+\frac{6B}{x^2}+18x^2\right)+12x^2$$

$$=0$$

Hence the given function is the general solution.

Substitute y and $\frac{d^2y}{dx^2}$ into the given differential equation.

The given function satisfies the differential equation for all values of A and B. Notice that it also contains two arbitrary constants, as stated in Key point 10.1.

b When $x=1$:

$$y=A+B+3=7$$

$$\frac{dy}{dx}=3A-2B+6=3$$

Substitute the given values of x, y and $\frac{dy}{dx}$ into the general solution.

$$\Leftrightarrow\begin{cases}A+B=4\\3A-2B=-3\end{cases}$$

Solve the simultaneous equations (you can use a calculator).

$$\therefore A=1, B=3$$

The particular solution is

$$y=x^3+\frac{3}{x^2}+3x^2$$

Non-homogeneous linear equations

In general, homogeneous equations are easier to solve than non-homogeneous ones. Fortunately, it turns out that, for linear equations, a general solution of a non-homogeneous equation can be found by using the general solution of the associated homogeneous equation, called the **complementary function**.

Once you have the complementary function, all you need is one solution of the full non-homogeneous equation. This is called a **particular integral**. Combining this with the complementary function gives the general solution of the full non-homogeneous equation.

For example, the differential equation $x^2\frac{d^2y}{dx^2}-6y+12x^2=0$ from Worked example 10.2 is non-homogeneous. You can check that $y_p=3x^2$ satisfies this equation, so it can be used as a particular integral.

The associated homogeneous equation is $x^2\frac{d^2y}{dx^2}-6y=0$ (obtained by removing the term without y). You can check that $y_c=Ax^3+\frac{B}{x^2}$ satisfies this homogeneous equation for all values of A and B; hence this is the complementary function. The general solution of the non-homogeneous equation is then $y=Ax^3+\frac{B}{x^2}+3x^2$, which is the sum of the particular integral and the complementary function.

> 💡 **Tip**
>
> The complementary function will contain arbitrary constants.

> ⏩ **Fast forward**
>
> In Section 4 you will learn how to 'guess' the form of a particular integral in some specific cases.

> 💡 **Tip**
>
> Particular integrals are not unique. For example, $y=3x^2+5x^3$, $y=3x^2+\frac{2}{x^2}$ and $y=3x^2+5x^3+\frac{2}{x^2}$ can all be taken as particular integrals for our equation. You may wish to investigate how using different particular integrals affects the values of the constants A and B for the particular solution in part **b** of Example 10.2.

🔑 Key point 10.2

For a linear differential equation, the general solution is given by

$$y = y_c + y_p$$

where y_c is the complementary function and y_p is a particular integral.

Tip

Don't confuse particular integrals with the particular solution. A particular integral is *any* solution of a differential equation. The particular solution needs to satisfy given initial conditions.

The proof of the result in Key point 10.2 is shown in Proof 6. It generalises the observations made in the discussion above. You do not need to learn (or even understand) this proof, but it might help to explain the result. It also shows you an example of a type of proof often seen in advanced mathematics.

Any linear differential equation can be written as $L[y] = f(x)$ where L is called a linear differential operator. For example: if $\dfrac{d^2 y}{dx} + x\dfrac{dy}{dx} + 3y = x^3$

then $L[y]$ is $\dfrac{d^2 y}{dx^2} + x\dfrac{dy}{dx} + 3y$ and $f(x) = x^3$.

Proof 6 uses the fact that $L[y_1 + y_2] = L[y_1] + L[y_2]$. This is because the derivative of a sum equals the sum of the derivatives.

PROOF 6

If y_c is the complementary function and y_p is the particular integral of a linear differential equation $L[y] = f(x)$, then $y = y_c + y_p$ will be a solution to the differential equation.

The complementary function, y_c, is defined by:

$L[y_c] = 0$ (1)

y_c is the solution of the associated homogeneous equation.

The particular integral is any function, y_p, satisfying

$L[y_p] = f(x)$ (2)

y_p is a solution of the full equation.

Then if $y = y_c + y_p$,

$L[y] = L[y_c + y_p]$

Use the given fact about linear differential operators.

$\quad = L[y_c] + L[y_p]$

$\quad = 0 + f(x)$

Use properties (1) and (2).

So y also satisfies $L[y] = f(x)$.

WORKED EXAMPLE 10.3

The differential equation $x\dfrac{dy}{dx} + y = \ln x$ is satisfied for $x > 0$.

a Find the complementary function.
b A particular integral has the form $y = a\ln x + b$. Find the values of a and b.
c Hence find the particular solution with initial condition $y = 3$ when $x = 1$.

a The associated homogenous differential equation is

$$x\frac{dy}{dx} + y = 0$$

$$\frac{dy}{dx} = -\frac{y}{x}$$

$$\frac{1}{y}\frac{dy}{dx} = -\frac{1}{x}$$

$$\int \frac{1}{y}dy = \int -\frac{1}{x}dx$$

$$\ln y = -\ln x + c$$

$$= \ln\left(\frac{1}{x}\right) + \ln A$$

$$= \ln\left(\frac{A}{x}\right)$$

$$\therefore y_c = \frac{A}{x}$$

> The given equation is non-homogeneous. The complementary function is the solution of the associated homogeneous equation, obtained by removing any terms which do not contain y.

> You need to be able to recognise that this differential equation is separable.

> Write c as $\ln A$ in order to use rules of logarithms.

> Remember that the complementary function should contain one arbitrary constant (since the equation is first order).

b If $y = a\ln x + b$, then $\dfrac{dy}{dx} = \dfrac{a}{x}$.

Substituting: $x \times \dfrac{a}{x} + a\ln x + b = \ln x$

So, $a + b + a\ln x = \ln x$

Comparing coefficients of $\ln x$: $a = 1$

> Frequently when finding the particular integral you look at the coefficients on both sides of the equation.

Comparing coefficients of the constant term and using the fact that $a = 1$: $a + b = 0$
$$b = -1$$

So the particular integral is $\ln x - 1$.

c The general solution is

$$y = \frac{A}{x} + \ln x - 1.$$

Using the initial condition, substituting in $x = 1$ when $y = 3$:

$$3 = A + \ln 1 - 1$$

$$A = 4$$

> The general solution is the sum of the complementary function and the particular integral.

> To find the particular solution, use the initial condition to find the value of the constant A.

Therefore the particular solution is $y = \dfrac{4}{x} + \ln x - 1$.

EXERCISE 10A

1 Write an example of each type of differential equation.

   a i Linear   **ii** Non-linear

   b i Second order   **ii** Third order

   c i Homogeneous   **ii** Non-homogeneous

2 Classify each differential equation, stating its order, whether or not it is linear, and whether it is homogeneous or non-homogeneous.

   a i $\dfrac{d^2y}{dx^2}+3\dfrac{dy}{dx}+4y=\sin x$ **ii** $\dfrac{d^2y}{dx^2}+3\dfrac{dy}{dx}+4x=0$

   b i $\dfrac{d^2y}{dx^2}+3y\dfrac{dy}{dx}+4y=0$ **ii** $\left(\dfrac{dy}{dx}\right)^2+4y=x^2$

   c i $5\dfrac{d^2z}{dt^2}+\dfrac{dz}{dt}+\sin z+e^t=0$ **ii** $t^3\dfrac{d^3z}{dt^3}+t^2\dfrac{d^2z}{dt^2}+t\dfrac{dz}{dt}+z=0$

   d i $\dfrac{d}{dx}\left(x\dfrac{dy}{dx}\right)=y$ **ii** $\dfrac{d}{dx}(x+y)=y^2$

3 Given these solutions to differential equations and the initial or boundary conditions, find the particular solution to each differential equation.

   a i $y=Ax^2+4$; $y=12$ when $x=2$ **ii** $y=A\cos x-2$; $y=6$ when $x=0$

   b i $y=Ae^{-x}+3x$; $\dfrac{dy}{dx}=2$ when $x=0$ **ii** $y=A\ln x-2x^2$; $\dfrac{dy}{dx}=2$ when $x=1$

   c i $y=Ax^2+Bx$; $y=1$ when $x=1$; $y=8$ when $x=2$

     ii $y=A\sin x+B\cos x$; $y=5$ when $x=0$; $y=10$ when $x=\dfrac{\pi}{2}$

   d i $y=Ae^{2x}+Be^x$; $y=2$ and $\dfrac{dy}{dx}=5$ when $x=0$

     ii $y=A\sin x+B\cos 2x$; $y=-2$ and $\dfrac{dy}{dx}=10$ when $x=0$

4 The differential equation $2x\dfrac{dy}{dx}+y=\ln x$ is defined for $x>0$.

   a Find the complementary function.

   b A particular integral has the form $y=a\ln x+b$. Find the values of a and b.

   c Hence find the particular solution with initial condition $y=3$ when $x=1$.

5 The differential equation $\cos x\dfrac{dy}{dx}+2\sin 2x=y\sin x$ is defined for $-\dfrac{\pi}{2}<x<\dfrac{\pi}{2}$.

   a Find the complementary function.

   b A particular integral exists of the form $y=a\sin x+b\cos x$. Find the values of a and b.

   c Hence find the general solution to the differential equation $\cos x\dfrac{dy}{dx}+2\sin 2x=y\sin x$ defined for $-\dfrac{\pi}{2}<x<\dfrac{\pi}{2}$.

6 The differential equation $y\dfrac{dy}{dx}+y^2=e^x$ is defined for $y>0$.

   a Show that this differential equation has a particular integral of the form $y=Ae^{Bx}$, stating the values of A and B.

   b Solve the associated homogenous differential equation.

c Explain why the general solution cannot be written as the sum of the complementary function and the particular integral.

d By considering the expression $\dfrac{d}{dx}\left(e^{2x}y^2\right)$, or otherwise, find the general solution of the differential equation.

 7 The differential equation $e^x\dfrac{dy}{dx}+y=2$ is defined for all x.

a Find the complementary function.

b Find a particular integral.

c Hence find the general solution.

Section 2: The integrating factor method for first order equations

You already have the necessary tools to solve a differential equation such as:

$$x^2\frac{dy}{dx}+2xy=e^x$$

because the left-hand side is of a convenient form. Notice that $2x$ is the derivative of x^2 and that $\dfrac{dy}{dx}$ is the derivative of y, which means you have an expression that has resulted from the differentiation of a product (x^2y) using the product rule. Therefore you can write the equation equivalently as

$$\frac{d}{dx}\left(x^2y\right)=e^x$$

Now, integrating both sides and rearranging:

$$x^2y=\int e^x\,dx$$

$$y=\frac{e^x+c}{x^2}$$

When faced with a differential equation like this where you cannot separate the variables, it will not often be the case that the left-hand side is quite so convenient. However, this method does suggest a way forward in such cases.

Consider, for example, the equation $\dfrac{dy}{dx}-\dfrac{y}{x}=x$. This can be rewritten as $\dfrac{1}{x}\dfrac{dy}{dx}-\dfrac{y}{x^2}=1$ by dividing throughout by x. This is $\dfrac{d}{dx}\left(\dfrac{y}{x}\right)=1$.

Consider, in general, a similar linear first order differential equation:

$$\frac{dy}{dx}+P(x)y=Q(x)$$

where $P(x)$ and $Q(x)$ are just functions of x. Note that if there is a function in front of $\dfrac{dy}{dx}$, you can divide through the equation by that function to get it in this form.

To make the left-hand side the derivative of a product as before, you can multiply through the equation by a function $I(x)$:

$$I(x)\frac{dy}{dx}+I(x)P(x)y=I(x)Q(x)$$

and then notice that if $I(x)$ is chosen such that $I'(x)=I(x)P(x)$ you have the left-hand side in the required form. From here you can proceed exactly as before:

$$\frac{d}{dx}(I(x)y)=I(x)Q(x)$$

$$y=\frac{1}{I(x)}\int I(x)Q(x)dx$$

The only remaining question is to decide on the function $I(x)$ to make this work.

You need

$$I'(x)=I(x)P(x)$$

$$\frac{I'(x)}{I(x)}=P(x)$$

$$\int\frac{I'(x)}{I(x)}dx=\int P(x)dx$$

$$\ln|I(x)|=\int P(x)dx$$

$$I(x)=e^{\int P(x)dx}$$

This function $I(x)$ is known as the **integrating factor**.

 Key point 10.3

Given a first order linear differential equation

$$\frac{dy}{dx}+P(x)y=Q(x)$$

multiply through by the integrating factor:

$$I(x)=e^{\int P(x)dx}$$

then the general solution will be:

$$y=\frac{1}{I(x)}\int I(x)Q(x)dx.$$

> **Tip**
>
> When calculating $\int P(x)dx$ you do not need to include the '$+c$'. It turns out that it does not matter whether there is a constant, as it would cancel later in the process.

WORKED EXAMPLE 10.4

Solve the differential equation

$$\cos x\frac{dy}{dx}-2y\sin x=3 \text{ for }-\frac{\pi}{2}<x<\frac{\pi}{2}$$

where $y=1$ when $x=0$.

Continues on next page ...

$$\cos x \frac{dy}{dx} - 2y\sin x = 3$$

You can't write the LHS as the derivative of a product: always check for this first. (Note that if the LHS had been $\cos x \frac{dy}{dx} - y\sin x$, i.e. without the 2, you could have written it as $\frac{d}{dx}(y\cos x)$.)

$$\frac{dy}{dx} - 2y\frac{\sin x}{\cos x} = \frac{3}{\cos x}$$

$$\frac{dy}{dx} - (2\tan x)y = 3\sec x$$

Therefore, start by dividing through by $\cos x$ to get the equation in the correct form for applying the integrating factor.

$$I(x) = e^{\int -2\tan x \, dx}$$

$$= e^{-2\ln|\sec x|}$$

$$= e^{\ln(\sec x)^{-2}}$$

$$= e^{\ln\cos^2 x}$$

$$= \cos^2 x$$

Find the integrating factor $I(x) = e^{\int P(x)\,dx}$, making sure not to miss the $-$ sign on $P(x)$.

So

$$\cos^2 x \frac{dy}{dx} - (2\cos^2 x \tan x)y = 3\cos^2 x \sec x$$

$$\cos^2 x \frac{dy}{dx} - (2\cos x \sin x)y = 3\cos x$$

$$\frac{d}{dx}(y\cos^2 x) = 3\cos x$$

Now multiply through by $\cos^2 x$ and check that the LHS is of the form $\frac{d}{dx}(y\cos^2 x) = \cos^2 x \frac{dy}{dx} - 2\cos x \sin x.$

$$y\cos^2 x = \int 3\cos x \, dx$$

$$= 3\sin x + c$$

Since $x = 0$, $y = 1$:

$$1\cos^2 0 = 3\sin 0 + c$$

$$c = 1$$

$$\therefore y\cos^2 x = 3\sin x + 1$$

$$y = \sec^2 x (3\sin x + 1)$$

You can now integrate both sides.

Finally, you need to find the constant c and rearrange into the form $y = f(x)$.

You can transform some differential equations into the required form by using a substitution. In an examination, you would generally be given the required substitution.

WORKED EXAMPLE 10.5

Show that the substitution $z = y^3$ transforms the differential equation

$$3y^2 \frac{dy}{dx} + \frac{y^3}{x} = \frac{e^x}{x}$$

into a linear differential equation. Hence find the general solution of the given differential equation.

If $z = y^3$ then $\frac{dz}{dx} = 3y^2 \frac{dy}{dx}$.

Continues on next page ...

Substituting this turns the given differential equation into:

$$\frac{dz}{dx} + \frac{z}{x} = \frac{e^x}{x}$$

which is a linear differential equation.

The integrating factor is $e^{\int \left(\frac{1}{x}\right)dx} = e^{\ln x} = x$.

Use Key point 10.3.

Therefore $z = \frac{1}{x}\int x \times \frac{e^x}{x} dx$

Use Key point 10.3 again.

$$= \frac{1}{x}\left(e^x + c\right)$$

Notice that the $+c$ is in the brackets.

Therefore $y^3 = \frac{1}{x}\left(e^x + c\right)$ or $y = \sqrt[3]{\frac{1}{x}\left(e^x + c\right)}$

You need to give the solution in terms of y and x. If you can easily rewrite it to make y the subject, this is the conventional thing to do.

EXERCISE 10B

1 Use an integrating factor to find the general solution to each linear differential equation.

a i $\dfrac{dy}{dx} + 2y = e^x$ **ii** $\dfrac{dy}{dx} - 4y = e^x$

b i $\dfrac{dy}{dx} + y\cot x = 1$ **ii** $\dfrac{dy}{dx} - (\tan x)y = \sec x$

c i $\dfrac{dy}{dx} + \dfrac{y}{x} = \dfrac{1}{x^2}$ **ii** $\dfrac{dy}{dx} + \dfrac{y}{x} = \dfrac{1}{x^3}$

2 Find the particular solution of the linear differential equation $\dfrac{dy}{dx} + y = e^x$ which has $y = e$ when $x = 1$.

3 Find the general solution to the differential equation $x^2\dfrac{dy}{dx} - 2xy = \dfrac{x^4}{x-3}$.

4 Find the general solution of the differential equation $\dfrac{dy}{dx} + y\sin x = e^{\cos x}$.

5 Find the particular solution of the linear differential equation $x^2\dfrac{dy}{dx} + xy = \dfrac{2}{x}$ that passes through the point $(1,1)$.

6 Given that $\cos x\dfrac{dy}{dx} + y\sin x = \cos^2 x$ and that $y = 2$ when $x = 0$, find y in terms of x.

7 Prove that when finding $\int P(x)dx$ in Key point 10.3, it does not matter whether or not the constant of integration is included.

8 Find the general solution to the differential equation $x\dfrac{dy}{dx} + 2y = 1 + \dfrac{1}{x}\dfrac{dy}{dx}$.

9 **a** Use the substitution $z = \dfrac{1}{y}$ to transform the equation

$$\frac{dy}{dx} + xy = xy^2$$

into a linear differential equation in x and z.

b Solve the resulting equation, writing z in terms of x.

c Find the particular solution to the original equation that has $y = 1$ when $x = 1$.

a Using the substitution $z = y^2$, or otherwise, solve the equation:

$$2y\frac{dy}{dx} + \frac{y^2}{x} = x^2$$

given that when $x = 4$, $y = -5$. Give your answer in the form $y = f(x)$.

b Use another substitution to find the general solution to the equation $\cos y\dfrac{dy}{dx} + \tan x\sin y = \sin x$.

Section 3: Homogeneous second order linear differential equations with constant coefficients

A differential equation of the form

$$a\frac{d^2y}{dx^2} + b\frac{dy}{dx} + cy = 0$$

is called a homogeneous second order linear differential equation with constant coefficients.

To find the solution to this type of differential equation, you need to create an **auxiliary equation**.

 Key point 10.4

The auxiliary equation of the differential equation

$$a\frac{d^2y}{dx^2} + b\frac{dy}{dx} + cy = 0$$

is

$$a\lambda^2 + b\lambda + c = 0.$$

> **Tip**
>
> How the auxiliary equation arises is shown in Proof 7.

Solving the auxiliary equation gives you important information about the solution of the differential equation, as set out in Proofs 7, 8 and 9. However, in most instances you will be able to just quote the results, which will be summarised in Key point 10.5.

If the auxiliary equation has real, distinct roots, λ_1 and λ_2, then the solution to the differential equation is $y = Ae^{\lambda_1 x} + Be^{\lambda_2 x}$.

PROOF 7

If $b^2 - 4ac > 0$ and $a\dfrac{d^2y}{dx^2} + b\dfrac{dy}{dx} + cy = 0$

then $y = Ae^{\lambda_1 x} + Be^{\lambda_2 x}$, where λ_1 and λ_2 are the roots of the equation.

Continues on next page ...

If $y = e^{\lambda x}$

Then

$\dfrac{dy}{dx} = \lambda e^{\lambda x}$

and

$\dfrac{d^2 y}{dx^2} = \lambda^2 e^{\lambda x}.$

One possible solution to the differential equation could occur if you had a function whose derivative and second derivative are proportional to the original function, allowing everything to 'cancel' and result in zero. $e^{\lambda x}$ is one example of a function which has this property (although you will see later that there are others).

Substituting these into the differential equation:

$a\lambda^2 e^{\lambda x} + b\lambda e^{\lambda x} + c e^{\lambda x} = 0$

$e^{\lambda x}\left(a\lambda^2 + b\lambda + c\right) = 0$

Taking out a factor of $e^{\lambda x}$.

$a\lambda^2 + b\lambda + c = 0$

Since $e^{\lambda x}$ can never be zero.
This is the auxiliary equation.

If $b^2 - 4ac > 0$ then the auxiliary equation will have two real solutions. Call these λ_1 and λ_2.

Therefore two possible solutions to the differential equation are $y = e^{\lambda_1 x}$ and $y = e^{\lambda_2 x}$.

$y = A e^{\lambda_1 x} + B e^{\lambda_2 x}$ will also be a solution, since any linear combination of solutions is also a solution.

This can be proved in a similar way to Proof 6.

This is a solution with two arbitrary constants, therefore it is the general solution.

Use Key point 10.1 to justify that your 'guess' gives the complete solution.

If the roots of the auxiliary equation are complex, you could still write the solution as $y = A e^{\lambda_1 x} + B e^{\lambda_2 x}$. However, you can then rewrite this in terms of trigonometric functions.

 Rewind

You learnt in Chapter 2, Section 2, that
$e^{p+iq} = e^p(\cos q + i \sin q)$.

PROOF 8

If $y = C e^{\lambda_1 x} + D e^{\lambda_2 x}$ with $\lambda_1 = \alpha + \beta i$ and $\lambda_2 = \alpha - \beta i$, then y can be written in the form
$y = e^{\alpha x}\left(A \cos(\beta x) + B \sin(\beta x)\right).$

Substituting in the given information:

$y = C e^{(\alpha+\beta i)x} + D e^{(\alpha-\beta i)x}$

Take out a factor of $e^{\alpha x}$.

$= e^{\alpha x}\left(C e^{\beta x i} + D e^{-\beta x i}\right)$

$= e^{\alpha x}\left(C\left(\cos(\beta x) + i\sin(\beta x)\right) + D\left(\cos(\beta x) - i\sin(\beta x)\right)\right)$

Rewrite the complex exponential into polar form.

$= e^{\alpha x}\left(A\cos(\beta x) + B\sin(\beta x)\right)$

Separate out the cosine and sine terms.

with $A = C + D$ and $B = i(C - D)$

If the auxiliary equation has equal roots, $\lambda_1 = \lambda_2 = \lambda$, the general solution becomes $y = A\,e^{\lambda x} + B\,e^{\lambda x} = C\,e^{\lambda x}$, which contains only one arbitrary constant. According to Key point 10.1, you need to find another complementary function. Proof 9 shows you how to do this.

PROOF 9

If $b^2 - 4ac = 0$ and $a\dfrac{d^2 y}{dx^2} + b\dfrac{dy}{dx} + cy = 0$, then $y = x e^{\lambda x}$ is a possible solution for a suitably chosen λ.

If $y = xe^{\lambda x}$

then

$$\frac{dy}{dx} = (1 + \lambda x)e^{\lambda x}$$

and

$$\frac{d^2 y}{dx^2} = \lambda(2 + \lambda x)e^{\lambda x}.$$

Substituting into the differential equation:

$$a\lambda(2 + \lambda x)e^{\lambda x} + b(1 + \lambda x)e^{\lambda x} + cxe^{\lambda x} = 0$$

$$2a\lambda + a\lambda^2 x + b + b\lambda x + cx = 0 \quad \cdots\cdots \text{ Divide through by } e^{\lambda x} \text{ (which can never be 0)}$$

$$2a\lambda + b + x(a\lambda^2 + b\lambda + c) = 0 \qquad\qquad \text{and tidy up.}$$

Comparing coefficients:

$x^0: 2a\lambda + b = 0$

$$\lambda = -\frac{b}{2a}$$

$x^1: a\lambda^2 + b\lambda + c = 0$

Checking $\lambda = -\dfrac{b}{2a}$ in the second equation:

$$a\left(-\frac{b}{2a}\right)^2 + b\left(-\frac{b}{2a}\right) + c = \frac{b^2}{4a} - \frac{b^2}{2a} + c$$

$$= \frac{-b^2 + 4ac}{4a} = 0 \quad \cdots\cdots \text{ You are given that } b^2 - 4ac = 0.$$

So $y = xe^{\left(-\frac{b}{2a}x\right)}$ is a solution to the differential equation in this case.

To get to the general solution a linear combination of the two possible values is required, leading to $y = Ae^{\lambda x} + Bxe^{\lambda x}$.

When solving differential equations normally you will just be able to write down the solution without going through the Proofs 7, 8 and 9.

Key point 10.5

Solution to auxiliary equation	General solution to differential equation
Two distinct roots, λ_1 and λ_2	$y = Ae^{\lambda_1 x} + Be^{\lambda_2 x}$
Repeated root, λ	$y = (A + Bx)e^{\lambda x}$
Complex roots, $\alpha + i\beta$	$y = e^{\alpha x}(A\sin\beta x + B\cos\beta x)$

WORKED EXAMPLE 10.6

Solve the differential equation $\dfrac{d^2 y}{dx^2} - 3\dfrac{dy}{dx} + 2y = 0$

given that $y = 1$ and $\dfrac{dy}{dx} = 0$ when $x = 0$.

The auxiliary equation is

$\lambda^2 - 3\lambda + 2 = 0$.

This has roots $\lambda = 1$ and $\lambda = 2$, so the general solution to the differential equation is
$y = Ae^x + Be^{2x}$.

> Since the roots are real and distinct you can write the solution to the differential equation in exponential form using Key point 10.5.

$\dfrac{dy}{dx} = Ae^x + 2Be^{2x}$

> You need to differentiate the expression to make use of the initial conditions.

Using the initial conditions, when $x = 0$:

$y = 1 = A + B$

$\dfrac{dy}{dx} = 0 = A + 2B$

Solving gives $A = 2$ and $B = -1$.

> You can use technology to solve these types of simultaneous equations.

So the particular solution is $y = 2e^x - e^{2x}$.

EXERCISE 10C

1   a   Write the auxiliary equation associated with the differential equation $\dfrac{d^2 y}{dx^2} + 5\dfrac{dy}{dx} + 6y = 0$.

   b   Hence find the general solution of the differential equation.

2   a   Write the auxiliary equation associated with the differential equation $\dfrac{d^2 y}{dx^2} + 4y = 0$.

   b   Hence find the general solution of the differential equation.

3   a   Write the auxiliary equation associated with the differential
       equation $y'' + 2y' + y = 0$.

   b   Hence find the general solution of the differential equation.

> Tip
>
> Remember that y' is another notation for $\dfrac{dy}{dx}$.

4 **a** Find the general solution to the differential equation $\dfrac{d^2y}{dx^2} + 8y = 6\dfrac{dy}{dx}$.

b Find the particular solution that satisfies $y = 5$ and $\dfrac{dy}{dx} = 12$ when $x = 0$.

5 **a** Find the general solution to the differential equation $y'' + 4y' + 4y = 0$.

b Find the particular solution that satisfies $y(0) = 1$ and $y'(0) = 0$.

6 **a** Find the general solution to the differential equation $\dfrac{d^2x}{dt^2} - 2\dfrac{dx}{dt} + 2x = 0$.

b Find the particular solution that satisfies $x(0) = 1$ and $\dot{x}(0) = 0$.

7 **a** Find the general solution to the differential equation $\ddot{x} + 3x = 4\dot{x}$.

b Given that $x(0) = 1$ and $x(1) = e$, find $x(2)$.

> **Tip**
>
> Remember $\ddot{x}$ that means $\dfrac{dx}{dt}$.

8 **a** Find the general solution to the differential equation $\dfrac{d^2y}{dt^2} - 6\dfrac{dy}{dt} + 9y = 0$.

b Find the particular solution that satisfies $y(0) = 0$ and $y(1) = p$, writing your answer in terms of p.

9 Find the general solution to the differential equation $y''' - 5y'' + 9y' = 5y$.

10 Find the general solution to the differential equation $y''' + 3y'' + 3y' + y = 0$.

11 By using the trial function $y = x^n$, find the general solution to the differential equation $x^2\dfrac{d^2y}{dx^2} + x\dfrac{dy}{dx} - 9y = 0$.

12 **a** Use the substitution $y = x^2$ to turn the differential equation $x\dfrac{d^2x}{dt^2} + \left(\dfrac{dx}{dt}\right)^2 + x\dfrac{dx}{dt} = 0$

into a second order differential equation with constant coefficients involving y and t.

b Solve the differential equation to find y as a function of t.

c Hence solve the original differential equation given that when $t = 0$, $x = 2$ and $\dfrac{dx}{dt} = \dfrac{1}{4}$.

Section 4: Non-homogeneous second order linear differential equations with constant coefficients

The second order differential equations you need to solve can all be written in the form

$$a\frac{d^2y}{dx^2} + b\frac{dy}{dx} + cy = f(x).$$

To solve these differential equations you use the method in Key point 10.2. You first of all solve the associated homogeneous equation to find a complementary function (using Key point 10.5) and then find a particular integral.

The form of the particular integral will depend on $f(x)$. Key point 10.6 gives trial functions for some common situations. This trial function needs to be substituted into the differential equation to find the unknown constants.

Key point 10.6

$f(x)$	Trial function
$ax+b$	$px+q$
Polynomial	General polynomial of the same order
ae^{bx}	ce^{bx}
$a\cos bx$ $a\sin bx$	$p\sin bx + q\sin bx$

Tip

You need to learn these forms of trial functions. If a different trial function is needed, it will be given in the question.

WORKED EXAMPLE 10.7

Find the general solution to the differential equation

$$\frac{d^2y}{dx^2}+7\frac{dy}{dx}+12y=24x+60e^{2x}.$$

The associated homogenous equation is

$$\frac{d^2y}{dx^2}+7\frac{dy}{dx}+12y=0.$$

First solve the associated homogenous equation to find the complementary function.

This has auxiliary equation

$$\lambda^2+7\lambda+12=0$$

which has roots -3 and -4.

Therefore, the complementary function is
$$y=Ae^{-3x}+Be^{-4x}.$$

The trial function associated with $60e^{2x}$ is $y=ce^{2x}$.

You can find the particular integral in two stages. Notice that the coefficient of x in the power of the trial function mirrors the original function.

Differentiating twice:

$$\frac{dy}{dx}=2ce^{2x}$$

$$\frac{d^2y}{dx^2}=4ce^{2x}.$$

Substituting into the left-hand side of the differential equation and comparing to the exponential part of the right-hand side:

$$4ce^{2x}+7\times2ce^{2x}+12\times ce^{2x}=60e^{2x}$$

$$30ce^{2x}=60e^{2x}$$

$$c=2$$

The trial function associated with $24x$ is $y=px+q$.

Notice that although the expression on the right only involves a term in x, you need the general linear expression in the trial function.

Differentiating twice:

$$\frac{dy}{dx}=p$$

$$\frac{d^2y}{dx^2}=0.$$

Continues on next page ...

Substituting these into the left-hand side of the differential equation and comparing to the linear part of the right-hand side:

$0+7\times p+12(px+q)=24x$

$\qquad 12px+7p+12q=24x$

Comparing the coefficient of x:

Compare coefficients to find p and q.

$12p=24$

$\qquad p=2$

Comparing the constant term:

You can use the fact that $p=2$ to solve for q.

$7p+12q=0$

$14+12q=0$

$\qquad q=-\dfrac{7}{6}$

The particular integral is $2e^{2x}+2x-\dfrac{7}{6}$.

The general solution is

$y=Ae^{-3x}+Be^{-4x}+2e^{2x}+2x-\dfrac{7}{6}$.

The general solution is the sum of the complementary function and the particular integral, from Key point 10.2.

Sometimes the trial function given in Key point 10.6 already appears as a part of the complementary function. In that case, you need to modify the particular integral.

 Key point 10.7

If your trial function is already part of the complementary function, try multiplying the trial function by x.

WORKED EXAMPLE 10.8

Find the general solution to the differential equation

$$\frac{\mathrm{d}^2y}{\mathrm{d}x^2}+y=16\sin x.$$

Continues on next page ...

The associated homogenous equation is

$$\frac{d^2y}{dx^2} + y = 0.$$

This has auxiliary equation

$$\lambda^2 + 1 = 0$$

which has roots i and −i.

Therefore, the complementary function is

$$y = A\sin x + B\cos x.$$

First solve the associated homogenous equation to find the complementary function.

From Key point 10.5.

The trial function associated with $16\sin x$ is $y = p\sin x + q\cos x$.

Although the right-hand side of the equation involves only sin x, you need to include both sin and cos in the trial function.

This already appears in the complementary function, so try $y = x(p\sin x + q\cos x)$.

You need to adjust the trial function according to Key point 10.7.

Differentiating twice:

$$\frac{dy}{dx} = p\sin x + q\cos x + x(p\cos x - q\sin x)$$

$$\frac{d^2y}{dx^2} = p\cos x - q\sin x + p\cos x - q\sin x + x(-p\sin x - q\cos x).$$

You need to use the product rule to differentiate.

Substituting into the left-hand side of the differential equation:

$$2p\cos x - 2q\sin x = 16\sin x$$

$$p = 0, q = -8$$

The particular integral is $-8x\cos x$.

The general solution is

$$y = A\sin x + B\cos x - 8x\cos x.$$

Notice that the terms containing $x\sin x$ and $x\cos x$ all cancel. This will always happen in the situation described in Key point 10.7.

The general solution is the sum of the complementary function and the particular integral, from Key point 10.2.

EXERCISE 10D

1 For the differential equation $\dfrac{d^2y}{dx^2} - 4\dfrac{dy}{dx} - 5y = e^{2x}$:

   a find the complementary function

   b find the particular integral

   c hence write down the general solution.

2 For the differential equation $y'' + 9y' + 20y = 60x$:

   a find the complementary function

   b find the particular integral

   c hence write down the general solution.

3 For the differential equation $\dfrac{d^2 y}{dx^2} + \dfrac{dy}{dx} + \sin x = 0$:

   a find the complementary function

   b find the particular integral

   c hence find the general solution.

4 For the differential equation $\dfrac{d^2 y}{dx^2} + 9y = 20\,e^{-x}$:

   a find the complementary function

   b hence find the general solution

   c find the particular solution given that $y = 7$ and $y' = 10$ when $x = 0$.

5 For the differential equation $\dfrac{d^2 y}{dx^2} + 4\dfrac{dy}{dx} + 4y = 12x + 25\sin x$, find:

   a the general solution

   b the particular solution given that $y = 0$ and $y' = 10$ when $x = 0$.

6 For the differential equation $y'' - 4y' + 8y = 32t^2$, find:

   a the general solution

   b the particular solution given that $y = 0$ and $y' = 0$ when $t = 0$.

7 For the differential equation $\dfrac{d^2 y}{dx^2} - 10\dfrac{dy}{dx} + 25y = e^{5x}$:

   a find the complementary function

   b show that there is a particular integral of the form $qx^2 e^{5x}$

   c hence find the general solution

   d find the particular solution given that $y = 4$ and $y' = 2$ when $x = 0$.

8 The function $f(x)$ satisfies the differential equation $f''(x) - 2f'(x) = 4e^x \sin x$ with boundary conditions $f(0) = f(\pi) = 3$. Given that there is a particular integral of the form $pe^x \sin x$, find the particular solution of the differential equation.

9 Find the general solution of the differential equation $\dfrac{d^2 y}{dx^2} + 3\dfrac{dy}{dx} - 4y = e^x$.

10 For the differential equation $\dfrac{d^2 y}{dx^2} + 4y = 12 \cos 2x$, find

   a the general solution

   b the particular solution which satisfies $y = 5$ and $\dfrac{dy}{dx} = 6$ when $x = 0$.

Checklist of learning and understanding

- The general solution to an nth-order differential equation has n arbitrary constants.
- For a linear differential equation, the general solution is given by $y = y_c + y_p$, where y_c is the complementary function and y_p is a particular integral.
  - The complementary function is the solution of the associated homogeneous equation, obtained from the original equation by removing the terms that do not contain y.
- Given a first order linear differential equation $\dfrac{dy}{dx} + P(x)y = Q(x)$, multiply through by the integrating factor $I(x) = e^{\int P(x)dx}$. The solution will be $y = \dfrac{1}{I(x)} \int I(x)Q(x)dx$.
- The auxiliary equation to the homogeneous differential equation $a\dfrac{d^2y}{dx^2} + b\dfrac{dy}{dx} + cy = 0$ is $a\lambda^2 + b\lambda + c = 0$.
  - The solution to the auxiliary equation gives the form of the general solution of the homogeneous equation:

Solution to auxiliary equation	General solution to differential equation
Two distinct roots, λ_1 and λ_2	$y = Ae^{\lambda_1 x} + Be^{\lambda_2 x}$
Repeated root, λ	$y = (A + Bx)e^{\lambda x}$
Complex roots, $\alpha + i\beta$	$y = e^{\alpha x}(A \sin \beta x + B \cos \beta x)$

- The form of the particular integral for the homogeneous differential equation $a\dfrac{d^2y}{dx^2} + b\dfrac{dy}{dx} + cy = f(x)$ depends on $f(x)$:

$f(x)$	Trial function
$ax + b$	$px + q$
Polynomial	General polynomial of the same order
ae^{bx}	pe^{bx}
$a\cos bx$ $a\sin bx$	$p\sin bx + q\sin bx$

- If the trial function is already part of the complementary function, multiply the trial function by x.

Mixed practice 10

1 Find the complementary function of the differential equation $4\dfrac{d^2y}{dx^2}+9y=\sin 3x$.

2 What is the integrating factor for the differential equation $\dfrac{dy}{dx}-\dfrac{3}{x}y=x^2$?

3 **a** Solve the quadratic equation $\lambda^2+6\lambda+5=0$.

  b Hence write down the general solution of the differential equation $\dfrac{d^2y}{dx^2}+6\dfrac{dy}{dx}+5y=0$.

4 **a** Show that the integrating factor for the differential equation $\dfrac{dy}{dx}+2xy=xe^{-x^2}$ is e^{x^2}.

  b Hence find the general solution of the differential equation.

5 The variables x and y satisfy the differential equation

$$\dfrac{dy}{dx}+4y=5\cos 3x.$$

  i Find the complementary function.

  ii Hence, or otherwise, find the general solution.

  iii Find the approximate range of values of y when x is large and positive.

© **OCR A Level Mathematics, Unit 4727 Further Pure Mathematics 3, June 2011**

6 The differential equation $y''+7y'+10y=e^x$ is defined for all x.

  a By considering the associated homogeneous differential equation, find the complementary function.

  b Show that a function of the form qe^x forms a particular integral, and find the value of q.

  c Hence write down the general solution of the differential equation.

  d Find the particular solution with initial conditions $y(0)=0$ and $y'(0)=6$.

7 **a** Find the value of the constant q for which $q\cos x$ is a particular integral of the differential equation $\dfrac{d^2y}{dx^2}+4y=\cos x$.

  b Hence find the general solution of the differential equation.

8 The differential equation $\dfrac{d^2y}{dx^2}+6\dfrac{dy}{dx}+25y=50x$ is defined for all x.

  a By considering the associated homogeneous differential equation, find the complementary function.

  b Show that a function of the form $px+q$ forms a particular integral, and find the values of p and q.

  c Hence write down the general solution of the differential equation.

  d Find the particular solution with initial conditions $y=-\dfrac{12}{25}$ and $y'=6$ when $x=0$.

9 Find the particular solution of the differential equation

$$x\dfrac{dy}{dx}+3y=x^2+x$$

for which $y=1$ when $x=1$, giving y in terms of x.

© **OCR A Level Mathematics, Unit 4727/01 Further Pure Mathematics 3, June 2015**

10 Solve the differential equation

$$\frac{d^2y}{dx^2} + 5\frac{dy}{dx} + 6y = e^{-x}$$

subject to the conditions $y = \frac{dy}{dx} = 0$ when $x = 0$.

© OCR A Level Mathematics, Unit 4727/01 Further Pure Mathematics 3, June 2014

11 Solve the differential equation $x\frac{dy}{dx} - 3y = x^4e^{2x}$ for y in terms of x, given that $y = 0$ when $x = 1$.

© OCR A Level Mathematics, Unit 4727/01 Further Pure Mathematics 3, January 2013

12 The variables x and y satisfy the differential equation

$$2\frac{d^2y}{dx^2} + 3\frac{dy}{dx} - 2y = 5e^{-2x}.$$

i Find the complementary function of the differential equation.

ii Given that there is a particular integral of the form $y = px\,e^{-2x}$, find the constant p.

iii Find the solution of the equation for which $y = 0$ and $\frac{dy}{dx} = 4$ when $x = 0$.

© OCR A Level Mathematics, Unit 4727 Further Pure Mathematics 3, January 2012

13 i Find the general solution of the differential equation

$$3\frac{d^2y}{dx^2} + 5\frac{dy}{dx} - 2y = -2x + 13$$

ii Find the particular solution for which $y = -\frac{7}{2}$ and $\frac{dy}{dx} = 0$ when $x = 0$.

iii Write down the function to which y approximates when x is large and positive.

© OCR A Level Mathematics, Unit 4727 Further Pure Mathematics 3, January 2011

14 a Find the general solution of $x\frac{du}{dx} + 3u = x$ for $x > 0$.

b Show that the substitution $u = \frac{dy}{dx}$ transforms the differential equation $x\frac{d^2y}{dx^2} + 3\frac{dy}{dx} = x$ into

$$x\frac{du}{dx} + 3u = x.$$

c Hence find the general solution of the differential equation $x\frac{d^2y}{dx^2} + 3\frac{dy}{dx} = x$ for $x > 0$.

15 a Find the general solution to the differential equation $\cos x\frac{dy}{dx} + y\sin x = \sin 2x$.

b Find the particular solution with $y(0) = 5$.

16 Find the general solution of the differential equation $y'' - 2y' = 5$.

11 Applications of differential equations

In this chapter you will learn how to:

- use differential equations in modelling, in kinematics and in other contexts
- solve the equation for simple harmonic motion and relate the solution to the motion
- model damped oscillations using second order differential equations and interpret their solution
- solve coupled first order differential equations and use them to model situations with two dependent variables.

Before you start…

Chapter 10	You should know how to solve second order differential equations.	1	Find the general solution to $y'' + 5y' + 4y = x$.
A Level Mathematics Student Book 1, Chapter 21	You should be able to use Newton's second law.	2	A falling object of mass 10 kg is subjected to a constant air resistance of 50 N. Find the acceleration of the object if $g = 9.8$ m s^{-2}.

Real world modelling

In reality, nearly everything of interest – be it the effect of a medicine or the price of a share – changes over time. The tool that mathematicians use to model these situations is a differential equation. In this chapter you will look at some common situations modelled by differential equations and how you can use the methods from Chapter 10 to solve them and interpret their solutions in context.

Section 1: Forming differential equations

When modelling real-life situations, it is often the case that the description can be interpreted in terms of differential equations.

You have already met many examples of setting up differential equations in A Level Mathematics Student Book 2, Chapter 13. In this section you will see further types of situations where differential equations arise, but this time you will often need to use methods from Chapter 10 to solve them. You will also look at the type of assumptions which are made when writing these differential equations.

⏪ **Rewind**

See A Level Mathematics Student Book 1, Chapter 21, for a reminder of using $F = ma$, and A Level Mathematics Student Book 2, Chapter 13, for its use in setting up differential equations.

WORKED EXAMPLE 11.1

A car, of mass m kg, is moving along a straight horizontal road. At time t seconds, the car has speed v m s^{-1}. The only force acting is a resistance, which is modelled as being proportional to $m(144+v^2)$ newtons.

Initially the car is moving with speed 12 m s^{-1} and deceleration 2 m s^{-2}.

Find the time taken for the car to come to rest.

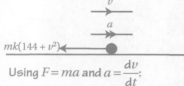

The resistance force is $mk(144+v^2)$ for some constant k.

Using $F = ma$ and $a = \dfrac{dv}{dt}$:

$$-mk(144+v^2) = m\dfrac{dv}{dt}$$

The resistance force is negative as the car is moving in the opposite direction to which this force acts.

$$-k(144+v^2) = \dfrac{dv}{dt}$$

Initially:

$$-k(144+12^2) = -2$$

$$k = \dfrac{1}{144}$$

Use the initial conditions $\left(v=12, \dfrac{dv}{dt}=-2\right)$ to find the value of k.

Separating the variables and integrating:

$$\int \dfrac{1}{144+v^2}\, dv = -\int \dfrac{1}{144}\, dt$$

$$\dfrac{1}{12}\arctan\left(\dfrac{v}{12}\right) = -\dfrac{1}{144}t + c$$

This is a standard arctan integral.

When $t = 0$, $v = 12$:

$$\dfrac{1}{12}\arctan\left(\dfrac{12}{12}\right) = 0 + c$$

Use the initial condition again to find c.

$$c = \dfrac{\pi}{48}$$

$$\therefore \dfrac{1}{12}\arctan\left(\dfrac{v}{12}\right) = -\dfrac{1}{144}t + \dfrac{\pi}{48}$$

$$\arctan\left(\dfrac{v}{12}\right) = -\dfrac{1}{12}t + \dfrac{\pi}{4}$$

When $v = 0$:

$$\arctan 0 = -\dfrac{1}{12}t + \dfrac{\pi}{4}$$

The car will come to rest when $v = 0$.

$$t = 3\pi \text{ seconds}$$

Tip

You can shortcut having to find c and then setting $v = 0$ by using definite instead of indefinite integration. After separating variables, integrate with limits 12 and 0 for v, and 0 and T for t:

$$\int_{12}^{0} \dfrac{1}{144+v^2}\, dv = -\int_{0}^{T} \dfrac{1}{144}\, dt$$

Then T will be the time taken for the car to stop.

EXERCISE 11A

1 A stone of mass m falls vertically downwards under gravity. At time t, the stone has speed v, and it experiences air resistance of magnitude kmv, where k is a constant.

  a Find an expression for $\dfrac{dv}{dt}$ in terms of v, g and k.

  b The initial speed of the stone is u. Find an expression for v at time t.

2 A car of mass m kg is moving along a straight horizontal road. At time t seconds, the car has speed v m s^{-1}. The magnitude of the resistance force, in newtons, is modelled by $3mv^{\frac{3}{2}}$. No other horizontal force acts on the car. The initial speed of the car is 9 m s^{-1}.

  a Show that, according to this model, $v = \left(\dfrac{6}{9t+2}\right)^2$.

  b A student performs an experiment to measure the speed of the car. She finds that the speed of the car after half a second is 0.8 m s^{-1} and the speed after two seconds is 0.3 m s^{-1}. Comment on the suitability of the model.

3 The current (I) at time t in a circuit with resistance ($2R$), capacitance (C) and inductance (L) is modelled by the differential equation:

$$L\frac{d^2 I}{dt^2} + 2R\frac{dI}{dt} + \frac{1}{C}I = 0$$

Solve to find I as a function of t and sketch the solution in each situation.

  a $R = 0$ **b** $R^2 < \dfrac{L}{C}$ **c** $R^2 > \dfrac{L}{C}$

4 The rate of immigration into a country is modelled as exponentially decreasing. The initial rate is 200 000 per year. One year later the rate is 50 000 per year.

  a Write a differential equation for the population (Y), assuming that changes in the population are due only to immigration.

  b Given that the initial population is 12 million, find the long-term population predicted by the model.

  c The model is refined by adding the term $0.02Y$ to the rate of change. Suggest what this term represents.

5 A chicken is to be cooked and is placed into an oven. The temperature of the oven, T_{oven} °C, follows the rule $T_{oven} = 25 + 20t$, where t is the time in minutes after the chicken is put into the oven. The rate of increase of the temperature of the chicken (T °C) is modelled as proportional to the difference between the chicken's temperature and the oven's temperature.

  a Write a differential equation for the temperature of the chicken.

  b If the temperature of the chicken is originally 5 °C and increasing at a rate of 10 °Cs^{-1}, find the particular solution of the differential equation.

  c Find an estimate of the chicken's temperature after 10 minutes, giving your answer to an appropriate degree of accuracy.

  d Describe one way in which the model is a simplification of the chicken's temperature.

6 A school has N students. The rate of spread of a rumour in a school is thought to be proportional to both the number of students who know the rumour (R) and the number who do not know the rumour.

  a Write this information as a differential equation.

  b Find the number of students who know the rumour when the rumour is spreading fastest.

  c Write down two assumptions that are being made in this situation.

7 A bacterium is modelled as a sphere. According to one biological model the volume of the bacterium (V) follows this differential equation:

$$\frac{dV}{dt} = 2V^{\frac{2}{3}} - V$$

a Explain the biological significance of the $V^{\frac{2}{3}}$ term.

b By using the substitution $u = V^{\frac{1}{3}}$, solve the differential equation given that initially $V = 1$.

c Sketch the solution and hence find the long-term volume of the bacterium.

 Did you know?

The model in question 7 is called Von Bertalanffy growth. It is very important in mathematical biology.

Section 2: Simple harmonic motion

In Chapter 10, you saw that some differential equations have solutions involving sines and cosines. These describe **oscillating behaviour**.

The differential equation which has pure sinusoidal behaviour is called **simple harmonic motion**. It occurs in a surprisingly wide range of physical situations.

 Tip

Simple harmonic motion is often abbreviated to SHM.

 Key point 11.1

The differential equation for simple harmonic motion is

$$\frac{d^2x}{dt^2} = -\omega^2 x$$

 Tip

Using the dot notation to represent differentiation with respect to time, you can also write this equation as $\ddot{x} = -\omega^2 x$.

In the equation in Key point 11.1, x represents the displacement of an object from its **equilibrium position** (the position where the acceleration of the object is zero).

To solve this differential equation you find the auxiliary equation:

$$\lambda^2 = -\omega^2$$

This has solutions $\lambda = \pm i\omega$, which lead to the general solution to the differential equation.

 Key point 11.2

The general solution to the simple harmonic motion differential equation is
$$x = A\sin\omega t + B\cos\omega t$$

Rewind

The general form of solutions for second order differential equations was given in Key point 10.5.

There is some terminology that is useful in describing these solutions:

- The average position around which the object oscillates (corresponding to $x = 0$) is the **equilibrium position**.
- The maximum distance from the equilibrium position is called the **amplitude**.
- The motion repeats itself after time, T, which is called the **period**.
- The value ω is called the **angular frequency**.

If initially the object is:

- at the equilibrium position, then the solution will be $x = a\sin\omega t$
- at the maximum displacement from the equilibrium position, then the solution will be $x = a\cos\omega t$.

In both of these cases the amplitude is given by a.

You know from A Level Mathematics Student Book 2, Chapter 8 that $A\sin\omega t + B\cos\omega t$ can also be written in the form $R\sin(\omega t + \varphi)$.

Key point 11.3

The general solution to the simple harmonic motion can also be written as $R\sin(\omega t + \varphi)$.

In the equation in Key point 11.3, the amplitude is R and φ is called the phase shift. $R\sin\varphi$ gives the initial displacement from the equilibrium position.

Since $\sin\theta$ and $\cos\theta$ repeat when θ gets to 2π, one full period, T, occurs when $\omega T = 2\pi$.

Key point 11.4

The period, T, of a particle moving with simple harmonic motion is

$$T = \frac{2\pi}{\omega}.$$

The object has its maximum speed as it is going through the equilibrium position, and it is instantaneously at rest when it reaches the maximum displacement, a.

Key point 11.5

The relationship between velocity and displacement for a particle moving with simple harmonic motion is

$$v^2 = \omega^2\left(a^2 - x^2\right).$$

PROOF 10

Prove that $v^2 = \omega^2\left(a^2 - x^2\right)$.

If $x = 0$ when $t = 0$, then $$x = a\sin\omega t.$$	Since you are only looking for a relationship between v and x, choose to start the time when the object moves through the equilibrium position.
$v = \dfrac{dx}{dt} = a\omega\cos\omega t$	Use the fact that $v = \dfrac{dx}{dt}$ from kinematics.
$\begin{aligned} v^2 &= \omega^2 a^2 \cos^2\omega t \\ &= \omega^2 a^2\left(1 - \sin^2\omega t\right) \end{aligned}$	Use $\cos^2\theta \equiv 1 - \sin^2\theta$.
$\begin{aligned} &= \omega^2\left(a^2 - \left(a\sin\omega t\right)^2\right) \\ &= \omega^2\left(a^2 - x^2\right) \end{aligned}$	Group the terms together to make a link with the expression for displacement.

A common context for simple harmonic motion is the situation with springs. One of the forces acting on the object is the tension, T, in the spring. The tension is always directed back towards the equilibrium position. There is a standard model in physics for the magnitude of the tension, but in this course you will always be told the form to use.

If the only force acting on the object is the tension from the spring (for example, when the object is moving on a smooth horizontal table) then in the equilibrium position the spring is neither extended nor compressed (it is at its natural length).

However, if there are additional forces, this spring might be extended or compressed at the equilibrium position.

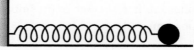

> ### 🔍 Explore
>
> The tension in an elastic spring can be modelled using Hooke's Law. You will learn about it if you study the Further Mechanics option.

WORKED EXAMPLE 11.2

A spring of natural length 10 cm is attached to a hook in the ceiling. A particle of mass 0.5 kg is attached to the other end of the spring. When the extension of the spring from its natural length is x m, the tension in the spring has magnitude $100x$ N.

Use $g = 10$ m s^{-2}, giving your final answers to an appropriate degree of accuracy.

a Show that, in the equilibrium position, the length of the spring is 15 cm.
b Show that, if the spring is displaced from the equilibrium, the particle will perform simple harmonic motion and find the time period of oscillations about this equilibrium.
c The spring is stretched 2 cm from the equilibrium position and then released. Find the maximum speed of the particle.

a

Draw a diagram to help visualise the situation.

Only tension and weight are acting on the mass. These must balance in equilibrium.

When the spring is in equilibrium:

$100x = 0.5g$

$x = \dfrac{5}{100}$

To keep consistent units you need to use metres for x.

So the extension is 5 cm and the equilibrium length is 15 cm.

Continues on next page ...

b

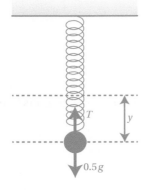

If y is the extension below the equilibrium position then:

$m\dfrac{d^2y}{dt^2} = mg - 100(0.05 + y)$

$\qquad = 0.5 \times 10 - 100 \times 0.05 - 100y$

$\qquad = -100y$

$\therefore \dfrac{d^2y}{dt^2} = -200y$

So, $\dfrac{d^2y}{dt^2} = -\omega^2 y$, where $\omega^2 = 200$.

This is the equation for simple harmonic motion.

Then $T = \dfrac{2\pi}{\omega}$

$T = \dfrac{2\pi}{\omega} = 0.44\,\text{s} \ (\text{2 d.p.})$

c If the spring is stretched an additional 2 cm, then the amplitude is 0.02 m.

$v^2 = \omega^2(a^2 - x^2) = 200(0.02^2 - x^2).$

This is maximised when $x = 0$, so the maximum speed is

$\sqrt{200 \times 0.02^2} = 0.28\,\text{ms}^{-1} \ (\text{2 d.p.})$

This is Newton's second law vertically. The acceleration is $\dfrac{d^2y}{dt^2}$.

The total extension of the spring is $0.05 + y$ so the magnitude of the tension is $100(0.05 + y)$.

If y is positive when below the equilibrium position, then you need to use down as positive, so the resultant force is weight − tension.

Rearrange into the standard form for simple harmonic motion.

Use $T = \dfrac{2\pi}{\omega}$ from Key point 11.4.

It is important to be consistent with units, in this case working only in metres.

Use $v^2 = \omega(a^2 - x^2)$ from Key point 11.5.

EXERCISE 11B

1 State the amplitude and the period of the simple harmonic motion described by each equation. Also state whether the particle is at rest, passing through the equilibrium position, or neither, when $t = 0$.

a i $x = 4.5 \cos 3t$ **ii** $x = 3 \sin 4t$

b i $x = 2.6 \sin \dfrac{t}{3}$ **ii** $x = 5 \cos \dfrac{t}{4}$

c i $x = 3.2 \sin\dfrac{2\pi t}{3}$ **ii** $x = 10.4 \cos\dfrac{3\pi t}{5}$

d i $x = 2.6\left(\sin\dfrac{t}{3} + 0.2\right)$ **ii** $x = 5\sin\left(\dfrac{t}{4} + 1.4\right)$

e i $x = 3.2 \sin\dfrac{5\pi t}{4} + 1.4 \cos\dfrac{5\pi t}{4}$ **ii** $x = 3 \sin\dfrac{2\pi t}{7} + 8 \cos\dfrac{2\pi t}{7}$

2 For each description of simple harmonic motion write an equation for x in terms of t (where x is in metres and t is in seconds).

a i Amplitude 0.6 m, period $\dfrac{\pi}{5}$ seconds; at rest when $t = 0$.

ii Amplitude 3.4 m, period $\dfrac{\pi}{7}$ seconds; at rest when $t = 0$.

b i Amplitude 0.7 m, period 6π seconds; in equilibrium when $t = 0$.

ii Amplitude 1.3 m, period 10π seconds; at in equilibrium when $t = 0$.

c i Amplitude 12.1 m, period 2.5 seconds; in equilibrium when $t = 0$.

ii Amplitude 0.3 m, period 0.6 seconds; at rest when $t = 0$.

3 Each differential equation models a particle performing simple harmonic motion. Find the period of the motion.

a i $\dfrac{d^2 x}{dt^2} + 25x = 0$ **ii** $\dfrac{d^2 x}{dt^2} + 9x = 0$

b i $\ddot{x} + 2x = 0$ **ii** $\ddot{x} + 8x = 0$

c i $3\dfrac{d^2 x}{dt^2} + 9x = 0$ **ii** $5\dfrac{d^2 x}{dt^2} + 45x = 0$

d i $4\ddot{x} = -4x$ **ii** $3\ddot{x} = -15x$

4 A particle performs simple harmonic motion with amplitude 0.2 m and angular frequency 5 s⁻¹. The particle passes through the equilibrium position when $t = 0$.

a Find the distance of the particle from the equilibrium position when $t = 4$ s.

b Find the maximum speed of the particle.

5 A small ball is attached to one end of an elastic spring. When $t = 0$ the ball is released from rest 0.6 m from the equilibrium position and performs simple harmonic motion with angular frequency 12 s⁻¹.

a Find the displacement of the ball from the equilibrium position after 3 seconds.

b Find the time when the ball first passes through the equilibrium position, and the speed of the ball at this time.

6 A small ball attached to the end of a spring performs simple harmonic motion with amplitude 8 cm and angular frequency 15 s⁻¹.

a Find the maximum speed of the ball.

b The ball is at rest when $t = 0$. Find the speed of the ball 5 seconds later. Find also the magnitude of acceleration of the ball at this time.

7 A particle performs simple harmonic motion with amplitude 12 cm. Its speed as it passes through the equilibrium position is 0.08 m s⁻¹.

a Find the angular frequency of the simple harmonic motion.

b Find the speed of the particle when its displacement from the equilibrium position is 8 cm.

8 A particle performs simple harmonic motion with amplitude 0.6 m and angular frequency 10 s⁻¹. The particle passes through the equilibrium position when $t = 0$ with positive displacement immediately after $t = 0$.

a Find the displacement of the particle when $t = 3.6$ s.

b Find the time when the particle is first 0.3 m from the equilibrium position.

c Find the speed of the particle at that point. Is it moving towards or away from the equilibrium position?

9 A particle is attached to one end of an elastic spring. It is displaced from its equilibrium position and performs simple harmonic motion with amplitude 0.5 m. When its displacement from the equilibrium position is 0.2 m the speed of the particle is 0.4 m s⁻¹.

a Find the angular frequency of the simple harmonic motion.

b Hence find the distance from the equilibrium position when the speed of the particle is 0.05 m s⁻¹.

10 A particle moves in a straight line between points A and B which are 0.6 m apart. The midpoint of AB is O and the displacement of the particle from O at time t seconds is x metres.

The motion of the particle is described by the equation $\dfrac{d^2x}{dt^2} + 0.16x = 0$. When $t = 0$ the particle is at A.

a Write down the amplitude and the period of the simple harmonic motion.

b Write down an expression for x in terms of t.

c Point C is between A and B, and $AC = 0.4$ m. Find the time when the particle first passes through C.

d The mass of the particle is 0.2 kg. Find the magnitude of the force acting on the particle when it passes through C.

11 A cart of mass 300 kg is moving in a straight line with a speed of 12 m s⁻¹ when it hits a buffer which is attached to a fixed wall by a light spring.

At time t seconds after the impact the compression of the spring is x metres and the force in the spring is given by $T = 192x$ newtons. Any other forces acting on the cart can be ignored.

a Show that the cart performs simple harmonic motion as long as it remains in contact with the buffer.

b Find the maximum compression of the spring and the magnitude of the force acting on the cart at that point.

c Find the time taken to reach the point of maximum compression.

12 A particle of mass m kg is attached to one end of a light spring and rests on a smooth horizontal table. The string is horizontal and its other end is attached to a fixed wall.

The particle is displaced away from the wall so that the extension of the spring is 0.6 m and then released. When the extension of the spring is e the elastic force in the spring is $T = mq^2e$, where q is a constant. All other forces on the particle can be ignored.

a Show that the particle performs simple harmonic motion and find, in terms of q, the period of the motion.

b Find the maximum speed and the maximum acceleration of the particle.

c Find the extension of the spring at the moment when the speed of the particle equals half of its maximum speed.

13 A particle of mass 0.5 kg rests on a smooth horizontal table. The particle is attached to two light springs and the other ends of the springs are attached to fixed points A and B, which are 0.8 m apart. The natural length of each spring is 0.3 m and the magnitude of the tension in each spring is given by $1.2e$, where e is the extension of the spring.

The particle is released from rest 0.04 m from O, the midpoint of AB.

At time t the displacement of the particle from O is x.

a Find the magnitude of the resultant force on the particle at time t.

b Hence show that the particle performs simple harmonic motion.

c Find an expression for x in terms of t.

14 A light spring is attached to a fixed point A. A particle of mass 0.2 kg is attached to the other end of the spring and hangs vertically below A.

When the extension of the spring is e metres, the magnitude of the tension in the spring is $T = 2ge$ N.

a The particle hangs in equilibrium at point B. Find the extension of the spring.

The particle is displaced x m downward from the equilibrium position.

b Write down the extension of the spring. Hence show that, as long as $|x| < 0.1$, the magnitude of the resultant force on the particle is $2gx$.

c Hence show that the particle performs simple harmonic motion and find the period of the motion.

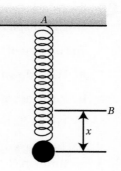

Section 3: Damping and damped oscillations

When objects are moving they are usually subjected to resistive forces such as air resistance or drag in water. There are several ways in which you can model this situation. One common model is to say that the drag force, D, is proportional to the speed, acting in the opposite direction.

 Key point 11.6

The drag force on an object moving with speed v is given by
$$D = -Kv$$
where K is a constant.

If you add this to the standard equation for simple harmonic motion, the differential equation becomes:

$$\frac{d^2x}{dt^2} + k\frac{dx}{dt} + \omega^2 x = 0$$

where $k = \dfrac{K}{m}$ is a positive constant. **Damped** oscillations result, or **damped simple harmonic motion**.

As you saw in Chapter 10, the solutions to this differential equation depend upon how many solutions there are to the auxiliary equation, $\lambda^2 + k\lambda + \omega^2 = 0$, and each case is given a different name.

Key point 11.7

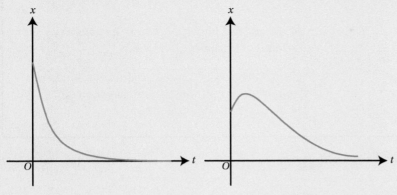

$k^2 - 4\omega^2 > 0$

Overdamping

$x = Ae^{\alpha t} + Be^{\beta t}$

$k^2 - 4\omega^2 = 0$

Critical damping

$x = (A + Bt)e^{-\frac{k}{2}t}$

$k^2 - 4\omega^2 < 0$

Underdamping

$x = e^{-\frac{k}{2}t}(A\sin qt + B\cos qt)$

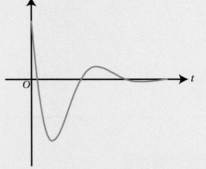 **Did you know?**

In physical situations, such as the suspension of a car, critical damping is often desirable as it minimises vibrations without too much jerkiness.

WORKED EXAMPLE 11.3

A bob of mass 0.1 kg is connected to a spring. In air the bob is found to follow simple harmonic motion with period π seconds. The bob is then placed into oil where there is a drag force of magnitude Kv. Find the value of K which produces critical damping.

If the period is T, then the value of ω is given by $= \dfrac{2\pi}{T} = 2$.

> Rearrange the formula in Key point 11.4 to express ω in terms of T.

Therefore, in air the differential equation is:
$$\frac{d^2 x}{dt^2} + 4x = 0$$

The force is given by:
$$F = ma = m\frac{d^2 x}{dt^2} = -4mx$$

In oil, there must be the additional drag force:
$$F = m\frac{d^2 x}{dt^2} = -4mx - K\frac{dx}{dt}$$

$$\therefore \frac{d^2 x}{dt^2} + \frac{K}{m}\frac{dx}{dt} + 4x = 0$$

> Divide through by m.

Continues on next page ...

253

$$\frac{d^2x}{dt^2}+10K\frac{dx}{dt}+4x=0 \quad\cdots\cdots\cdots\cdots\cdots$$ Since $m=0.1$.

Critical damping occurs when $\quad\cdots\cdots\cdots\cdots$

$$(10K)^2-4\times4=0$$

$\therefore K=0.4 \quad\cdots\cdots\cdots\cdots\cdots\cdots\cdots\cdots$

Critical damping occurs when the auxiliary equation has a repeated root.

Only the positive solution to the equation is required, since from the context you need $K>0$.

EXERCISE 11C

1 Each differential equation describes damped harmonic motion. In each case determine whether the damping is critical, underdamping or overdamping.

a i $\dfrac{d^2x}{dt^2}+2\dfrac{dx}{dt}+5x=0$ **ii** $\dfrac{d^2x}{dt^2}+8\dfrac{dx}{dt}+3x=0$

b i $\ddot{x}+4\dot{x}+4x=0$ **ii** $\ddot{x}+3\dot{x}+4x=0$

c i $3\dfrac{d^2x}{dt^2}+3\dfrac{dx}{dt}+9x=0$ **ii** $5\dfrac{d^2x}{dt^2}+30\dfrac{dx}{dt}+45x=0$

d i $4\ddot{x}=-8\dot{x}-4x$ **ii** $3\ddot{x}=-6\dot{x}-15x$

> **Tip**
>
> Remember that $\ddot{x}$ is an alternative notation for $\dfrac{d^2x}{dt^2}$, and $\dot{x}$ is an alternative notation for $\dfrac{dx}{dt}$.

2 A particle performs damped oscillations described by the differential equation $\dfrac{d^2x}{dt^2}+3n\dfrac{dx}{dt}+6nx=0$. Given that the damping is critical, find the value of n.

3 A particle of mass 0.2 kg is attached to one end of a light spring and rests on a horizontal table, with the spring horizontal. When the extension of the spring is x metres the tension in the spring has magnitude $3.6x$ N. The resistance force acting on the particle has magnitude kv N, where v m s^{-1} is the speed of the particle.

a Show that the equation of motion of the particle is $\ddot{x}+5k\dot{x}+18x=0$.

b Given that the motion of the particle is critically damped, find the exact value of k.

c Name the type of damping that occurs when $k=1.8$.

4 A particle P of mass m kg is attached to one end of a spring. When the displacement of P from its equilibrium position is x metres, the magnitude of the tension in the spring is $4nx$ N and the resistance force on P has magnitude $5c\dot{x}$ N.

a Write down a differential equation that models the motion of the particle.

b Given that the motion of the particle is critically damped, express n in terms of m and c.

5 A particle is attached to one end of a spring and moves under the action of a tension and a resistance force. The motion of the particle is described by the differential equation $\dfrac{d^2x}{dt^2}+4\dfrac{dx}{dt}+13x=0$, when $t=0$, $x=0$ and $\dfrac{dx}{dt}=2.7$.

a Find an expression for x in terms of t.

b Name the type of damping that occurs and sketch the graph of x as a function of t.

6 A particle of mass 0.2 kg is attached to one end of a spring and moves in a straight line on a horizontal table. When the displacement of the particle from a fixed point O is x m the tension in the spring has magnitude $1.2x$ N. The resistance force acting on the particle has magnitude $1.4v$ N, where v m s^{-1} is the speed of the particle.

   a Show that the equation of motion for the particle is $\dfrac{d^2x}{dt^2}+7\dfrac{dx}{dt}+6x=0$.

   When $t=0$ the particle is at rest, 1 m from O.

   b Find an equation for x in terms of t.

   c Show that the particle never reaches O.

   d Name the type of damping that occurs in this case.

7 A particle of mass 3 kg moves in a straight line under the action of two forces. When the particle's displacement from a fixed point O is x m there is a force towards O of magnitude $2.43x$ N as well as a resistance force of magnitude $12kv$ m s^{-1} (where v is the speed of the particle). When $t=0$ the particle is at rest 0.8 m from O.

   a Show that the motion of the particle is described by the equation $\ddot{x}+4k\dot{x}+0.81x=0$.

   b Given that the motion of the particle is critically damped, find the value of k.

   c In this case, find an expression for x in terms of t.

8 A particle P of mass 0.16 kg is suspended by a light elastic string, and the other end of the string is attached to a fixed point A vertically above P. The natural length of the string is 1.2 m. When the extension of the string is d m, the magnitude of the tension in the string is $T=4d$ N.

   a P hangs in equilibrium at a point B. Taking $g=10$ m s^{-2}, find the extension of the string at this point.

   P is held at rest with the string at its natural length, and then released. When the speed of P is v m s^{-1} the resistance force acting on P has magnitude $1.28v$ N.

   b Show that the subsequent motion of P can be modelled by the differential equation $\ddot{x}+8\dot{x}+25x=0$.

   c Name the type of damping that occurs in this case and find an expression for x in terms of t.

   d According to this model, what will the length of the string be in the long term?

   e Find the speed of P when it passes through B for the first time.

9 A particle is attached to one end of a light spring and performs damped oscillations described by the differential equation $\ddot{x}+k\dot{x}+c^2x=0$, where x is the extension of the spring beyond the equilibrium position. It is given that $k=\dfrac{8c}{5}$.

   a Determine the type of damping that occurs.

   At $t=0$, $x=0$ and $\dot{x}=u$.

   b Find an expression for x in terms of t.

   c Show that the maximum extension of the spring is approximately $\dfrac{0.424u}{c}$.

Section 4: Linear systems

There are many situations where two variables are linked by coupled differential equations; for example, each variable might change with time, but the rate of change might depend of the value of the other variable. If both of these differential equations are linear and first order, then you can eliminate one of the variables to form a second order linear differential equation.

 Rewind

You learnt how to solve linear second order differential equations in Chapter 10, Sections 3 and 4.

WORKED EXAMPLE 11.4

In a population of foxes (f thousands) and rabbits (r thousands), the foxes have a birth rate $3r$ and a death rate $6f$. The rabbits have a birth rate of $4r$ and a death rate of $8f$.

a Write this information in the form of a pair of differential equations.

b Rewrite these differential equations as a second order differential equation for f.

c Solve this second order differential equation given that initially $f = 2$ and $\dfrac{df}{dt} = 2$.

d Hence find the solution for r, given that the initial population of rabbits is five thousand.

e What is the long-term population of foxes and rabbits?

a $\dfrac{df}{dt} = 3r - 6f$　　　(1) ....

The rate of change of the fox population will be (birth rate – death rate), and likewise for the rabbit population.

$\dfrac{dr}{dt} = 4r - 8f$　　　(2)

b Differentiating (1) with respect to t:

$\dfrac{d^2 f}{dt^2} = 3\dfrac{dr}{dt} - 6\dfrac{df}{dt}$

Substituting in $\dfrac{dr}{dt}$ from (2):

$\dfrac{d^2 f}{dt^2} = 12r - 24f - 6\dfrac{df}{dt}$

Rearranging (1):

$3r = \dfrac{df}{dt} + 6f$

Substituting this in:

$\dfrac{d^2 f}{dt^2} = 4 \times \left(\dfrac{df}{dt} + 6f \right) - 24f - 6\dfrac{df}{dt}$

$\phantom{\dfrac{d^2 f}{dt^2}} = -2\dfrac{df}{dt}$

So $\dfrac{d^2 f}{dt^2} + 2\dfrac{df}{dt} = 0$

c Auxiliary equation is:

$\lambda^2 + 2\lambda = 0$

$\lambda(\lambda + 2) = 0$

$\lambda = 0 \text{ or } -2$

$\therefore f = A + Be^{-2t}$

Continues on next page ...

$$\frac{df}{dt} = -2Be^{-2t}$$

When $t = 0, \frac{df}{dt} = 2$ so $B = -1$.

When $t = 0, f = 2$ so $A = 3$.

So the solution is $f = 3 - e^{-2t}$.

d Substituting the solution from part c into (2):

$$\frac{dr}{dt} = 4r - 24 + 8e^{-2t}$$

$$\frac{dr}{dt} - 4r = 8e^{-2t} - 24$$

> This is a first order linear differential equation, so you can write it in an appropriate form to use integrating factors.

The integrating factor is e^{-4t}, so:

$$re^{-4t} = \int e^{-4t}\left(8e^{-2t} - 24\right)dt$$

$$= \int 8e^{-6t} - 24e^{-4t}\, dt$$

$$= -\frac{4}{3}e^{-6t} + 6e^{-4t} + c$$

$$\therefore r = -\frac{4}{3}e^{-2t} + 6 + ce^{4t}$$

When $t = 0, r = 5$ so $c = \frac{1}{3}$.

$$\therefore r = -\frac{4}{3}e^{-2t} + 6 + \frac{1}{3}e^{4t}$$

e As t gets very large e^{-2t} gets very small, but e^{4t} gets very large. The population of foxes tends towards 3000, but the population of rabbits grows without limit.

EXERCISE 11D

1 Write each pair of differential equations as a single second order equation for x. Hence find the general solution for x and y in terms of t.

a i $\dfrac{dx}{dt} = 5x - 2y, \dfrac{dy}{dt} = x + 2y$ **ii** $\dfrac{dx}{dt} = x + 2y, \dfrac{dy}{dt} = 2x + y$

b i $\dot{x} = 4y - 3x, \dot{y} = y - 2x$ **ii** $\dot{x} = 3x - y, \dot{y} = 8x - y$

c i $\dot{x} = 4y - 5x + e^{-3t}, \dot{y} = 2y - 3x + 2e^{-3t}$ **ii** $\dot{x} = 2y - 3x + 5, \dot{y} = 2y - 2x - 8$

2 Find the general solution of $\dfrac{dy}{dt} = x + \cos t, \dfrac{dx}{dt} = y + \sin t$.

3 Find the general solution for x and y in terms of t for this system of differential equations:

$$\frac{dx}{dt} = -2y, \quad \frac{dy}{dt} = -8x.$$

4 The variables x and y satisfy the differential equations

$$\frac{dx}{dt} = 35 - 5y, \quad 5\frac{dy}{dt} = 16x - 192.$$

When $t = 0$, $x = 17$ and $y = 7$.

Find expressions for x and y in terms of t.

5 Consider the system of differential equations

$$\frac{dx}{dt} = 3x + y, \quad \frac{dy}{dt} = 6x - 2y.$$

a Find a second order differential equation for x.

When $t = 0$, $x = 1$ and $y = 15$.

b Find expressions for x and y in terms of t.

6 Three identical cylindrical buckets, each with cross-sectional area 0.25 m², are placed vertically above each other. A hole is drilled in the base of each of the top two buckets so that water can flow from the top bucket to the middle one and from the middle one to the bottom one.

For each of the top two buckets, when the height of water in the bucket is h m, the rate of flow of water out of the bucket is $0.5h$ m³ s⁻¹. Initially, the height of water in the top bucket is 30 cm and the middle bucket is empty.

Let x be the height of water in the top bucket and y be the height of water in the middle bucket at time t.

The time taken for water to fall between buckets can be ignored.

a Show that $x = 0.3e^{-2t}$ and write a differential equation for y in terms of t.

b Find an expression for y in terms of t and show that this model predicts that the second bucket never empties.

c Find the maximum height of water in the second bucket.

7 A system contains sharks (S thousand) and fish (F million). The sharks have a birth rate given by $0.1F + 1$ and a death rate given by $0.2S$. The fish have a birth rate given by $0.2F + 4$ and a death rate given by $0.5S$.

Focus on ...

You can find out how this model can be improved in Focus on ... Modelling 2.

a Write this information in the form of a pair of differential equations.

b Rewrite these differential equations as a second order differential equation for S.

c Solve this second order differential equation given that initially $S = 17$ and $F = 28$.

d By writing the solution for S in the form $S = A + B\cos(kt - \alpha)$, where $\alpha \in [0, \pi)$, find the time of the first peak in the shark population. Find the equivalent time at which the fish population first peaks.

e Describe the long-term behaviour of the two populations.

8 A predator-prey system is of the form $\dfrac{dx}{dt} = ax + by$, $\dfrac{dy}{dt} = cx + dy$.

Prove that the system will only oscillate if $(a + d)^2 < 4(ad - bc)$.

Checklist of learning and understanding

- The differential equation for simple harmonic motion is $\dfrac{d^2 x}{dt^2} = -\omega^2 x$.

- The general solution to the simple harmonic motion differential equation is $x = A\sin\omega t + B\cos\omega t$, which can also be written as $x = R\sin(\omega t + \varphi)$.

- Period of the solution: $T = \dfrac{2\pi}{\omega}$

- Speed, v, is given by: $v^2 = \omega^2 \left(a^2 - x^2 \right)$.

- Drag force is given by $D = -Kv$.

- If there is a drag force there can be underdamping, overdamping or critical damping depending on the number of solutions to the auxiliary equation.

- You can rewrite coupled pairs of linear first order differential equations as a second order differential equation in one variable.

Mixed practice 11

1 Find the period of the oscillations of a particle whose motion is modelled by the differential equation

$$\frac{d^2 y}{dt^2} + 4y = 0.$$

2 Find the value of q which would result in critical damping in the system modelled by

$$\frac{d^2 x}{dt^2} + 16\frac{dx}{dt} + qx = 0.$$

3 A particle of mass 5 kg is acted on by a force $F = 10\sin t$ newtons, where t is the time measured in seconds.

a Write down a differential equation satisfied by the displacement, x metres, of the particle from its initial position.

b Given that the particle is initially at rest, find its displacement after 3 seconds.

4 A ball is attached to one end of an elastic string and performs simple harmonic motion with amplitude 0.3 m and angular frequency 6 s^{-1}.

a Find the maximum speed of the ball.

b Find the speed of the ball when its displacement from the equilibrium position is 0.2 m.

c The mass of the ball is 0.3 kg. Find the magnitude of the maximum force acting on the ball during the motion.

5 A particle of mass 2 kg moves in a straight line so that, when the displacement of the particle from the origin is x m, the force acting on the particle is directed towards the origin and has magnitude $18x$ N.

a Show that the displacement of the particle satisfies the differential equation $\dfrac{d^2 x}{dt^2} = -9x$.

b Verify that, for some value of ω which you should state, $x = A\cos\omega t + B\sin\omega t$, where A and B are constants, satisfies this differential equation.

c The particle is initially at rest 0.3 m from the origin. Find the value of the constants A and B.

d Hence find the maximum speed of the particle.

6 A particle P of mass 0.2 kg moves on a smooth horizontal plane. Initially it is projected with velocity 0.8 m s^{-1} from a fixed point O towards another fixed point A. At time t s after projection, P is x m from O and is moving with velocity v m s^{-1}, with the direction OA being positive. A force of $(1.5t - 1)$ N acts on P in the direction parallel to OA.

i Find an expression for v in terms of t.

ii Find the time when the velocity of P is next 0.8 m s^{-1}.

iii Find the times when P subsequently passes through O.

iv Find the distance P travels in the third second of its motion.

© OCR A Level Mathematics, Unit 4730/01 Mechanics 3, June 2013

7 One end of a light elastic spring is attached to a fixed wall and a small ball is attached to the other end. The ball rests on a smooth horizontal table.

At $t = 0$ the ball is given the velocity of 15 m s^{-1} away from the equilibrium position. When the displacement of the ball from the equilibrium position is x m the force acting on the particle is $5x$ N.

a Given that the mass of the ball is 0.2 kg, show that the equation of motion of the ball is $\dfrac{d^2x}{dt^2} = -25x$.

b Show that $x = R\sin(5t + \varphi)$ satisfies the equation and find the value of the constants R and φ.

c Find the time when the particle first returns to the equilibrium position.

8 The spread of a disease through a population is modelled using the following differential equations:

$$\begin{cases} \dfrac{dS}{dt} = -2I \\ \dfrac{dI}{dt} = 2I \end{cases}$$

where S is the number of uninfected individuals and I is the number of infected individuals in the population at time t months.

Initially there are 199 uninfected individuals and 1 infected individual. According to this model, how long will it take for half the population to become infected?

9 Solve this system of differential equations:

$$\begin{cases} \dot{x} = 3x - 5y \\ \dot{y} = 5x - 3y \end{cases}$$

given that $x(0) = 1$ and $y(0) = 1$.

10 Two particles, P and Q, each have a mass of 1 kg and are initially at rest. P moves under the action of a force F_P newtons, modelled by $F_P(t) = t + 1$, where t is the time measured in seconds. Q moves under the action of a force F_Q newtons, modelled by $F_Q(x) = x + 1$, where x metres is the displacement from the initial position. Which particle travels further in the first five seconds?

11 A particle moves with simple harmonic motion in a straight line between points A and B, which are 1.2 m apart. The midpoint of AB is O.

The motion of the particle satisfies the differential equation $\dfrac{d^2x}{dt^2} = -\omega^2 x$, where x is the displacement of the particle from O.

a Show that $x = 0.6\cos\omega t$ satisfies the differential equation. Hence show that $v^2 = \omega^2(0.36 - x^2)$.

b Given that the particle takes four seconds to travel from A to B, find the value of ω.

c Given that the mass of the particle is 400 grams, find the maximum force acting on the particle.

12 One end of a light spring is attached to a fixed wall. A ball of mass 0.25 kg is attached to the other end of the spring and rests on a smooth horizontal table. The ball is displaced 0.2 m from the equilibrium position and then released. When the extension of the spring is x m, the magnitude of the tension in the spring is given by $T = 64x$ N.

a Show that the equation of motion of the ball can be written as $\dfrac{d^2x}{dt^2} = -256x$.

b Find the maximum speed of the ball.

13 One end of a light spring is attached to a fixed wall. A particle P of mass m kg is attached to the other end of the spring and rests on a smooth horizontal table with the spring horizontal. P is displaced 30 cm from its equilibrium position and released from rest. When the displacement of P from equilibrium is x m the tension in the spring has magnitude $6.25mx$ N.

a Show that $\dfrac{d^2x}{dt^2} - 6.25x = 0$.

b Show that $x = A\sin 2.5t + B\cos 2.5t$ satisfies the differential equation and find the values of A and B. Hence show that $v^2 = 6.25(0.09 - x^2)$.

c Find the maximum speed of the particle.

14 A cart of mass 13 kg is attached to one end of a horizontal spring. When the extension of the spring is x m the tension in the spring is $13x$ N. Initially the cart is displaced 5 m from its equilibrium position along the axis of the spring. It is held at rest and then released.

In a simple model the only force acting on the cart is the tension in the spring.

a Find an expression for x in terms of time.

b How long does it take for the cart to reach the equilibrium position for the first time?

In an improved model there is also a resistance force on the cart of magnitude $10v$ N, where $v\,\text{ms}^{-1}$ is the speed of the cart.

c Find an expression for x in terms of t for the second model.

d Which model predicts the cart reaching the equilibrium position later?

15 Find the general solution of this system of differential equations:

$$\frac{dx}{dt} = x - y, \frac{dy}{dt} = 2x + y$$

16 Snakes and badgers are in competition for resources on a plain. There are no other types of animals on this plain. The populations snakes (S) and badgers (B) at time t months are modelled by these differential equations:

$$\frac{dB}{dt} = B - S, \frac{dS}{dt} = S - B$$

Initially there are 1000 badgers and 3000 snakes on the plain. Find the total number of animals on the plain after three months.

17 A particle P starts from rest from a point A and moves in a straight line with simple harmonic motion about a point O. At time t seconds after the motion starts the displacement of P from O is x m towards A. The particle P is next at rest when $t = 0.25\pi$ having travelled a distance of 1.2 m.

i Find the maximum velocity of P.

ii Find the value of x and the velocity of P when $t = 0.7$.

iii Find the other values of t, for $0 < t < 1$, at which P's speed is the same as when $t = 0.7$. Find also the corresponding values of x.

© OCR A Level Mathematics, Unit 4730/01 Mechanics 3, June 2015

18 O is a fixed point on a horizontal plane. A particle P of mass 0.25 kg is released from rest at O and moves in a straight line on the plane. At time t s after release the only horizontal force acting on P has magnitude

$$\frac{1}{2400}\left(144 - t^2\right) \text{ N for } 0 \leqslant t \leqslant 12$$

and

$$\frac{1}{2400}\left(t^2 - 144\right) \text{ N for } t \geqslant 12.$$

The force acts in the direction of P's motion. P's velocity at time t s is $v\,\text{ms}^{-1}$.

i Find an expression for v in terms of t, valid for $t \geqslant 12$, and hence show that v is three times greater when $t = 24$ than it is when $t = 12$.

ii Sketch the (t, v) graph for $0 \leqslant t \leqslant 24$.

© OCR A Level Mathematics, Unit 4730 Mechanics 3, June 2010

A particle of mass 3 kg is attached to two identical springs, each of natural length 1 m. The magnitude of the tension in each spring is $24e$, where e is the extension of the spring.

The other ends of the springs are attached to points A and B, which are 2.6 m apart on a smooth horizontal surface. The midpoint of AB is C.

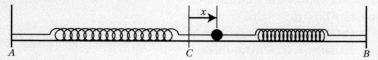

The particle is released from rest 0.15 m from C.

a Show that, when the displacement of the particle from C is x, the magnitude of the force acting on the particle is $48x$.

b Hence show that the particle performs simple harmonic motion, and find the period of the motion.

c Find the speed of the particle when it is 0.05 m from C.

 In a strongman competition the competitors pull a truck (initially at rest) for 20 seconds. The winner is the person who pulls the truck furthest.

The truck has a mass of 2000 kg and is subject to a constant resistance force of 2000 N. Brawny Bill initially pulls the truck with a force of 3000 N, but by the end of the 20 seconds he is pulling it with a force of 1000 N.

a State one assumption needed to model this force as a linear function of time. Comment on the appropriateness of this assumption.

b Given the assumption from part **a**, write down a differential equation satisfied by the displacement, x, of the truck from its initial position.

c Solve your differential equation and hence find the displacement of the truck at the end of the 20 seconds.

d Muscly Mike's force, F newtons, is modified as $F = 3000 \times \left(\dfrac{1}{3} \right)^{\frac{t}{20}}$ at time t seconds. Determine who wins the competition.

Elements of area and Gaussian integrals

You have seen that you can find areas under a curve using an integral which you thought of as summing up lots of little rectangles. In more advanced work it is useful to sum up lots of little elements of area instead and do a double sum over all coordinates. You can write this as:

$$A = \iint dA$$

where, in Cartesian coordinates, $dA = dy\,dx$.

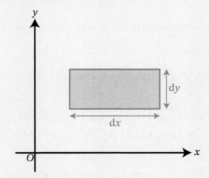

 Tip

This Focus on ... section extends significantly beyond the scope of the specification, but it will be of interest to anyone wanting to go on to study Mathematics, Physics, Chemistry, Engineering or Theoretical Economics.

The double integrals become

$$A = \int_{x=a}^{x=b} \left(\int_{y=c}^{y=d} dy \right) dx$$

If you are looking for the area between a curve and the x-axis then the limits on y are from 0 to $f(x)$ so the area is:

$$A = \int_{x=a}^{x=b} \left(\int_{y=0}^{y=f(x)} dy \right) dx$$

$$= \int_{x=a}^{x=b} [y]_0^{f(x)}\, dx$$

$$= \int_{x=a}^{x=b} f(x)\, dx$$

which is the formula you are used to using.

In Chapter 9 you found that the area between two half-lines in polar coordinates is given by $A = \int_\alpha^\beta \frac{1}{2} r^2\, d\theta$.

You can derive this using a similar method to the one shown for Cartesian coordinates. In the diagram the shaded area is approximately a rectangle with one dimension $r\,d\theta$ (using the formula for arc length in radians) and the other dr.

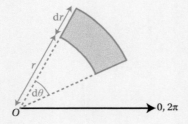

The area element in polar coordinates is therefore:

$$dA = r \, dr \, d\theta$$

Question

1 Prove that the area bounded by the lines $\theta = \alpha$, $\theta = \beta$ and $r = r(\theta)$

is given by the formula $A = \displaystyle\int_\alpha^\beta \frac{1}{2} r(\theta)^2 \, d\theta$.

These area elements have some lovely consequences, including allowing you to evaluate otherwise impossible integrals.

Consider the integral $I = \displaystyle\int_{x=-\infty}^{x=\infty} e^{-x^2} \, dx$.

You cannot find the indefinite integral of e^{-x^2} using standard functions, however over this range you can evaluate the integral exactly. The x in the integral is just a dummy variable. You could also write:

$$I = \int_{y=-\infty}^{y=\infty} e^{-y^2} \, dy$$

Multiplying the two expressions together:

$$I^2 = \int_{x=-\infty}^{x=\infty} e^{-x^2} \, dx \int_{y=-\infty}^{y=\infty} e^{-y^2} \, dy$$

It turns out that you can combine these two integrals into one double integral:

$$I^2 = \int_{x=-\infty}^{x=\infty} \int_{y=-\infty}^{y=\infty} e^{-y^2} e^{-x^2} \, dy \, dx$$

$$= \int_{x=-\infty}^{x=\infty} \int_{y=-\infty}^{y=\infty} e^{-y^2 - x^2} \, dy \, dx$$

But $dx \, dy = dA$ is just an element of area, so you could rewrite it as $r \, dr \, d\theta$. You can recast the whole expression in terms of polar coordinates, noting that $x^2 + y^2 = r^2$ and that the limits represent the whole plane:

$$I^2 = \int_{\theta=0}^{\theta=2\pi} \left(\int_{r=0}^{r=\infty} e^{-r^2} r \, dr \right) d\theta$$

Questions

2 Complete the proof to evaluate I.

3 Hence evaluate $\displaystyle\int_{-\infty}^{\infty} e^{-\frac{x^2}{2\sigma^2}} \, dx$ where σ is a constant.

> ◄◄ **Rewind**
>
> This is an example of an improper integral which you met in Chapter 8.

> ◄◄ **Rewind**
>
> The integral in question 3 is of vital importance in working with the normal distribution, which you met in A Level Mathematics Student Book 2, Chapter 17.

Finding the shape of a hanging chain

Consider this problem:

> A uniform chain is suspended from two fixed points at the same height and hangs under its own weight. Find the shape of the chain.

The first step is to express the question in a mathematical form. If you set up the coordinate axes so that the two end points have the same y-coordinate, then you can describe the shape of the chain by a function $y = f(x)$. The task is thens to find an expression for $f(x)$.

It is clear that the shape of the chain will be symmetrical, with the lowest point halfway between the end points. Note that the position of the x-axis is irrelevant, since the shape of the chain does not change if the end points are moved vertically.

Next you need to introduce some parameters: what could the exact shape of the chain depend on? It seems reasonable to consider these factors:

- the mass of the chain (M)
- the length of the chain (L)
- the distance between the end points ($2D$).

As already noted, the height of the end points does not affect the shape of the chain.

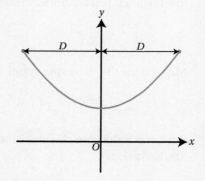

The shape of the chain is determined by the forces acing on it. As well as the mass of the chain, there is a tension force acting along the chain. At each point the tension acts along the tangent to the chain. So, if you can determine the direction of the tension at each point, you will know the gradient of the tangent, which is $\dfrac{dy}{dx}$. Knowing the gradient will enable you to find the equation for y in terms of x.

Consider the part of the chain between the lowest point and another point with a variable x-coordinate. The forces acting on this part of the chain are shown in the diagram (m is the mass of this part of the chain). The force T_0 is fixed (it is the force from the left half of the chain on the right half of the chain), but T changes with x.

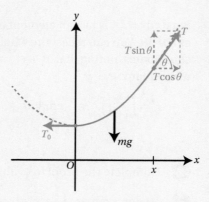

Resolving forces horizontally and vertically gives:

$$T\cos\theta = T_0, \ T\sin\theta = mg$$

and therefore $\tan\theta = \dfrac{mg}{T_0}$. But, since the force T is directed along the tangent to the curve, $\tan\theta$ equals the gradient of the curve at that point. Hence $\dfrac{dy}{dx} = \dfrac{mg}{T_0}$.

◄◄ **Rewind**

For a reminder of resolving forces, see A Level Mathematics Student Book 2, Chapter 21.

In the expression for the gradient, g and T_0 are constants, but m (the mass of this part of the chain) depends on the x-coordinate. If you can express m in terms of x, you can then integrate $\dfrac{dy}{dx}$ to obtain your required equation for the shape of the chain.

Since the chain is uniform, the mass of a part of the chain is proportional to the length of that part. The whole chain has length L and mass M, so $m = \dfrac{Ms}{L}$ where s is the length of the section of the chain between x-coordinates 0 and x.

To find an expression for the length of the curve in terms of x, consider a small section of the curve between points with coordinates (x, y) and $(x + \Delta x, y + \Delta y)$, and denote the length of this small section Δs. The small section of the curve is close to a straight line, so

$$\Delta s \approx \sqrt{(\Delta x)^2 + (\Delta y)^2} = (\Delta x)\sqrt{1 + \left(\frac{\Delta y}{\Delta x}\right)^2}$$

$$\Rightarrow \frac{\Delta s}{\Delta x} \approx \sqrt{1 + \left(\frac{\Delta y}{\Delta x}\right)^2}$$

As $\Delta x \to 0$, $\dfrac{\Delta s}{\Delta x} \to \dfrac{ds}{dx}$ and $\dfrac{\Delta y}{\Delta x} \to \dfrac{dy}{dx}$, and so

$$\frac{ds}{dx} = \sqrt{1 + \left(\frac{dy}{dx}\right)^2}$$

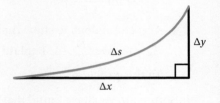

You now have the equation $\dfrac{dy}{dx} = \dfrac{mg}{T_0} = \dfrac{Mg}{T_0 L}s$, since $m = \dfrac{Ms}{L}$.

Differentiating this gives $\dfrac{d^2 y}{dx^2} = \dfrac{gM}{T_0 L}\dfrac{ds}{dx}$, and so

$$\frac{d^2 y}{dx^2} = \frac{gM}{T_0 L}\sqrt{1 + \left(\frac{dy}{dx}\right)^2}$$

You can now proceed to solve this differential equation.

Questions

1 Make a substitution $u = \dfrac{dy}{dx}$ and show that

$$\int \frac{1}{\sqrt{1 + u^2}}\, du = \frac{gM}{T_0 L}\int 1\, dx.$$

2 Explain why the constant of integration is zero. Hence show that $u = \sinh\left(\dfrac{gM}{T_0 L}x\right)$.

Rewind

You met integrals of this type in Chapter 7, Section 3.

3 Hence find an expression for y in terms of x. Explain why the constant of integration can be taken to be zero.

In the expression you found in question 3, g is a constant and M and L are fixed properties of the chain. However, you don't yet know what T_0 is; you defined it as the magnitude of the tension acting at the lowest point of the chain. You should also notice that you have not yet used the condition that the end points of the chain are a distance $2D$ apart. It seems reasonable that the tension in the chain will depend on how far apart the end points are.

Questions

4 Show that the length of the curve $y = k\cosh\left(\dfrac{x}{k}\right)$

between points with coordinates $x = a$ and $x = b$ is

$$k\left(\sinh\left(\dfrac{b}{k}\right) - \sinh\left(\dfrac{a}{k}\right)\right).$$

5 Use the fact that the total length of the chain is L, and that the end points are at $x = -D$ and $x = D$, to show that
$$\dfrac{2T_0}{gM}\sinh\left(\dfrac{gMD}{LT_0}\right) = 1.$$

6 Use technology to show that this equation has a solution for T_0 whenever $\dfrac{D}{L} < \dfrac{1}{2}$. Explain why this condition always holds in this problem.

In summary, you have found that a chain suspended freely from two fixed points hangs in the shape of a cosh curve, $y = k\cosh\left(\dfrac{x}{k}\right)$, where k is a constant depending on the mass and the length of the chain and the distance between the end points.

> 💡 **Tip**
>
> You have seen that the length of the curve satisfies
>
> $\dfrac{ds}{dx} = \sqrt{1 + \left(\dfrac{dy}{dx}\right)^2}$. Integrating this expression, you find that
>
> $s = \displaystyle\int_a^x \sqrt{1 + \left(\dfrac{dy}{dx}\right)^2}\, dx.$

> ℹ️ **Did you know?**
>
> The cosh curve is called a **catenary**, meaning 'relating to a chain'.

The Lotka–Volterra model and phase planes

During World War I the marine biologist Umberto D'Ancona noticed something puzzling about fish in the Adriatic Sea. Although they were being fished less (and so their natural death rate decreased), the numbers of small fish were actually decreasing while the numbers of predator fish were increasing. His father-in-law, Vito Volterra, applied the work of Alfred Lotka to try to explain this observation.

Consider a population of a species of fish (F million) and sharks (S thousand).

The natural net birth rate of the fish (i.e. the birth rate minus the death rate) is proportional to the number of fish, with constant of proportionality a. There is also a death rate due to predation which is proportional to both the number of fish and the number of sharks, with constant of proportionality b. This means that:

$$\frac{\mathrm{d}F}{\mathrm{d}t} = aF - bFS$$

A similar differential equation governs the population of sharks:

$$\frac{\mathrm{d}S}{\mathrm{d}t} = cFS - kS$$

where the cFS term represents the growth in the shark population due to their predation on the fish and the $-kS$ term is the natural net death rate of the sharks.

Question

1 Describe some modelling assumptions that have been made in creating this model.

When analysing systems like this, it is often the case that solving the differential equation is less important than finding fixed points of the system (values of the population where there is no change in the population i.e. places where $\frac{\mathrm{d}F}{\mathrm{d}t} = 0$ and $\frac{\mathrm{d}S}{\mathrm{d}t} = 0$.)

Questions

2 Find all fixed points of the differential equations in the Lotka–Volterra model. Which correspond to the biological equilibrium values if the populations do not go extinct?

3 When trawler fishing is reduced, the net birth rate of the fish will increase and the net death rate of the sharks will decrease. Use the Lokta–Volterra model to explain this.

A common way to visualise these systems of equations is to use a phase plane. These plot the 'flow' of the system at each value of F and S. You can find phase plane plotters online. For $a = b = c = k = 1$, the phase plane for Lotka–Volterra is shown in the diagram.

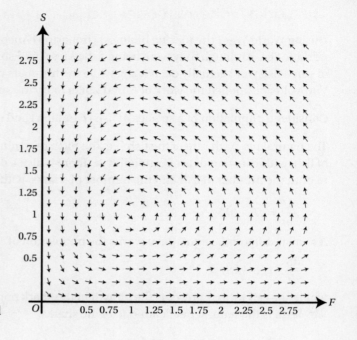

Questions

4 Sketch the curve in the phase plane above, corresponding to the initial values $F = 0.5$ and $S = 1$. Use this curve to estimate the maximum fish population.

5 Hence sketch the behaviour of F against t and of S against t for these initial conditions.

6 The effect of competition amongst the fish can be included in the model by adding another term in F^2 to the original differential equation:

$$\frac{dF}{dt} = aF - eF^2 - bFS$$

$$\frac{dS}{dt} = cFS - kS$$

Assuming that all parameters are positive, explain why this adaptation introduces a competition effect into the differential equations.

7 By using online technology, investigate this system with $a = b = c = k = 1$ and $e = 0.5$. How has the introduction of competition changed the behaviour of the system?

1 The curve C has polar equation $r^2 = a\sin 4\theta$, where $0 \leqslant \theta < 2\pi$ and $a > 0$.

   a Sketch C, clearly stating the range of values of θ for which it is defined.

   b Find the total area enclosed by C.

2 Solve the equation $3\sinh x = 2\cosh x$, giving your answer in the form $x = \ln\sqrt{a}$.

3 Solve the equation $3\sinh^2 x + 2\sinh x - 8 = 0$, giving your answer in terms of natural logarithms.

4 The Cartesian equation of a circle is $(x+4)^2 + (y-7)^2 = 65$.

Using the origin O as the pole and the positive x-axis as the initial line, find the polar equation of this circle, giving your answer in the form $r = p\sin\theta + q\cos\theta$.

5 The shaded region in the diagram is bounded by the curve with equation $y = 4x^{-\frac{3}{2}} + 1$, the x-axis and lines $x = 1$ and $x = 4$.

Calculate the volume of revolution when the shaded region is rotated 360° about the x-axis.

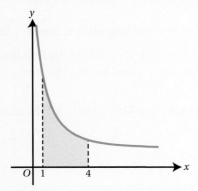

6 Express $\sinh 2x$ in terms of exponentials and hence, by using the substitution $u = e^{2x}$,

find $\displaystyle\int \frac{1}{\sinh 2x}\, dx$.

7 By first completing the square in the denominator, find the exact value of

$$\int_{\frac{1}{2}}^{\frac{3}{2}} \frac{1}{4x^2 - 4x + 5}\, dx.$$

© OCR A Level Mathematics, Unit 4726 Further Pure Mathematics 2, January 2012

8

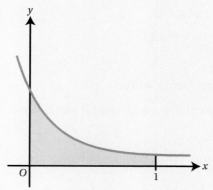

The diagram shows part of the curve $y = \dfrac{6}{(2x+1)^2}$. The shaded region is bounded by the curve and the lines $x=0$, $x=1$ and $y=0$. Find the exact volume of the solid produced when this shaded region is rotated completely about the x-axis.

© OCR A Level Mathematics, Unit 4723 Core Mathematics 3, January 2012

9 Given that the first three terms of the Maclaurin series for $(1+\sin x)\mathrm{e}^{2x}$ are identical to the first three terms of the binomial series for $(1+ax)^n$, find the values of the constants a and n. (You may use appropriate results given in the List of Formulae (MFl).)

© OCR A Level Mathematics, Unit 4726 Further Pure Mathematics 2, June 2010

10 a By using the substitution $u = \sinh x$, show that

$$\int \frac{1}{\cosh x}\,\mathrm{d}x = \arctan(\sinh x) + c$$

The part of the curve $y = \sqrt{\dfrac{1}{\cosh x}}$ between $x=0$ and $x=k$, where k is a positive constant, is rotated through $360°$ about the x-axis. The volume of the solid formed is $\dfrac{\pi^2}{6}$.

b Find the exact value of k.

11 Show that $\sinh(\ln \sin x) = -\dfrac{\cos x}{2\tan x}$.

12 a Show that $9\sinh x - \cosh x = 4\mathrm{e}^x - 5\mathrm{e}^{-x}$.

b Given that $9\sinh x - \cosh x = 8$, find the exact value of $\tanh x$.

13 i Use the definitions of hyperbolic function in terms of exponentials to prove that

$$8\sinh^4 x \equiv \cosh 4x - 4\cosh 2x + 3.$$

ii Solve the equation

$$\cosh 4x - 3\cosh 2x + 1 = 0,$$

giving your answer in logarithmic form.

© OCR A Level Mathematics, Unit 4726 Further Pure Mathematics 2, January 2011

14 **i** Show that $\dfrac{d}{dx}(\sinh^{-1} x) = \dfrac{1}{\sqrt{x^2+1}}$.

ii Given that $y = \cosh(a\sinh^{-1} x)$, where a is a constant, show that

$$(x^2+1)\frac{d^2 y}{dx^2} + x\frac{dy}{dx} - a^2 y = 0.$$

© OCR A Level Mathematics, Unit 4726 Further Pure Mathematics 2, June 2010

15 **i** Prove that, if $y = \sin^{-1} x$, then $\dfrac{dy}{dx} = \dfrac{1}{\sqrt{1-x^2}}$.

ii Find the Maclaurin series for $\sin^{-1} x$, up to and including the term in x^3.

iii Use the result of part **ii** and the Maclaurin series for $\ln(1 + x)$ to find the Maclaurin series for $(\sin^{-1} x)\ln(1 + x)$ up to and including the term in x^4.

© OCR A Level Mathematics, Unit 4726 Further Pure Mathematics 2, June 2011

16 It is given that $f(x) = \tanh^{-1}\left(\dfrac{1-x}{3+x}\right)$ for $x > -1$.

i Show that $f''(x) = \dfrac{1}{2(x+1)^2}$.

ii Hence find the Maclaurin series for $f(x)$ up to and including the term in x^2.

© OCR A Level Mathematics, Unit 4726/01 Further Pure Mathematics 2, June 2013

17 The equation of a curve in polar coordinates is $r = 2\sin 3\theta$ for $0 \leqslant \theta \leqslant \dfrac{1}{3}\pi$.

i Sketch the curve.

ii Find the area of the region enclosed by this curve.

iii By expressing $\sin 3\theta$ in terms of $\sin\theta$, show that a Cartesian equation for the curve is

$$\left(x^2 + y^2\right)^2 = 6x^2 y - 2y^3.$$

© OCR A Level Mathematics, Unit 4726/01 Further Pure Mathematics 2, June 2015

18 **i** Find the general solution of the differential equation

$$\frac{d^2 y}{dx^2} + 2\frac{dy}{dx} + 17y = 17x + 36.$$

ii Show that, when x is large and positive, the solution approximates to a linear function, and state its equation.

© OCR A Level Mathematics, Unit 4727 Further Pure Mathematics 3, June 2010

19 Find the solution of the differential equation $\dfrac{d^2 y}{dx^2} + 2\dfrac{dy}{dx} + 5y = e^{-x}$ for which $y = \dfrac{dy}{dx} = 0$ when $x = 0$.

© OCR A Level Mathematics, Unit 4727/01 Further Pure Mathematics 3, June 2013

20 Find the solution of the differential equation

$$\frac{dy}{dx} + y\cot x = 2x$$

for which $y = 2$ when $x = \dfrac{1}{6}\pi$. Give your answer in the form $y = f(x)$.

© OCR A Level Mathematics, Unit 4727 Further Pure Mathematics 3, June 2012

21 At time $t = 0$ s a particle P, of mass 0.3 kg, is 1 m away from a point O on a smooth horizontal plane and is moving away from O with speed $\sqrt{5}$ m s^{-1}. The only horizontal force acting on P has magnitude $1.5x$ N, where x is the distance OP, and acts away from O.

   i Show that the speed of P, v m s^{-1}, is given by $v = \sqrt{5}x$.

   ii Find an expression for v in terms of t.

© OCR A Level Mathematics, Unit 4730/01 Mechanics 3, January 2013

22 A particle P starts from rest at a point A and moves in a straight line with simple harmonic motion. At time t s after the motion starts, P's displacement from a point O on the line is x m towards A. The particle P returns to A for the first time when $t = 0.4\pi$. The maximum speed of P is 4 m s^{-1} and occurs when P passes through O.

   i Find the distance OA.

   ii Find the values of x and the velocity of P when $t = 1$.

   iii Find the number of occasions in the interval $0 < t < 1$ at which P's speed is the same as that when $t = 1$, and find the corresponding values of x and t.

© OCR A Level Mathematics, Unit 4730 Mechanics 3, January 2012

23 A particle P of mass 0.25 kg is projected horizontally with speed 5 m s^{-1} from a fixed point O on a smooth horizontal surface and moves in a straight line on the surface. The only horizontal force acting on P has magnitude $0.2v^2$ N, where v m s^{-1} is the velocity of P at time t s after it is projected from O. This force is directed towards O.

   i Find an expression for v in terms of t.

The particle P passes through a point X with speed 0.2 m s^{-1}.

   ii Find the average speed of P for its motion between O and X.

© OCR A Level Mathematics, Unit 4730 Mechanics 3, June 2011

24 Find the set of values of k for which

$$2\sinh x + 3\cosh x = k$$

has at least one solution.

25 The mean value of the function $\mathrm{f}(x) = 2 - \dfrac{1}{2\sqrt{x}}$ between 1 and k is $\dfrac{8}{5}$.

Find the value of k.

26 **a** Find, up to the term in x^3, the Maclaurin series for $\ln\left(\dfrac{2+x}{2-x}\right)$.

   b Find the set of x values for which the expansion is valid.

   c By evaluating the series in part **a** at an appropriate value of x, find a rational approximation to $\ln 3$.

27 Prove that if $y = \ln(\tan x)$, then $\tanh y = -\cos 2x$.

28 **a** Use the substitution $x = \sinh\theta$ to show that

$$\int \frac{1}{x^2\sqrt{1+x^2}}\,\mathrm{d}x = -\frac{\sqrt{1+x^2}}{x} + c$$

   b Hence find $\displaystyle\int \frac{\sqrt{1+x^2}}{x^2}\,\mathrm{d}x$.

29 Evaluate the improper integral $\displaystyle\int_0^\infty \frac{6x-4}{(3x^2+2)(x+1)}\,dx$, clearly showing the limiting process used.

30 **i** Using the definition of $\cosh x$ in terms of e^x and e^{-x}, show that

$$4\cosh^3 x - 3\cosh x \equiv \cosh 3x.$$

ii Use the substitution $u=\cosh x$ to find, in terms of $5^{\frac{1}{3}}$, the real root of the equation

$$20u^3 - 15u - 13 = 0.$$

© OCR A Level Mathematics, Unit 4726 Further Pure Mathematics 2, June 2010

31 **i** Use the substitution $x=\cosh^2 u$ to find $\displaystyle\int \sqrt{\frac{x}{x-1}}\,dx$, giving your answer in the form $f(x)+\ln\big(g(x)\big)$.

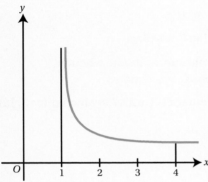

ii Hence calculate the exact area of the region between the curve $y=\sqrt{\dfrac{x}{x-1}}$, the x-axis and the lines $x=1$ and $x=4$ (see diagram).

iii What can you say about the solid of revolution obtained when the region defined in part **ii** is rotated completely about the x-axis? Justify your answer.

© OCR A Level Mathematics, Unit 4726 Further Pure Mathematics 2, June 2011

32 A curve has polar equation $r=5\sin 2\theta$ for $0\leqslant\theta\leqslant\dfrac{1}{2}\pi$.

i Sketch the curve, indicating the line of symmetry and stating the polar coordinates of the point P on the curve which is furthest away from the pole.

ii Calculate the area enclosed by the curve.

iii Find the Cartesian equation of the tangent to the curve at P.

iv Show that a Cartesian equation of the curve is $\left(x^2+y^2\right)^3 = (10xy)^2$.

© OCR A Level Mathematics, Unit 4726/01 Further Pure Mathematics 2, January 2013

33 The differential equation $\dfrac{d^2y}{dx^2}+4y=\sin kx$ is to be solved, where k is a constant.

i In the case $k=2$, by using a particular integral of the form $ax\cos 2x+bx\sin 2x$, find the general solution.

ii Describe briefly the behaviour of y when $x\to\infty$.

iii In the case $k\neq 2$, explain whether y would exhibit the same behaviour as in part **ii** when $x\to\infty$.

© OCR A Level Mathematics, Unit 4727/01 Further Pure Mathematics 3, January 2013

34

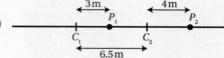

Particles P_1 and P_2 are each moving with simple harmonic motion along the same straight line. P_1's motion has centre C_1, period 2π s and amplitude 3 m; P_2's motion has centre C_2, period $\frac{4}{3}\pi$ s and amplitude 4 m. The points C_1 and C_2 are 6.5 m apart. The displacements of P_1 and P_2 from their centres of oscillation at time t s are denoted by x_1 m and x_2 m respectively. The diagram shows the positions of the particles at time $t=0$, when $x_1 = 3$ and $x_2 = 4$.

i State expressions for x_1 and x_2 in terms of t, which are valid until the particles collide.

The particles collide when $t = 5.99$, correct to 3 significant figures.

ii Find the distance travelled by P_1 and P_2 before the collision takes place.

iii Find the velocities of P_1 and P_2 immediately before the collision, and state whether the particles are travelling in the same direction or in opposite directions.

© OCR A Level Mathematics, Unit 4730 Mechanics 3, June 2010

35 **i** Given that $y = \cosh^{-1} x$, show that $y = \ln\left(x + \sqrt{x^2 - 1}\right)$.

ii Show that $\dfrac{\mathrm{d}}{\mathrm{d}x}\left(\cosh^{-1} x\right) = \dfrac{1}{\sqrt{x^2 - 1}}$

iii Solve the equation $\cosh x = 3$, giving your answer in logarithmic form.

© OCR A Level Mathematics, Unit 4726/01 Further Pure Mathematics 2, June 2014

36 A function is defined by $\mathrm{f}(x) = \sinh^{-1} x + \sinh^{-1}\left(\dfrac{1}{x}\right)$, for $x = 0$.

i When $x > 0$, show that the value of $\mathrm{f}(x)$ for which $\mathrm{f}'(x) = 0$ is $2\ln\left(1 + \sqrt{2}\right)$.

ii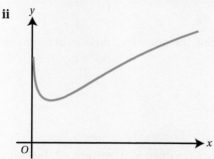

The diagram shows the graph of $y = \mathrm{f}(x)$ for $x > 0$. Sketch the graph of $y = \mathrm{f}(x)$ for $x < 0$ and state the range of values that $\mathrm{f}(x)$ can take for $x \neq 0$.

© OCR A Level Mathematics, Unit 4726 Further Pure Mathematics 2, June 2012

37   **a**   Find $\int \arcsin x \, dx$.

     b   Show that $\int \sin^2 x \, dx = \dfrac{1}{2}(x - \sin x \cos x) + c$.

The area A is bounded by the curve with equation $y = \sin^2 x$, the y-axis and the line $y = p$ as shown.

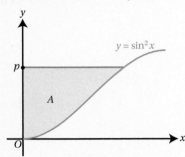

   c   **i**   Find the area A in terms of p.

       ii   Hence state $\int \arcsin \sqrt{x} \, dx$, $0 < x < 1$.

  38

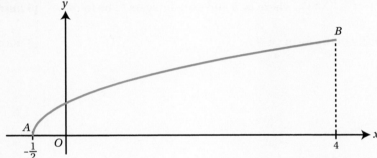

The diagram shows the curve with equation $y = \sqrt{2x+1}$ between the points $A\left(-\tfrac{1}{2}, 0\right)$ and $B(4, 3)$.

   i   Find the area of the region bounded by the curve, the x-axis and the line $x = 4$. Hence find the area of the region bounded by the curve and the lines OA and OB, where O is the origin.

   ii   Show that the curve between B and A can be expressed in polar coordinates as

$$r = \frac{1}{1 - \cos\theta}, \text{ where } \tan^{-1}\left(\tfrac{3}{4}\right) \leqslant \theta \leqslant \pi.$$

   iii   Deduce from parts **i** and **ii** that $\displaystyle\int_{\tan^{-1}\left(\frac{3}{4}\right)}^{\pi} \operatorname{cosec}^4\left(\tfrac{1}{2}\theta\right) d\theta = 24$.

© OCR A Level Mathematics, Unit 4726 Further Pure Mathematics 2, June 2010

1 hour 30 minutes, 75 marks

1 Let $\mathbf{a} = \begin{pmatrix} 3 \\ -1 \\ 2 \end{pmatrix}$, $\mathbf{b} = \begin{pmatrix} 1 \\ 1 \\ k \end{pmatrix}$ and $\mathbf{c} = \begin{pmatrix} 2 \\ 22 \\ 8 \end{pmatrix}$.

Find the value of k such that $\mathbf{c}$ is perpendicular to $\mathbf{a}$ and $\mathbf{b}$. **[3 marks]**

2 Use the definitions of $\sinh x$ and $\cosh x$ to prove that

$\cosh(x + y) \equiv \cosh x \cosh y + \sinh x \sinh y$. **[3 marks]**

3 **In this question you must show detailed reasoning.**

Evaluate $\int_0^9 \dfrac{1}{\sqrt{x}}\, dx$, explaining clearly why the integral converges. **[3 marks]**

4 **In this question you must show detailed reasoning.**

Given that α, β and γ are roots of the equation $2x^3 - x + 5 = 0$, find the value of $\alpha^2 + \beta^2 + \gamma^2$. **[4 marks]**

5 The region bounded by the curve $y = \dfrac{1}{\sqrt[4]{x}} + 1$, the x-axis and the lines $x = 1$ and $x = 4$ is rotated through $360°$ about the x-axis.

Show that the volume generated is $\dfrac{(a + b\sqrt{2})\pi}{c}$, where a, b and c are integers to be found. **[5 marks]**

6 **a** Write down the 7th roots of unity in the form $\operatorname{cis} \theta$. **[3 marks]**

b

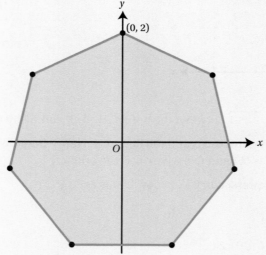

The diagram shows a regular seven-sided polygon with the centre at the origin and one vertex at $(0, 2)$, whose vertices represent the roots of the equation $z^n = w$, with $n \in \mathbb{N}$ and $w \in \mathbb{C}$. Find the values of n and w. **[2 marks]**

7 Find the general solution of the system of differential equations:

$$\begin{cases} \dfrac{dx}{dt} = 2y \\[2mm] \dfrac{dy}{dt} = 2x \end{cases}$$ **[5 marks]**

8 **a** Write $\dfrac{2x^2 - x + 3}{(x-1)(x^2+1)}$ in partial fractions. **[4 marks]**

    b Hence find $\displaystyle\int \dfrac{2x^2 - x + 3}{(x-1)(x^2+1)}\,\mathrm{d}x$. **[3 marks]**

9 Plane Π contains the points $A(-1, 1, 2)$, $B(3, 5, -1)$ and $C(2, 2, 1)$.

    a Find the Cartesian equation of Π. **[5 marks]**

    b Point D has coordinates $(3, -1, 1)$. Find the angle between Π and the line AD, giving your answer to the nearest $0.1°$. **[4 marks]**

10 A curve C has polar equation $r(1 - \cos\theta) = 3$.

    a Find its Cartesian equation in the form $y^2 = \mathrm{f}(x)$.

    The curve C intersects the line $3r = \dfrac{4}{\cos\theta}$. **[4 marks]**

    b Find the value of r at the points of intersection. **[3 marks]**

11 Consider the matrix $\mathbf{A} = \begin{pmatrix} a & 2 & 1 \\ 1 & a & 3 \\ 1 & 1 & 1 \end{pmatrix}$.

    a Show that $\mathbf{A}$ is non-singular for all values of a. **[2 marks]**

    b Find $\mathbf{A}^{-1}$ in terms of a. **[5 marks]**

    c Hence solve the simultaneous equations

$$\begin{cases} ax + 2y + z = 1 \\ x + ay + 3z = 0 \\ x + y + z = 0 \end{cases}$$ **[3 marks]**

12 Given that $y = 1$ when $x = 0$, solve the differential equation

$$(1 - x^2)\dfrac{\mathrm{d}y}{\mathrm{d}x} - xy = 2,\ |x| < 1.$$

Give your answer in the form $y = \mathrm{f}(x)$. **[6 marks]**

13 **a** Prove by induction that, for $n \in \mathbb{Z}^+$,

$$\cos\theta + \cos(3\theta) + \cos(5\theta) + \ldots + \cos((2n-1)\theta) = \dfrac{\sin(2n\theta)}{2\sin\theta}.$$ **[6 marks]**

    b Hence find the exact value of $\cos\dfrac{\pi}{7} + \cos\dfrac{3\pi}{7} + \ldots + \cos\dfrac{13\pi}{7}$. **[2 marks]**

1 hour 30 minutes, 75 marks

1 In this question you must show detailed reasoning.

Let $z = \dfrac{1-2i}{1+3i}$.

a Find z in the form $a + bi$. [2 marks]

b Find the modulus and argument of z. [3 marks]

2 A transformation is described by the matrix $\mathbf{M} = \begin{pmatrix} \dfrac{1}{2} & -\dfrac{\sqrt{3}}{2} \\ \dfrac{\sqrt{3}}{2} & \dfrac{1}{2} \end{pmatrix}$.

a The image of point A is the point $(1, -1)$. Find the coordinates of A. [2 marks]

b Describe the transformation fully. [2 marks]

3 Find the Cartesian equation of the curve with polar equation $r^3 = 8\cos\theta$. [2 marks]

4 Use the formulae for $\displaystyle\sum_{r=1}^{n} r$ and $\displaystyle\sum_{r=1}^{n} r^2$ to show that $\displaystyle\sum_{r=1}^{n}(2r-1)^2 = \dfrac{n}{3}(2n-1)(2n+1)$. [5 marks]

5 In this question you must show detailed reasoning.

By first completing the square, find the exact value of $\displaystyle\int_{0}^{8} \dfrac{1}{\sqrt{x^2 - 8x + 25}}\, dx$. [6 marks]

6 a Show that the Maclaurin series of the function $\ln(1 + \sin x)$ up to the

term in x^4 is $x - \dfrac{x^2}{2} + \dfrac{x^3}{6} - \dfrac{x^4}{12} + \cdots$. [6 marks]

b A student claims that this series is valid for all $x \in \mathbb{R}$. Show by means of a counterexample that he is wrong. [2 marks]

7 Matrix $\mathbf{A}$ is given by $\mathbf{A} = \begin{pmatrix} 1 & 5 \\ 0 & 1 \end{pmatrix}$.

a Find $\mathbf{A}^2$, $\mathbf{A}^3$ and $\mathbf{A}^4$. [2 marks]

b Conjecture an expression for $\mathbf{A}^n$ for $n \in \mathbb{N}$. [1 mark]

c Use mathematical induction to prove your conjecture. [5 marks]

8 Show that the lines with Cartesian equations $\dfrac{x-2}{5} = \dfrac{y+1}{-1} = \dfrac{z-1}{1}$ and

$\dfrac{x+1}{2} = \dfrac{y-1}{2} = \dfrac{z-2}{7}$ are skew and find the shortest distance between them. [7 marks]

9 Show that the mean value of the function $f(x) = \dfrac{3x^2 + 2x - 5}{(2x+1)(x^2+5)}$ between 0 and 4 is $a \ln b$,

where a and b are constants to be found. [7 marks]

10 a If $z = \cos\theta + i\sin\theta$, show that $\dfrac{1}{z} = \cos\theta - i\sin\theta$. [1 mark]

b Show that $\cos(n\theta) = \dfrac{1}{2}\left(z^n + \dfrac{1}{z^n}\right)$ for $n \in \mathbb{N}$. [4 marks]

c Hence solve $z^4 - 3z^3 + 4z^2 - 3z + 1 = 0$. [3 marks]

11 Three planes have equations $\Pi_1 : x - 2y + z = 0$, $\Pi_2 : 3x - z = 4$, $\Pi_3 : x + y - z = k$.

   a Show that, for all values of k, the planes do not intersect at a unique point. **[2 marks]**

   b Find the value of k for which the intersection of the three planes is a line. **[4 marks]**

12 A particle P of mass m is attached to one end of a light horizontal spring. The other end of the spring is attached to a fixed point.

The magnitude of the tension in the spring is given by $2mk^2 x$, where x is the extension in the spring at time t seconds and $k > 0$ is a constant.

The particle experiences a resistance to motion of magnitude $3kmv$, where v is the speed of the particle at time t seconds.

   a Show that $\dfrac{d^2 x}{dt^2} + 3k \dfrac{dx}{dt} + 2k^2 x = 0$. **[3 marks]**

   b Given that when $t = 0$, $x = 4$ and $v = -3k$:

     i find x in terms of t and k **[5 marks]**

     ii state whether the damping is underdamping, overdamping or critical. **[1 mark]**

FORMULAE

Learners will be given the following formulae in the Formulae Booklet in each assessment.

Pure Mathematics

Arithmetic series

$$S_n = \frac{1}{2}n(a+l) = \frac{1}{2}n\{2a+(n-1)d\}$$

Geometric series

$$S_n = \frac{a(1-r^n)}{1-r}$$

$$S_\infty = \frac{a}{1-r} \text{ for } |r| < 1$$

Binomial series

$$(a+b)^n = a^n + {}^nC_1 a^{n-1}b + {}^nC_2 a^{n-2}b^2 + \ldots + {}^nC_r a^{n-r}b^r + \ldots + b^n \ (n \in \mathbb{N}),$$

where $\displaystyle {}^nC_r = \binom{n}{r} = \frac{n!}{r!(n-r)!}$

$$(1+x)^n = 1 + nx + \frac{n(n-1)}{2!}x^2 + \ldots + \frac{n(n-1)\ldots(n-r+1)}{r!}x^r + \ldots \ (|x| < 1, \ n \in \mathbb{R})$$

Series

$$\sum_{r=1}^{n} r^2 = \frac{1}{6}n(n+1)(2n+1), \ \sum_{r=1}^{n} r^3 = \frac{1}{4}n^2(n+1)^2$$

Maclaurin series

$$f(x) = f(0) + f'(0)x + \frac{f''(0)}{2!}x^2 + \ldots + \frac{f^{(r)}(0)}{r!}x^r + \ldots$$

$$e^x = \exp(x) = 1 + x + \frac{x^2}{2!} + \ldots + \frac{x^r}{r!} + \ldots \text{ for all } x$$

$$\ln(1+x) = x - \frac{x^2}{2} + \frac{x^3}{3} - \ldots + (-1)^{r+1}\frac{x^r}{r} + \ldots \ (-1 < x \leqslant 1)$$

$$\sin x = x - \frac{x^3}{3!} + \frac{x^5}{5!} - \ldots + (-1)^r \frac{x^{2r+1}}{(2r+1)!} + \ldots \text{ for all } x$$

$$\cos x = 1 - \frac{x^2}{2!} + \frac{x^4}{4!} - \ldots + (-1)^r \frac{x^{2r}}{(2r)!} + \ldots \text{ for all } x$$

$$(1+x)^n = 1 + nx + \frac{n(n-1)}{2!}x^2 + \ldots + \frac{n(n-1)\ldots(n-r+1)}{r!}x^r + \ldots \ (|x| < 1, \ n \in \mathbb{R})$$

Matrix transformations

Reflection in the line $y = \pm x$: $\begin{pmatrix} 0 & \pm 1 \\ \pm 1 & 0 \end{pmatrix}$

Rotations through θ about the coordinate axes. The direction of positive rotation is taken to be anticlockwise when looking towards the origin from the positive side of the axis of rotation.

$$\mathbf{R}_x = \begin{pmatrix} 1 & 0 & 0 \\ 0 & \cos\theta & \sin\theta \\ 0 & -\sin\theta & \cos\theta \end{pmatrix}$$

$$\mathbf{R}_y = \begin{pmatrix} \cos\theta & 0 & -\sin\theta \\ 0 & 1 & 0 \\ \sin\theta & 0 & \cos\theta \end{pmatrix}$$

$$\mathbf{R}_z = \begin{pmatrix} \cos\theta & \sin\theta & 0 \\ -\sin\theta & \cos\theta & 0 \\ 0 & 0 & 1 \end{pmatrix}$$

Differentiation

$f(x)$	$f'(x)$
$\tan kx$	$k \sec^2 kx$
$\sec x$	$\sec x \tan x$
$\cot x$	$-\csc^2 x$
$\csc x$	$-\csc x \cot x$
$\arcsin x$ or $\sin^{-1} x$	$\dfrac{1}{\sqrt{1-x^2}}$
$\arccos x$ or $\cos^{-1} x$	$-\dfrac{1}{\sqrt{1-x^2}}$
$\arctan x$ or $\tan^{-1} x$	$\dfrac{1}{1+x^2}$

Quotient rule $y = \dfrac{u}{v}$, $\dfrac{dy}{dx} = \dfrac{v\dfrac{du}{dx} - u\dfrac{dv}{dx}}{v^2}$

Differentiation from first principles

$$f'(x) = \lim_{h \to 0} \frac{f(x+h) - f(x)}{h}$$

Integration

$$\int \frac{f'(x)}{f(x)} \, dx = \ln|f(x)| + c$$

283

$$\int f'(x)\big(f(x)\big)^{n}\,dx = \frac{1}{n+1}\big(f(x)\big)^{n+1} + c$$

Integration by parts $\int u\dfrac{dv}{dx}\,dx = uv - \int v\dfrac{du}{dx}\,dx$

The mean value of f(x) on the interval $[a, b]$ is $\dfrac{1}{b-a}\int_{a}^{b} f(x)\,dx$

Area of sector enclosed by polar curve is $\dfrac{1}{2}\int r^{2}\,d\theta$

f(x)	$\int f(x)\,dx$
$\dfrac{1}{\sqrt{a^{2}-x^{2}}}$	$\sin^{-1}\left(\dfrac{x}{a}\right)\ (|x|<a)$
$\dfrac{1}{a^{2}+x^{2}}$	$\dfrac{1}{a}\tan^{-1}\left(\dfrac{x}{a}\right)$
$\dfrac{1}{\sqrt{a^{2}+x^{2}}}$	$\sinh^{-1}\left(\dfrac{x}{y}\right)$ or $\ln\left(x+\sqrt{x^{2}+a^{2}}\right)$
$\dfrac{1}{\sqrt{x^{2}-a^{2}}}$	$\cosh^{-1}\left(\dfrac{x}{a}\right)$ or $\ln\left(x+\sqrt{x^{2}-a^{2}}\right)\ (x>a)$

Numerical methods

Trapezium rule: $\int_{a}^{b} y\,dx \approx \dfrac{1}{2}h\big\{(y_{0}+y_{n})+2(y_{1}+y_{2}+\ldots+y_{n-1})\big\}$, where $h = \dfrac{b-a}{n}$

The Newton-Raphson iteration for solving $f(x)=0$: $x_{n+1} = x_{n} - \dfrac{f(x_{n})}{f'(x_{n})}$

Complex numbers

Circles: $|z-a|=k$

Half-lines: $\arg(z-a)=\alpha$

Lines: $|z-a|=|z-b|$

De Moivre's theorem: $\big\{r(\cos\theta+i\sin\theta)\big\}^{n} = r^{n}(\cos n\theta+i\sin n\theta)$

Roots of unity: The roots of $z^{n}=1$ are given by $z = \exp\left(\dfrac{2\pi k}{n}i\right)$ for $k=0,1,2,\ldots,n-1$

Vectors and 3D coordinate geometry

Cartesian equation of the line through the point A with position vector $\mathbf{a}=a_{1}\mathbf{i}+a_{2}\mathbf{j}+a_{3}\mathbf{k}$ in direction $\mathbf{u}=u_{1}\mathbf{i}+u_{2}\mathbf{j}+u_{3}\mathbf{k}$ is $\dfrac{x-a_{1}}{u_{1}}=\dfrac{y-a_{2}}{u_{2}}=\dfrac{z-a_{3}}{u_{3}}(=\lambda)$

Cartesian equation of a plane is $n_{1}x+n_{2}y+n_{3}z+d=0$

Vector product: $\mathbf{a}\times\mathbf{b}=\begin{pmatrix}a_{1}\\a_{2}\\a_{3}\end{pmatrix}\times\begin{pmatrix}b_{1}\\b_{2}\\b_{3}\end{pmatrix}=\begin{vmatrix}\mathbf{i}&a_{1}&b_{1}\\\mathbf{j}&a_{2}&b_{2}\\\mathbf{k}&a_{3}&b_{3}\end{vmatrix}=\begin{pmatrix}a_{2}b_{3}-a_{3}b_{2}\\a_{3}b_{1}-a_{1}b_{3}\\a_{1}b_{2}-a_{2}b_{1}\end{pmatrix}$

The distance between skew lines is $D=\dfrac{|(\mathbf{b}-\mathbf{a})\boldsymbol{\cdot}\mathbf{n}|}{|\mathbf{n}|}$, where $\mathbf{a}$ and $\mathbf{b}$ are position vectors of points on each line and $\mathbf{n}$ is a mutual perpendicular to both lines

The distance between a point and a line is $D = \dfrac{|ax_1 + by_1 - c|}{\sqrt{a^2 + b^2}}$, where the coordinates of the point are (x_1, y_1) and the equation of the line is given by $ax + by = c$

The distance between a point and a plane is $D = \dfrac{|\mathbf{b} \cdot \mathbf{n} - p|}{|\mathbf{n}|}$, where $\mathbf{b}$ is the position vector of the point and the equation of the plane is given by $\mathbf{r} \cdot \mathbf{n} = p$

Small angle approximations

$\sin\theta \approx \theta$, $\cos\theta \approx 1 - \dfrac{1}{2}\theta^2$, $\tan\theta \approx \theta$ where θ is small and measured in radians

Trigonometric identities

$\sin(A \pm B) = \sin A \cos B \pm \cos A \sin B$

$\cos(A \pm B) = \cos A \cos B \mp \sin A \sin B$

$\tan(A \pm B) = \dfrac{\tan A \pm \tan B}{1 \mp \tan A \tan B} \left(A \pm B \neq \left(k + \dfrac{1}{2} \right)\pi \right)$

Hyperbolic functions

$\cosh^2 x - \sinh^2 x = 1$

$\sinh^{-1} x = \ln\left[x + \sqrt{(x^2 + 1)} \right]$

$\cosh^{-1} x = \ln\left[x + \sqrt{(x^2 - 1)} \right]$, $x \geqslant 1$

$\tanh^{-1} x = \dfrac{1}{2}\ln\left(\dfrac{1+x}{1-x} \right)$, $-1 < x < 1$

Simple harmonic motion

$x = A\cos(\omega t) + B\sin(\omega t)$

$x = R\sin(\omega t + \varphi)$

Answers

Chapter 1

Before you start...

1 Proof

2 $u_1 = 3$, $u_2 = 9$, $u_3 = 17$

3 $3n^2(n+1)$

4 62

5 $(5+6x)e^{3x}$

6 $\dfrac{1}{r} - \dfrac{1}{r+1}$

Exercise 1A

1, 2 Proof

3 a 4, 24, 124, 624   **b** $u_n = 5^n - 1$; Proof

4 a $\begin{pmatrix} 1 & 0 \\ 2 & 1 \end{pmatrix}, \begin{pmatrix} 1 & 0 \\ 3 & 1 \end{pmatrix}, \begin{pmatrix} 1 & 0 \\ 4 & 1 \end{pmatrix}$

    b $\begin{pmatrix} 1 & 0 \\ n & 1 \end{pmatrix}$; Proof

5 a 4, 24, 124, 624

    b 4   **c** Proof

6, 7 Proof

8 a $\begin{pmatrix} 2 & 2 \\ 2 & 2 \end{pmatrix}, \begin{pmatrix} 4 & 4 \\ 4 & 4 \end{pmatrix}, \begin{pmatrix} 8 & 8 \\ 8 & 8 \end{pmatrix}$

    b $\begin{pmatrix} 2^{n-1} & 2^{n-1} \\ 2^{n-1} & 2^{n-1} \end{pmatrix}$; Proof

9 a 5   **b** Proof

10–15 Proof

Exercise 1B

1–10 Proof

Work it out 1.1

The correct answer is Solution 2.

Exercise 1C

1 a i 9455   **ii** 44 100

    b i 1 379 609   **ii** 4750

2 a i $2n(4n+1)$ **ii** $\dfrac{n}{2}(3n+1)(6n+1)$

    b i $\dfrac{n}{6}(n-1)(2n-1)$ **ii** $\dfrac{(n+1)^2(n+2)^2}{4}$

3, 4 Proof

5 a $3n^2 + 10n$ **b** 27

6 a Proof   **b** 25 225

7 Proof; $k = 3$

8 a Proof   **b** $n(2n+1)(n-1)(2n+3)$

9 a Proof   **b** $\ln 3^{2660}$

10 Proof; $a = 4$

Exercise 1D

1, 2 Proof

3 a Proof   **b i** Proof   **ii** $\dfrac{7}{78}$

4 a $\dfrac{1}{2r-1} - \dfrac{1}{2r+1}$ **b** Proof

    c 1

5 Proof

6 a Proof   **b** $\dfrac{3}{2}$

7 a Proof   **b** $\dfrac{n}{3(2n+3)}$

    c Proof

8 $\dfrac{n^2 + 5n}{12(n+2)(n+3)}$

9 a Proof

    b Proof; $a = 2$, $b = 3$, $c = 4$

    c $\dfrac{5}{1848}$

10 a $\ln(n+1)$ **b** Proof

Mixed practice 1

1 a 16, 88, 736, 6568; 8

    b Proof

2 Proof

3 a $3e^{3x}, 9e^{3x}, 27e^{3x}; 3^n e^{3x}$

    b Proof

4 $3n^2 + 2n$

5 Proof

6 1 278 270

7 a Proof   **b** Proof; $a = 1$, $b = 5$

8 $2n^2(4n+3)$

9–11 Proof

12 a Proof   **b** 603 330

13 a Proof   **b** Proof

14 a Proof   **b** $1 - \dfrac{1}{(n+1)!}$

    c 1

15 i $6, 27, 129$ **ii** 3 **iii** Proof

16–18 Proof

19 7; Proof

20, 21 Proof

22 i Proof   **ii** $\dfrac{n}{n+1}$ **iii** $\dfrac{1}{n+1}$

23 a $\dfrac{1}{r-1}-\dfrac{1}{r+2}$ **b** Proof; $a=99, b=144, c=49$

24 Proof; $a=5, b=9, c=2$

Chapter 2

Before you start...

1 5; 2.21 radians

2 $-3+2i$; $-3i$

3 a $1-3i$ **b** $\dfrac{4}{5}-\dfrac{7}{5}i$

4 a $20\left(\cos\left(-\dfrac{7\pi}{12}\right)+i\sin\left(-\dfrac{7\pi}{12}\right)\right)$

b $5\left(\cos\dfrac{\pi}{12}+i\sin\dfrac{\pi}{12}\right)$

5 a $-3-5i$ **b** $3\left(\cos\left(-\dfrac{\pi}{4}\right)+i\sin\left(-\dfrac{\pi}{4}\right)\right)$

6 a Reflection in the real axis.

b Translation by $\begin{pmatrix}2\\1\end{pmatrix}$.

Exercise 2A

1 a i $64\left(\cos\left(\dfrac{-4\pi}{5}\right)+i\sin\left(\dfrac{-4\pi}{5}\right)\right)$

ii $81\left(\cos\dfrac{2\pi}{3}+i\sin\dfrac{2\pi}{3}\right)$

b i $\cos\left(\dfrac{-11\pi}{12}\right)+i\sin\left(\dfrac{-11\pi}{12}\right)$

ii $\cos\left(\dfrac{-5\pi}{6}\right)+i\sin\left(\dfrac{-5\pi}{6}\right)$

c i $\cos\left(\dfrac{-\pi}{2}\right)+i\sin\left(\dfrac{-\pi}{2}\right)$

ii $\cos\dfrac{\pi}{2}+i\sin\dfrac{\pi}{2}$

2 a $z^2=\cos\dfrac{\pi}{3}+i\sin\dfrac{\pi}{3}$; $z^3=\cos\dfrac{\pi}{2}+i\sin\dfrac{\pi}{2}$;

$z^4=\cos\dfrac{2\pi}{3}+i\sin\dfrac{2\pi}{3}$

b

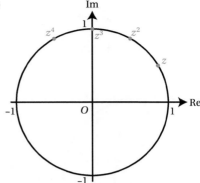

3 a i $z^2=\cos\left(-\dfrac{2\pi}{3}\right)+i\sin\left(-\dfrac{2\pi}{3}\right)$; $z^3=1$,

$z^4=\cos\dfrac{2\pi}{3}+i\sin\dfrac{2\pi}{3}$

ii

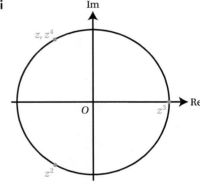

b $n=1+3k, k\in\mathbb{Z}^+$

4 a $\text{mod}=2$, $\arg=\dfrac{\pi}{3}$

b $32\left(\cos\dfrac{5\pi}{3}+i\sin\dfrac{5\pi}{3}\right)$ **c** $16-16\sqrt{3}i$

5 a $2\text{cis}\left(\dfrac{3\pi}{4}\right)$ **b** $64i$

6 12

7 14

Exercise 2B

1 a i $\dfrac{3\sqrt{3}}{2}+\dfrac{3}{2}i$ **ii** $2\sqrt{2}+2\sqrt{2}i$

b i -4 **ii** 5

c i $-\dfrac{1}{2}+\dfrac{\sqrt{3}}{2}i$ **ii** $-2i$

2 a i $5\sqrt{2}\,e^{i\frac{\pi}{4}}$ **ii** $4e^{-i\frac{\pi}{6}}$

b i $\dfrac{1}{\sqrt{2}}e^{i\frac{3\pi}{4}}$ **ii** $\sqrt{13}\,e^{0.983i}$

c i $4e^{-i\frac{\pi}{2}}$ **ii** $5e^{i\pi}$

3 a i $20e^{i\frac{5\pi}{12}}$ **ii** $\frac{1}{2}e^{i\frac{\pi}{2}}$

b i $\frac{8}{25}e^{i\frac{\pi}{12}}$ **ii** $2e^{-i\frac{\pi}{2}}$

4

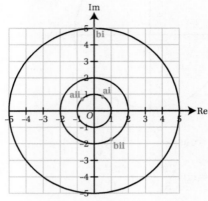

5 Proof

6 a $\frac{2}{3}i$ **b** $-432\sqrt{3}-432i$

7 $-54.1+7.70i$

8 $\frac{e^2}{2}-\frac{e^2\sqrt{3}}{2}i$

9 $a=-3,\ b=3,\ c=-2$

10 $x^4-\left(2+\sqrt{3}\right)x^3+\left(5+2\sqrt{3}\right)x^2-\left(2+4\sqrt{3}\right)x+4=0$

11 $\cos(\ln 5)+i\sin(\ln 5)$

12 $9\cos(\ln 3)-9i\sin(\ln 3)$

Exercise 2C

1 a i $3,\ 3e^{\frac{2\pi i}{3}},\ 3e^{-\frac{2\pi i}{3}}$

   ii $\sqrt[3]{100},\ \sqrt[3]{100}\,e^{\frac{2\pi i}{3}},\ \sqrt[3]{100}\,e^{-\frac{2\pi i}{3}}$

b i $2e^{\frac{\pi i}{6}},\ 2e^{\frac{5\pi i}{6}},\ 2e^{\frac{3\pi i}{2}}$ **ii** $e^{\frac{\pi i}{6}},\ e^{\frac{5\pi i}{6}},\ e^{\frac{3\pi i}{2}}$

c i $2^{\frac{1}{6}}e^{\frac{\pi i}{12}},\ 2^{\frac{1}{6}}e^{\frac{3\pi i}{4}},\ 2^{\frac{1}{6}}e^{\frac{17\pi i}{12}}$

   ii $7^{\frac{1}{6}}e^{-0.238i},\ 7^{\frac{1}{6}}e^{1.86i},\ 7^{\frac{1}{6}}e^{-2.33i}$

2 a i $2\mathrm{cis}\frac{\pi}{4},\ 2\mathrm{cis}\frac{3\pi}{4},\ 2\mathrm{cis}\frac{5\pi}{4},\ 2\mathrm{cis}\frac{7\pi}{4};$

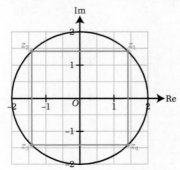

ii $3\mathrm{cis}\frac{\pi}{8},\ 3\mathrm{cis}\frac{5\pi}{8},\ 3\mathrm{cis}\frac{9\pi}{8},\ 3\mathrm{cis}\frac{13\pi}{8};$

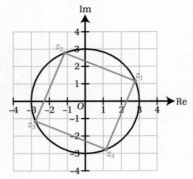

b i $2\mathrm{cis}\frac{\pi}{16},\ 2\mathrm{cis}\frac{9\pi}{16},\ 2\mathrm{cis}\frac{17\pi}{16},\ 2\mathrm{cis}\frac{25\pi}{16};$

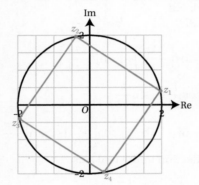

ii $\mathrm{cis}\frac{\pi}{12},\ \mathrm{cis}\frac{7\pi}{12},\ \mathrm{cis}\frac{13\pi}{12},\ \mathrm{cis}\frac{19\pi}{12};$

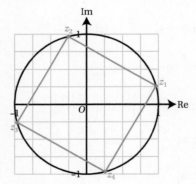

3 $-2,\ 1+\sqrt{3}i,\ 1-\sqrt{3}i$

4 a $16;\ -\frac{\pi}{6}$

   b $2\mathrm{cis}\left(-\frac{\pi}{24}\right),\ 2\mathrm{cis}\left(\frac{11\pi}{24}\right),\ 2\mathrm{cis}\left(\frac{23\pi}{24}\right),\ 2\mathrm{cis}\left(-\frac{13\pi}{24}\right)$

5 $\dfrac{\sqrt{2}+\sqrt{6}}{2}+\left(\dfrac{\sqrt{2}-\sqrt{6}}{2}\right)i,\ \dfrac{\sqrt{2}-\sqrt{6}}{2}+\left(\dfrac{\sqrt{2}+\sqrt{6}}{2}\right)i,$

   $-\sqrt{2}-\sqrt{2}i$

6 $3\left(\cos\left(\dfrac{3\pi}{8}\right)+i\sin\left(\dfrac{3\pi}{8}\right)\right), 3\left(\cos\left(\dfrac{7\pi}{8}\right)+i\sin\left(\dfrac{7\pi}{8}\right)\right),$

$3\left(\cos\left(\dfrac{11\pi}{8}\right)+i\sin\left(\dfrac{11\pi}{8}\right)\right), 3\left(\cos\left(\dfrac{15\pi}{8}\right)+i\sin\left(\dfrac{15\pi}{8}\right)\right)$

7 a $8e^{i\frac{\pi}{3}}$

b $8^{\frac{1}{4}}e^{i\frac{\pi}{12}}, 8^{\frac{1}{4}}e^{i\frac{7\pi}{12}}, 8^{\frac{1}{4}}e^{i\frac{13\pi}{12}}, 8^{\frac{1}{4}}e^{i\frac{19\pi}{12}}$

c

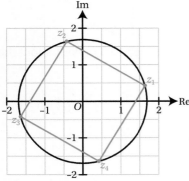

8 $n=4, w=-64$

9 a $\sqrt{2}\pm\sqrt{2}i, -\sqrt{2}\pm\sqrt{2}i$

b $\left(z^2+2\sqrt{2}z+4\right)\left(z^2-2\sqrt{2}z+4\right)$

10 a $2i, -\sqrt{3}-i, \sqrt{3}-i$

b $\dfrac{4}{5}-\dfrac{2}{5}i, \dfrac{14-3\sqrt{3}}{13}+\dfrac{\left(5-2\sqrt{3}\right)}{13}i, \dfrac{14+3\sqrt{3}}{13}+\dfrac{\left(5+2\sqrt{3}\right)}{13}i$

11 a $2\left(\cos\left(\dfrac{\pi}{4}\right)+i\sin\left(\dfrac{\pi}{4}\right)\right),$

$2\left(\cos\left(\dfrac{11\pi}{12}\right)+i\sin\left(\dfrac{11\pi}{12}\right)\right),$

$2\left(\cos\left(\dfrac{19\pi}{12}\right)+i\sin\left(\dfrac{19\pi}{12}\right)\right)$

b $1; \dfrac{7\pi}{12}$ **c** $\dfrac{\sqrt{2}}{2}-\dfrac{\sqrt{2}}{2}i$

12 a $-1, e^{\frac{i\pi}{3}}, e^{-\frac{i\pi}{3}}$ **b** $x^3+6x^2+12x+8$

c $-3, -\dfrac{3}{2}+\dfrac{\sqrt{3}}{2}i, -\dfrac{3}{2}-\dfrac{\sqrt{3}}{2}i$

Exercise 2D

1 a i $\cos 0+i\sin 0, \cos\left(\dfrac{2\pi}{3}\right)+i\sin\left(\dfrac{2\pi}{3}\right),$

$\cos\left(\dfrac{4\pi}{3}\right)+i\sin\left(\dfrac{4\pi}{3}\right)$

ii $\cos 0+i\sin 0, \cos\pi+i\sin\pi$

b i $\cos 0+i\sin 0, \cos\left(\dfrac{\pi}{3}\right)+i\sin\left(\dfrac{\pi}{3}\right),$

$\cos\left(\dfrac{2\pi}{3}\right)+i\sin\left(\dfrac{2\pi}{3}\right), \cos\pi+i\sin\pi,$

$\cos\left(\dfrac{4\pi}{3}\right)+i\sin\left(\dfrac{4\pi}{3}\right),$

$\cos\left(\dfrac{5\pi}{3}\right)+i\sin\left(\dfrac{5\pi}{3}\right)$

ii $\cos 0+i\sin 0, \cos\left(\dfrac{\pi}{2}\right)+i\sin\left(\dfrac{\pi}{2}\right),$

$\cos\pi+i\sin\pi, \cos\left(\dfrac{3\pi}{2}\right)+i\sin\left(\dfrac{3\pi}{2}\right)$

2 a i $1, -\dfrac{1}{2}\pm i\dfrac{\sqrt{3}}{2}$ **ii** ± 1

b i $\pm 1, \dfrac{1}{2}\pm i\dfrac{\sqrt{3}}{2}, -\dfrac{1}{2}\pm i\dfrac{\sqrt{3}}{2}$ **ii** $\pm 1, \pm i$

3 a $1, e^{\frac{2\pi i}{5}}, e^{\frac{4\pi i}{5}}, e^{\frac{6\pi i}{5}}, e^{\frac{8\pi i}{5}}$

b

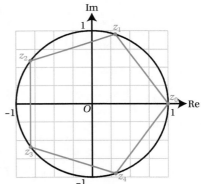

4 a 5 **b** -1

c A, B, C

5 a 1 (or ω^0), $\omega, \omega^2, \omega^3, \omega^4, \omega^5, \omega^6$

b No. Consider $\omega^7=1$, or an Argand diagram.

c 3 **d** 5

6 a, b Proof

7 a $1, -\dfrac{1}{2}\pm\dfrac{\sqrt{3}}{2}i$ **b** $\dfrac{-1\pm\sqrt{3}i}{2}$

8 a^2+b^2+ab

9 a $(1), \omega, \omega^2, \omega^3, \omega^4$

b $\dfrac{1+\omega^k}{1-\omega^k}$ for $k=1, 2, 3, 4$

c–e Proof

10 a

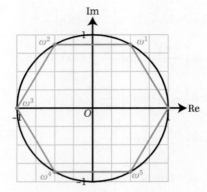

b i $\dfrac{\sqrt{3}}{2}e^{i\frac{\pi}{6}}$ **ii** $\dfrac{\sqrt{3}}{2}e^{i\frac{7\pi}{6}}$

11 a Proof

  b i Proof **ii** $-\dfrac{1}{2}$

  c Proof

Exercise 2E

1 a $2e^{i\frac{\pi}{4}}, 2e^{i\frac{3\pi}{4}}, 2e^{i\frac{5\pi}{4}}, 2e^{i\frac{7\pi}{4}}$

  b $\sqrt{2}+i\sqrt{2}, \sqrt{2}-i\sqrt{2}, -\sqrt{2}+i\sqrt{2}, -\sqrt{2}-i\sqrt{2}$

  c $\left(z^2+2\sqrt{2}z+4\right)\left(z^2-2\sqrt{2}z+4\right)$

2 $\left(z^2-2z+2\right)\left(z^2+2z+2\right)\left(z^2-2\right)\left(z^2+2\right)=0$

3 Proof; $\theta=\dfrac{2\pi}{5}, \phi=\dfrac{4\pi}{5}$

4 a $1, \omega, \omega^2, \omega^3, \omega^4$ **b** 31

5 a Proof **b** $e^{\frac{i\pi}{6}}, e^{\frac{2i\pi}{3}}, e^{\frac{7i\pi}{6}}, e^{\frac{5i\pi}{3}}$

  c $\left(z^2+z+1\right)\left(z^2-z+1\right)\left(z^2+\sqrt{3}z+1\right)\left(z^2-\sqrt{3}z+1\right)$

6 a $\omega, \omega^2, \omega^3, \omega^4, \omega^5, \omega^6$
  (or $\omega, \omega^2, \omega^3, \omega^*, \omega^{*2}, \omega^{*3}$)

  b, c Proof

Exercise 2F

1 a $\sqrt{17}, 0.245; \sqrt{34}, 0.540$

  b $\sqrt{2}, 0.295\,(16.9°)$

2 a Proof

  b Rotation 1.76 radians $(101°)$ about the origin.

3 $\dfrac{3\sqrt{3}-2}{2}+i\dfrac{3+2\sqrt{3}}{2}$

4 $(7,-3), (2,-5)$

5 $b=az, c=az^3, d=\dfrac{a}{z^2}$

6 a $\sqrt{60}$

  b $\left(6-\sqrt{3}, 3+2\sqrt{3}\right)$

7 a

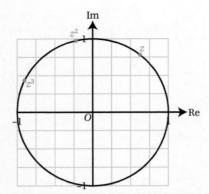

  b Rotation through 1.85 radians about the origin.

8 a $\dfrac{\pi}{3}$ **b** $\dfrac{\pi}{6}$

  c $\left(\dfrac{\sqrt{6}-\sqrt{2}}{2}, \dfrac{\sqrt{6}+\sqrt{2}}{2}\right)$

9 a $4-i$

  b $B\left(\dfrac{\sqrt{3}-4}{2}, \dfrac{4\sqrt{3}+1}{2}\right), C\left(-\dfrac{4+\sqrt{3}}{2}, -\dfrac{4\sqrt{3}-1}{2}\right)$

10 $2\text{cis}\left(\dfrac{2\pi}{5}\right), 2\text{cis}\left(\dfrac{4\pi}{5}\right), 2\text{cis}\left(\dfrac{6\pi}{5}\right), 2\text{cis}\left(\dfrac{8\pi}{5}\right)$

11 a iz^* **b** Proof

12 a Proof **b** $\left(\dfrac{3-4\sqrt{3}}{2}, \dfrac{2-\sqrt{3}}{2}\right)$

13 a $c-a=(b-a)e^{i\theta}$ **b** $0.935+4.89i$

14 $\dfrac{1-\sqrt{3}}{4}+\dfrac{1+\sqrt{3}}{4}i$

Mixed practice 2

1 $\dfrac{1}{r}e^{i\theta}$

2 a $2; \dfrac{2\pi}{3}$ **b** $-16-16\sqrt{3}i$

3 a $e^{\frac{2k\pi i}{5}}$ for $k=0,1,2,3,4$

  b

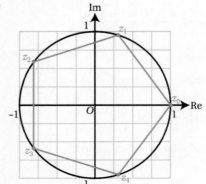

4 $e^{\frac{7\pi i}{12}}$

5 a $8\sqrt{2}; \dfrac{7\pi}{4}$

b $2^{\frac{7}{8}} e^{i\left(\frac{(8k-1)\pi}{16}\right)}$ for $k = 0, 1, 2, 3$

6 a $\sqrt{2}, \dfrac{\pi}{4}$ **b** $z^6 = -8i$

7 i $e^{\frac{i\pi}{3}}$ **ii** 6

8 $\dfrac{\sqrt{3}}{3}$

9 $-\dfrac{1}{64}$

10 a $\cos\left(-\dfrac{\pi}{6}\right) + i\sin\left(-\dfrac{\pi}{6}\right)$

b Proof; $c = 1$
c $m = 6, n = 4$

11, 12 Proof

13 θ

14 Proof

15 a $e^{i\frac{\pi}{2}}$ **b** $e^{-\frac{\pi}{2}}$

16 i

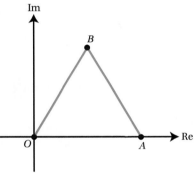

Proof
ii $3e^{-i\frac{\pi}{3}}$ **iii** $\dfrac{243}{2} + \dfrac{243}{2}i\sqrt{3}$

17 a $\omega^2 = e^{\frac{4\pi i}{5}}, \omega^3 = e^{\frac{6\pi i}{5}}, \omega^4 = e^{\frac{8\pi i}{5}}$
b, c Proof

d $4\cos^2\alpha + 2\cos\alpha - 1 = 0 \left(\text{where } \alpha = \dfrac{2\pi}{5}\right)$

18 a Proof
b i 1   **ii** 1
c $z^3 - 4z^2 + 4z - 3 = 0$

19 a $1 + 2i$
b $\left(\sqrt{3} - 2, 2\sqrt{3} + 1\right), \left(\sqrt{3} + 2, 2\sqrt{3} - 1\right)$

20 Proof; it equals $2|a|\cos\dfrac{\theta}{2}$.

21 i Proof

ii $1, e^{i\frac{2\pi}{7}}, e^{i\frac{4\pi}{7}}, e^{i\frac{6\pi}{7}}, e^{i\frac{8\pi}{7}}, e^{i\frac{10\pi}{7}}, e^{i\frac{12\pi}{7}};$

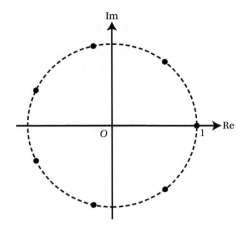

iii $(z-1)\left(z^2 - \left(2\cos\dfrac{2\pi}{7}\right)z + 1\right)$

$\times \left(z^2 - \left(2\cos\dfrac{4\pi}{7}\right)z + 1\right) \times \left(z^2 - \left(2\cos\dfrac{6\pi}{7}\right)z + 1\right)$

22 a $\dfrac{3-\sqrt{3}}{2} + \dfrac{1+3\sqrt{3}}{2}i$ **b** 5.35

23 a Proof
b i a **ii** $b(\cos\theta + i\sin\theta)$
iii $AB = \sqrt{b^2\sin^2\theta + (a - b\cos\theta)^2}$
iv Proof

Chapter 3

Before you start...

1 $32\left(\cos\dfrac{5\pi}{7} + i\sin\dfrac{5\pi}{7}\right)$

2 a $2 - i2\sqrt{3}$ **b** $2 + e^{-3i}$

3 $x^5 - 10x^4y + 40x^3y^2 - 80x^2y^3 + 80xy^4 - 32y^5$

4 $\text{Re} = 0; \text{Im} = -\dfrac{\sin x}{1 + \cos x}$

5 a $\dfrac{e^x(1 - e^{nx})}{1 - e^x}$ **b** $x < 0$

Exercise 3A

1 a $4\cos^3\theta\sin\theta - 4\cos\theta\sin^3\theta$
b Proof

2 $\sin 3\theta = 3\sin\theta - 4\sin^3\theta$

3 a $\cos^5\theta + 5i\cos^4\theta\sin\theta - 10\cos^3\theta\sin^2\theta$
$- 10i\cos^2\theta\sin^3\theta + 5\cos\theta\sin^4\theta + i\sin^5\theta$
b $16\sin^5\theta - 20\sin^3\theta + 5\sin\theta$

4 a Proof   **b** $\dfrac{\pi}{2}, \dfrac{3\pi}{2}$

5 a $A = 16, B = 20, C = 5$ **b** $0, \pm\dfrac{\sqrt{2}}{2}$

6 a Real: $\cos^4\theta - 6\sin^2\theta\cos^2\theta + \sin^4\theta$;
Imaginary: $4\cos^3\theta\sin\theta - 4\cos\theta\sin^3\theta$

b $\dfrac{4\tan\theta - 4\tan^3\theta}{1 - 6\tan^2\theta + \tan^4\theta}$

7 a Proof **b** $\dfrac{\pi}{24}, \dfrac{5\pi}{24}, \dfrac{3\pi}{8}$

8 a Real: $\cos^5\theta - 10\cos^3\theta\sin^2\theta + 5\cos\theta\sin^4\theta$;
Imaginary: $5\cos^4\theta\sin\theta - 10\cos^2\theta\sin^3\theta + \sin^5\theta$

b Proof **c** $5 - 20\theta^2$

Exercise 3B

1 a $2\cos^2\theta - 1$ **b** $2c^2 - \left(1 + \dfrac{\sqrt{3}}{2}\right) = 0$

c $\dfrac{\sqrt{2 + \sqrt{3}}}{2}$

2 a Proof **b** $\dfrac{\pi}{8}, \dfrac{5\pi}{8}$

c $-1 - \sqrt{2}$

3 a $\dfrac{\pi}{10}, \dfrac{3\pi}{10}, \dfrac{7\pi}{10}, \dfrac{9\pi}{10}$ **b** Proof

4 a Proof

b $\dfrac{\pi}{18}, \dfrac{13\pi}{18}, \dfrac{25\pi}{18}$ or $\dfrac{5\pi}{18}, \dfrac{17\pi}{18}, \dfrac{29\pi}{18}$

c Proof; $\sin\dfrac{5\pi}{18}, \sin\dfrac{25\pi}{18}$

5 a Proof

b $\tan 3\theta = \dfrac{3t - t^3}{1 - 3t^2}$; $\tan 4\theta = \dfrac{4t - 4t^3}{1 - 6t^2 + t^4}$; proof

6 a Proof **b** $\dfrac{\sqrt{7}}{8}$

Exercise 3C

1 a i $2\cos 3\theta + 6\cos\theta$
ii $2\cos 4\theta + 8\cos 2\theta + 6$
b i $2\cos 4\theta - 8\cos 2\theta + 6$
ii $2i\sin 5\theta - 10i\sin 3\theta + 20i\sin\theta$

2 a Proof
b Proof; $A = 2, B = 10, C = 20$

3 a Proof **b** $\dfrac{5\pi}{48} - \dfrac{9\sqrt{3}}{64}$

4 a i, ii Proof

b i $z^5 - 5z^3 + 10z - \dfrac{10}{z} + \dfrac{5}{z^3} - \dfrac{1}{z^5}$

ii $a = 1, b = -5, c = 10$

c $\dfrac{1}{16}\left(-\dfrac{1}{10}\cos 10x + \dfrac{5}{6}\cos 6x - 5\cos 2x\right) + c$

5 a Proof

b $\left(z + z^{-1}\right)^6 = z^6 + 6z^4 + 15z^2 + 20 + 15z^{-2} + 6z^{-4} + z^{-6}$
$\left(z - z^{-1}\right)^6 = z^6 - 6z^4 + 15z^2 - 20 + 15z^{-2} - 6z^{-4} + z^{-6}$

c Proof

6 a $\sin x = \dfrac{e^{ix} - e^{-ix}}{2i}$, $\cos x = \dfrac{e^{ix} + e^{-ix}}{2}$

b $\dfrac{4}{35}$

Exercise 3D

1 a $\dfrac{3}{3 - e^{i\theta}}$ or $\dfrac{3\left(3 - e^{-i\theta}\right)}{10 - 6\cos\theta}$

b $\dfrac{9 - 3\cos 1}{10 - 6\cos 1}(\approx 1.09)$

2 a Proof; $\dfrac{2}{2 - e^{i\theta}}$ or $\dfrac{2\left(2 - e^{-i\theta}\right)}{5 - 4\cos\theta}$

b Proof

3 $\dfrac{2\sin 1}{5 + 4\cos 2}(\approx 0.505)$

4, 5 Proof

6 a $\dfrac{e^{i\theta}\left(1 - e^{2ni\theta}\right)}{1 - e^{2i\theta}}$ **b** Proof

c $\theta = \dfrac{\pi}{6}, \dfrac{2\pi}{6}, \dfrac{3\pi}{6}, \dfrac{4\pi}{6}, \dfrac{5\pi}{6}$

Mixed practice 3

1 a $\cos^4\theta + 4i\cos^3\theta\sin\theta - 6\cos^2\theta\sin^2\theta$
$- 4i\cos\theta\sin^3\theta + \sin^4\theta$
b $A = 4, B = 8$

2 Proof; $\dfrac{1}{5}, -\dfrac{1}{5}$

3 a $A = \dfrac{1}{16}, B = \dfrac{5}{16}, C = \dfrac{5}{8}$ **b** $\dfrac{8}{15}$

4–6 Proof
7 i Proof **ii** $\dfrac{\pi}{3}, \dfrac{\pi}{2}, \dfrac{2\pi}{3}$

8 a, b Proof
c i Proof **ii** $\dfrac{2}{3} \pm \dfrac{\sqrt{5}}{3}i, \dfrac{-1}{2} \pm \dfrac{\sqrt{3}}{2}i$

9 a $\cos 3\theta = 4\cos^3\theta - 3\cos\theta$
$\sin 3\theta = 3\sin\theta - 4\sin^3\theta$
b, c Proof
d Proof; $-1, 2 \pm \sqrt{3}$
e Proof
f $2 - \sqrt{3}$

10 i Proof **ii** $\cos\left(\dfrac{\pi}{18}\right)$

11 i Proof
ii Proof; $S = \dfrac{2\sin\theta}{5 - 4\cos\theta}$

Chapter 4

Before you start...

1 a $r = \begin{pmatrix} 3 \\ -1 \\ 2 \end{pmatrix} + \lambda \begin{pmatrix} 1 \\ 1 \\ 3 \end{pmatrix}$ **b** $\dfrac{x-3}{1} = \dfrac{y+1}{1} = \dfrac{z-2}{3}$

2 $(4, 0, 5)$

3 $42.4°$

4 $-2\mathbf{i} - 10\mathbf{j} + 4\mathbf{k}$ (or $\mathbf{i} + 5\mathbf{j} - 2\mathbf{k}$)

Exercise 4A

1 a i $r = \begin{pmatrix} 1 \\ 0 \\ 2 \end{pmatrix} + \lambda \begin{pmatrix} -1 \\ 5 \\ 2 \end{pmatrix} + \mu \begin{pmatrix} 1 \\ -2 \\ 3 \end{pmatrix}$

ii $r = \begin{pmatrix} 0 \\ 2 \\ 0 \end{pmatrix} + \lambda \begin{pmatrix} 0 \\ 4 \\ -1 \end{pmatrix} + \mu \begin{pmatrix} 5 \\ 3 \\ 0 \end{pmatrix}$

b i $r = (\mathbf{j}+\mathbf{k}) + \lambda(3\mathbf{i}+\mathbf{j}-3\mathbf{k}) + \mu(\mathbf{i}-3\mathbf{j})$

ii $r = (\mathbf{i}-6\mathbf{j}+2\mathbf{k}) + \lambda(5\mathbf{i}-6\mathbf{j}) + \mu(-\mathbf{i}+3\mathbf{j}-\mathbf{k})$

2 a i $r = \begin{pmatrix} 3 \\ -1 \\ 3 \end{pmatrix} + \lambda \begin{pmatrix} -2 \\ 2 \\ -1 \end{pmatrix} + \mu \begin{pmatrix} 1 \\ 0 \\ -1 \end{pmatrix}$

ii $r = \begin{pmatrix} -1 \\ -1 \\ 5 \end{pmatrix} + \lambda \begin{pmatrix} 5 \\ 2 \\ -3 \end{pmatrix} + \mu \begin{pmatrix} -6 \\ 2 \\ -4 \end{pmatrix}$

b i $r = \begin{pmatrix} 9 \\ 0 \\ 0 \end{pmatrix} + \lambda \begin{pmatrix} -11 \\ 1 \\ 0 \end{pmatrix} + \mu \begin{pmatrix} -8 \\ -1 \\ 2 \end{pmatrix}$

ii $r = \begin{pmatrix} 11 \\ -7 \\ 3 \end{pmatrix} + \lambda \begin{pmatrix} -10 \\ 21 \\ -1 \end{pmatrix} + \mu \begin{pmatrix} -16 \\ 17 \\ -3 \end{pmatrix}$

3 a i $r = \begin{pmatrix} -1 \\ 4 \\ 3 \end{pmatrix} + \lambda \begin{pmatrix} 4 \\ 1 \\ 2 \end{pmatrix} + \mu \begin{pmatrix} 2 \\ -1 \\ 2 \end{pmatrix}$

ii $r = \begin{pmatrix} 11 \\ 12 \\ 13 \end{pmatrix} + \lambda \begin{pmatrix} 6 \\ -3 \\ 1 \end{pmatrix} + \mu \begin{pmatrix} 2 \\ 15 \\ 6 \end{pmatrix}$

b i $r = \begin{pmatrix} -3 \\ 1 \\ 0 \end{pmatrix} + \lambda \begin{pmatrix} 0 \\ 0 \\ 1 \end{pmatrix} + \mu \begin{pmatrix} -7 \\ -3 \\ -1 \end{pmatrix}$

ii $r = \begin{pmatrix} 4 \\ 0 \\ 2 \end{pmatrix} + \lambda \begin{pmatrix} 2 \\ 1 \\ 1 \end{pmatrix} + \mu \begin{pmatrix} 4 \\ 0 \\ 2 \end{pmatrix}$

4 a i $r \cdot \begin{pmatrix} 3 \\ -5 \\ 2 \end{pmatrix} = -4$ **ii** $r \cdot \begin{pmatrix} 6 \\ -1 \\ 2 \end{pmatrix} = 19$

b i $r \cdot \begin{pmatrix} 3 \\ -1 \\ 0 \end{pmatrix} = -9$ **ii** $r \cdot \begin{pmatrix} 4 \\ 0 \\ -5 \end{pmatrix} = -10$

5 a i $\begin{pmatrix} 10 \\ 13 \\ -12 \end{pmatrix}$ **ii** $\begin{pmatrix} 10 \\ 4 \\ 3 \end{pmatrix}$

b i $\begin{pmatrix} 1 \\ 5 \\ 0 \end{pmatrix}$ **ii** $\begin{pmatrix} 1 \\ 20 \\ 7 \end{pmatrix}$

6 a i $r \cdot \begin{pmatrix} 10 \\ 13 \\ -12 \end{pmatrix} = 38$ **ii** $r \cdot \begin{pmatrix} 10 \\ 4 \\ 3 \end{pmatrix} = 3$

b i $r \cdot \begin{pmatrix} 1 \\ 5 \\ 0 \end{pmatrix} = 22$ **ii** $r \cdot \begin{pmatrix} 1 \\ 20 \\ 7 \end{pmatrix} = 152$

7 a i $10x + 13y - 12z = 38$

ii $10x + 4y + 3z = 3$

b i $x + 5y = 22$ **ii** $x + 20y + 7z = 152$

8 a i $x + y + z = 10$ **ii** $z = 2$

b i $40x + 5y + 8z = 580$

ii $x + y + z = 1$

9 a–c Proof

10 $6x + y - 3z = 1$

11 $r = \begin{pmatrix} 5 \\ 1 \\ 5 \end{pmatrix} + \lambda \begin{pmatrix} 8 \\ 0 \\ 3 \end{pmatrix} + \mu \begin{pmatrix} 5 \\ 0 \\ 0 \end{pmatrix}$

12 a $\begin{pmatrix} -1 \\ -4 \\ -17 \end{pmatrix}$ **b** $x + 4y + 17z = 37$

13 a $r \cdot \begin{pmatrix} -11 \\ 7 \\ 13 \end{pmatrix} = 39$ **b** No

14 a $\begin{pmatrix} 13 \\ -11 \\ -8 \end{pmatrix}$ **b** $-13x + 11y + 8z = 38$

15 a $\begin{pmatrix} -2 \\ 3 \\ -1 \end{pmatrix}$

b i Proof   **ii** $(1, -3, 14)$

c $2x - 3y + z = 25$

16 No

17 a $\begin{pmatrix} 1 \\ -3 \\ 4 \end{pmatrix}$ **b** $p = -\dfrac{1}{4}, q = \dfrac{3}{4}$

c $\mathbf{r} = \begin{pmatrix} 0 \\ 0 \\ 4 \end{pmatrix} + \lambda \begin{pmatrix} 4 \\ 0 \\ -1 \end{pmatrix} + \mu \begin{pmatrix} 0 \\ 4 \\ 3 \end{pmatrix}$

18 a $8x - 10y + 17z = 75$

b For example: $\mathbf{r} = \begin{pmatrix} 0 \\ -1 \\ 4 \end{pmatrix} + \lambda \begin{pmatrix} 5 \\ 2 \\ 1 \end{pmatrix} + \mu \begin{pmatrix} -1 \\ 1 \\ 4 \end{pmatrix}$

19 For example: $\mathbf{r} = \begin{pmatrix} 0 \\ 0 \\ -5 \end{pmatrix} + \lambda \begin{pmatrix} 1 \\ 0 \\ 0 \end{pmatrix} + \mu \begin{pmatrix} 0 \\ 1 \\ 3 \end{pmatrix}$

Exercise 4B

1 a i $(7, 1, 1)$ **ii** $(-19, -5, 7)$

b i $\left(-\dfrac{4}{3}, -\dfrac{7}{3}, -4 \right)$ **ii** $(8, -3, 2)$

2 a–d Proof

3 $(15, 5, 8)$

4 a $\begin{pmatrix} -1 \\ 2 \\ 1 \end{pmatrix}$ **b** $(0.2, 2.6, 3.8)$

5 $(5, 3, 0)$

6 a $(5, 0, 0), (0, -20, 0), (0, 0, 12)$

b $133 \, (3 \text{ s.f.})$

Exercise 4C

1 a i $46.4°$ **ii** $17.5°$

b i $47.6°$ **ii** $10.8°$

2 a $75.8°$ **b** $60°$

3 a $\begin{pmatrix} 2 \\ 3 \\ -1 \end{pmatrix}$ **b** $32.8°$

4 a $\begin{pmatrix} 3 \\ -1 \\ 1 \end{pmatrix}$ **b** $57°$

5 a $\begin{pmatrix} 4 \\ 2 \\ 3 \end{pmatrix}$ **b** $28.3°$

6 a $\begin{pmatrix} 13 \\ 7 \\ -8 \end{pmatrix}$ **b** $3.46°$

7 Proof

8 a $\begin{pmatrix} -5 \\ 0 \\ 1 \end{pmatrix}$ **b** $64.4°$

9 a Proof **b** $\dfrac{\sqrt{7}}{3}$

c $3\sqrt{5}$ **d** $\sqrt{35}$

Exercise 4D

1 a i $\dfrac{19}{\sqrt{6}}$ **ii** $\dfrac{12}{\sqrt{37}}$

b i $\dfrac{\sqrt{14}}{7}$ **ii** $\dfrac{12}{\sqrt{17}}$

2 a i $\dfrac{27}{\sqrt{73}}$ **ii** $\dfrac{24}{\sqrt{10}}$

b i $\dfrac{23}{\sqrt{17}}$ **ii** $\dfrac{19}{\sqrt{10}}$

3 a i 0.894 **ii** 0.596

b i 1.23 **ii** 3.77

4 a i Proof; 1.94 **ii** Proof; 3

b i Proof; 4.60 **ii** Proof; 3.11

5 1.52

6 $\dfrac{8}{\sqrt{11}}$

7 $\sqrt{2}$

8 $\dfrac{16}{\sqrt{41}}$

9 Proof; 5.30

10 $\dfrac{47}{\sqrt{122}}; \dfrac{47}{2}$

11 Proof; 2.57

12 a, b Proof

c $\dfrac{6\sqrt{11}}{11}$

13 a Proof **b** 0

c $6\sqrt{2}$

14 a $\mathbf{r} = \begin{pmatrix} -3 \\ -3 \\ 4 \end{pmatrix} + \lambda \begin{pmatrix} 2 \\ 2 \\ -1 \end{pmatrix}$ **b** $(3, 3, 1)$

c 9

15 a $\left(\dfrac{96}{41}, -\dfrac{32}{41}, \dfrac{16}{41} \right)$ **b** $\dfrac{16\sqrt{41}}{41}$

16 $\left(\dfrac{64}{9}, \dfrac{4}{9}, \dfrac{19}{9} \right); \dfrac{\sqrt{29}}{3}$

17 a, b Proof

c $\left(\dfrac{184}{11}, \dfrac{-32}{11}, \dfrac{-1}{11} \right)$ **d** 6.99

18 a Proof   **b** $11\mu - 6\lambda = 21$

   c $\sqrt{30}$

Mixed practice 4

1 $\dfrac{6\sqrt{10}}{5}$

2 $\dfrac{2}{\sqrt{19}}$

3 a $3x + y - z = 6$ **b** $\dfrac{5}{4}$

4 a $\begin{pmatrix} 0 \\ 5 \\ 5 \end{pmatrix}$ **b** $2x - y + z = 0$

   c Proof   **d** $47.1° \,(3\text{ s.f.})$

5 i $\mathbf{r} = \begin{pmatrix} 1 \\ 6 \\ 2 \end{pmatrix} + \lambda \begin{pmatrix} 4 \\ -4 \\ -1 \end{pmatrix} + \mu \begin{pmatrix} 0 \\ 3 \\ 2 \end{pmatrix}$

   ii $5x + 8y - 12z = 29$

6 i $2\mathbf{i} - \mathbf{j} - \mathbf{k}$ **ii** $\dfrac{7\sqrt{6}}{6}$

7 a $\begin{pmatrix} -2 \\ 7 \\ -3 \end{pmatrix}$ **b** $(3, 3, 8)$

   c $\begin{pmatrix} -2 \\ 7 \\ -3 \end{pmatrix}$ **d** $2x - 7y + 3z = 9$

8 a $\mathbf{r} = \begin{pmatrix} 4 \\ -1 \\ 2 \end{pmatrix} + \lambda \begin{pmatrix} 1 \\ -2 \\ 1 \end{pmatrix}$ **b** $(6, -5, 4)$

   c $2\sqrt{6}$

9 a Proof

   b $\mathbf{r} = (5\mathbf{i} + \mathbf{j} + 3\mathbf{k}) + t(4\mathbf{i} - 8\mathbf{j} + 3\mathbf{k})$

   c $\mathbf{r} = (9\mathbf{i} - 7\mathbf{j} + 6\mathbf{k}) + t(\mathbf{i} - 4\mathbf{j} + 2\mathbf{k})$

   d $(7, 1, 2)$

   e $2\sqrt{21}$

10 $\sqrt{14}$

11 a $-2, 2$ **b** 1.58

   c 5.91

12 a $(10, 11, -6)$ **b** $\begin{pmatrix} 7 \\ -9 \\ -5 \end{pmatrix}$

   c $7x - 9y - 5z = 1$

13 a $\dfrac{x-3}{3} = \dfrac{y-1}{-1} = \dfrac{z+4}{-1}$

   b $(0, 2, -3)$ **c** $(-3, 3, -2)$

   d Proof   **e** $3\sqrt{2}$

14 i $(2, 1, -3)$ **ii** $12x + 13y - 8z = 61$

15 i $(1, -3, -2); 6$ **ii** $41.8°$

16 a $\mathbf{r} = \begin{pmatrix} -1 \\ 1 \\ 4 \end{pmatrix} + \lambda \begin{pmatrix} 6 \\ 1 \\ 5 \end{pmatrix}$ **b** Proof

   c $\begin{pmatrix} 13 \\ -38 \\ -8 \end{pmatrix}$ **d** $13x - 38y - 8z = -83$

17 $k = 8$

18 $7x + 2y - 3z = 3$

19 a $\begin{pmatrix} -1 \\ 4 \\ 7 \end{pmatrix}$ **b, c** Proof

   d $\mathbf{r} = \begin{pmatrix} 1 \\ 1 \\ 2 \end{pmatrix} + \lambda \begin{pmatrix} -1 \\ 4 \\ 7 \end{pmatrix}$

20 a Proof   **b** $\mathbf{r} \cdot \begin{pmatrix} -1 \\ 5 \\ 2 \end{pmatrix} = -5$

   c $\sqrt{30}$ **d** $(8, -5, -1)$

21 a $\begin{pmatrix} -3 \\ -10 \\ 2 \end{pmatrix}$ **b** 5.32

   c $3x + 10y - 2z = 16$ **d** $\mathbf{r} = \begin{pmatrix} -7 \\ -28 \\ 11 \end{pmatrix} + \lambda \begin{pmatrix} -3 \\ -10 \\ 2 \end{pmatrix}$

   e $(2, 2, 5); 31.9\,(3\text{ s.f.})$ **f** 56.5

22 i Proof

   ii Symmetry in the plane $y = 0$.

   iii $\dfrac{1}{3}$

23 i, ii Proof

   iii $\mathbf{r} = \dfrac{1}{3}(\mathbf{u} + \mathbf{v} + \mathbf{w}) + t(\mathbf{u} - \mathbf{v}) \times (\mathbf{u} - \mathbf{w})$

   iv $\dfrac{\sqrt{3}}{3}$

Chapter 5

Before you start...

1 -5

2 $\begin{pmatrix} 2 & -3 \\ 5 & -8 \end{pmatrix}\begin{pmatrix} x \\ y \end{pmatrix} = \begin{pmatrix} 2 \\ 3 \end{pmatrix}; \mathbf{M}^{-1} = \begin{pmatrix} 8 & -3 \\ 5 & -2 \end{pmatrix}; x = 7, y = 4$

3 -5

4 $x = 7, y = 4$

5 a $4x - y + 2z = 3$ **b** $3\mathbf{i} - 4\mathbf{k}$

Exercise 5A

1 a i Unique   **ii** Unique
  b i No solutions   **ii** Infinitely many
  c i Infinitely many   **ii** No solutions

2 a i Unique; $x = \dfrac{36}{5}, y = 7, z = \dfrac{122}{5}$

    ii Unique; $x = 3, y = -1, z = -2$

  b i Unique; $x = \dfrac{5}{3}, y = \dfrac{16}{3}, z = -\dfrac{7}{3}$

    ii Not unique; inconsistent

  c i Not unique; consistent

    ii Not unique; consistent

3 Proof
4 a $2, -3$
  b No solutions for both
5 a Proof   **b** $\pm 1, -2$
  c $x = 2, y = -1, z = 5$ **d** Inconsistent
6 a, b Proof
7 $k = 2, c = 1$

Exercise 5B

1 a i Consistent; unique solution:
       $x = 3, y = 2, z = 2$
    ii Consistent; unique solution:
       $x = 1, y = 1, z = 4$
  b i Inconsistent; two parallel planes with a single intersecting plane.
    ii Consistent; line intersection of three distinct planes (sheaf)
  c i Consistent; unique solution;
       $x = -1, y = -\dfrac{1}{3}, z = \dfrac{13}{3}$
    ii Inconsistent; two parallel planes with a single intersecting plane
  d i Consistent; unique solution;
       $x = \dfrac{1}{6}, y = \dfrac{1}{6}, z = \dfrac{7}{6}$
    ii Consistent; unique solution:
       $x = 0.5, y = 0.5, z = 4$

2 a Proof $(\det \mathbf{M} \neq 0)$; $x = \dfrac{5}{3}, y = \dfrac{16}{3}, z = -\dfrac{7}{3}$

  b The planes intersect at a single point.
3 a Proof
  b The planes intersect at a single point.

4 $\left(\dfrac{3}{2}, -\dfrac{11}{6}, -\dfrac{1}{6} \right)$

5 a, b Proof
  c Triangular prism
6 Π_1 and Π_3 are parallel, Π_2 intersects them.
7 a $k = 25$ **b** Triangular prism

8 a Proof   **b** -2
  c Intersect along a line (sheaf)
9 a Proof
  b Intersect along a line (sheaf)

10 a $\begin{pmatrix} 0.5 & 0.5 & 0.5 \\ -0.5 & 0.5 & 0.5 \\ 0.5 & 0.5 & -0.5 \end{pmatrix}$ **b** $\left(\dfrac{5+d}{2}, \dfrac{d-3}{2}, \dfrac{5-d}{2} \right)$

11 a 2
   b Inconsistent; triangular prism
12 a -4 **b** 2
   c Intersect in a line (form a sheaf)
13 $a = -3, b = 15$

Mixed practice 5

1 $(6, 1, 0)$
2 $k = 4, -4$
3 a Proof   **b** $k = 9$
4 a $a = 3, -3$

  b $\left(\dfrac{-9(2a+3)}{a^2 - 9}, \dfrac{3a}{a^2 - 9}, \dfrac{4a^2 - 9}{a^2 - 9} \right)$

  c $k = 1.5$
5 i $a^2 - 7a + 6$
  ii $1, 6$
  iii Infinitely many
6 i $a^3 - 4a$
  ii a Unique
     b Not unique, inconsistent
     c Not unique, consistent

Focus on ... 1

Focus on ... Proof 1

1, 2 Proof

Focus on ... Problem solving 1

1 $\begin{pmatrix} -\dfrac{1}{2}x - \dfrac{\sqrt{3}}{2}y \\ \dfrac{\sqrt{3}}{2}x - \dfrac{1}{2}y \end{pmatrix}$

2 The velocity is parallel to $S_2 - S_1$; proof
3–7 Proof

8 $t = \dfrac{2}{\sqrt{3}v}$; $\theta \to \infty$

9 Proof; $\dfrac{dy}{dt} = \dfrac{dr}{dt}\sin\theta + r\dfrac{d\theta}{dt}\cos\theta$

10 $\begin{cases} \dfrac{dr}{dt}\cos\theta - r\dfrac{d\theta}{dt}\sin\theta = -\dfrac{v\sqrt{3}}{2}\cos\theta - \dfrac{v}{2}\sin\theta \\[2mm] \dfrac{dr}{dt}\sin\theta + r\dfrac{d\theta}{dt}\cos\theta = \dfrac{v}{2}\cos\theta - \dfrac{v\sqrt{3}}{2}\sin\theta \end{cases}$; proof

11 $\dfrac{dr}{d\theta} = -r\sqrt{3}$; proof

Focus on ... Modelling 1

1 Proof

2 $j_{n+1} = 3a_n$

3 $\begin{pmatrix} 0.9 & 0.8 \\ 3 & 0 \end{pmatrix}$

4 a 180   **b** 179 108

5 2.06

6 1.45

7 0.125

8 For example: all adults are the same; there is no reference to gender; the average of 3 might not give a good prediction with small numbers; no randomness; there are no limiting factors such as the size of the island; there are no direct effects of predators.

9 Investigation

Cross-topic review exercise 1

1 a Proof   **b** 3.76

2 a $8e^{-i\frac{\pi}{2}}$

   b $\sqrt{2}e^{-i\frac{\pi}{12}}, \sqrt{2}e^{i\frac{\pi}{4}}, \sqrt{2}e^{i\frac{7\pi}{12}}, \sqrt{2}e^{i\frac{11\pi}{12}}, \sqrt{2}e^{-i\frac{5\pi}{12}}, \sqrt{2}e^{-i\frac{3\pi}{4}}$

3 a $6x - 2y + 3z = 4$ **b** $180° - 99.2° = 80.8°$

4 $a = 4, b = -4$

5 $n^3(n+1)$

6 i Proof

   ii $\left(z + e^{\frac{i\pi}{6}}\right)\left(z - e^{\frac{i\pi}{6}}\right)\left(z + e^{\frac{5i\pi}{6}}\right)\left(z - e^{\frac{5i\pi}{6}}\right)$

7 i $z_1 = \sqrt{2}\operatorname{cis}\left(\dfrac{\pi}{12}\right)$ $z_2 = \sqrt{2}\operatorname{cis}\left(\dfrac{7\pi}{12}\right)$

     $z_3 = \sqrt{2}\operatorname{cis}\left(\dfrac{13\pi}{12}\right)$ and $z_4 = \sqrt{2}\operatorname{cis}\left(\dfrac{19\pi}{12}\right)$

   ii

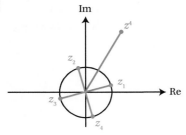

8 $\dfrac{6\sqrt{6}}{5}$

9 $\lambda = \dfrac{1}{3}$ or 2

10 a Proof   **b** $5\arctan\left(\dfrac{1}{a}\right)$

   c Proof

11 i Proof

   ii $\dfrac{1}{2}\left(\sqrt{n+2} + \sqrt{n+1} - 1 - \sqrt{2}\right)$

   iii Does not converge;

     as $n \to \infty, \displaystyle\sum_{r=1}^{n} \dfrac{1}{\sqrt{r+2} + \sqrt{r}} \to \infty$

12 i Proof

   ii $\dfrac{3}{2} - \dfrac{2n+3}{(n+1)(n+2)}$

   iii $N = 4$

13 i Proof

   ii $\dfrac{5}{4} - \dfrac{1}{(n+1)^2} - \dfrac{1}{(n+2)^2}$

   iii $\dfrac{61}{900}$

14 i $u_2 = \dfrac{2}{3}, u_3 = \dfrac{2}{5}$; proof

   ii $u_n = \dfrac{2}{2n-1}$

   iii Proof

15 i

   ii Proof

   iii a 3   **b** 1

   iv $3z^3 - 9z^2 + 7z - 2 = 0$

16 i $z = \pm 2$ or $\pm 2i$

   ii $\dfrac{2}{3}, 2, \dfrac{4+2i}{5}, \dfrac{4-2i}{5}$

17 i Proof

   ii Rotation of a point in the Argand plane by $\dfrac{2\pi}{3}$ about the origin; proof

   iii Proof

18 i $z = 1, e^{\frac{2\pi i}{5}}, e^{\frac{4\pi i}{5}}, e^{\frac{6\pi i}{5}}$ or $e^{\frac{8\pi i}{5}}$

   ii Proof; $\theta = \dfrac{2\pi}{5}, \dfrac{4\pi}{5}, \dfrac{6\pi}{5}$ or $\dfrac{8\pi}{5}$

19 i

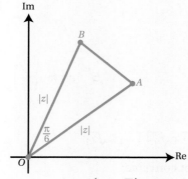

ii $\omega = \frac{1}{2} + 2\sqrt{3} + i\left(3 + \frac{\sqrt{3}}{2}\right)$ or

$\omega = \frac{3}{2} + 2\sqrt{3} + i\left(-1 + \frac{\sqrt{3}}{2}\right)$

20 i Proof
ii Proof; $k = 2$
21 i Proof
ii $\theta = 0$ or ± 0.899
22 i $M(5, 7, 3)$; 6
ii $(5.5, 6, 4)$

23 i $\mathbf{r} \cdot \begin{pmatrix} 1 \\ 4 \\ -2 \end{pmatrix} = 11$

ii $(1, 4, 3)$

iii $\mathbf{c} = k\begin{pmatrix} 2 \\ 1 \\ 3 \end{pmatrix}$

24 $\mathbf{r} = \begin{pmatrix} 1 \\ 4 \\ 2 \end{pmatrix} + t\begin{pmatrix} -1 \\ 1 \\ 1 \end{pmatrix}$

25 i $\frac{\sqrt{6}}{9}$
ii $2x + y + 7z = 11$

26 a $\frac{1}{k}e^{kx} + c$ **b** Proof

c $\frac{3 - e^{\frac{\pi}{2}}}{10}$

27 a Proof   **b** $-i\ln\left(2 \pm \sqrt{3}\right)$

28 a Proof   **b** $\dfrac{1}{1 - \frac{1}{2}e^{i\theta}}$
c Proof
29 a 4   **b** Proof
30 a Proof   **b** 0

31 Proof
32 a Proof   **b** $\dfrac{1}{2} - \dfrac{1}{n+1} + \dfrac{1}{n+2}$
c Proof
33 Proof; $S = \dfrac{3 - 2e^{\pi}}{13}$
34 i, ii Proof
iii Proof; $a = \dfrac{1}{6}$, $b = 2$. So $a = \dfrac{1}{6}$, $b = 2$
35 i $\theta = \dfrac{\pi}{12}, \dfrac{\pi}{4}, \dfrac{5\pi}{12}, \dfrac{7\pi}{12}, \dfrac{3\pi}{4}, \dfrac{11\pi}{12}$
ii Proof
iii $\dfrac{1}{16}$
36 i $8\cos^4\theta - 8\cos^2\theta + 1$
ii–iv Proof
37 i Proof
ii $\theta = \dfrac{\pi}{20}, \dfrac{5\pi}{20} = \dfrac{\pi}{4}, \dfrac{9\pi}{20}, \dfrac{13\pi}{20}, \dfrac{17\pi}{20}$
iii $t = \tan\left(\dfrac{\pi}{20}\right), \tan\left(\dfrac{9\pi}{20}\right), \tan\left(\dfrac{13\pi}{20}\right), \tan\left(\dfrac{17\pi}{20}\right)$
38 i a Proof   **b** $S = 10$
ii Proof
iii Proof; $\theta = \dfrac{\pi}{5}$

Chapter 6

Before you start...

1 a $x \geqslant 3$
b $f(x) \geqslant 0$

2

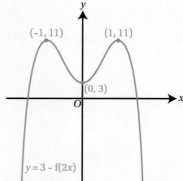

3 a $2e^{2x}$ **b** $-e^{-x} + c$
4 a $\sec^2 x$ **b** $\sin x + c$
5 a $6\sin 3x \cos 3x$ **b** $\cos x - x\sin x$
c $\dfrac{2x\sec^2 2x - \tan 2x}{x^2}$

Exercise 6A

1 a

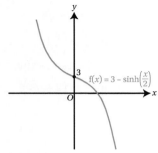

Domain: $x \in \mathbb{R}$; range: $f(x) \in \mathbb{R}$

b

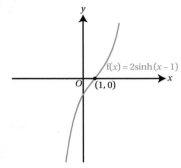

Domain: $x \in \mathbb{R}$; range: $f(x) \in \mathbb{R}$

c

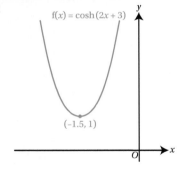

Domain: $x \in \mathbb{R}$; range: $f(x) \geqslant 1$

d

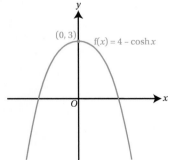

Domain: $x \in \mathbb{R}$; range: $f(x) \leqslant 3$

e

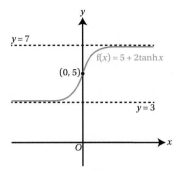

Domain: $x \in \mathbb{R}$; range: $3 < f(x) < 7$

f

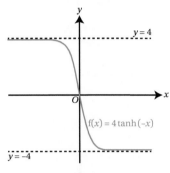

Domain: $x \in \mathbb{R}$; range: $-4 < f(x) < 4$

2 $a = 4, b = -2$

3 $a = -3, b = 1$

Exercise 6B

1 a i

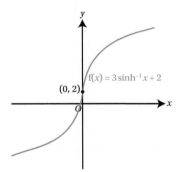

Domain: $x \in \mathbb{R}$; range: $f(x) \in \mathbb{R}$

ii

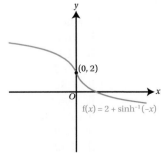

Domain: $x \in \mathbb{R}$; range: $f(x) \in \mathbb{R}$

b i

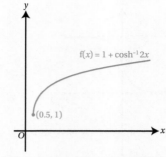

$f(x) = 1 + \cosh^{-1} 2x$

(0.5, 1)

Domain: $x \geqslant 0.5$; range: $f(x) \geqslant 1$

ii

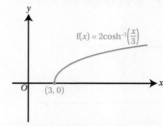

$f(x) = 2\cosh^{-1}\left(\frac{x}{3}\right)$

(3, 0)

Domain: $x \geqslant 3$; range: $f(x) \geqslant 0$

c i

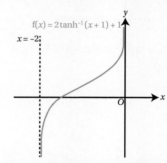

$f(x) = 2\tanh^{-1}(x+1) + 1$

$x = -2$

Domain: $-2 < x < 0$; range: $f(x) \in \mathbb{R}$

ii

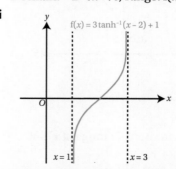

$f(x) = 3\tanh^{-1}(x-2) + 1$

$x = 1$ $x = 3$

Domain: $1 < x < 3$; range: $f(x) \in \mathbb{R}$

2 a i 1.54   **ii** 10.0
 b i 0.580   **ii** 101
 c i 1.60   **ii** 10.3
 d i 0.481   **ii** 1.32
 e i Not possible   **ii** Not possible
3 a i −1.44   **ii** 0.0998
 b i ±1.57   **ii** ±2.06
 c i 0.973   **ii** 0.424
 d i No solution   **ii** No solution
 e i 74.2   **ii** 27.3

4 a i $\ln(1+\sqrt{2})$ **ii** $\ln(2+\sqrt{5})$
 b i $\ln(2+\sqrt{3})$ **ii** $\ln(3+\sqrt{8})$
 c i $\frac{1}{2}\ln 2$ **ii** $\frac{1}{2}\ln\left(\frac{5}{3}\right)$
 d i Doesn't exist   **ii** Doesn't exist
 e i $\ln(\sqrt{2}+\sqrt{3})$ **ii** $\frac{1}{2}\ln(2+\sqrt{3})$

5 2.10 or −0.0986

6 $\frac{5}{4}$

7 $\frac{4}{5}$

8 $b \leqslant a - 2$

9 ±0.515

10 0.549

11 $\sqrt{1+x^2}$

12–14 Proof

Exercise 6C

1 Proof

2 $\cosh x$

3–8 Proof

9 a, b Proof   **c** $4\cosh^3 x - 3\cosh x$

10 Proof

Work it out 6.1

Solution 3 is correct.

Exercise 6D

1 $\ln 5$

2 $\ln\frac{1}{2}$

3 0.481, 2.06, −2.06

4 $\ln\frac{1}{2}$

5 $\ln\sqrt{3}$

6 $0, \ln\left(\frac{3\pm\sqrt{5}}{2}\right)$

7 $\ln 3$

8 $\ln 4$

9 $\ln\left(\frac{\sqrt{5}-1}{2}\right)$ or $\ln(3+\sqrt{10})$

10 $\ln(2\pm\sqrt{3})$

11 $\ln(1+\sqrt{2})$

12 $\ln 4$

13 $\ln(2\pm\sqrt{3})$

14 a Proof

   b $x = \ln 2,\ y = \ln 4$ or $x = \ln 4,\ y = \ln 2$

15 $r^4 \geqslant p^4 - q^4$

16 a Proof   **b** $\dfrac{1}{2}\ln\left(1+\sqrt{2}\right)$

17 a Proof   **b** $\dfrac{1}{6}\ln\left(3\pm2\sqrt{2}\right)$

Exercise 6E

1 a i $3\cosh 3x$ **ii** $\dfrac{1}{2}\cosh\dfrac{1}{2}x$

  b i $4\sinh(4x+1)$ **ii** $\dfrac{1}{3}\sinh\dfrac{1}{3}x$

  c i $\dfrac{2}{3}\operatorname{sech}^2\dfrac{2}{3}x$ **ii** $-2\operatorname{sech}^2(1-2x)$

2 a $2x\tanh 3x + \dfrac{3x^2}{\cosh^2 3x}$ **b** $-\dfrac{10}{\tanh 5x \sinh^2 5x}$

3 $(0,\ e-1)$

4 $(-\ln 2,\ 4)$

5 Proof

6 $x + 2y - \ln 3 - 2 = 0$

7 a $\pm\dfrac{1}{2}\ln\left(\sqrt{2}+1\right)$ **b** Proof

8 $\left(\ln 3,\ \dfrac{\sqrt{3}}{9}\right)$

9 Proof; $k = 1+\sqrt{2}$

10 a $\pm\ln\left(\dfrac{3+\sqrt{5}}{2}\right)$ **b** Proof

Exercise 6F

1 a i $\dfrac{1}{3}\cosh 3x + c$ **ii** $2\cosh\dfrac{x}{2} + c$

  b i $\dfrac{1}{2}\sinh(2x+1) + c$ **ii** $\dfrac{1}{4}\sinh 4x + c$

  c i $-\dfrac{1}{2}\ln\cosh(2x) + c$ **ii** $\dfrac{1}{3}\ln\cosh(3x-2) + c$

2 a i $\dfrac{e^4 - 2e^2 + 1}{2e^2}$ **ii** $\dfrac{e^{10} - 1}{2e^5}$

  b i $\dfrac{e^4 - 2e^2 + 1}{4e^2}$ **ii** $\dfrac{e^{12} - 1}{4e^6}$

  c i $\dfrac{1197}{128}$ **ii** $\dfrac{175}{144}$

3 a i $\dfrac{1}{8}\sinh 4x - \dfrac{1}{2}x + c$ **ii** $\dfrac{1}{12}\sinh 6x + \dfrac{1}{2}x + c$

  b i $x - 2\tanh\dfrac{x}{2} + c$ **ii** $x - \dfrac{1}{3}\tanh 3x + c$

c i $\dfrac{1}{4}\cosh 2x + c$ **ii** $\dfrac{1}{12}\cosh 6x + c$

4 a i $x\cosh x - \sinh x + c$

   ii $\dfrac{1}{2}x\cosh 2x - \dfrac{1}{4}\sinh 2x + c$

  b i $3x\sinh x - 3\cosh x + c$

   ii $2x\sinh\dfrac{x}{2} - 4\cosh\dfrac{x}{2} + c$

  c i $x^2\cosh x - 2x\sinh x + 2\cosh x + c$

   ii $\dfrac{1}{3}x^2\cosh 3x - \dfrac{2}{9}x\sinh 3x + \dfrac{2}{27}\cosh 3x + c$

  d i $\dfrac{1}{2}x^2\sinh 2x - \dfrac{1}{2}x\cosh 2x + \dfrac{1}{4}\sinh 2x + c$

   ii $3x^2\sinh x - 6x\cosh x + 6\sinh x + c$

5 a i $\dfrac{1}{6}e^{3x} + \dfrac{1}{2}e^{-x} + c$ **ii** $\dfrac{1}{6}e^{3x} + \dfrac{1}{2}e^{x} + c$

  b i $\dfrac{1}{20}e^{5x} - \dfrac{1}{20}e^{-5x} - \dfrac{1}{12}e^{3x} + \dfrac{1}{12}e^{-3x} + c$

   ii $\dfrac{1}{20}e^{5x} - \dfrac{1}{20}e^{-5x} + \dfrac{1}{4}e^{x} - \dfrac{1}{4}e^{-x} + c$

6 $\dfrac{1}{4}(\ln(\cosh x) + x) + c$

7 $1 - e^{-1}$

8 Proof

9 a $\dfrac{1}{5}\sinh^5 x + \dfrac{1}{3}\sinh^3 x + c$

  b $\sinh x - \dfrac{1}{\sinh x} + c$

10 $x\tanh x - \ln(\cosh x) + c$

11 $2\pi(5\ln 2 - 3)$

12, 13 Proof

14 a $\dfrac{1}{\sqrt{x^2+1}}$ **b** Proof

Mixed practice 6

1 a

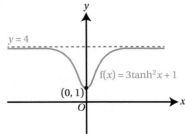

  b $1 \leqslant f(x) < 4$

2 $\ln k$

3 $\dfrac{e^2 p^2 - 1}{e^2 p^2 + 1}$

4 $-1\pm\ln(3+\sqrt{8})$

5 0.128

6 $\pm\ln 2$

7 $x=\dfrac{1}{2}\ln(2+\sqrt{5})$

8 $18\cosh 6x$

9, 10 Proof

11 $\ln(2\sqrt{14}-7)$

12 $-\dfrac{1}{3\cosh 3x}+c$

13 Proof

14 0 or $\dfrac{1}{3}\ln(\sqrt{5}\pm 2)$

15 $\ln(4\pm\sqrt{15})$

16 Proof

17 $\dfrac{x}{\sqrt{1+x^2}}$

18 Proof

19 a

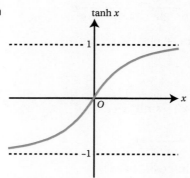

b Proof

c i Proof   **ii** Proof; $\dfrac{1}{2}\ln 2$

20 a Proof   **b** $\ln\sqrt{3},\,-\ln\sqrt{5}$

21 i Proof   **ii** Proof; $\dfrac{5\sqrt{6}}{12}$

22 $\dfrac{2}{3}\tan^{-1}(3e^x)+c$

23 $7\ln 6-10$

24 a Proof   **b** $\pm\dfrac{1}{3}\ln\dfrac{3}{2}$ **c** $\dfrac{1}{2}\left(\sqrt[3]{\dfrac{3}{2}}+\sqrt[3]{\dfrac{2}{3}}\right)$

25 $x=\ln 2,\ y=\ln 5$ or $x=\ln 5,\ y=\ln 2$

26–28 Proof

Chapter 7

Before you start...

1 $\dfrac{2x-5}{3y^2}$

2 $\dfrac{1}{9}(3\sqrt{3}-1)$

3 $\ln|(x-1)(x-2)|+\dfrac{2}{x-2}+c$

Exercise 7A

1 a i $\dfrac{-3}{\sqrt{1-9x^2}}$ **ii** $\dfrac{-2}{\sqrt{1-4x^2}}$

   b i $\dfrac{2}{4+x^2}$ **ii** $\dfrac{10}{25+4x^2}$

   c i $\arcsin x+\dfrac{x}{\sqrt{1-x^2}}$ **ii** $2x\arcsin x+\dfrac{x^2}{\sqrt{1-x^2}}$

   d i $\dfrac{2x}{(2+2x^2+x^4)}$ **ii** $-\dfrac{2}{\sqrt{2-x^2}}$

2 $-\dfrac{3}{\sqrt{35}}$

3 $\dfrac{3\pi-2}{4}$

4 $\dfrac{3}{9x^2+12x+5}$

5 $\dfrac{2x}{\sqrt{-x^4+6x^2-8}};\ x\in(-2,-\sqrt{2})\cup(\sqrt{2},2)$

6 a Proof   **b** $-\dfrac{1}{x^2+1}$

7 Proof; $|x|<\dfrac{2}{3}$

8 $-\dfrac{1+\tan^2\left(\dfrac{1}{x}\right)}{x^2}$

9 a $\sin^{-1}x+\dfrac{x}{\sqrt{1-x^2}}$ **b** $x\sin^{-1}x+\sqrt{1-x^2}+c$

10 Proof

Exercise 7B

1 a i $\dfrac{2}{\sqrt{4x^2+1}}$ **ii** $\dfrac{1}{\sqrt{(x+2)^2+1}}$

   b i $\dfrac{-1}{\sqrt{x^2-1}}$ **ii** $\dfrac{3}{\sqrt{9x^2-1}}$

   c i $\dfrac{4}{1-16x^2}$ **ii** $\dfrac{1}{2x(x-1)}$

2 $\dfrac{\sinh x}{\sqrt{\cosh^2 x+1}}$

3 $\operatorname{arcosh}(x^2)+\dfrac{2x^2}{\sqrt{x^4-1}}$

4 Proof; $a = 2$, $b = 4$

5 $25x - 16y + 16\ln 2 - 15 = 0$

6 Proof

7 $(-1, 0)$

8 Proof

9 Proof; $a = -\dfrac{1}{2}$

Exercise 7C

1 a i $\dfrac{3}{2}\arctan\left(\dfrac{x}{2}\right) + c$ **ii** $\dfrac{5}{6}\arctan\left(\dfrac{x}{6}\right) + c$

b i $\dfrac{1}{6}\arctan\left(\dfrac{3x}{2}\right) + c$ **ii** $\dfrac{2}{5}\arctan\left(\dfrac{2x}{5}\right) + c$

c i $\sqrt{6}\arctan\left(\dfrac{\sqrt{6}x}{3}\right) + c$

ii $\sqrt{10}\arctan\left(\dfrac{\sqrt{10}x}{2}\right) + c$

d i $2\arcsin\left(\dfrac{x}{3}\right) + c$ **ii** $5\arcsin\left(\dfrac{x}{2}\right) + c$

e i $\dfrac{1}{2}\arcsin\left(\dfrac{2x}{3}\right) + c$ **ii** $\arcsin\left(\dfrac{3x}{5}\right) + c$

f i $5\sqrt{3}\arcsin\left(\dfrac{\sqrt{15}x}{5}\right) + c$

ii $\sqrt{3}\arcsin\left(\dfrac{\sqrt{84}x}{7}\right) + c$

2 a i $3\sinh^{-1}\left(\dfrac{x}{4}\right) + c$ **ii** $5\sinh^{-1}\left(\dfrac{x}{5}\right) + c$

b i $\dfrac{10}{3}\sinh^{-1}\left(\dfrac{3x}{5}\right) + c$ **ii** $\dfrac{3}{2}\sinh^{-1}\left(\dfrac{2x}{3}\right) + c$

c i $2\sqrt{2}\sinh^{-1}\left(\sqrt{\dfrac{2}{3}}x\right) + c$

ii $\dfrac{6\sqrt{7}}{7}\sinh^{-1}\left(\sqrt{\dfrac{7}{5}}x\right) + c$

d i $2\cosh^{-1}\left(\dfrac{x}{7}\right) + c$ **ii** $7\cosh^{-1}\left(\dfrac{x}{6}\right) + c$

e i $\dfrac{1}{3}\cosh^{-1}\left(\dfrac{3x}{4}\right) + c$ **ii** $3\cosh^{-1}\left(\dfrac{5x}{6}\right) + c$

f i $\dfrac{5\sqrt{3}}{3}\cosh^{-1}\left(\sqrt{\dfrac{3}{7}}x\right) + c$

ii $\dfrac{2\sqrt{7}}{7}\cosh^{-1}\left(\sqrt{\dfrac{7}{11}}x\right) + c$

3 a i $\arctan(x+2) + c$ **ii** $\arctan(x-3) + c$

b i $\arcsin(x-4) + c$ **ii** $\arcsin(x-1) + c$

c i $3\sqrt{2}\arctan\left(\dfrac{x+5}{\sqrt{2}}\right) + c$

ii $\dfrac{5}{2}\arcsin\left(\dfrac{2x+3}{3}\right) + c$

d i $\sinh^{-1}(x+3) + c$ **ii** $\sinh^{-1}(x+2) + c$

e i $\cosh^{-1}\left(\dfrac{x-2}{4}\right) + c$ **ii** $\cosh^{-1}(x-1) + c$

f i $3\cosh^{-1}\left(\dfrac{2x-3}{\sqrt{5}}\right) + c$

ii $3\sinh^{-1}\left(\dfrac{x+1}{2}\right) + c$

4 $\ln\left(1 + \sqrt{2}\right)$

5 $\dfrac{\pi}{2}$

6 $\dfrac{\pi\sqrt{3}}{18}$

7 a $\dfrac{1}{3}\arctan(3x) + c$ **b** $4\arctan\left(\dfrac{x}{4}\right) + c$

8 a Proof **b** $\dfrac{5\pi}{8}$

9 a Proof **b** $2\ln(2 + \text{sqrt}(3))$

10 a $2(x+1)^2 + 9$

b $\dfrac{1}{\sqrt{2}}\arctan\left(\dfrac{\sqrt{2}(x+1)}{3}\right) + c$

11 a $2^2 - 3(x-1)^2$ **b** $\dfrac{\sqrt{3}\pi}{9}$

12 a Proof **b** $\dfrac{3}{2}\sin^{-1}\left(\dfrac{2x+1}{3}\right) + c$

13 Proof

14 $\arctan(x+1) + c$

15 Proof

16 $-4\sqrt{1-x^2} + 5\arcsin x + c$

17 $\sqrt{x^2 - 1} + \cosh^{-1} x + c$

18 $3\ln(x^2 + 9) - \dfrac{5}{3}\arctan\left(\dfrac{x}{3}\right) + c$

19 a $2(x-2)^2 + 9$

b $\dfrac{1}{2}\ln\left|2x^2 - 8x + 17\right| + 2\sqrt{2}\arctan\left(\dfrac{\sqrt{2}(x-2)}{3}\right) + c$

20, 21 Proof

22 a $\cos u = \sqrt{\dfrac{1}{1+x^2}}$, $\sin u = \dfrac{x}{\sqrt{1+x^2}}$

b Proof

Exercise 7D

1 a i $\dfrac{1}{\sqrt{2}}\arctan\left(\dfrac{x}{\sqrt{2}}\right)+2\ln|x+3|+c$

  ii $2\arctan x-\ln|x-2|+c$

  b i $2\ln|x+1|+\arctan(x+3)+c$

  ii $\ln|x-2|+2\arctan\left(\dfrac{2}{x+1}\right)+c$

  c i $\ln|x^2+1|+\arctan x-3\ln|x+1|+c$

  ii $\dfrac{1}{2}\ln|x^2+4|-\arctan\left(\dfrac{x}{2}\right)-\ln|x-1|+c$

  d i $\ln|x+1|-\dfrac{2}{x+1}-\dfrac{1}{\sqrt{3}}\arctan\left(\dfrac{x}{\sqrt{3}}\right)+c$

  ii $\ln|x-2|-\dfrac{1}{x-2}+2\arctan x+c$

2 $\dfrac{\pi}{4}-\ln 4$

3 a $\dfrac{1}{x-2}-\dfrac{1}{x^2+9}$

  b $y=\ln\left|\dfrac{x-2}{2}\right|-\dfrac{1}{3}\arctan\left(\dfrac{x}{3}\right)$

4 a $\ln|x-2|+2\ln|x+1|-\dfrac{1}{x+1}+c$

  b $\ln|x-2|+2\arctan(x+1)+c$

5 a $\dfrac{1}{x-2}+\dfrac{1}{x+2}+\dfrac{1}{x^2+4}$

  b $\ln 2+\dfrac{\pi}{6}$

6 $\ln 2+1+\dfrac{\pi}{4}$

7 $\ln\left|\dfrac{x-1}{x+3}\right|-\sqrt{2}\arctan\left(\dfrac{x+1}{\sqrt{2}}\right)+c$

8 Proof; $P=\dfrac{3}{2},Q=-\dfrac{1}{2},R=-1$

Mixed practice 7

1 $\dfrac{e^x}{1+e^{2x}}$

2 $2x\sin^{-1}x+\dfrac{x^2}{\sqrt{1-x^2}}$

3 $\dfrac{2x}{\sqrt{1-\left(1-x^2\right)^2}}$

4 $\pm\sqrt{3}$

5 $\dfrac{\pi}{6}$

6 i $\dfrac{1}{x-1}+\dfrac{9}{x^2+9}$ **ii** $\ln|x-1|+3\arctan\left(\dfrac{x}{3}\right)+c$

7 $\dfrac{2\left(1-3x^4\right)}{\left(1+x^4\right)^2}$

8 Proof

9 $3\ln\left(x^2+4\right)+2\arctan\left(\dfrac{x}{2}\right)+c$

10 $\arctan(x-1)+c$

11 $108^{\frac{1}{6}}$

12 i $2\sqrt{1-x^2}$ **ii** $\dfrac{\pi}{2}$

13 i $\dfrac{1}{1-x}+\dfrac{1}{1+x}+\dfrac{2}{1+x^2}$ **ii** Proof

14 a Proof

  b $\dfrac{1}{3}\left(\arcsin 3x+\sqrt{1-9x^2}\right)+c$

15 Proof; $A=10$

16 a $\dfrac{2}{x+2}-\dfrac{2x-1}{x^2+1}$

  b $2\ln|x+2|-\ln|x^2+1|+\arctan x+c$

  c $\dfrac{4\pi}{3}-\dfrac{3}{2}$

17 a, b Proof

18 i Proof

  ii $\dfrac{1}{2}\cosh^{-1}2x+c$

  iii $\dfrac{x}{2}\sqrt{4x^2-1}-\dfrac{1}{4}\cosh^{-1}2x+c$

Chapter 8

Before you start...

1 $10x\left(x^2+3\right)^4$

2 a i $-2e^{-2x}$ **ii** $4e^{-2x}$

  b i $\dfrac{1}{x}$ **ii** $-\dfrac{1}{x^2}$

  c i $-3\sin 3x$ **ii** $-9\cos 3x$

3 a $\operatorname{sech}^2 x$ **b** $-2\operatorname{sech}^2 x\tanh x$

4 a $\dfrac{1}{\sqrt{x^2-1}}$ **b** $-x\left(x^2-1\right)^{-\frac{3}{2}}$

5 a $\dfrac{1}{\sqrt{1-x^2}}$ **b** $x\left(1-x^2\right)^{-\frac{3}{2}}$

Exercise 8A

1 a i $1+x+\dfrac{x^2}{2!}+\dfrac{x^3}{3!}+\ldots+\dfrac{x^n}{n!}$

ii $1-3x+\dfrac{9}{2}x^2-\dfrac{9}{2}x^3+\ldots+\dfrac{(-3)^n}{n!}x^n$

b i $-x+\dfrac{x^3}{3!}-\dfrac{x^5}{5!}+\dfrac{x^7}{7!}+\ldots+\dfrac{(-1)^{n+1}x^{2n+1}}{(2n+1)!}$

ii $2x-\dfrac{4}{3}x^3+\dfrac{4}{15}x^5-\dfrac{8}{315}x^7+\ldots$
$+\dfrac{(-1)^n 2^{2n+1}}{(2n+1)!}x^{2n+1}$

c i $1-\dfrac{x^2}{2!}+\dfrac{x^4}{4!}-\dfrac{x^6}{6!}+\ldots+\dfrac{(-1)^n x^{2n}}{(2n)!}$

ii $1-\dfrac{9}{2}x^2+\dfrac{27}{8}x^4-\dfrac{81}{80}x^6+\ldots+\dfrac{(-1)^n 3^{2n}}{(2n)!}x^{2n}$

d i $-x-\dfrac{x^2}{2}-\dfrac{x^3}{3}-\dfrac{x^4}{4}+\ldots+-\dfrac{x^n}{n}$

ii $2x-2x^2+\dfrac{8}{3}x^3-4x^4+\ldots+\dfrac{-(-2)^n x^n}{n}$

e i $x+\dfrac{x^3}{3!}+\dfrac{x^5}{5!}+\dfrac{x^7}{7!}+\ldots+\dfrac{x^{2n+1}}{(2n+1)!}$

ii $2x+\dfrac{8x^3}{3!}+\dfrac{32x^5}{5!}+\dfrac{128x^7}{7!}+\ldots+\dfrac{2^{2n+1}x^{2n+1}}{(2n+1)!}$

f i $1+\dfrac{x^2}{2!}+\dfrac{x^4}{4!}+\dfrac{x^6}{6!}+\ldots+\dfrac{x^{2n}}{(2n)!}$

ii $1+\dfrac{x^2}{2!}+\dfrac{x^4}{4!}+\dfrac{x^6}{6!}+\ldots+\dfrac{x^{2n}}{(2n)!}$

2 $2+\dfrac{1}{4}x+\dfrac{7}{64}x^2$

3 a Proof   **b** 0.324

4 a i $f'(x)=-2xe^{-x^2}; f''(x)=-2e^{-x^2}+4x^2e^{-x^2};$
$f'''(x)=12xe^{-x^2}-8x^3e^{-x^2};$
$f^{(4)}(x)=\left(16x^4-48x^2+12\right)e^{-x^2}$

ii $1-x^2+\dfrac{1}{2}x^4$

b $\dfrac{23}{30}$

5 a $1-x^2+\dfrac{1}{3}x^4-\dfrac{2}{45}x^6$

b $x^2-\dfrac{1}{3}x^4+\dfrac{2}{45}x^6$

6 a i Proof

ii $f'''(x)=\dfrac{\cos x}{(1+\sin x)^2};$
$f^{(4)}(x)=-\dfrac{1+\sin x+\cos^2 x}{(1+\sin x)^3}$

b $x-\dfrac{1}{2}x^2+\dfrac{1}{6}x^3-\dfrac{1}{12}x^4$

c 0.116

7 a i $f'(x)=\dfrac{1}{1-x}; f''(x)=\dfrac{1}{(1-x)^2};$
$f'''(x)=\dfrac{2}{(1-x)^3}$

ii Proof

b $\dfrac{80}{81}$

8 a Proof   **b** $\dfrac{x^n}{(n-1)!}$

9 a Proof   **b** $5^n x^n$

10 a $x+\dfrac{1}{6}x^3+\dfrac{3}{40}x^5$

b i $f^{(n)}(x)=-g^{(n)}(x)$ **ii** Proof; $k=\dfrac{\pi}{2}$

11 a Not equal to f(0).

b f(x) is an increasing function at $x=0$, but first derivative of series is negative at $x=0$.

Exercise 8B

1 a i $1-3x+\dfrac{9x^2}{2}+\ldots+\dfrac{(-3)^n}{n!}x^n$

ii $1+x^3+\dfrac{x^6}{2}+\ldots+\dfrac{x^{3n}}{n!}$

b i $3x-\dfrac{9x^2}{2}+9x^3+\ldots+\dfrac{(-1)^{(n+1)}3^n}{n}x^n$

ii $-2x-2x^2-\dfrac{8}{3}x^3+\ldots+\dfrac{-2^n}{n}x^n$

c i $-\dfrac{x}{2}+\dfrac{x^3}{48}-\dfrac{x^5}{3840}+\ldots+\dfrac{(-1)^n}{2^{2n+1}(2n+1)!}x^{2n+1}$

ii $3x^2-\dfrac{9x^6}{2}+\dfrac{81x^{10}}{40}+\ldots+\dfrac{(-1)^n 3^{2n+1}}{(2n+1)!}x^{4n+2}$

d i $1-\dfrac{x^4}{18}+\dfrac{x^8}{1944}+\ldots+\dfrac{(-1)^n}{3^{2n}(2n)!}x^{4n}$

ii $1-2x^2+\dfrac{2x^4}{3}+\ldots+\dfrac{(-1)^n 2^{2n}}{(2n)!}x^{2n}$

e i $1-2x-2x^2+\ldots+\dfrac{\left(\dfrac{1}{2}\right)\left(-\dfrac{1}{2}\right)\ldots\left(\dfrac{3}{2}-n\right)}{n!}(-4)^n x^n$

ii $1-\dfrac{4x}{3}+\dfrac{10x^2}{9}+\ldots+\dfrac{(-4)(-5)\ldots(-3+n)}{3^n n!}x^n$

2 a i $\ln 3+\dfrac{x}{3}-\dfrac{x^2}{18}$ **ii** $-\ln 2-2x-2x^2$

b i $\dfrac{1}{8}+\dfrac{9x}{16}+\dfrac{27x^2}{16}$ **ii** $2-8x+48x^2$

c i $-3+\dfrac{8x}{27}+\dfrac{64x^2}{2187}$ **ii** $\dfrac{1}{16}+\dfrac{3x}{32}+\dfrac{27x^2}{256}$

3 a i $2x^2 - x^3 - \dfrac{2}{3}x^4$

ii $-x - \dfrac{1}{2}x^2 + \dfrac{25}{6}x^3 + 2x^4$

b i $1 + \dfrac{1}{2}x^2 - \dfrac{1}{3}x^3 + \dfrac{3}{8}x^4$

ii $x + 2x^2 + \dfrac{23}{6}x^3 + \dfrac{23}{3}x^4$

c i $x - \dfrac{x^2}{2} + \dfrac{x^3}{6} - \dfrac{x^4}{12}$

ii $-\dfrac{x^2}{2} - \dfrac{x^4}{12}$

4 $4x - 4x^2 + \dfrac{16}{3}x^3 - 8x^4 + ...; \; -\dfrac{1}{2} < x \leqslant \dfrac{1}{2}$

5 $2x + 6x^2 + \dfrac{23}{3}x^3 + 5x^4$

6 Proof

7 a $x + \dfrac{x^3}{3}$

b $1 + x + \dfrac{x^2}{2} + \dfrac{x^3}{2} + \dfrac{3}{8}x^4$

8 a $-\dfrac{x^2}{2} - \dfrac{x^4}{12}$

b $\dfrac{x^2}{2} + \dfrac{x^4}{12}$

c $x + \dfrac{x^3}{3}$

9 a $\ln 8 - \dfrac{3}{2}x - \dfrac{39}{8}x^2 - \dfrac{71}{8}x^3$

b $y = \ln 8 - 1.5x$

10 a $\displaystyle\sum_{k=1}^{\infty} \dfrac{x^{2k-1}}{2k-1};$ convergence for $|x| < 1$

b $x = \dfrac{3}{5}; \ln 2 \approx 0.688$

Exercise 8C

1 a 1   **b** 4

c Integral diverges.   **d** $\dfrac{1}{2}$

2 a $p < 0$ **b** $p > 1$

3 Proof; 4

4 1

5 $\dfrac{\pi}{2}$

6 $\ln\dfrac{4}{45}$

Exercise 8D

1 a i 0.4π **ii** $\dfrac{128\pi}{7}$

b i 304.8π **ii** $\dfrac{18\pi}{7}$

c i $\dfrac{\pi}{2}$ **ii** $\dfrac{21\pi}{64}$

2 a i $\dfrac{\pi}{2}(e^2 - 1)$ **ii** $\dfrac{\pi}{2}(1 - e^{-6})$

b i $\pi\left(\dfrac{e^4}{4} + e^2 - \dfrac{1}{4}\right)$ **ii** $\pi\left(\dfrac{25}{2} - 4e^{-2} - \dfrac{e^{-4}}{2}\right)$

c i 2π **ii** π

3 a i 32π **ii** $\dfrac{85}{2}\pi$

b i $\dfrac{96}{5}\pi$ **ii** $\dfrac{28\sqrt{2}}{3}\pi$

c i 3π **ii** $\dfrac{35}{3}\pi$

4 a i $\dfrac{\pi}{2}(e^4 - 1)$ **ii** $\dfrac{\pi}{8}(e^8 + 4e^4 + 3)$

b i $\pi \ln 2$ **ii** $\pi \ln 3$

c i $\dfrac{\pi^2}{2}$ **ii** $(\pi - 2)\dfrac{\pi}{4}$

5 a i 2304π **ii** 0.5π

b i $\left(\dfrac{27}{2} + 2\ln 2\right)\pi$ **ii** $\dfrac{527}{5}\pi$

c i $\dfrac{\pi^2}{4}$ **ii** $\dfrac{\pi^2}{3}$

6 a i $\dfrac{18432\pi}{7}$ **ii** $\dfrac{3\pi}{14}$

b i $\dfrac{487\pi}{480}$ **ii** $\dfrac{2103\pi}{35}$

c i $\dfrac{\pi^2}{4}$ **ii** $\dfrac{\pi}{2}$

7 a $(4, 0)$ **b** $\dfrac{11\pi}{6}$

8 75.4

9 π

10 2

11 $\dfrac{4\pi a^5}{15}$

12 $\dfrac{4}{3}$

13 a $(0, 3), (4, 19)$ **b** 630 (3 s.f.)

14 184 (3 s.f.)

15 a $(1, 4), (9, 12)$ **b** $\dfrac{736\pi}{15}$

16 Proof

17 $\dfrac{197}{2}\pi$

18 $2\pi\left(\ln\dfrac{3}{2} - \dfrac{1}{6}\right)$

19 $\dfrac{8}{15}\pi$

20 Proof; use $y = \dfrac{rx}{h}$.

21 $\pi\left(\dfrac{1}{2}e^2 - 2e + \dfrac{5}{2}\right)$

Exercise 8E

1 a i $\dfrac{1}{3}$ **ii** $\dfrac{13}{3}$

 b i $\dfrac{4}{3}$ **ii** $\dfrac{1}{5}$

 c i 17 **ii** 1995

2 a i $\dfrac{2}{\pi}$ **ii** 0

 b i $e-1$ **ii** $\dfrac{1}{e-1}$

 c i $\dfrac{38}{15}$ **ii** $\dfrac{1}{\sqrt{\pi}}$

3 $20\sqrt{T}$

4 1.5

5 a $\dfrac{a^2}{3}$ **b** $\dfrac{a}{\sqrt{3}}$

6 Proof

7 $1:2$

8 Proof

9 a

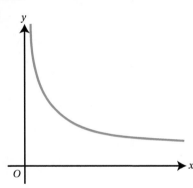

 b Curve is concave up.

 c Proof

10 Not true. For example: $f(x)=x^2-1$ between -1 and 1.

Mixed practice 8

1 a, b Proof

2 a $f'(x)=(1+x)^{-1}, f''(x)=-(1+x)^{-2},$
 $f'''(x)=2(1+x)^{-3}, f^{(4)}(x)=-6(1+x)^{-4}$

 b $f(x)\approx x-\dfrac{1}{2}x^2+\dfrac{1}{3}x^3-\dfrac{1}{4}x^4$

 c $\ln 2$

3 a The integrand is not defined at $x=0$.

 b $\displaystyle\lim_{a\to 0}\left\{\int_a^4 \dfrac{5-x}{\sqrt{x^3}}\,dx\right\}$ does not converge to a finite value.

4 $-\dfrac{9}{2}x^2$

5 6

6 57.8

7 $\dfrac{3}{2}$

8 4

9 $x<0$

10 a $-\dfrac{1}{2}x^2-\dfrac{1}{12}x^4$ **b** Proof

11 a $f'(x)=\dfrac{\cos x}{1+\sin x}, f''(x)=-\dfrac{1}{1+\sin x},$
 $f'''(x)=\dfrac{\cos x}{(1+\sin x)^2}$

 b $x-\dfrac{1}{2}x^2+\dfrac{1}{6}x^3$ **c** $-\dfrac{1}{2}$

12 i $f(0)=0, f'(0)=1$

 ii Proof; $f''(0)=-2$

 iii $f'''(x)=-2f''(x)-2f'(x); f'''(0)=2$

 iv $f(x)=x-x^2+\dfrac{1}{3}x^3$

13 $\dfrac{\left|\pi a^5\right|}{30}$

14 a Proof **b** $\pi\left(\dfrac{5e^2}{6}-\dfrac{1}{2}\right)$

15 $\dfrac{\pi}{60}$

16 i $\dfrac{16\sqrt{3}}{9}$

 ii $\left(3\ln 3-\dfrac{20}{27}\right)\pi$

17 i Proof

 ii $\dfrac{3e^4+1}{2}\pi$ **iii** $\dfrac{\pi}{2}\left(e^4-1\right)$

18 6π

19 $\dfrac{4}{3}\pi ab^2$

20 $\dfrac{\pi}{2}\left(1-\dfrac{3}{e^2}\right)$

21 a $x+\dfrac{x^2}{1!}+\dfrac{x^3}{2!}+\dfrac{x^4}{3!}+\dots+\dfrac{x^n}{(n-1)!}+\dots$

 b $\dfrac{x^2}{2}+\dfrac{x^3}{3(1!)}+\dfrac{x^4}{4(2!)}+\dots+\dfrac{x^n}{n(n-2)!}+\dots$

 c Proof

22 $3+5\sqrt{2}$

23 a $(0,12)$ and $(4.5,-3.75)$

b $\pi \int_0^{4.5} (14x^3 - 111x^2 + 216x)\, dx$

c 787

24 a

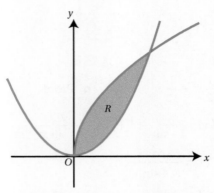

b $\dfrac{3\pi}{10}$ **c** $\dfrac{3\pi}{10}$

Chapter 9

Before you start...

1 a 210°   **b** $-\dfrac{\sqrt{3}}{2}$

2 a $\theta \in \left(\dfrac{\pi}{2}, \dfrac{3\pi}{2} \right)$ **b** 7

3 a $\dfrac{1}{3}$ **b** $\dfrac{\pi}{4}$

Exercise 9A

1 a–c

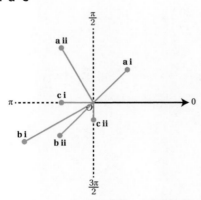

2 a i Distance $AB = 2.53$; area $AOB = 4.53$

   ii Distance $AB = 3.42$; area $AOB = 2.5$

 b i Distance $AB = 17.8$; area $AOB = 10.4$

   ii Distance $AB = 8.92$; area $AOB = 2.59$

c i Distance $AB = 2.91$; area $AOB = 0.5$

  ii Distance $AB = 7.21$; area $AOB = 12$

3 a i

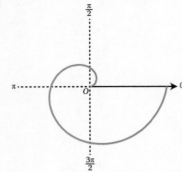

  ii

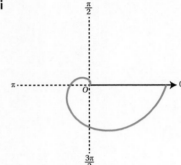

 b i

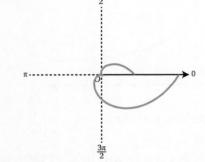

  ii

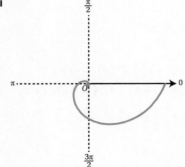

c i

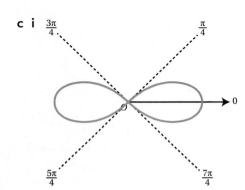

ii

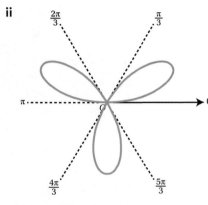

4 a

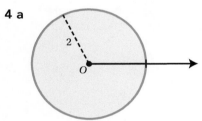

b

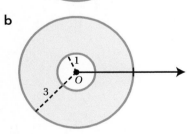

c

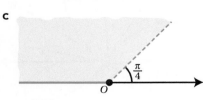

5 a $\dfrac{\pi}{4} < \theta < \dfrac{3\pi}{4}$ and $\dfrac{5\pi}{4} < \theta < \dfrac{7\pi}{4}$

b

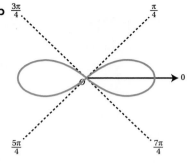

6 a $\pi < \theta < 2\pi$ **b** Proof

c

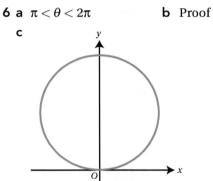

d $2\sqrt{3}$

Exercise 9B

1 a i Maximum $\left(5, \dfrac{\pi}{2}\right)$; minimum $\left(1, \dfrac{3\pi}{2}\right)$

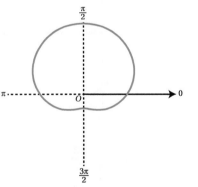

ii Maximum $(6, 0)$; minimum $(4, \pi)$

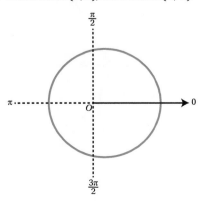

b i Maxima $\left(10, \dfrac{\pi}{2}\right)$ and $\left(10, \dfrac{3\pi}{2}\right)$;

minima $(4, 0)$ and $(4, \pi)$

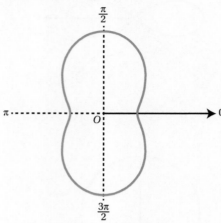

ii Maxima $\left(7, \dfrac{3\pi}{4}\right)$ and $\left(7, \dfrac{7\pi}{4}\right)$;

minima $\left(3, \dfrac{\pi}{4}\right)$ and $\left(3, \dfrac{5\pi}{4}\right)$

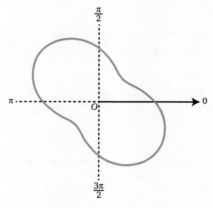

2 a i $\theta = 0, \dfrac{\pi}{3}, \dfrac{2\pi}{3}, \pi, \dfrac{4\pi}{3}, \dfrac{5\pi}{3}$

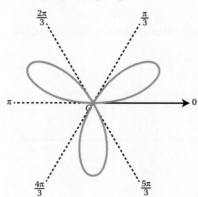

ii $\theta = \dfrac{\pi}{4}, \dfrac{3\pi}{4}, \dfrac{5\pi}{4}, \dfrac{7\pi}{4}$

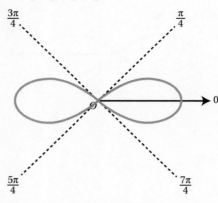

b i $\theta = \dfrac{2\pi}{9}, \dfrac{4\pi}{9}, \dfrac{8\pi}{9}, \dfrac{10\pi}{9}, \dfrac{14\pi}{9}, \dfrac{16\pi}{9}$

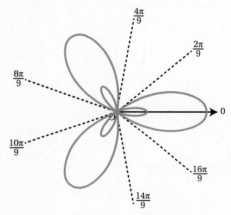

ii $\theta = \dfrac{\pi}{16}, \dfrac{3\pi}{16}, \dfrac{9\pi}{16}, \dfrac{11\pi}{16}, \dfrac{17\pi}{16}, \dfrac{19\pi}{16},$

$\dfrac{25\pi}{16}, \dfrac{27\pi}{16}$

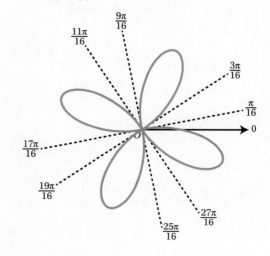

3 a $\theta = \dfrac{\pi}{8}, \dfrac{3\pi}{8}, \dfrac{5\pi}{8}, \dfrac{7\pi}{8}, \dfrac{9\pi}{8}, \dfrac{11\pi}{8}, \dfrac{13\pi}{8}, \dfrac{15\pi}{8}$

b $\dfrac{\pi}{8} < \theta < \dfrac{3\pi}{8}, \dfrac{5\pi}{8} < \theta < \dfrac{7\pi}{8}, \dfrac{9\pi}{8} < \theta < \dfrac{11\pi}{8}$ and $\dfrac{13\pi}{8} < \theta < \dfrac{15\pi}{8}$

c

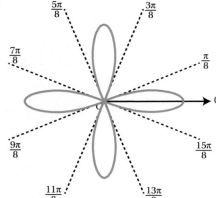

4 a

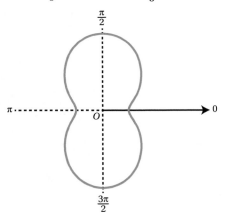

b $1 \leqslant r \leqslant 3$

5 a $\theta \in \left[0, \dfrac{7\pi}{12} \right] \cup \left[\dfrac{11\pi}{12}, \dfrac{19\pi}{12} \right] \cup \left[\dfrac{23\pi}{12}, 2\pi \right]$

b $\theta = \dfrac{7\pi}{12}, \dfrac{11\pi}{12}, \dfrac{19\pi}{12}, \dfrac{23\pi}{12}$; maximum r at $\left(3, \dfrac{\pi}{4}\right)$ and $\left(3, \dfrac{5\pi}{4}\right)$

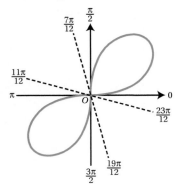

6 a Largest $r = 3$ when $\theta = \dfrac{\pi}{2}$; smallest $r = 1$ when $\theta = \dfrac{3\pi}{2}$.

b

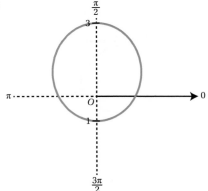

7 a

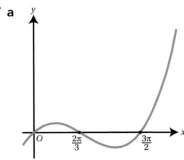

b

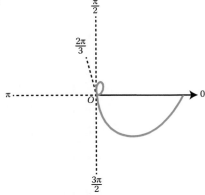

8 a Maximum y is $4\pi^2$; minimum y is π^2

b

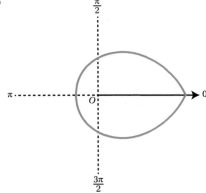

9

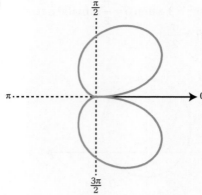

10

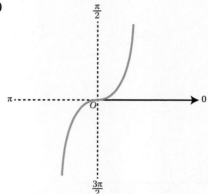

Exercise 9C

1 a i $\left(\dfrac{5}{\sqrt{2}}, \dfrac{5}{\sqrt{2}}\right)$ **ii** $\left(\dfrac{3}{2}, \dfrac{3\sqrt{3}}{2}\right)$

b i $(-1, 1)$ **ii** $\left(-\dfrac{3}{2}, \dfrac{\sqrt{3}}{2}\right)$

c i $(-3.45, -4.91)$ **ii** $(2.50, -1.65)$

2 a i $(\sqrt{29}, 0.381)$ **ii** $(5, 0.927)$

b i $\left(2, \dfrac{\pi}{2}\right)$ **ii** $\left(3, \dfrac{3\pi}{2}\right)$

c i $(\sqrt{26}, 4.51)$ **ii** $(\sqrt{17}, 6.04)$

3 a i $\sin 2\theta = \dfrac{2}{3}$ **ii** $r = 2\cos^2\theta\sin\theta$

b i $r = 5(\sec\theta + \operatorname{cosec}\theta)$

 ii $r = \left(\dfrac{3}{\sin^3\theta + \cos^3\theta}\right)^{\frac{1}{3}}$

c i $r = \dfrac{1}{\sin\theta - 3\cos\theta}$ **ii** $r = \sqrt{6}$

4 a i $x^2 + y^2 = 4\left(\tan^{-1}\dfrac{y}{x}\right)^2$

 ii $x^2 + y^2 = 9\left(\tan^{-1}\dfrac{y}{x}\right)^4$

b i $x^2 + y^2 = 4y$ **ii** $y^2 = 2x - x^2$

c i $x^4 + x^2y^2 - 4y^2 = 0$ **ii** $x^2 + y^2 = \dfrac{y}{x}$

5 a 0.841 **b** $\left(\dfrac{4}{3}, \dfrac{2\sqrt{5}}{3}\right)$

 c $x^2 + y^2 = 3x$

6 $r = 2(\cos\theta + \sin\theta)$

7 $x^4 + x^2y^2 - 9y^2 = 0$

8 Proof

9 a $y = \sqrt{x\sqrt{x} - x^2}$ **b** $y^2 = x^3 - x^2$

Exercise 9D

1 a i $\dfrac{1}{2}$ **ii** $\dfrac{1}{3}$

 b i $\dfrac{2\pi^3}{3}$ **ii** $\dfrac{\pi^5}{10}$

 c i $e^{4\pi} - 1$ **ii** $\dfrac{e^{2\pi} - 1}{2}$

 d i $\dfrac{\pi}{8}$ **ii** $\dfrac{2 + \pi}{16}$

 e i $\dfrac{3\pi}{4}$ **ii** $\dfrac{3\pi}{2}$

2 a $r = a$ **b** Proof

3 $\dfrac{4 - \pi}{8}$

4 Proof

5 27π

6 a

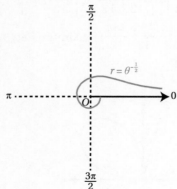

b Proof

7 a

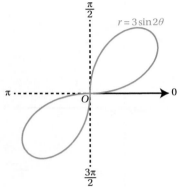

$r = 3\sin 2\theta$

b $\dfrac{9\pi}{4}$

8 a

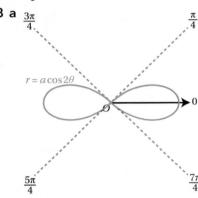

$r = a\cos 2\theta$

Tangents: $\theta = \dfrac{\pi}{4}, \dfrac{3\pi}{4}, \dfrac{5\pi}{4}, \dfrac{7\pi}{4}$

b $\dfrac{a^2\pi}{4}$

9 $\dfrac{\pi}{3}$

10 Proof

Exercise 9E

1 a $\left(2, \dfrac{\pi}{6}\right)$

b i $\dfrac{\sqrt{3}}{2}$ **ii** Proof

2 $\dfrac{3\pi a^2}{8}$

3 a $\left(a, \dfrac{\pi}{12}\right)$ and $\left(a, \dfrac{5\pi}{12}\right)$

b $\dfrac{a^2}{12}\left(4\pi - 3\sqrt{3}\right)$

4 a $\left(\dfrac{1}{2}, \dfrac{\pi}{6}\right), \left(\dfrac{1}{2}, \dfrac{5\pi}{6}\right)$ **b** $\dfrac{16\pi - 21\sqrt{3}}{24}$

5 a $\left(3, \dfrac{\pi}{3}\right), \left(3, \dfrac{5\pi}{3}\right)$ **b** Proof

6 a

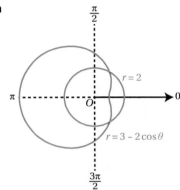

$r = 2$

$r = 3 - 2\cos\theta$

b Proof

Mixed practice 9

1 16

2 $r = a(\cos\theta - \sin\theta)$

3 a 8.92 **b** 13.5

4

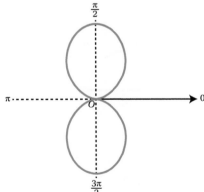

5 $a\left(e^{2\pi} - 1\right)$

313

6 a

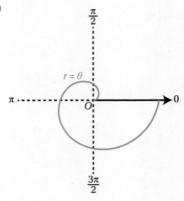

b Proof

7 a

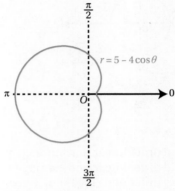

b 33π

8 a Proof   **b** $\theta = \dfrac{2\pi}{3}$ or $\dfrac{4\pi}{3}$

c

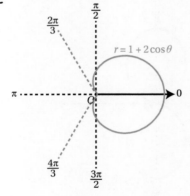

d Proof

9 $\left(x^2 + y^2\right)^{\frac{3}{2}} = 3x^2$

10 a $\theta = \dfrac{7\pi}{6}$ and $\theta = \dfrac{11\pi}{6}$

b

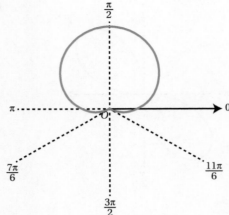

c $(x^2 + y^2 - 4y)^2 = 4(x^2 + y^2)$

11 a

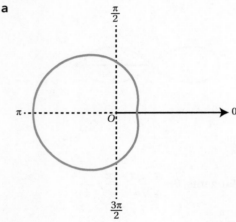

b $(-8, 0)$

12 a $\theta = \dfrac{\pi}{12}, \dfrac{5\pi}{12}, \dfrac{13\pi}{12}, \dfrac{17\pi}{12}$

b $\left(6, \dfrac{3\pi}{4}\right)$ and $\left(6, \dfrac{7\pi}{4}\right)$

c

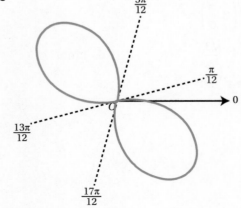

13 a

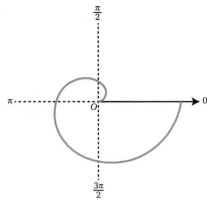

b $(-\pi, \pi\sqrt{3})$

14

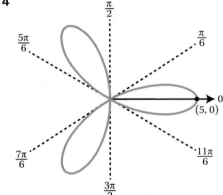

15 $8\pi + 6\sqrt{3}$

16 a Proof

b $\left(5, \dfrac{\pi}{3}\right)$ and $\left(5, \dfrac{5\pi}{3}\right)$

c $\dfrac{200\pi}{3} - \dfrac{175\sqrt{3}}{2}$

17 a i Proof

ii $\theta = \dfrac{\pi}{4}, \dfrac{\pi}{2}, \dfrac{3\pi}{4}, \dfrac{5\pi}{4}, \dfrac{3\pi}{2}, \dfrac{7\pi}{4}$

b Proof

18 i $r = 1 + \cos\theta$

ii

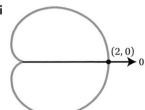

iii $1:3$

19 i, ii Proof

Chapter 10

Before you start...

1 $y = A\mathrm{e}^{\frac{1}{2}x^2}$

2 $\dfrac{\mathrm{d}y}{\mathrm{d}x} = \mathrm{e}^{3x} + 3x\mathrm{e}^{3x}$

3 $\mathrm{e}^x(x-1) + c$

Exercise 10A

1 a i For example: $\dfrac{\mathrm{d}^2 y}{\mathrm{d}x^2} + 2\dfrac{\mathrm{d}y}{\mathrm{d}x} + y = 0$

  ii For example: $\dfrac{\mathrm{d}^2 y}{\mathrm{d}x^2} + 2\dfrac{\mathrm{d}y}{\mathrm{d}x} + \cos y = 0$

b i For example: $\dfrac{\mathrm{d}^2 y}{\mathrm{d}x^2} + 2\dfrac{\mathrm{d}y}{\mathrm{d}x} + y = 0$

  ii For example: $\dfrac{\mathrm{d}^3 y}{\mathrm{d}x^3} + 2\dfrac{\mathrm{d}y}{\mathrm{d}x} + y = 0$

c i For example: $\dfrac{\mathrm{d}^2 y}{\mathrm{d}x^2} + 2\dfrac{\mathrm{d}y}{\mathrm{d}x} + y = 0$

  ii For example: $\dfrac{\mathrm{d}^2 y}{\mathrm{d}x^2} + 2\dfrac{\mathrm{d}y}{\mathrm{d}x} + y = x$

2 a i Second order linear non-homogeneous
  ii Second order linear non-homogeneous
b i Second order non-linear homogeneous
  ii First order non-linear non-homogeneous
c i Second order non-linear non-homogeneous
  ii Third order linear homogeneous
d i Second order linear homogeneous
  ii First order non-linear non-homogeneous

3 a i $y = 2x^2 + 4$
  ii $y = 8\cos x - 2$
b i $y = \mathrm{e}^{-x} + 3x$
  ii $y = 6\ln x - 2x^2$
c i $y = 3x^2 - 2x$
  ii $y = 10\sin x + 5\cos x$
d i $y = 3\mathrm{e}^{2x} - \mathrm{e}^x$
  ii $y = 10\sin x - 2\cos x$

4 a $y = \dfrac{A}{\sqrt{x}}$ **b** $a = 1, b = -2$

c $y = \dfrac{5}{\sqrt{x}} + \ln x - 2$

5 a $y = \dfrac{A}{\cos x}$ **b** $a = 0, b = 2$

c $y = \dfrac{A}{\cos x} + 2\cos x$

6 a Proof; $A = \dfrac{1}{\sqrt{2}}, B = 1$ **b** $y = C\mathrm{e}^{-x}$

c The equation is not linear.

d $y=\sqrt{\dfrac{2}{3}e^x+ce^{-2x}}$

7 a $y=Ae^{e^{-x}}$ **b** 2

c $y=Ae^{e^{-x}}+2$

Exercise 10B

1 a i $y=\dfrac{1}{3}e^x+ce^{-2x}$ **ii** $y=-\dfrac{1}{3}e^x+ce^{4x}$

b i $y=-\cot x+c\cosec x$

ii $y=\dfrac{x+c}{\cos x}$

c i $y=\dfrac{\ln|x|}{x}+\dfrac{c}{x}$ **ii** $-\dfrac{1}{x^2}+\dfrac{c}{x}$

2 $y=\dfrac{1}{2}e^x+\dfrac{1}{2}e^{2-x}$

3 $y=x^2\ln|x-3|+cx^2$

4 $y=e^{\cos x}(x+c)$

5 $y=-\dfrac{2}{x^2}+\dfrac{3}{x}$

6 $y=(x+2)\cos x$

7 Proof

8 $y=\dfrac{x^2+c}{2(x^2-1)}$

9 a $\dfrac{dz}{dx}-xz=-x$

b $z=1+ce^{\frac{x^2}{2}}$ **c** 1

10 a $y=-\sqrt{\dfrac{x^3}{4}+\dfrac{36}{x}}$

b $\sin y=\cos x(\ln\sec x+c)$

Exercise 10C

1 a $\lambda^2+5\lambda+6=0$ **b** $y=Ae^{-3x}+Be^{-2x}$

2 a $\lambda^2+4=0$

b $y=A\cos(2x)+B\sin(2x)$

3 a $\lambda^2+2\lambda+1=0$ **b** $y=(Ax+B)e^{-x}$

4 a $y=Ae^{4x}+Be^{2x}$ **b** $y=e^{4x}+4e^{2x}$

5 a $y=(A+Bx)e^{-2x}$ **b** $y=(1+2x)e^{-2x}$

6 a $x=e^t(A\cos t+B\sin t)$

b $x=e^t(\cos t-\sin t)$

7 a $x=Ae^t+Be^{3t}$ **b** e^2

8 a $y=(A+Bt)e^{3t}$ **b** $y=pte^{3(t-1)}$

9 $y=Ae^x+e^{2x}(B\sin x+C\cos x)$

10 $y=(A+Bx+Cx^2)e^{-x}$

11 $y=Ax^3+\dfrac{B}{x^3}$

12 a $\dfrac{d^2y}{dt^2}+\dfrac{dy}{dt}=0$ **b** $y=A+Be^{-t}$

c $x=\sqrt{5-e^{-t}}$

Exercise 10D

1 a $Ae^{5x}+Be^{-x}$ **b** $-\dfrac{1}{9}e^{2x}$

c $y=Ae^{5x}+Be^{-x}-\dfrac{1}{9}e^{2x}$

2 a $Ae^{-5x}+Be^{-4x}$ **b** $3x-\dfrac{27}{20}$

c $y=Ae^{-5x}+Be^{-4x}+3x-\dfrac{27}{20}$

3 a $Ae^{-x}+B$ **b** $\dfrac{1}{2}\sin x+\dfrac{1}{2}\cos x$

c $y=Ae^{-x}+B+\dfrac{1}{2}\sin x+\dfrac{1}{2}\cos x$

4 a $A\sin 3x+B\cos 3x$

b $y=A\sin 3x+B\cos 3x+2e^{-x}$

c $y=4\sin 3x+5\cos 3x+2e^{-x}$

5 a $y=(A+Bx)e^{-2x}+3x-3+3\sin x-4\cos x$

b $y=(7+18x)e^{-2x}+3x-3+3\sin x-4\cos x$

6 a $y=e^{2t}(A\sin 2t+B\cos 2t)+4t^2+4t+1$

b $y=e^{2t}(-\sin 2t-\cos 2t)+4t^2+4t+1$

7 a $(A+Bx)e^{5x}$

b Proof

c $y=(A+Bx)e^{5x}+\dfrac{1}{2}x^2e^{5x}$

d $y=(4-18x)e^{5x}+\dfrac{1}{2}x^2e^{5x}$

8 $f(x)=3-2e^x\sin x$

9 $Ae^{-4x}+Be^x+0.2xe^x$

10 a $A\sin 2x+B\cos 2x+3x\sin 2x$

b $3\sin 2x+5\cos 2x+3x\sin 2x$

Mixed practice 10

1 $A\cos\left(\dfrac{3}{2}x\right)+B\sin\left(\dfrac{3}{2}x\right)$

2 $\dfrac{1}{x^3}$

3 a $\lambda = -5, -1$ **b** $y = Ae^{-5x} + Be^{-x}$

4 a Proof   **b** $y = e^{-x^2}\left(\dfrac{x^2}{2} + c\right)$

5 i $y = Ae^{-4x}$

  ii $y = Ae^{-4x} + \dfrac{1}{5}(4\cos 3x + 3\sin 3x)$

  iii For large x, the function oscillates approximately between -1 and $+1$.

6 a $Ae^{-2x} + Be^{-5x}$

  b Proof; $\dfrac{1}{18}$

  c $y = Ae^{-2x} + Be^{-5x} + \dfrac{e^x}{18}$

  d $y = \dfrac{34}{18}e^{-2x} - \dfrac{35}{18}e^{-5x} + \dfrac{e^x}{18}$

7 a $\dfrac{1}{3}$

  b $y = A\cos 2x + B\sin 2x + \dfrac{\cos x}{3}$

8 a $e^{-3x}(A\cos 4x + B\sin 4x)$

  b Proof; $p = 2, q = -\dfrac{12}{25}$

  c $y = e^{-3x}(A\cos 4x + B\sin 4x) + 2x - \dfrac{12}{25}$

  d $y = e^{-3x}\sin 4x + 2x - \dfrac{12}{25}$

9 $y = \dfrac{1}{20}\left(4x^2 + 5x + 11x^{-3}\right)$

10 $y = \dfrac{1}{2}e^{-x} - e^{-2x} + \dfrac{1}{2}e^{-3x}$

11 $y = \dfrac{1}{2}x^3\left(e^{2x} - e^2\right)$

12 i $y = Ae^{\frac{x}{2}} + Be^{-2x}$

  ii $p = -1$

  iii $y = 2e^{\frac{x}{2}} - (2 + x)e^{-2x}$

13 i $y = Ae^{\frac{x}{3}} + Be^{-2x} + x - 4$

  ii $y = \dfrac{1}{2}e^{-2x} + x - 4$

  iii $y = x - 4$

14 a $\dfrac{A}{x^3} + \dfrac{x}{4}$

  b Proof

  c $y = \dfrac{B}{x^2} + C + \dfrac{x^2}{8}$

15 a $y = A\cos x - 2\cos x \ln|\cos x|$

  b $y = 5\cos x - 2\cos x \ln|\cos x|$

16 $A + Be^{2x} - 2.5x$

Chapter 11

Before you start...

1 $y = Ae^{-4x} + Be^{-x} + \dfrac{x}{4} - \dfrac{5}{16}$

2 $4.8\ \text{m s}^{-2}$

Exercise 11A

1 a $\dfrac{dv}{dt} = g - kv$

  b $v = \dfrac{1}{k}\left(g - (g - ku)e^{-kt}\right)$

2 a Proof

  b The model seems suitable initially, but is not accurate for later times.

3 a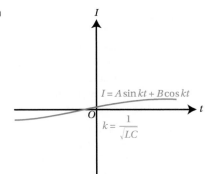

  b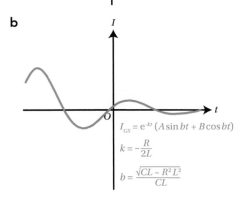

c

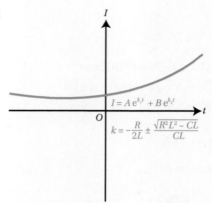

$I = A e^{k_1 t} + B e^{k_2 t}$

$k = -\dfrac{R}{2L} \pm \dfrac{\sqrt{R^2 L^2 - CL}}{CL}$

4 a $\dfrac{dY}{dt} = 200\,000 \times e^{-t\ln 4}$

b 12 144 270

c A natural net birth rate of the population

5 a $\dfrac{dT}{dt} = k(25 + 20t - T)$

b $T = 20t - 15 + 20 e^{-\frac{t}{2}}$

c 185 °C

d Different parts of the chicken are likely to have different temperatures.

6 a $\dfrac{dR}{dt} = kR(N - R)$ **b** $\dfrac{N}{2}$

c For example: interest in the rumour remains constant; the number of students who know the rumour is modelled as a continuous variable; there are no people outside the school spreading the rumour.

7 a This is proportional to the surface area of the bacterium. Larger surface areas make the bacterium more efficient in taking up nutrients so it will grow faster.

b $V = \left(2 - e^{-\frac{t}{3}}\right)^3$

c

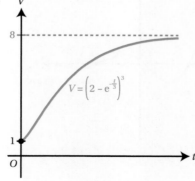

$V = \left(2 - e^{-\frac{t}{3}}\right)^3$

Exercise 11B

1 a i $A = 4.5$, $T = \dfrac{2\pi}{3}$; at rest

   ii $A = 3$, $T = \dfrac{\pi}{2}$; equilibrium

 b i $A = 2.6$, $T = 6\pi$; equilibrium
   ii $A = 5$, $T = 8\pi$; at rest
 c i $A = 3.2$, $T = 3$; equilibrium

   ii $A = 10.4$, $T = \dfrac{10}{3}$; at rest

 d i $A = 2.6$, $T = 6\pi$; neither
   ii $A = 5$, $T = 8\pi$; neither
 e i $A = 3.49$, $T = 1.6$; neither
   ii $A = 8.54$, $T = 7$; neither

2 a i $x = 0.6\cos 10t$
   ii $x = 3.4\cos 14t$

 b i $x = 0.7\sin\dfrac{t}{3}$

   ii $x = 1.3\sin\dfrac{t}{5}$

 c i $x = 12.1\sin\dfrac{4\pi t}{5}$

   ii $x = 0.3\cos\dfrac{10\pi t}{3}$

3 a i $\dfrac{2\pi}{5}$ **ii** $\dfrac{2\pi}{3}$

 b i $\pi\sqrt{2}$ **ii** $\dfrac{\pi}{\sqrt{2}}$

 c i $\dfrac{2\pi}{\sqrt{3}}$ **ii** $\dfrac{2\pi}{3}$

 d i 2π **ii** $\dfrac{2\pi}{\sqrt{5}}$

4 a 0.183 m   **b** $1\,\text{m s}^{-1}$
5 a −0.0768 m   **b** 0.131 s; $7.2\,\text{m s}^{-1}$
6 a $1.2\,\text{m s}^{-1}$ **b** $0.465\,\text{m s}^{-1}$; $16.6\,\text{m s}^{-2}$
7 a $0.667\,\text{s}^{-1}$ **b** $0.0596\,\text{m s}^{-1}$
8 a −0.595 m   **b** 0.0524 s

 c $5.20\,\text{m s}^{-1}$; away

9 a $0.873\,\text{s}^{-1}$ **b** 0.497 m
10 a 0.3 m; 15.7 s   **b** $x = 0.3\cos 0.4t$

  c 4.78 s   **d** 0.0032 N

11 a Proof   **b** 15 m; 2880 N

  c 1.96 s

12 a Proof; $\dfrac{2\pi}{q}$ **b** $0.6q\,\text{m s}^{-1}$; $0.6q^2\,\text{m s}^{-2}$

  c 0.520 m

13 a $2.4x$ **b** Proof

  c $x = 0.04\cos 2.19t$

14 a 0.1 m   **b** $0.1 + x$; proof

  c Proof; $T = \dfrac{2\pi}{\sqrt{10g}}$ s

Exercise 11C

1 a i Underdamping   **ii** Overdamping
  b i Critical   **ii** Underdamping
  c i Underdamping   **ii** Critical
  d i Critical   **ii** Underdamping

2 $\dfrac{8}{3}$

3 a Proof   **b** $\dfrac{6\sqrt{2}}{5}$

  c Overdamping

4 a $m\dfrac{d^2x}{dt^2} + 5c\dfrac{dx}{dt} + 4nx = 0$

  b $n = \dfrac{25c^2}{16m}$

5 a $x = 0.9e^{-2t}\sin 3t$ **b** Underdamping

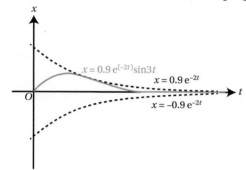

6 a Proof   **b** $x = 1.2e^{-t} - 0.2e^{-6t}$

  c Proof   **d** Overdamping

7 a Proof   **b** 0.45

  c $x = (0.8 + 0.72t)e^{-0.9t}$

8 a 0.4 m   **b** Proof

  c Underdamping;

    $x = -0.4e^{-4t}\left(\dfrac{4}{3}\sin 3t + \cos 3t\right)$

  d 0.4 m   **e** 0.0714 m s^{-1}

9 a Underdamping   **b** $x = \dfrac{5u}{3c}e^{-\frac{4ct}{5}}\sin\dfrac{3ct}{5}$

  c Proof

Exercise 11D

1 a i $\dfrac{d^2x}{dt^2} - 7\dfrac{dx}{dt} + 12x = 0$;

    $x = Ae^{3t} + Be^{4t},\ y = Ae^{3t} + \dfrac{B}{2}e^{4t}$

  ii $\dfrac{d^2x}{dt^2} - 2\dfrac{dx}{dt} - 3x = 0$;

    $x = Ae^{3t} + Be^{-t},\ y = Ae^{3t} - Be^{-t}$

  b i $\ddot{x} + 2\dot{x} + 5x = 0$;

    $x = e^{-t}(A\cos 2t + B\sin 2t)$,

    $y = 2e^{-t}((A+B)\cos 2t - (A-B)\sin 2t)$

  ii $\ddot{x} - 2\dot{x} + 5x = 0$; $x = e^t(A\cos 2t + B\sin 2t)$,

    $y = 2e^t((A+B)\cos 2t + (B-A)\sin 2t)$

  c i $\ddot{x} + 3\dot{x} + 2x = 3e^{-3t}$; $x = Ae^{-t} + Be^{-2t} + \dfrac{3}{2}e^{-3t}$,

    $y = Ae^{-t} + \dfrac{3B}{4}e^{-2t} + \dfrac{1}{2}e^{-3t}$

  ii $\ddot{x} + \dot{x} - 2x = -26$;

    $x = Ae^t + Be^{-2t} + 13,\ y = 2Ae^t + \dfrac{B}{2}e^{-2t} + 17$

2 $x = Ae^t + Be^{-t} - \cos t,\ y = Ae^t - Be^{-t}$

3 $x = Ae^{4t} + Be^{-4t},\ y = -2Ae^{4t} + 2Be^{-4t}$

4 $x = 12 + 5\cos 4t,\ y = 7 + 4\sin 4t$

5 a $\dfrac{d^2x}{dt^2} - \dfrac{dx}{dt} - 12x = 0$

  b $x = 3e^{4t} - 2e^{-3t},\ y = 3e^{4t} + 12e^{-3t}$

6 a Proof; $\dfrac{dy}{dt} + 2y = 0.6e^{-2t}$

  b $y = 0.6te^{-2t}$; proof

  c 11.0 cm

7 a $\dfrac{dS}{dt} = 0.1F - 0.2S + 1$

    $\dfrac{dF}{dt} = 0.2F - 0.5S + 4$

  b $\dfrac{d^2S}{dt^2} + 0.01S = 0.2$

  c $S = 20 - 3\cos 0.1t + 4\sin 0.1t$

    $F = 30 - 2\cos 0.1t + 11\sin 0.1t$

  d $S = 20 + 5\cos(0.1t - 2.21)$; shark peak at $t = 22.1$, fish peak at $t = 17.5$

  e The populations oscillate with the same period (62.8 time units), and with a phase delay of 4.6 time units between fish population peaking and shark population peaking.

8 Proof

Mixed practice 11

1 π

2 64

3 a $\ddot{x} = 2\sin t$ **b** 5.72 m

4 a 1.8 m s^{-1} **b** 1.34 m s^{-1}

  c 3.24 N

5 a Proof   **b** Proof; $\omega = 3$

  c $A = 0.3, B = 0$ **d** 0.9 m s^{-1}

6 i $v = \dfrac{15}{4}t^2 - 5t + 0.8$ **ii** $\dfrac{4}{3}$ s

  iii 0.4 s, 1.6 s   **iv** 12.1 m

7 a Proof   **b** Proof; $R = 3, \varphi = 0$

  c $\dfrac{\pi}{5}$ seconds

8 $2.30 \approx 2$ months

9 $x = \cos 4t - \dfrac{1}{2}\sin 4t,\, y = \cos 4t + \dfrac{1}{2}\sin 4t$

10 $Q\,(x_P = 33.3 \text{ m},\, x_Q = 74.2 \text{ m})$

11 a Proof   **b** 0.785 s^{-1}

  c 0.148 N

12 a Proof   **b** 3.2 m s^{-1}

13 a Proof

  b $A = 0, B = 0.3$; proof   **c** 0.75 m s^{-1}

14 a $x = 5\cos t$ **b** 1.57 s

  c $x = e^{-\frac{5}{13}t}\left(5\cos\left(\dfrac{12}{13}t\right) + \dfrac{25}{12}\sin\left(\dfrac{12}{13}t\right)\right)$

  d The second model (after 2.13 s)

15 $x = e^t\left(A\cos\left(t\sqrt{2}\right) + B\sin\left(t\sqrt{2}\right)\right),$

  $y = e^t\sqrt{2}\left(A\sin\left(t\sqrt{2}\right) - B\cos\left(t\sqrt{2}\right)\right)$

16 4000

17 i 2.4 m s^{-1}

  ii $x = -0.565$ m, $v = -0.804$ m s^{-1}

  iii $t = 0.0854$ s $(x = 0.565$ m, $v = -0.804$ m s$^{-1})$,
     $t = 0.871$ s $(x = -0.565$ m, $v = 0.804$ m s$^{-1})$

18 i $v = \dfrac{t^3 - 432t + 6912}{1800}$; proof

  ii v

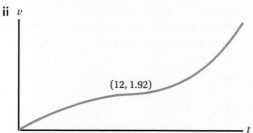

(12, 1.92)

19 a Proof   **b** Proof; $\dfrac{\pi}{2}$

  c 0.566 m s^{-1}

20 a The force decreases at a constant rate. In reality the force will vary over each stride; he might be more motivated towards the end.

  b $2000\ddot{x} = 1000 - 100t$

  c $x = \dfrac{1}{4}t^2 - \dfrac{1}{120}t^3$; 33.3 m

  d Bill (Mike's distance is 14.7 m but you don't need to find this. A sketch of both forces makes it clear that Mike is never pulling harder.)

Focus on ... 2

Focus on ... Proof 2

1 Proof

2 $\sqrt{\pi}$

3 $\sqrt{2\pi\sigma}$

Focus on ... Problem solving 2

1 Proof

2 The tangent to the chain at $x = 0$ is horizontal; proof

3 $y = \dfrac{T_0 L}{gM}\cosh\left(\dfrac{gM}{T_0 L}x\right)$; moving the chain vertically does not change its shape.

4 Proof

5 Proof

6 Investigation (using graphing software); the distance between the end-points ($2D$) has to be smaller than the length of the chain (L).

Focus on ... Modelling 2

1 For example: all fish and sharks are treated as equivalent so that the effects of age or disease average out over the population; there is no randomness, which might be acceptable if the populations are large enough; there are no external populations (i.e. no other predators or sources of food); there is no seasonality so the birth rate stays constant over time.

2 $F = 0, S = 0$ or $F = \dfrac{k}{c}, S = \dfrac{a}{b}$; the second solution is the biologically relevant one.

3 The equilibrium value of the fish goes down when k decreases. The equilibrium value of the sharks goes up when a increases.

4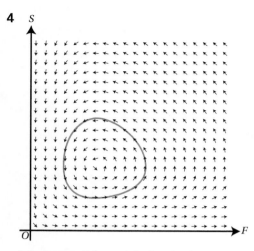

Maximum fish population is about 1.75 million.

5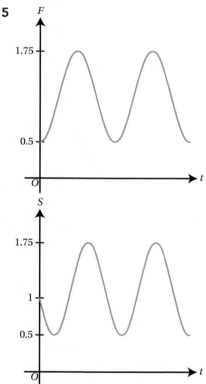

6 When F is small the aF term will be relatively more important. When F is large the eF^2 term will dominate, meaning that when the population is too large there is a net death, as would be expected with internal competition.

7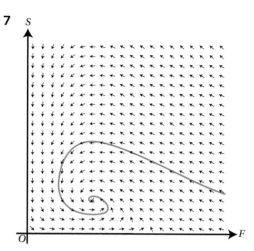

The system tends to an equilibrium at $F = 1, S = 0.5$.

Cross-topic review exercise 2

1 a $0 \leqslant \theta \leqslant \dfrac{\pi}{4}, \dfrac{\pi}{2} \leqslant \theta \leqslant \dfrac{3\pi}{4}, \pi \leqslant \theta \leqslant \dfrac{5\pi}{4}, \dfrac{3\pi}{2} \leqslant \theta \leqslant \dfrac{7\pi}{4}$

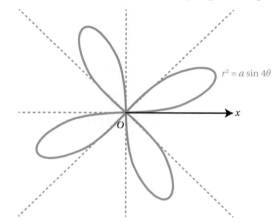

b a

2 $\ln \sqrt{5}$

3 $\ln 3$ or $\ln(\sqrt{5} - 2)$

4 $r = 14\sin\theta - 8\cos\theta$

5 $\dfrac{37\pi}{2}$

6 $\dfrac{1}{2}\ln\dfrac{e^x - e^{-x}}{e^x + e^{-x}} + c = \dfrac{1}{2}\ln(\tanh x) + c$

7 $(2x - 1)^2 + 4; \dfrac{\pi}{16}$

8 $\dfrac{52\pi}{9}$

9 $a=\dfrac{1}{3}, n=9$

10 a Proof   **b** $\ln\sqrt{3}$

11 Proof

12 a Proof   **b** $\dfrac{21}{29}$

13 i Proof   **ii** $\ln\left(\dfrac{\sqrt{5}\pm1}{2}\right)$

14 i, ii Proof

15 i Proof   **ii** $x+\dfrac{1}{6}x^3$

     iii $x^2-\dfrac{1}{2}x^3+\dfrac{1}{2}x^4$

16 i Proof   **ii** $\ln\sqrt{2}-\dfrac{1}{2}x+\dfrac{1}{4}x^2$

17 i

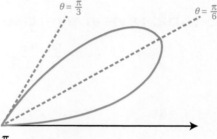

$\theta=\dfrac{\pi}{3}$ $\theta=\dfrac{\pi}{6}$

     ii $\dfrac{\pi}{3}$

     iii Proof

18 i $y=e^{-x}(A\cos4x+B\sin4x)+x+2$

     ii Proof; $y=x+2$

19 $y=\dfrac{e^{-x}}{4}(1-\cos2x)$

20 $y=2-2x\cot x+\dfrac{\pi\sqrt{3}}{6}\operatorname{cosec} x$

21 i Proof

     ii $v=\sqrt{5}\,e^{\sqrt{5}t}$

22 i $0.8\,\mathrm{m}$

     ii $x=0.227$, velocity $3.84\ \mathrm{ms^{-1}}$

     iii $3; t=0.257$ and $x=0.227$, $t=0.372$ and $x=-0.227$, $t=0.885$ and $x=-0.227$

23 i $v=\dfrac{1}{0.8t+0.2}=\dfrac{5}{4t+1}$

     ii $0.671\ \mathrm{ms^{-1}}$ (3 s.f.)

24 $k\geqslant\sqrt{5}$

25 $\dfrac{9}{4}$

26 a $x+\dfrac{x^3}{12}$ **b** $-2<x<2$

    c $\dfrac{13}{12}$

27 Proof

28 a Proof

     b $\operatorname{arsinh} x-\dfrac{\sqrt{1+x^2}}{x}+c$

29 $\ln\dfrac{3}{2}$

30 i Proof

     ii $u=\dfrac{1}{2}\left(5^{\frac{1}{3}}+\dfrac{1}{5^{\frac{1}{3}}}\right)$

31 i $\sqrt{x(x-1)}+\ln\left(\sqrt{x}+\sqrt{x^2-1}\right)+c$

     ii $2\sqrt{3}+\ln\left(2+\sqrt{3}\right)$

     iii The volume of revolution is infinite.

32 i

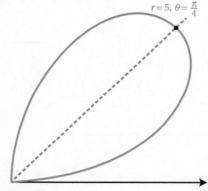

$r=5, \theta=\dfrac{\pi}{4}$

     ii $\dfrac{25\pi}{8}$

     iii $y=5\sqrt{2}-x$

     iv Proof

33 i $y=\left(A-\dfrac{1}{4}x\right)\cos2x+B\sin2x$

     ii y oscillates increasingly widely, with amplitude proportional to x.

     iii y oscillates with a stable amplitude throughout all values of x, and does not grow without limit.

34 i $x_1=3\cos t, x_2=4\cos1.5t$

     ii The period of P_1 is $2\pi>5.99$ so the particle has not completed a full cycle. $23.6\ \mathrm{m}$

     iii $v_{P_1}=-0.867\ \mathrm{ms^{-1}}, v_{P_2}=2.55\ \mathrm{ms^{-1}}$. The particles are travelling in opposite directions.

35 i, ii Proof

iii $\pm\ln\left(3+2\sqrt{2}\right)$

36 i Proof

ii

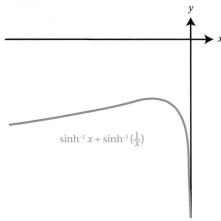

$$\sinh^{-1}x+\sinh^{-1}\left(\tfrac{1}{x}\right)$$

$$\left(-\infty,-2\ln\left(1+\sqrt{2}\right)\right]\cup\left[2\ln\left(1+\sqrt{2}\right),\infty\right)$$

37 a $x\arcsin x+\sqrt{1-x^2}+c$

b Proof

c i $p\arcsin\sqrt{p}-\dfrac{1}{2}\arcsin\sqrt{p}+\dfrac{1}{2}\sqrt{p-p^2}$

ii $x\arcsin\sqrt{x}-\dfrac{1}{2}\arcsin\sqrt{x}+\dfrac{1}{2}\sqrt{x-x^2}+c$

38 i 9; 3

ii, iii Proof

Practice paper 1

1 $k=-3$

2 Proof

3 6; proof

4 1

5 Proof; $a=7$, $b=16$, $c=3$

6 a $1,\operatorname{cis}\left(\dfrac{2\pi}{7}\right),\operatorname{cis}\left(\dfrac{4\pi}{7}\right),\operatorname{cis}\left(\dfrac{6\pi}{7}\right),$

$\operatorname{cis}\left(\dfrac{8\pi}{7}\right),\operatorname{cis}\left(\dfrac{10\pi}{7}\right),\operatorname{cis}\left(\dfrac{12\pi}{7}\right)$

b $n=7$, $w=-128i$

7 $x=Ae^{2t}+Be^{-2t}$, $y=Ae^{2t}-Be^{-2t}$

8 a $\dfrac{2}{x-1}-\dfrac{1}{x^2+1}$

b $2\ln|x-1|-\arctan x+c$

9 a $x+5y+8z=20$ **b** $18.8°$

10 a $y^2=6x+9$ **b** $r=\dfrac{13}{3}$

11 a Proof

b $\dfrac{1}{a^2-4a+5}\begin{pmatrix} a-3 & -1 & 6-a \\ 2 & a-1 & 1-3a \\ 1-a & 2-a & a^2-2 \end{pmatrix}$

c $x=\dfrac{a-3}{a^2-4a+5},y=\dfrac{2}{a^2-4a+5},z=\dfrac{1-a}{a^2-4a+5}$

12 $y=\dfrac{2\arcsin x+1}{\sqrt{1-x^2}}$

13 a Proof **b** 0

Practice paper 2

1 a $-\dfrac{1}{2}-\dfrac{1}{2}i$ **b** $\dfrac{\sqrt{2}}{2},\dfrac{5\pi}{4}$

2 a $\left(\dfrac{1-\sqrt{3}}{2},\dfrac{-\sqrt{3}-1}{2}\right)$

b Rotation through 60° anticlockwise about the origin

3 $\left(x^2+y^2\right)^2=8x$

4 Proof

5 $\ln 9$

6 a Proof

b For example, $x=\dfrac{3\pi}{2}$

7 a $\begin{pmatrix} 1 & 10 \\ 0 & 1 \end{pmatrix},\begin{pmatrix} 1 & 15 \\ 0 & 1 \end{pmatrix},\begin{pmatrix} 1 & 20 \\ 0 & 1 \end{pmatrix}.$

b $\begin{pmatrix} 1 & 5n \\ 0 & 1 \end{pmatrix}$ **c** Proof

8 Proof; 0.745

9 Proof; $a=\dfrac{1}{4}$, $b=\dfrac{7}{5}$

10 a, b Proof

c $1,\dfrac{1}{2}\pm i\dfrac{\sqrt{3}}{2}$

11 a Proof **b** $k=2$

12 a Proof

b i $x=5e^{-kt}-e^{-2kt}$ **ii** Overdamping

Glossary

amplitude (of an object moving with SHM): The maximum distance from the equilibrium position.

angular frequency: The constant ω in the simple harmonic motion equation $\dfrac{d^2x}{dt^2} = -\omega^2 x$.

auxiliary equation: The quadratic equation $a\lambda^2 + b\lambda + c = 0$ associated with the second order differential equation $a\dfrac{d^2y}{dx^2} + b\dfrac{dy}{dx} + c = 0$.

circular functions: A name sometimes given to trigonometric functions, related to points on a unit circle (with equation $x^2 + y^2 = 1$).

complementary function: The solution to the homogeneous differential equation associated with a non-homogenous differential equation.

consistent (system of equations): A set of simultaneous equations that have (a) solution(s).

converges: When a series approaches a finite value as more terms are added.

damped harmonic motion: Simple harmonic motion in which a resistive force proportional to the object's velocity is added, causing the amplitude to decay with time.

De Moivre's theorem: A theorem for finding powers of complex numbers: $z^n = r^n (\cos n\theta + i \sin n\theta)$ for any integer n.

dependent variable (in a differential equation): The variable on the top of the derivatives.

equilibrium position: The position where the acceleration of an object is zero.

exponential form (of a complex number): A way of expressing a complex number, z, in terms of its modulus, r, and argument, θ: $z = re^{i\theta}$

finite series: The sum of a finite number of terms in a sequence.

general solution (of a differential equation): The solution involving all the necessary arbitrary constants.

general term (in a Maclaurin series): The expression for the general term in a Maclaurin series is $\dfrac{f^{(r)}(0)}{r!} x^r$.

homogeneous differential equation: A differential equation in which every term involves the dependent variable.

hyperbola: A curve consisting of two branches. Coordinates of points on the curve are of the form $(\cosh\theta, \sinh\theta)$.

hyperbolic functions: The functions $\sinh x$, $\cosh x$ and $\tanh x$.

improper integral: An integral where either the range of integration is infinite or the integrand is undefined at a point within the range of integration.

inconsistent (system of equations): A set of simultaneous equations that have no solution.

independent variable (in a differential equation): The variable on the bottom of the derivatives.

infinite series: The sum of the terms of an infinite sequence (this may have a finite sum).

initial line: In polar coordinates, a fixed line from the pole from which the angle to a point is measured.

integrating factor: A function that is multiplied through a first order linear differential equation so that the side containing the dependent variable can be expressed as the derivative of a product.

inverse functions: A function denoted by f^{-1} that reverses the effect of function f. The inverse hyperbolic functions are $\operatorname{arshin} x$, $\operatorname{arcosh} x$ and $\operatorname{artanh} x$.

irreducible (quadratic): A quadratic that does not factorise.

linear differential equation: A differential equation in which the dependent variable only appears to the power 1 in any expression.

Maclaurin series: An expansion of a function as a series in powers of x.

non-homogeneous differential equation: A differential equation in which at least one term doesn't involve the dependent variable.

normal vector (of a plane): A vector that is perpendicular to the plane.

order (of a differential equation): The largest number of times the dependent variable is differentiated.

oscillating behaviour: To vary in magnitude or position in a regular manner about a central (equilibrium) point.

particular integral: Any solution of a differential equation.

particular solution: The general solution with the values of all constants found to fit a set of specific conditions.

period (of an object moving with SHM): The time after which the motion repeats itself.

polar coordinates: A way of describing the position of a point by means of its distance from the origin and the angle relative to a fixed line.

pole: In polar coordinates, an origin from which the distance of a point is measured.

roots of unity: The n solutions of the equation $z^n = 1$, where z is a complex number.

scalar product equation: A form of writing an equation of a plane, using the scalar (dot) product, denoted $\mathbf{r} \cdot \mathbf{n} = \mathbf{a} \cdot \mathbf{n}$, where $\mathbf{n}$ is the normal to the plane and $\mathbf{a}$ is the position vector of a point in the plane.

series: The sum of the terms of a sequence.

sigma notation: A shorter way of writing a series, using a large Greek sigma with limits.

simple harmonic motion: Oscillating motion where the acceleration of the object is proportional to the displacement from a central (equilibrium) position and is in the direction opposite to that of the displacement.

solid of revolution: A 3D shape formed by rotating a curve, usually around the x- or y-axis.

vector product: A way of multiplying two vectors $\mathbf{a}$ and $\mathbf{b}$, denoted as $\mathbf{a} \times \mathbf{b}$ where $\times$ is the cross product. The direction of the product is perpendicular to both $\mathbf{a}$ and $\mathbf{b}$.

volume of revolution: The volume of a solid of revolution.

Index

Acknowledgements

The authors and publishers acknowledge the following sources of copyright material and are grateful for the permissions granted. While every effort has been made, it has not always been possible to identify the sources of all the material used, or to trace all copyright holders. If any omissions are brought to our notice, we will be happy to include the appropriate acknowledgements on reprinting.

Thanks to the following for permission to reproduce images:

Cover image: huskyomega/Getty Images

Back cover: Fabian Oefner www.fabianoefner.com

Mondadori Portfolio/Contributor; Sakkmesterke/Getty Images; Laguna Design/Getty Images; Chris Clor/Getty Images; Phillippe Bourseiller/ Getty Images; Universal Images Group/Contributor/Getty Images; Hani Alahmadi/EyeEm/Getty Images; Wangwukong/Getty Images; Alter Your Reality/Getty Images; Anna Bliokh/Getty Images; Nobi Prizue/Getty Images; Cuppuppycake/Getty Images